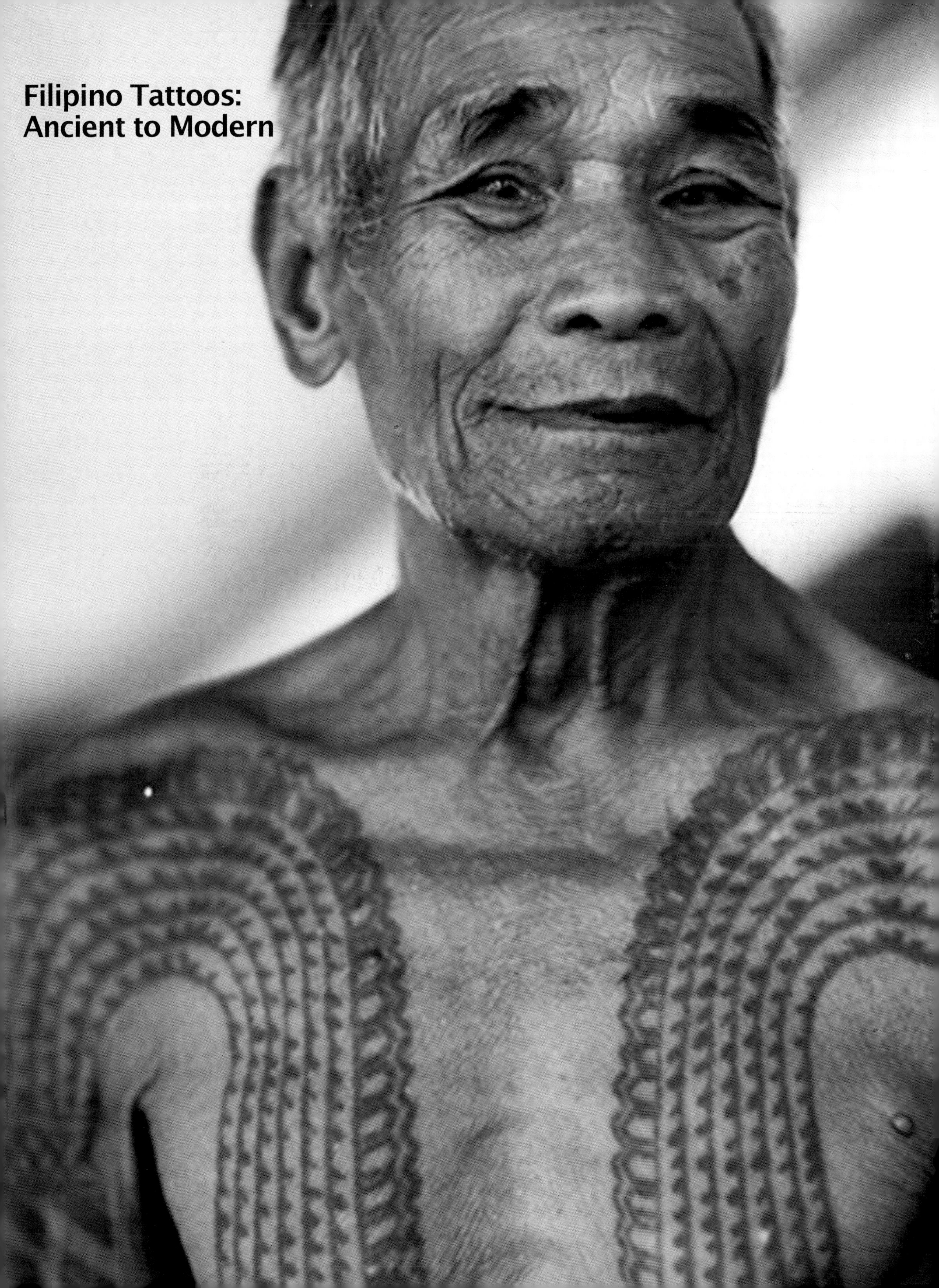

Filipino Tattoos:
Ancient to Modern

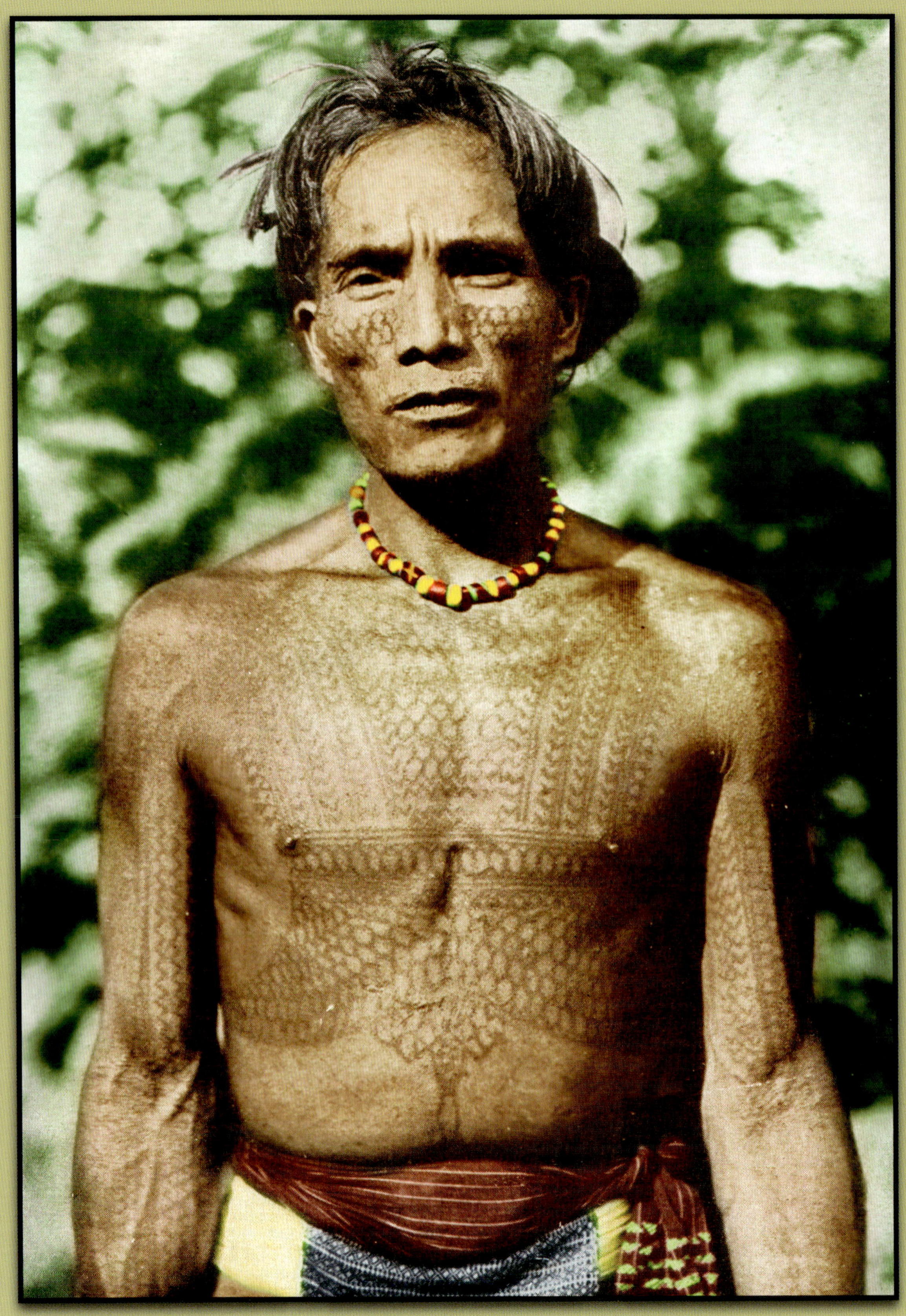

Filipino Tattoos:
Ancient to Modern

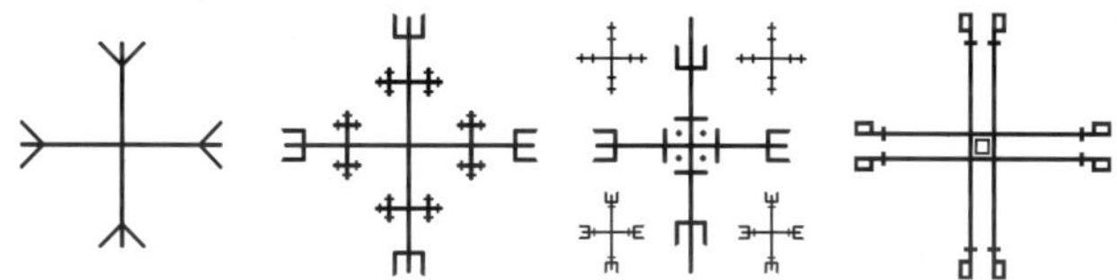

Lane Wilcken

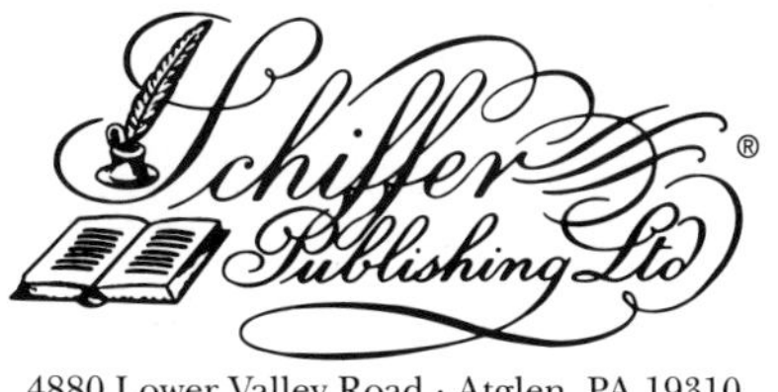

4880 Lower Valley Road · Atglen, PA 19310

Copyright © 2010 by Lane Wilcken.
Library of Congress Catalog Number: 2010936994.

Printed in India
ISBN: 978-0-7643-3602-7

We are always looking for people to write books on new and related subjects.
If you have an idea for a book, please contact us at the address below.

Published by Schiffer Publishing Ltd.
4880 Lower Valley Road
Atglen, PA 19310
Phone: (610) 593-1777
FAX: (610) 593-2002
E-mail: Info@schifferbooks.com.
Visit our web site at: www.schifferbooks.com
Please write for a free catalog.
This book may be purchased from the publisher.
Try your bookstore first.

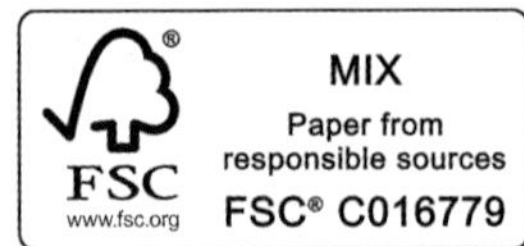

Contents

Foreword

by Su'a Suluape Alaiva'a Petelo

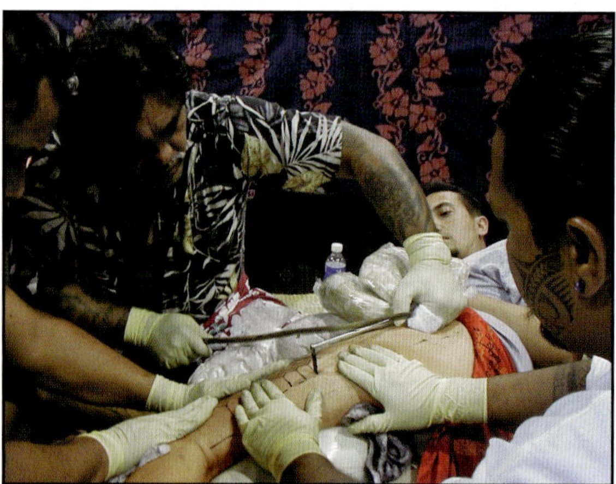

Su'a Suluape Alaiva'a Petelo, Master tattoo expert from Samoa tattooing the
Author. Su'a Suluape Alaiva'a Petelo comes from the oldest tattooing family of
Samoa whose practice of the art stretches back thousands of years.

The history of traditional tattooing began over 5,000 years ago and is diverse as the people who wear them. The word "tattoo" however is believed to have originated from the Polynesian term tatau which means "to mark something." Nevertheless, together with this diversity exists particular similarities in tattooing designs and techniques which affirms the idea that tattooing must indeed have a beginning; whether that beginning is in the Bronze Age or with the Pazyryk culture north of the border between Russia and China. Origins can also be arguably traced along the patterns of migration from Southeast Asia (China, Japan, Borneo, Thailand, and the Philippines) to the Pacific with Samoa being the oldest culture in terms of traditional tattooing methods and symbolism. Samoan traditional tattooing has been the most resilient in that it did not falter nor perish in the face of Christianity and colonialism.

Regarding Pacific cultures in general, tattooing has a tremendous historic significance. Polynesian tattooing is considered the most intricate and skillful tattooing of the ancient world. Polynesian people believe that their spiritual life force or power, otherwise known as 'mana' is expressed through their tattoo. Much of what we know today about these ancient arts has been passed down through generations in the form of legends, songs and ritual ceremonies. As such, as it is in Samoa, the art of applying tatau rests in the hands of only a few traditionally recognized tattooing families and their direct descendants.

It is always disheartening to hear stories of the gradual fading or already extinct practices of traditional tattooing in various cultures of Southeast Asia and the Pacific. This is even more so with the ever expanding reaches of globalization in a world where spiritual power or mana is becoming easily absorbed by the hollows of economic and financial burden. The silver lining is with people such as the Maori of New Zealand and individuals from the Philippines like Lane Wilcken, who are now, in the 21st century, trying to revive a tradition lost. It is this silver lining coupled with the continued resilience of Samoan traditional tattooing that will surely foster the beauty of the art for generations to come.

Su'a Suluape Alaiva'a Petelo

Foreword
by Keone Nunes

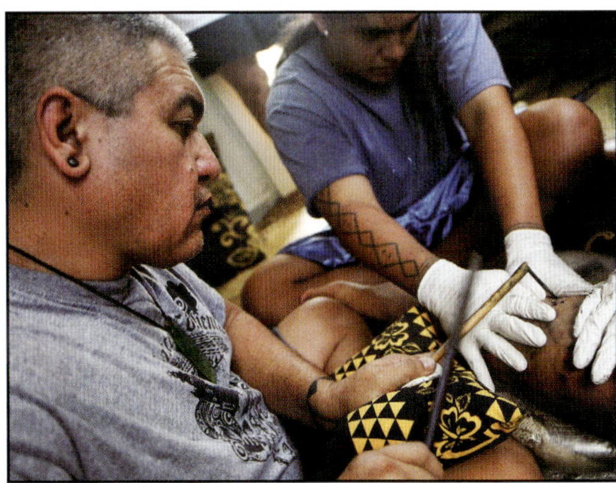

Keone Nunes is a traditional tattoo practitioner from the Hawaiian Islands.
Photo by Stephanie Young Mertze.

The practice of tattoo is as old as mankind itself, from the tattooed "Ice Man" found in the Alps of Europe to the rainforests of Brazil, and the shores of the emerald green islands of the Pacific. Tattooing was, and in many cases still is, an essential part of life, death, aesthetic beauty and sacred rituals of thousands of peoples and the cultures in which they belong.

When thinking of tattoo traditions in the Pacific many will look at Polynesia with the long-standing tradition of the Moko and Puhoro in Aotearoa, the Pe'a and Malu of Samoa, the Pahu Tiki of Nukuhiwa and the Uhi of Hawai'i. All of these traditions were seen by early European explores and their fascination was so great that they coined the word "tattoo' from the Polynesian word "tatau." These traditions did not originate in Polynesia however, the Samoan story of the twins Taema and Tilafaiga who brought the tattoo tools to Falealupo on the island of Savai'i from "Fiti" (Fiji) gives us clear indication from cultural sources that the practice of tattooing originated from areas outside of Polynesia and was introduced to early Polynesians by others.

In tracing back the origins of Polynesian tattooing one finds that the family tree of tattoo traditions is a bit more complex than would be imagined. The "hand-pricking" style of tattooing gave birth to a long stick piercing approach that is still being used in areas of Southeast Asia and in Japan. The "tapping" method used in Polynesian tattoo traditions was also developed in areas of Southeast Asia, but found its growth in the fertile waters of the Pacific. Borneo, Micronesia, Melanesia, Taiwan and the Philippines along with Polynesia gave life to the rhythmic sound of the tapping on of sacred designs.

The Philippines traditions bear designs that are geometric in nature and could well be the foundation of the tattooing traditions in the Pacific. It is a tradition that has been left literally in the mountains for centuries with no outside interest until recently. The history of the Philippines is one of strong colonization, ethnic and cultural genocide, missionization and westernization. All of these factors make the survival of Philippine traditional tattoo practices of any kind all that much more amazing.

Modernization and westernization is prevalent throughout the world and as such traditional practices are very much endangered in many cultures. There are, fortunately, a handful of people that decide to look back into these traditions to give us a clear roadmap to the future, Lane Wilcken has that foresight to look back. This book, which he has dedicated much time in research and speaking to individuals knowledgeable on Filipino tattoo traditions, is an important insight to these "aural" tattoo traditions of the Philippines. It gives us the opportunity to understand the importance of the role of the tattoo practice within the remaining traditional thought, culture and intellect of the indigenous Filipino.

In this book Lane gives us a taste of the uniqueness of this practice and its long-standing struggle to survive. It also brings to light the practices, beliefs and understandings that are the unseen foundation of contemporary Filipino life, and clarifies the cultural connections between the Philippines and the rest of the Pacific. In recent years, there have been many books that have exploited the popularity of traditional tattooing in contemporary cultures. Some of these books have increased our knowledge in understanding the spirituality, aesthetics and diversity of thought in the practice of tattooing. Others, unfortunately just rehash known information in a different package. Lane Wilcken has brought to the forefront the traditional practice of tattooing from an area of the world that previously has not been looked at and has added to our knowledge base of this tattooing tradition that may have well have been practiced for thousands of years.

As you read this book open your mind to what may have been, what is, and the possibility of what can be.

Aloha,
Keone Nunes

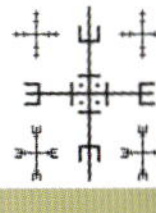

Testimonial
by Leo Zulueta

When Lane asked me to do this for his book, I felt honored to be included in such a project. As an American Filipino I have always hoped to add to my heritage via my long career as a contemporary tattoo artist. When Lane sent me some of the material in his book to review, I was pleased to see that his work appears very thorough and beneficial to Filipino culture.

Ten years ago, the great Sua Suluape Paulo asked me to learn Samoan tattooing from him; as it was his hope that I would in the future take back to the Philippines a heritage of hand (non-electric) tattooing. Unfortunately Paulo was taken from all of us unexpectedly shortly after our meeting. We had settled on me visiting him in New Zealand several months after that initial meeting, so I could familiarize myself with the process as a possible addition to my machine work. Paulo was also writing a paper on the migration of tattooing from Southeast Asia, traveling southward into the Philippines and Borneo, then eastward into Polynesia. Again it truly was Su'a Suluape Paulo's dream that a Filipino help to restore the ancient art of tattooing.

It has always been my hope that my contemporary Tribal style tattooing has added to the interest and preservation of all traditional tattooing around the world. Thank you Lane for this book and all your efforts and studies to help understand, revitalize and retain the ancient and beautiful art of traditional Filipino tattooing.

Leo Zulueta
Spiral Tattoo
Ann Arbor, Michigan

Acknowledgments

There is a saying that it takes a village to raise a child. In like manner, it takes more than one person's knowledge and experience to create a book. I would first and foremost like to deeply thank Apo Ama A Nailangitan for providing me with the desire, guidance, and strength to write this book. I would also like to thank my ancestors for their love and commitment to their families, which led to my birth. I hope this work honors them. I am also very grateful to my parents who taught me to honor my elders, both living and dead, to be proud of my heritage, how to think outside of the norm, and provided me with love and a moral compass through my life. Thank you, Inang, for finding answers to all my pestering questions about the old ways. I am especially grateful to my dear wife Rebekah for her support and encouragement to finish this book. Her patience and sacrifice have allowed me the freedom to write. I love you. I want to express my gratitude to Su'a Suluape Alaiva'a Petelo and Keone Nunes for their kindness and friendship in writing the Forewords. Their commitment to their cultural arts has been truly inspiring to me. I also want to thank Professor Analyn "Ikin" Salvadore-Amores, whose groundbreaking work on tattooing in the Philippines and generosity of her knowledge laid the foundation for a large amount of my research. I am grateful to my friend, Virgil Mayor Apostol, for his insight into our spiritual beliefs and for keeping me laughing through this project. There are a few others I would like to name in gratitude for their contributions to my knowledge and work in no particular order:

Uncle (Jun) Roque Coloma Rivera Junior
Apo Maria Whang-od
Uncle (Sam) Samuel Coloma Rivera
Manang Caridad Fiar-od
Su'a Suluape Aisea Toetu'u
Manang Gabie M. Buduhan
Suluape Angela Bolson
Michael Fatutoa
Margarita Alcantara
Manong Jaime Buyayo
Mary Ann Ubaldo
Su'a Peter Suluape
Manong Jotoc
Claudell Duldulao
Manong Arthur B. Butic
Manong Hospicio Binlingan Dulnuan
Leo Zulueta

I am also grateful for all the Lakays and Bakets who still wear these sacred designs and have shared their knowledge to others for the rest of us to learn from. Thank you to Nancy and Peter at Schiffer Publishing for making my dream a reality. I also want to express my appreciation to all the people who generously contributed information and pictures.

There are so many people who made this book possible in one way or another. It would be impossible to name them all. If I have forgotten anyone, please forgive me. There are also people who have humbly asked to remain anonymous. Thank you all for your friendship, insight and support.

"Agyamanak Kadakayo Amin"

Introduction

attooing is an extremely old art form that has existed among many different cultures around the world. Over the centuries some cultures maintained the art form while others abandoned it. Wherever tattooing existed, the art was performed in similar ways. It was created by injecting ink usually made of soot into the skin whether by puncturing the skin with needles or by cutting and placing ink in the wounds. It is closely related to scarification which involves cutting the skin and sometimes introducing foreign matter to produce raised scars (keloid) in various patterns and designs. There are some individuals who believe that tattooing may have developed from the practice of scarification.

Both scarification and tattooing were practiced in the Philippines. After many centuries of not being practiced in Europe the art of tattooing was re-introduced to the Western world through the inhabitants of the Pacific Ocean. Beginning in the sixteenth century Europeans exploring the various islands of Oceania came across many peoples who practiced tattooing as an integral portion of their cultures. In much of Polynesia the word to describe tattooing is usually some form of the word "*tatau*" (*tah-tah-oo* or *tah-taw*) which has several interpretations, depending on the island group. Definitions range from meaning "to mark or strike," to "doing what is right or correct," and the interpretation of the sound of the tapping of the tattooing tools as the ink is pushed into the skin. The corrupted form of this word *tatau* has made its way into the European languages as the word "*tattoo.*"

My interest in tattooing began when I was living in Hawaii several years ago. I saw many Hawaiians and Samoans proudly wearing the tattoos of their native cultures. A few of them explained to me some of the deep spiritual symbolisms of the unfading marks upon their skin. As I felt their pride in their heritage I wondered, "Did the Philippines have this ancient practice as well?" I asked my grandparents and mother about it and I was told that there were indeed Filipinos who tattooed!

As I researched the subject I found at first, very little information. Then one day I was in the library at Southern Utah University looking through some old National Geographic magazines (*National Geographic Magazine*, "Head-Hunters of Northern Luzon," Vol.XXIII, No.9, September, 1912) and to my amazement I saw old photographs of some exquisite tattooing from the Philippines. Since then I have searched through any information I could get my hands on concerning the subject of tattooing in the Philippines as well as the Pacific isles. Often the information I found was scanty and I had to read through related works about mythology and pre-Hispanic beliefs to gain pieces here and there. Over the years as my education continued, the pieces of the tattooing culture of the Philippines became more and more clear. I interviewed people from some of the last places in the Philippines that tattooed as well as representatives from other tattooing cultures in the Pacific. This amazing personal journey into the history of tattooing has become a rewarding insight into the lives of my ancestors. Unfortunately many people in the Philippines see our tattooing through the eyes of the foreign regimes who once occupied our islands. They see our traditional tattoos as barbaric or primitive.

Much of the early manuscripts about the Philippines and its tattooing were written from a Western ethnocentric perspective. Often, when interviewed by Westerners, those with tattoos only gave the superficial meanings because they did not believe that people who lived outside of their culture would be interested in the deeper meanings, let alone understand them. Other times the people would not explain meanings of specific tattoos because of the sacred nature of the designs. Because of the deep symbolism and metaphoric nature of tattoos, the full context of the tattoo could not be understood by simple identification. An appreciation of the culture as a whole is necessary to fully comprehend the significance and context of the tattoo designs and motifs.

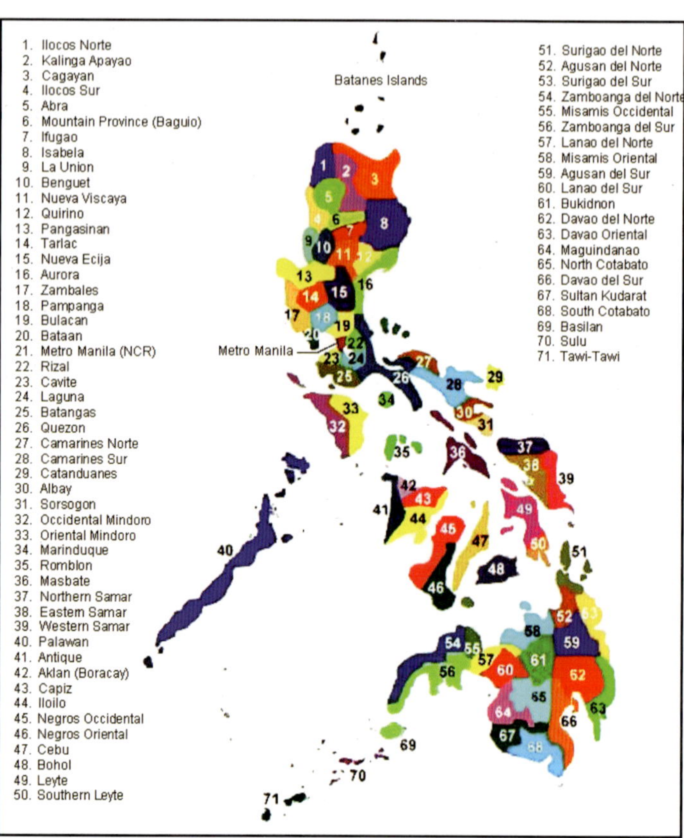

Map of the Philippines by ethnic groups

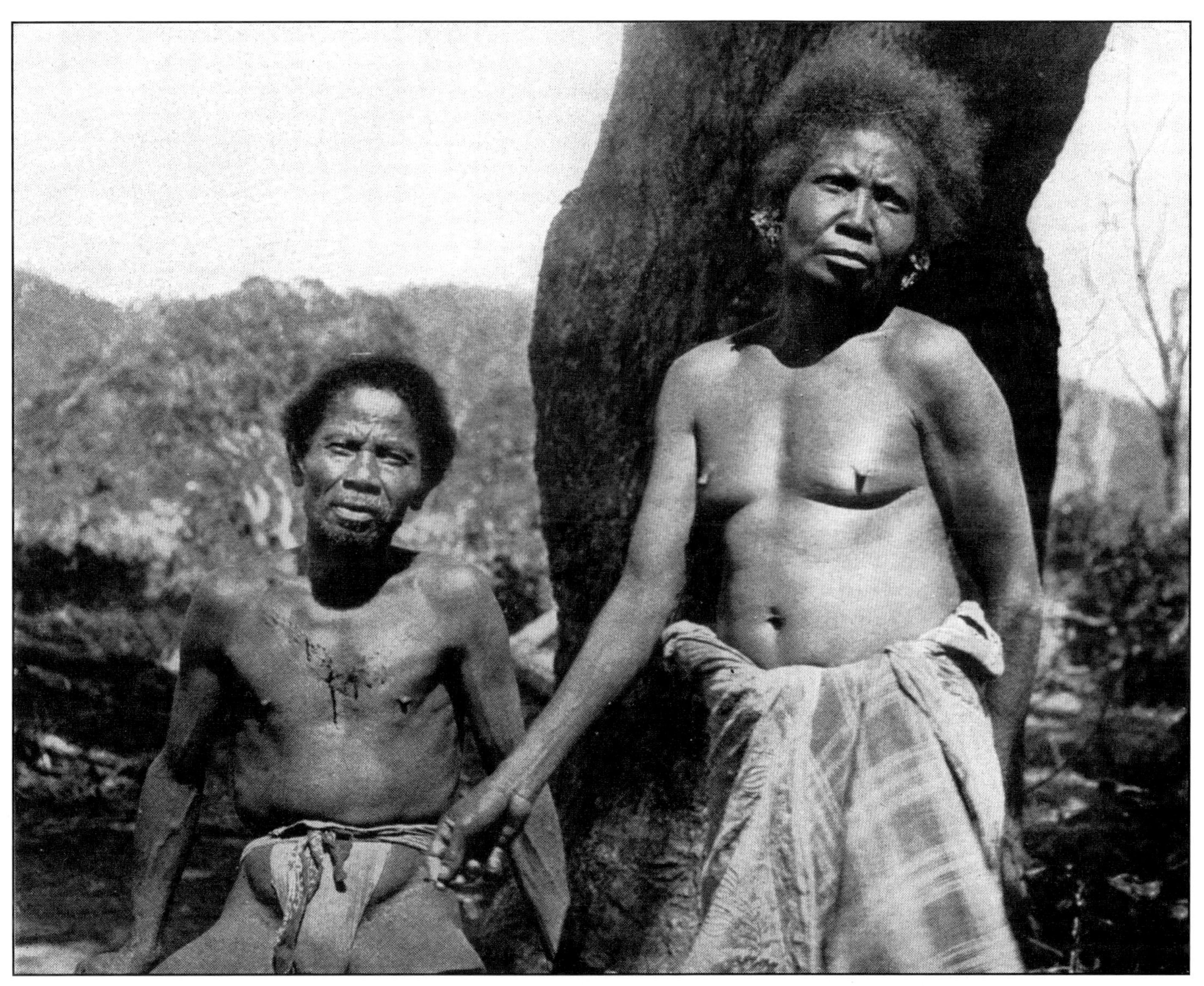

Aeta scarification in process. Both Aeta men and women of the Philippines formerly practiced scarification using the sharp edge of a bamboo knife.

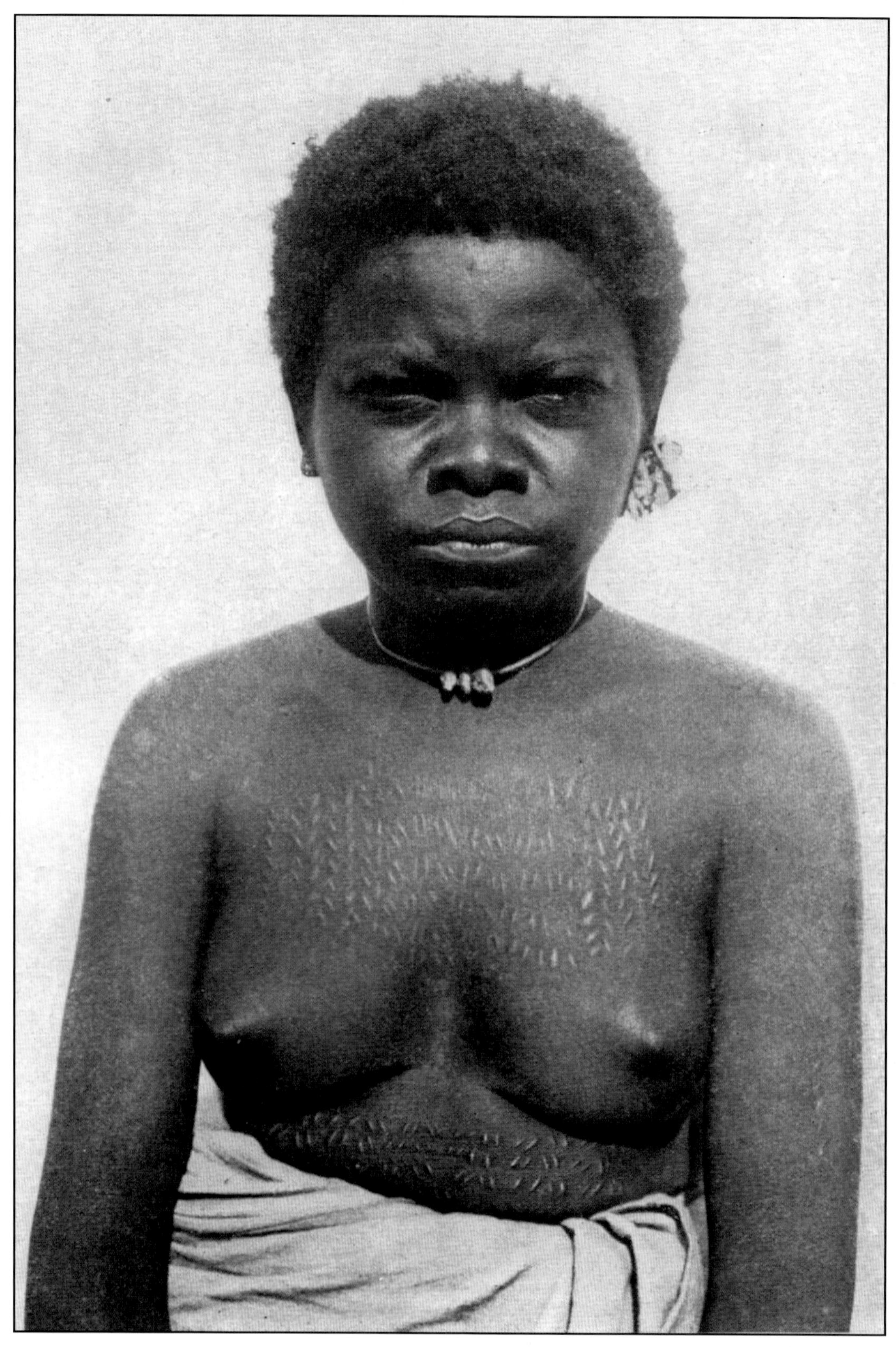

Aeta woman with scarification

Filipino Tattoos: Ancient to Modern

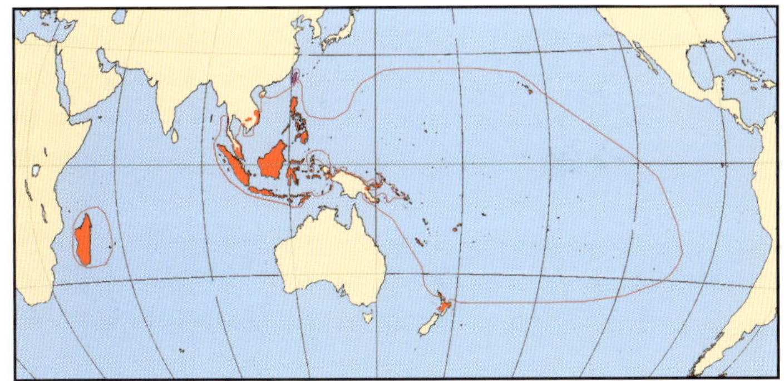

Above: Map of Austronesia by Vrata. http://commons.wikimedia. org/wiki/File:Austroneske_jazyky.jpg Used under licence of creative commons share and share alike 3.0. http://creativecommons.org/ licenses/by-sa/3.0/. *Right*: Map of the Phil-ippines. Author's collection

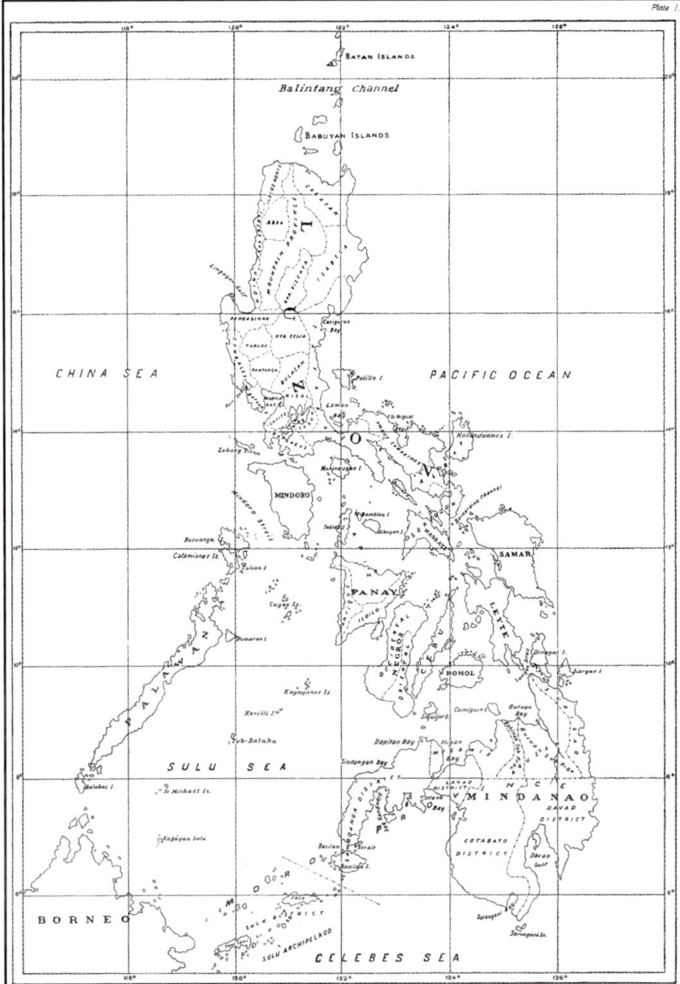

The younger generation of Filipinos in America and the Philippines tend to be ignorant of our tattooing heritage or they are embarrassed that our people tattooed in the past. Often they say that, "only criminals are tattooed." It is a shame that a practice that conveys so much prestige, beauty and history is now spoken of with embarrassment. Although this practice has largely disappeared from the Philippines it should not, by any means, be forgotten. Because many Filipinos do not realize the importance tattooing once played as part of our archipelago's culture, let us first review a little of the history of tattooing in the Philippines while comparing what we learn with our extended Austronesian family in the Pacific Isles.

Austronesians are the peoples who inhabit or inhabited Oceania and Southeast Asia who speak or whose ancestors spoke one of the Austronesian languages. The term *Austronesia* comes from the Latin word "*auster*" meaning "southern wind" and the Greek word "*nêsos*" meaning "islands." Austronesia as a geographical area includes the islands of Indonesia, Malaysia, Madagascar, Philippines, Taiwan, Micronesia, Melanesia, and Polynesia. Anthropologists, archeologists and linguists still debate on the exact origins of the Austronesian speaking peoples. In addition to their tattooing, Austronesian peoples share not only linguistic similarities but also similarities culturally in their spiritual beliefs, oral traditions and technology.

The majority of Austronesian peoples practiced tattooing to one extent or another either in the past or currently. Some groups tattooed from head to foot while others were very limited in their tattoos. In my research I have found that in some cases one particular group of Austronesians may remember aspects of a shared tradition one way while another group may understand the same tradition with altered or additional meanings. For example, while in Hawai'i in 1989 I met a Hawaiian woman that asked me if I knew the true meaning of the word "*Aloha*." I thought it was just a greeting word like "hello" or meant "love," but she pointed out to me that the true meaning related to the traditional way of greeting in Hawai'i. This greeting was done by two people touching noses on the side or on the cheek and inhaling. The practice was called "*honi*." (ho-nee) However, the *meaning* of it was *aloha* which came from two words, *alo* meaning "to share," and *ha,* "the breath of life."

This explanation brought back memories of my grandmother from the Philippines. When she would visit us she would sniff the sides of our faces. I asked my mother about the practice and she said it was called, in Ilokano, "*ungngo*" (ong-ngo). She did not know of any meaning behind it. She only said it was just the way the old people greet. In New Zealand the Maori people there call this type of greeting "*hongi*" very similar to the Hawaiian word "*honi*" but they press noses to inhale instead of pressing the cheek. Some groups in New Zealand do not aspirate the "H" sound, so it is pronouced "*o-ngee,*" very similar to the Ilokano word pronounced "*ong-ngo.*"

While this traditional greeting was being practiced in the Philippines, the meaning was lost. At the same time, until relatively recently, the Hawaiian practice of the honi was uncommon but the meaning was still known. By cross-referencing Austronesian cultures, missing elements or aspects of cultural practices can be found for a fuller understanding of our cultures. I believe this applies also to our tattooing practices. For this reason I use this methodology in this book to bring fuller understanding to the poorly remembered tattooing culture of the Philippines. In the same process I have found the reciprocal to be true as well. Some of the meanings remembered in the Philippines bring greater understanding to the tattooing practices of other Austronesian cultures.

Chapter 1

Early Accounts and Fragments of Philippine Tattoo Culture

When Ferdinand Magellan and his men landed on the shores of Homonhon Island on March 17, 1521, the first natives they saw wore tattoos and Magellan mistakenly thought the designs were painted on. Because of this, natives were called "*pintados,*" meaning "painted people." In fact, before the Spanish re-named the archipelago the "Philippines," they originally called the archipelago, "*Las Islas de los Pintados,*" which means "The Islands of the Painted Ones" because of the abundance of tattooing they saw. But the arrival of the Spaniards in the islands forever changed the customs and traditions of the Philippines.

In the modern world, Filipino people have been so deeply influenced by nearly 400 years of Spanish occupation that many believe that only the Visayan and Igorot peoples practiced tattooing. However, nearly all of the ancient Filipinos tattooed. According to the late William H. Scott, a leading researcher in pre-Hispanic Philippine history, only the Tagalog people and some of the people in Muslim areas did not practice tattooing at the time of the Spanish advent. Still, the word "to mark, stamp or print" in Tagalog is "*tatak,*" which is similar to its Polynesian counterpart "*tatau,*" from which comes the modern word "tattoo."

The Tagalog people may have abandoned the practice of tattooing due to their mercantile and trading lifestyle, which exposed them to the many Islamic Asian peoples via Borneo who did not practice tattooing. This also may be the reason Tagalog peoples also wore mustaches, unlike other groups in the Philippines that by-and-large removed body and facial hair. The Boxer Codex refers to the Tagalog people as "Moros," due to a superficial conversion to Islam.[1] There is also the possibility that the tattoos of the Tagalog people were never recorded. Due to the similarity of language and traditions of the Tagalog people and the Visayans it is likely that their tattooing in the past was similar to the Visayan tattoos.

Until recently tattooing was practiced in more remote parts of the Philippines but has fallen out of practice due to Western influence. Other ethnic groups in the Philippines lost the art of tattooing many years or even centuries ago but retained some of the words and designs in other artwork. An excellent example of this is the Ilokano "abel" (weaving) patterns. The Ilokanos tattooed in the past according to Jesuit chronicler Francisco Colin. He mentions Ilokano tattooing in his book, *Labor Evangelica,* printed in Madrid in 1663. Ilokanos most likely discontinued the practice due to Spanish influence and conversion to Christianity.

The tattooing patterns in the highlands above and adjacent to the Ilocos lowland are very similar, if not identical, to the patterns woven into Ilokano cloth. It is thought that the Isneg (also known as *Apayao*) people and the Itneg peoples, who inhabit the mountainous areas near the Ilokanos, were of the same ancestry as the Ilokanos but refused to be Christianized and so retreated deeper into to the mountains. When the efforts of the Spanish friars converted the Isneg and Itneg to Catholic faith they often were relocated from the highlands and intermarried freely into Ilokano communities.

The arm tattoos called *Andori* of the Isneg people are very similar to some of the weaving patterns of the Ilokanos. Since the Isneg didn't weave, they depended on the Ilokanos for their abel/lupot (cloth) that contained the motifs of their tattooing. Also, the Ilokanos provided many other highland tribes with their woven g-strings, skirts, and blankets that were

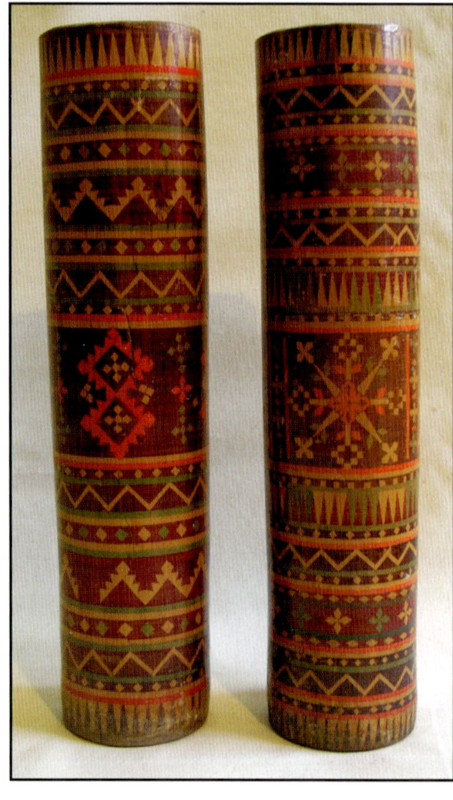

Bamboo containers called lakub from Mindanao with Manobo tattoo motifs. Courtesy of Virgil Mayor Apostol

Filipino Tattoos: Ancient to Modern

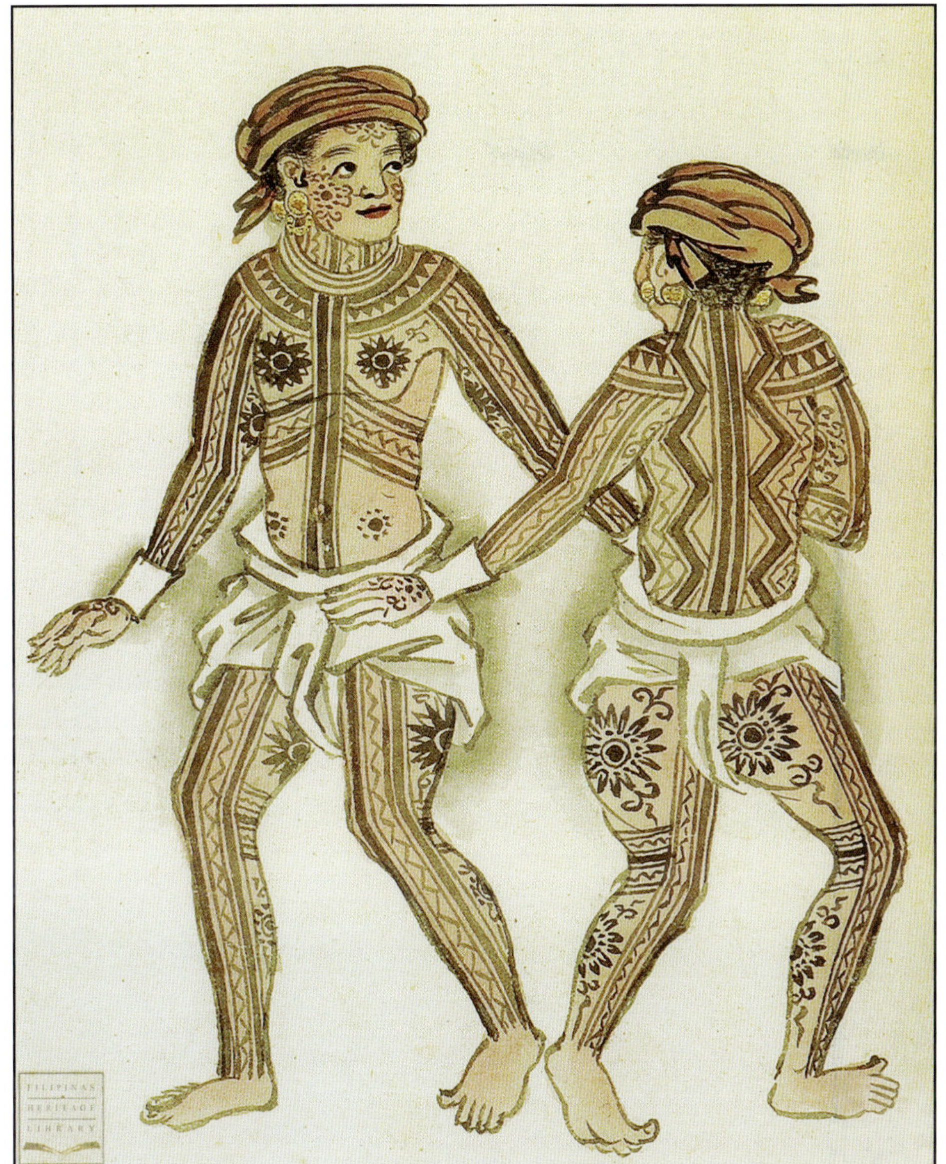

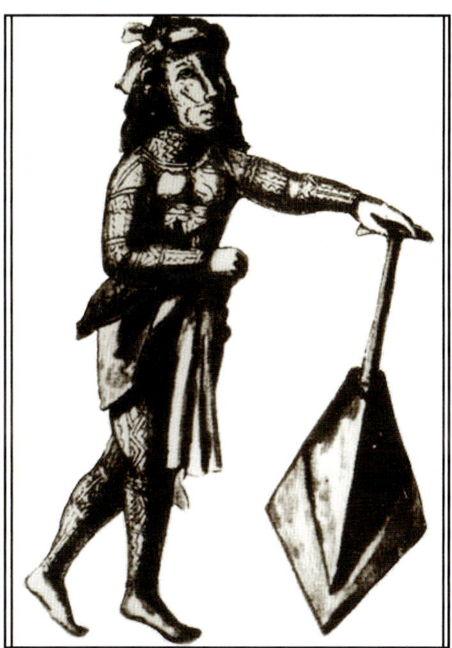

A tattooed Visayan warrior with canoe paddle from Francisco Alcina's Historiade las Islas e Indios de Bisayas, 1668

Fully tattooed Visayan warriors from the Boxer Codex, circa 1590. One of the few illustrations of Visayan tattooing, it is likely fairly accurate due to similarities (particularly the large sun-like designs) to documented symbols in other mediums throughout the Philippines. Early manu-scripts also describe the long, inch-wide stripes called "labid" that ran up the legs from the ankles to the waist. Courtesy of the Filipinas Heritage Library

decorated with tattoo motifs common to many groups. Because tattoos in the Philippines were thought of as a type of clothing or an extension of a man's loincloth or a woman's skirt, the patterns placed on both the skin and cloth were nearly identical. This seems to be the case throughout the Philippine archipelago. These same tattoo patterns were also incised into other implements, such as bamboo containers and flutes, axe handles, shields, etc.[2]

There is also terminology left over in the languages of the Philippines that comes from tattooing practices of the past. One such word in Ilokano is *iro*, (ee-roh), which means "soot" in Ilokano. "Iro" is similar to the word *biro* (bee-roh) in Visayan, which describes the soot from which the ink for tattooing was made. Biro was also the name for the tattooing ink in Visayan. It is also similar to the Kalinga word for tattooing ink, *biyug*.[3] There is also the word *puraw* ("poo-raoo") in Ilokano that has come to mean "white." In Visayan the same word, *puraw*, means "natural colored, un-dyed cloth" or "plain." Puraw in the Visayas was also used anciently to describe untattooed men.[4] Similarly, in the islands of Samoa in Polynesia, a similar word, *pula'u* ("poo-lah'-oo"), was used to describe untattooed men.[5] It therefore seems likely that the Ilokano "puraw" most likely was used in the same context in the past as in the Visayas prior to tattooing being exterminated in the Ilocos.

In the old Ilokano language, the term for tattoo is *batek.* Batek is similar to the Tagalog word *tatak*, meaning "to mark, stamp or print." The Ilokano word batek is even more similar to the Kalinga word for tattoo, *batok* or *fatok,* or the Visayan word for tattoo, *batuk* or *patik.* Among Ilokanos there is also a family surname, *Butac* or *Butak* (boo-tahk), which means "identifying mark." Since it is phonetically similar to *batek* (tattoo), it may be possible that the surname "*Butac*" also described tattooing.

There is also the word *burik* in Ilokano, which in the present means "engraving" or "spotted" but in the old Ilokano epic "Biag ni Lam-ang" *burikan* means tattooed. Among the Benguet peoples whose lands border the homelands of the Ilokanos, *burik* is the word for tattoo. The Gaddang people also use the word *burik* to describe their tattooing. Spanish Lieutenant Colonel Guillermo Galvey, in the early 1800s, described a group of unchristianized people whom he called "*Buriks*" who inhabited the part of the Cordillera from Ilocos Sur to the crest of the central ridge and were bordered by the Igorots in the south and in the north by the Busao people east of Santa Cruz. Galvey states, "They have the custom of painting their whole bodies with decorations exactly like a coat of mail with its breastplate and backplate."[6] It was likely these "Buriks" were unchristianized Ilokanos or Itneg people. This terminology and the existence of tattooing peoples in and surrounding the Ilocos area, and the existence of patterns in Ilokano produced textiles that resemble the tattooing patterns of the nearby peoples, display the remnants of tattooing that was once practiced among the Ilokanos but was lost sometime in the past.

There are a few early accounts from the Spanish that describe the tattooing of the Filipinos. In Jesuit chronicler Francisco Colin's book, *Labor Evangelica,* printed in Madrid in 1663, a chapter of his work is devoted to customs of the ancient Filipinos that describe the tattooing processes of the Visayans:

> Besides the exterior clothing and dress, some of these nations wore another inside dress, which could not be removed after it was once put on. These are the tattoos of the body so greatly practiced among the Visayans, whom we call Pintados for that reason. For it was a custom among them, and was a mark of nobility and bravery, to tattoo the whole body from top to toe when they were of an age and strength sufficient to endure the tortures of the tattooing which was done (after being carefully designed by the artists, and in accordance with the proportion of the parts of the body and the sex) with instruments like brushes or small twigs, with very fine points of bamboo.
>
> The body was pricked and marked with them until blood was drawn. Upon that a black powder or soot made from pitch, which never faded, was put on. The whole body was not tattooed at one time, but it was done gradually. In olden times no tattooing was begun until some brave deed had been performed; and after that, for each one of the parts of the body which was tattooed some new deed had to be

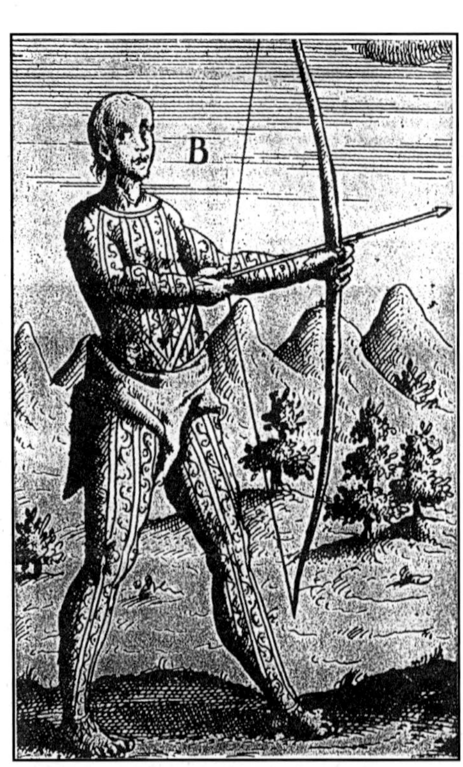

"A native of Capul" from A Voyage to the East Indies, written in 1600. This depiction shares some of the elements of the Boxer Codex illustration such as the long "labid" stripes running up the legs and the tattooed collar around on the upper chest. It is likely that the artist embellished his work due to the presence of the bow and arrow which were typically not used as weapons in the Visayan Islands.

Filipino Tattoos: Ancient to Modern

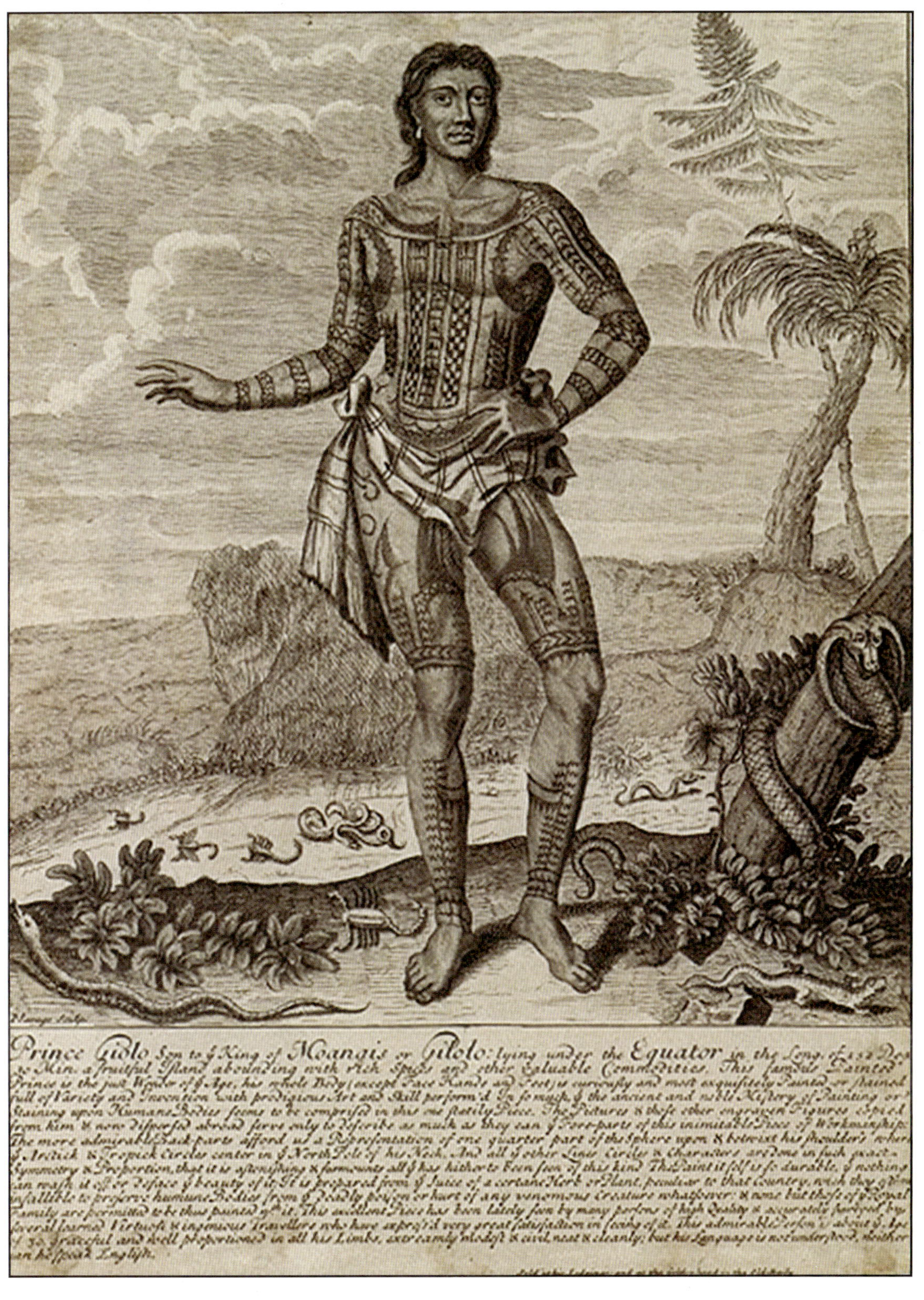

Prince Giolo from the engraving made for his exhibition in 1692

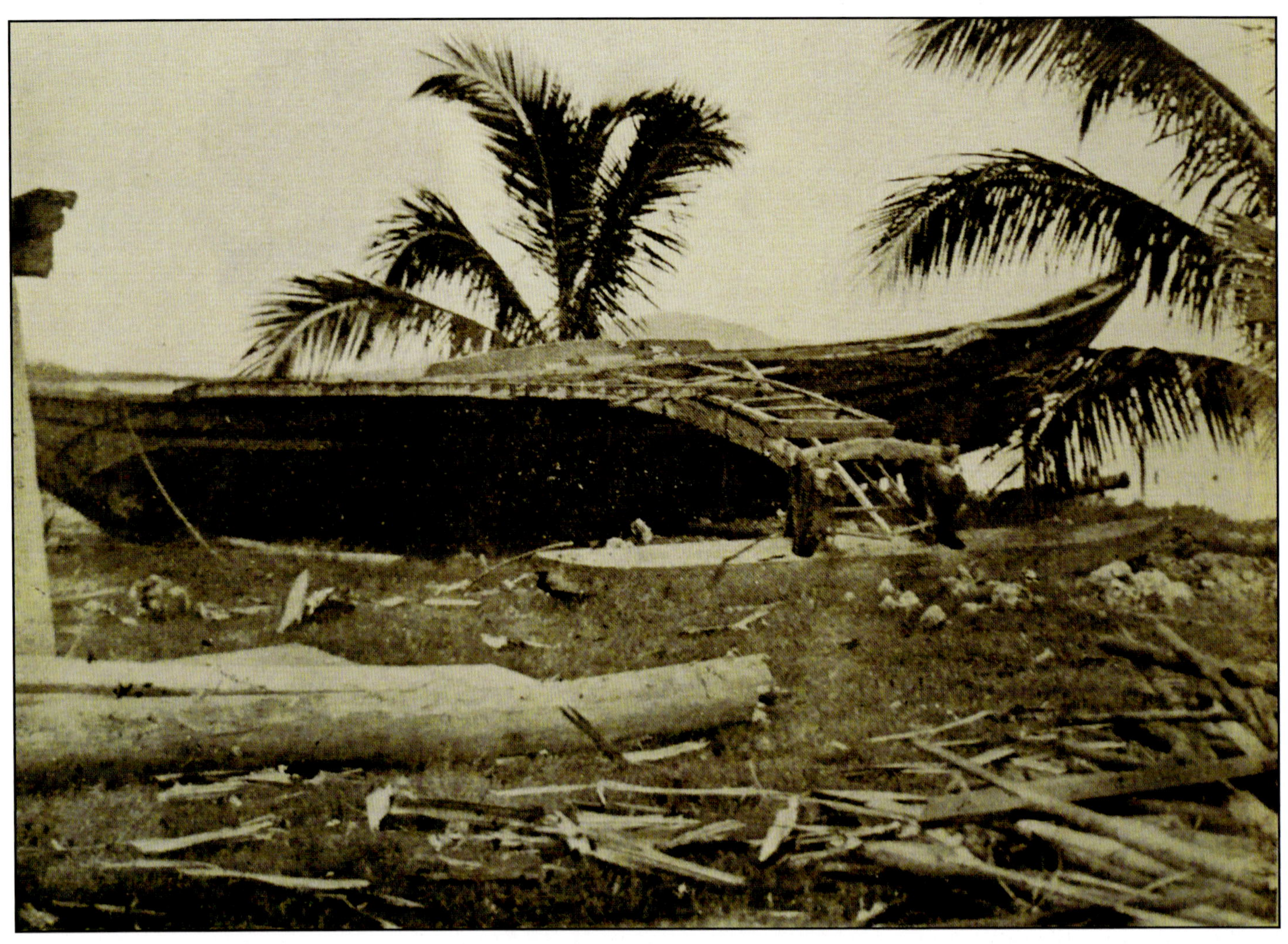

A Caroline Islands outrigger canoe in Mayo Bay in Mindanao in the Philippines ca. 1905. Photo by Faye-Cooper Cole

performed. The men tattooed even their chins and about the eyes so that they appeared to be masked. Children were not tattooed, and the women only one hand and part of the other. The Ilocanos in this island of Manila also tattooed themselves but not to the same extent as the Visayans.[7]

An old manuscript about the Philippines and neighboring areas that was procured by Charles Ralph Boxer, called *The Boxer Codex*, had some illustrations of what the men's tattoos of the Visayan Islands of the Philippines may have looked like. These illustrations depicted thick and fine black lines running up the legs and arms of the men, with zigzag lines placed among them. On the chest, buttocks and calves were matching floral or sun-like geometrical patterns. These patterns were also depicted on the forehead and cheeks of the face. (We explore these circular patterns in greater detail in Chapter 4.) Tattoos were shown covering the whole of the back. There were also bands of tattoos on the sides of the rib cages with a band of tattooing running up the center of the torso to a wide collar of tattooing. The shapes of the tattoos were geometric in nature, according to the illustrations.

Filipino Tattoos: Ancient to Modern

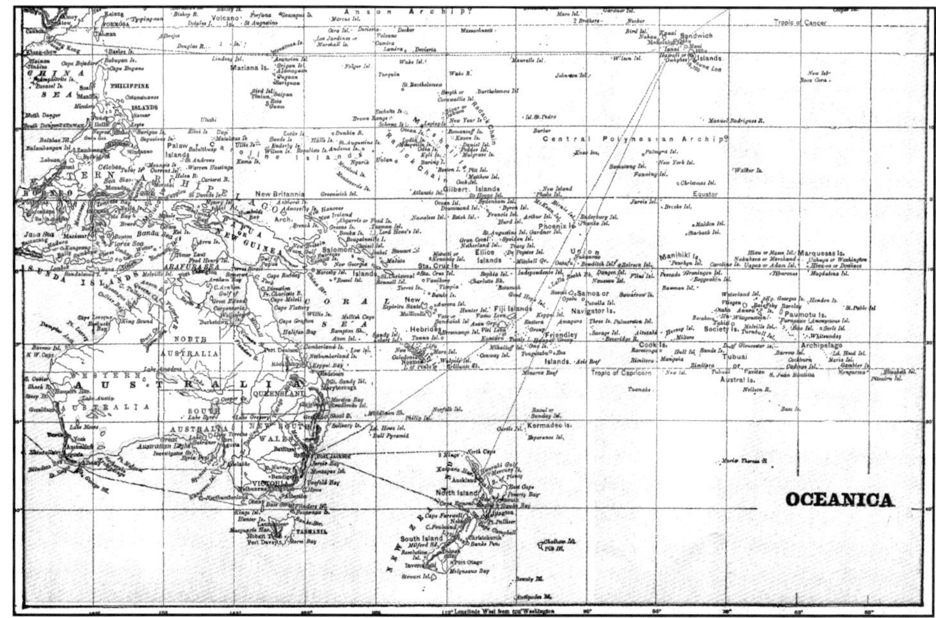

Jeoly or Prince Giolo

The art of tattooing has enjoyed recent popularity as the practice has become more mainstream in Western society. Many cultural groups throughout the world have tattooed in the past, but it was through the Austronesian family that it was reintroduced to Western society. The Philippines played a role in reintroducing tattooing to the Western world. The first tattooed Austronesian was brought to Europe in 1692. This tattooed man was called "Jeoly" and later re-named "Prince Giolo" by an English privateer, William Dampier. Jeoly was bought as a slave with his mother by the privateer Dampier on the Philippine Island of Mindanao. Dampier intended to put Jeoly on display and earn a profit from exhibitions of the tattooed prince. Unfortunately, Giolo died from smallpox soon after a few public appearances.[8]

Dampier records that Jeoly originally was from the island of Miangas, a small island about seventy-five miles east of the Sarangani Islands of the Philippines, also known as Pulau Miangas or Las Palmas Island. It was originally included in the boundaries of the Philippines when Spain ceded the Philippines to the United States after the Spanish-American War. However, after a territorial dispute in 1928, Miangas was awarded to Indonesia. The language of the inhabitants of Miangas is close to the language spoken on the Sarangani Islands.

From engravings made of Jeoly for his public exhibition in England, his tattoos show the designs and framing commonly found on the island of Yap in Micronesia. Travel to southern islands from Yap for trade was common to mine stone money. In the past, Caroline Islanders in Micronesia would sometimes be tattooed at locations they visited, including Yap. They would also adopt tattooing motifs or patterns from other islands. Just like today, cultural exchange among people occurred in the past. Whether Jeoly was actually from Miangas, the Caroline Islands or from Yap we may never know. The island of Miangas is close enough to Mindanao for island-to-island raiding or trade, which was common in the past. Although not a Filipino in the modern sense, Jeoly was the first tattooed member of the Austronesian family to be seen in Europe.

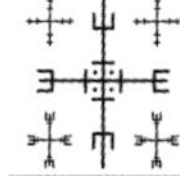

Early Accounts and Fragments of Philippine Tattoo Culture

Chapter 2

The Tattoo Process and Tools

The tattooing kit of Lakay Jacob Angnganai of Lubo Tanudan. Lakay Jacob last used these tools in 2000 at more than 90 years of age to tattoo his grandson. Halfway through the tattooing session Lakay Jacob broke down and tearfully stated "Adipon manbatek" (I cannot tattoo any more). His age and eyesight were hindering him. After finishing the tattooing of his grandson he gave the tools to Professor Analyn "Ikin" Salvadore-Amores of University of the Philippines Baguio as a gift. He passed away shortly thereafter. The coconut shell was used to hold the ink and the pieces of string were used as stencils to create straight lines. Photo courtesy of Professor Analyn Salvadore-Amores

Much of the original information on tattooing practices among peoples of the Philippines has been lost. In some areas Spanish colonization efforts so thoroughly exterminated the practice that only fragments remain to reconstruct the art of those people. There has been limited information academically about the application of tattoos, and even less about specific meanings behind the designs. From peoples of the Cordillera we learn that tattoos were applied much as they are in other parts of the Pacific region. A tattoo artist would be paid in advance with livestock, heirloom beads or coined silver, etc.[9] This sacred event then required a sacrifice by the butchering of an animal, such as a chicken or a hog. Before the tattooing began, often omens and signs were observed to ensure that the tattooing date and recipients had blessings from the *anito*, or ancestor spirits. According to tattoo anthropologist Lars Krutak, if the tattoo artist or recipient sneezed prior to the beginning of the tattooing, that was a sign that there was disapproval by a spirit and the tattooing should be postponed. Sneezing in general was a sign throughout the Philippines of a possible hazard or that a particular endeavor would not be successful. A practical interpretation of this belief was that sneezing indicated poor health or oncoming illness. Krutak also explains that according to Apo Maria Whang-Od, the last remaining traditional tattoo artist of the Kalinga, abstinence from alcohol was required prior to tattooing. Prior to tattooing, prayers or chants invoked the gods to bless the tattooing and protect the recipient from harm. Among the Kalinga, tattooing was conducted in the winter months to reduce the chance of serious or life-threatening infection. There were both male and female tattoo artists in the Cordillera region of Luzon. Although regional terms varied, male tattoo artists were called *manfatek*, *manbatek*[10], *mambabatok*,[11] *bumafatek*,[12] etc. and usually came from a family of warriors. Female tattoo artists were called *manfattong*[13] depending on locality.

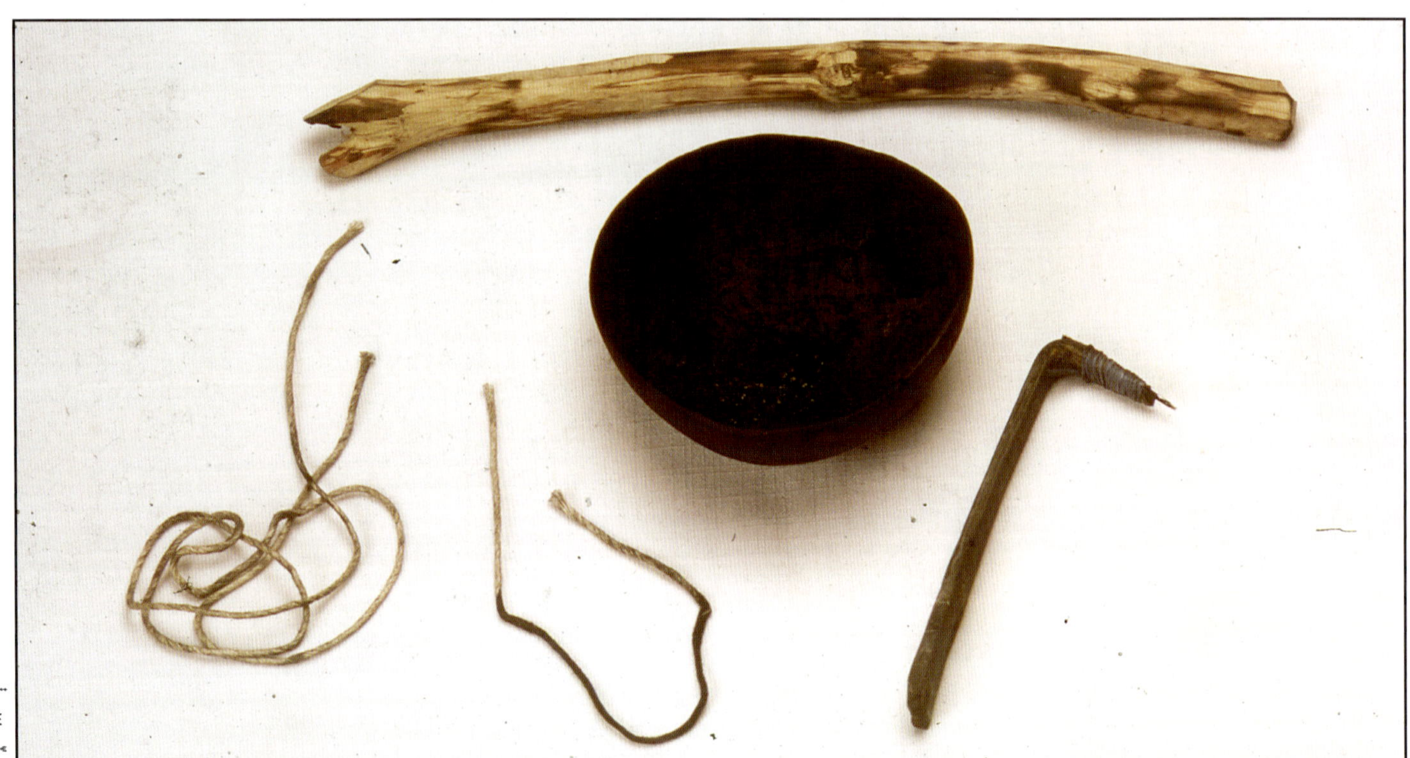

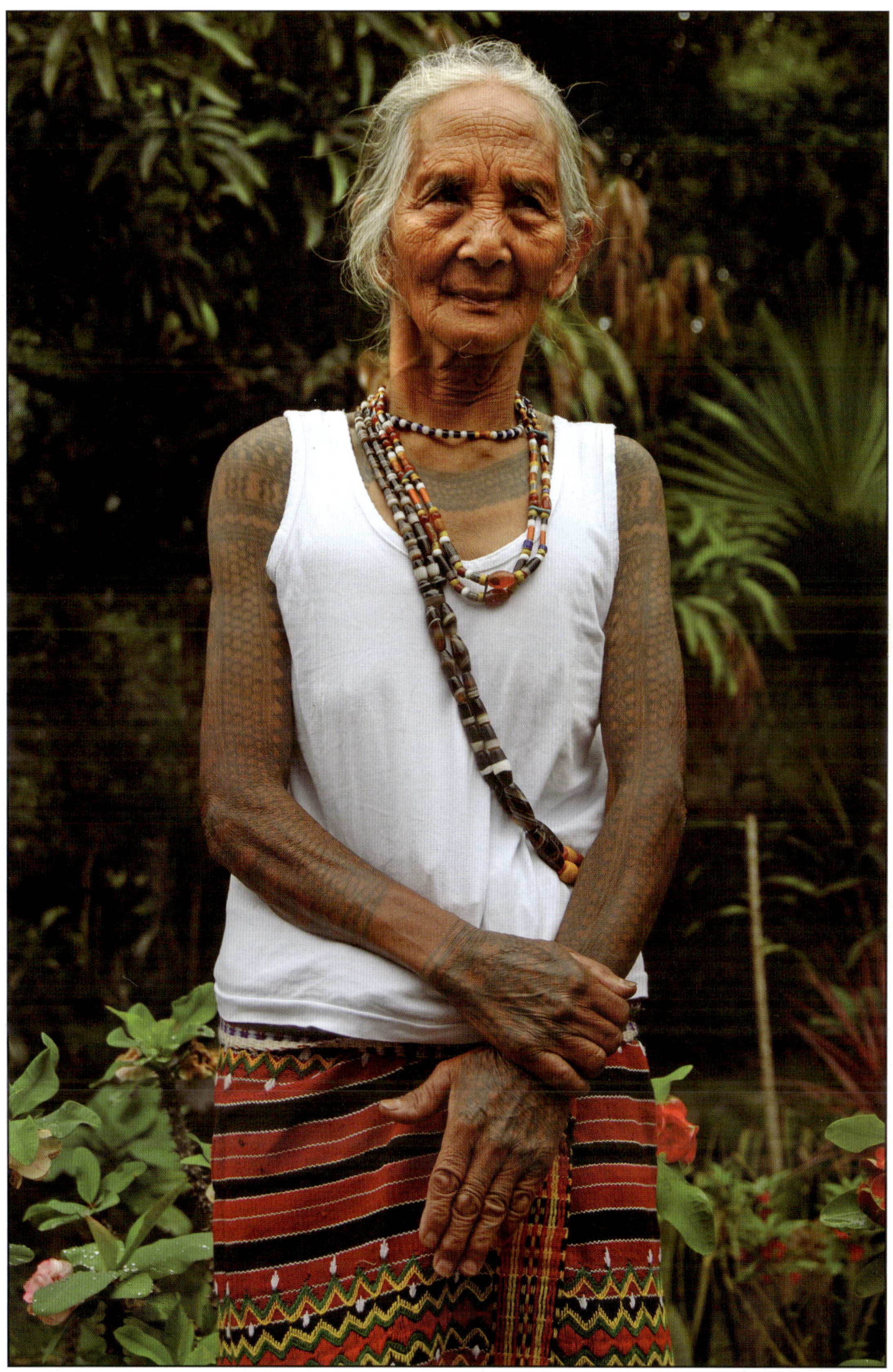

A Kalinga woman with heirloom beads used to pay for tattooing. Photo courtesy of Sidney Snoeck

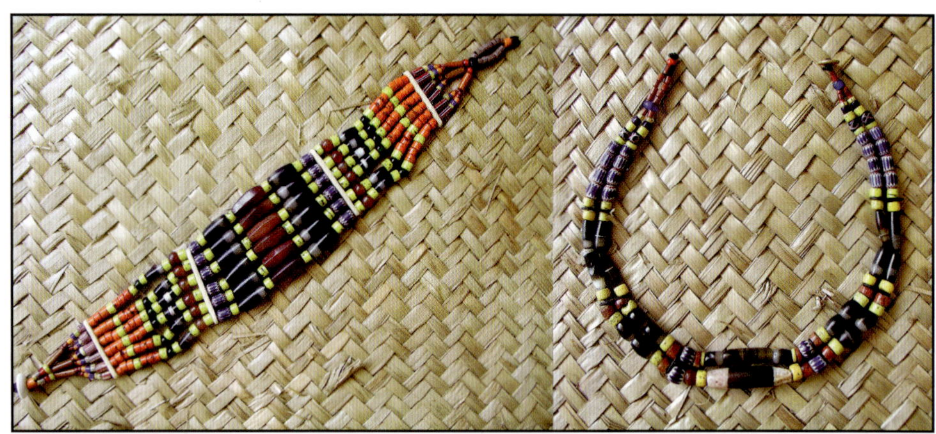

Making Tattooing Ink

Before a tattoo could be made, the tattooing ink had to be prepared. The ink, called variations of "*iro, biro, biyug, bidu*" etc., was usually made from pine soot and water. Other ingredients sometimes included, such as oil, sugarcane juice, chicken excrement and hog bile. In addition, the Ifugao added the juice of an edible plant called "*latong.*"[14]

Pine soot was collected from the bottoms of pots that sat over a fire where pine logs full of resin were being burned. The soot that accumulated on the pots was scraped off i (usually into a coconut shell) to be made into the tattooing ink.

In the Pacific Isles, tattooing ink was prepared in a similar way by collecting soot from stones or pebbles sitting underneath burning candlenuts. Candlenut or *Kukui*, as it is called in Hawai'i, is full of a resinous substance similar to pine pitch that produces black smoke when burned. P.F. Kwiatkowski, a native Hawaiian and the author of *The Hawaiian Tattoo,* states that coconut and sugarcane juice was added to the soot as preparation for the ink.[15] There are also references to Hawaiians using shellfish bile as a tattooing ink,[16] similar to using hog bile in the preparation of Philippine tattooing inks. In French Polynesia, among the Marquesan Islanders, similar tattoo ink recipes were used and the ink was called *hinu,*[17] similar to Philippine words for tattoo ink, *bidu* or *biro.*

After the ink was prepared, tattoo artists traced the design onto the skin with the ink. The Kalinga sometimes used stencils, called "*kammai,*" for certain zig-zag patterns. Pieces of string or long blades of grass were also dipped into the ink and used as stencils to make straight lines. Then the *manbatek* was prepared to begin tattooing. The tattooing comb was ready to be dipped into the ink.

Tattooing Tools

Throughout most of Austronesia, tattooing tools were similar. Most incorporated a comb of needles set at a right angle to the length of an L-shaped stick. In the Philippines combs were similar to those used by Pacific Islanders. An adze-like tool was made of wood or carabao horn (Philippine water buffalo) with needles made of iron, steel, brass, bamboo or thorns of the orange tree lashed to the tool.

The name of the tattooing comb varied. Among the Kalinga and Kankana-ey, the tattooing comb was commonly called *gisi* or *kisi*. The

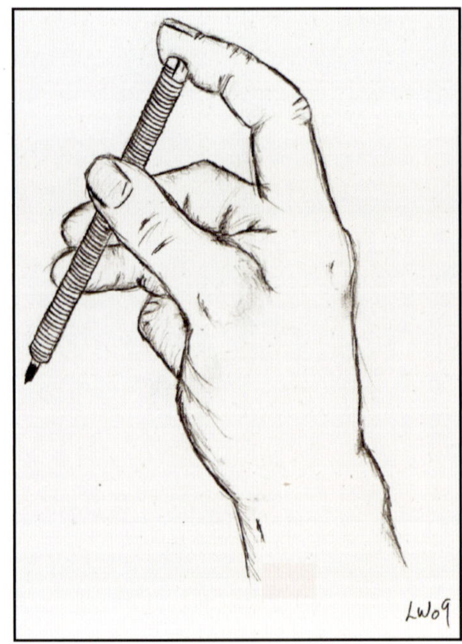

The Ifugao ukmok tool – by the author

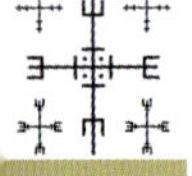

Filipino Tattoos: Ancient to Modern

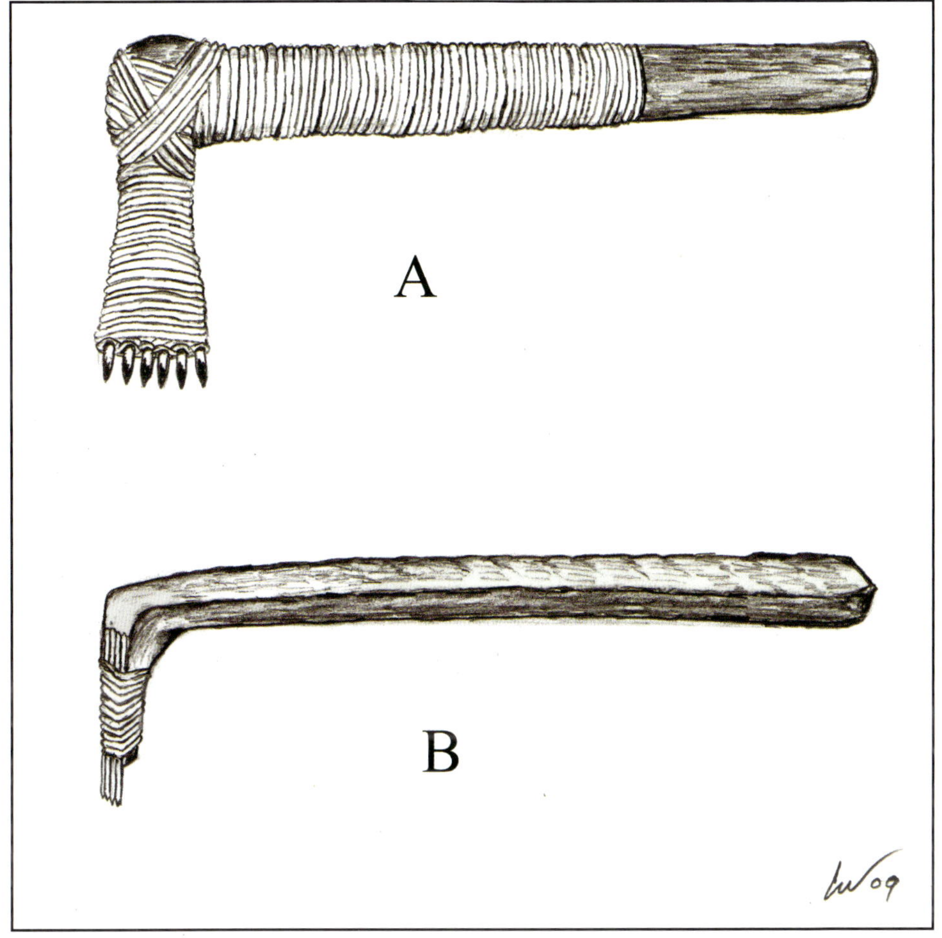

A

B

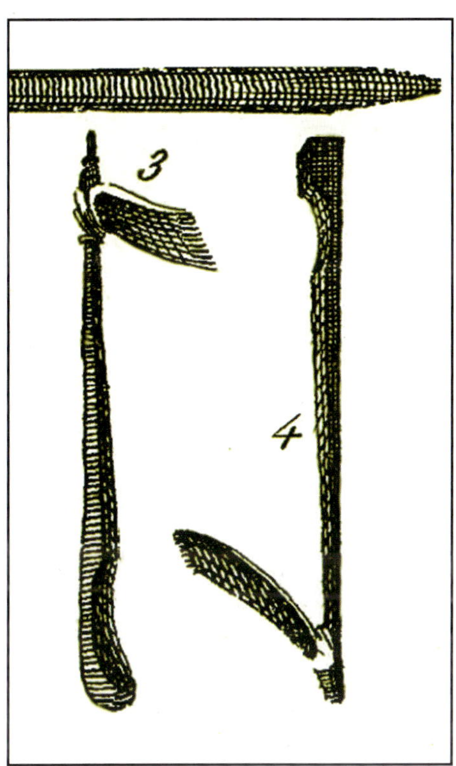

Left: The Bontoc tattoo tool called lufan with its needles set parallel to the shaft of the tool. (above) A Kalinga tattoo comb called gisi made from carabao horn with the needles set perpendicular to the length of the tool. By the author

Above: Tahitian tattoo tools drawn by Syndey Parkinson ca. 1769

Isneg called the same tool "*igihisi.*"[18] The Ilokano word for "comb," *sagaysay*, is a cognate of *gisi* (*sagaysay* = gisi). There are similar words in Maori and Hawaiian for "comb" or a comb made of fish bones, called *kahi*. According to Papa Henry Auwae, noted *Kahuna La'au Lapa'au* (herbal medicine) expert, told P.F. Kwiatkowski that fish bones were used for making tattooing needles. Due to the lack of the "s" sound in Maori and Hawaiian, "h" was used as a substitute. When the "h" sound is replaced by the "s" sound, *kahi* becomes *kasi*, which is similar to the word *kisi*. A variation of this tool was the *lufan*, used in Bontoc and Kalinga provinces, which was an orange or lemon thorn attached to a stick in the same adze-like arrangement.

The Ifugao people used a needle tied to the tip of a stick, called *ukmok*, to perform a stabbing motion, similar to Asian methods of tattooing. Differently sized combs were used for different types of detail work. Combs for women's tattoos were as small as one, two or three needles. In the Bontoc region as many as twelve needles were sometimes used. Samoan tattoo combs, called *au*, can have more that thirty teeth in the comb, but this was probably due to the extensive solid black areas of their tattooing, which would take considerably longer to apply with a smaller comb. It is thought that since the Pacific Islands did not have metal ores on many of the islands, the skill to extract and refine metallic ores was lost some time in the past. Consequently, tattooing needles of the Pacific Islands were usually made from the bones of fishes, birds and small animals. Human

The Tattoo Process and Tools

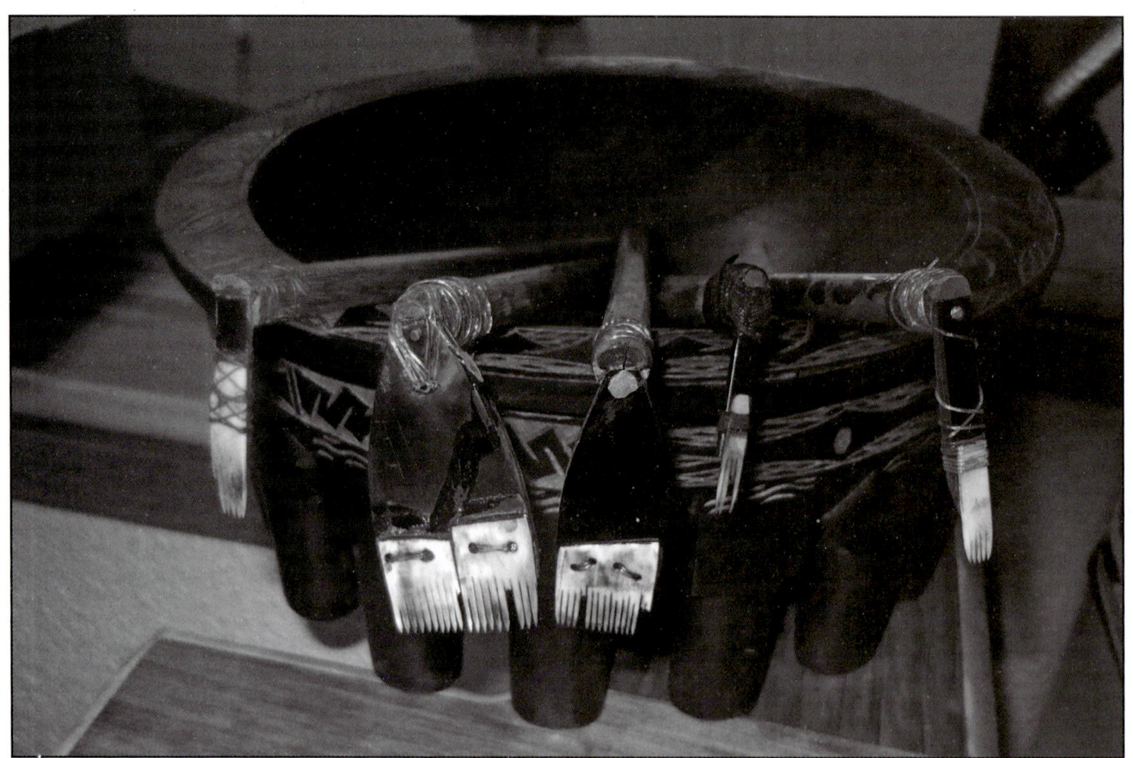

Samoan tattooing tools called au – Courtesy of Michael Fatutoa

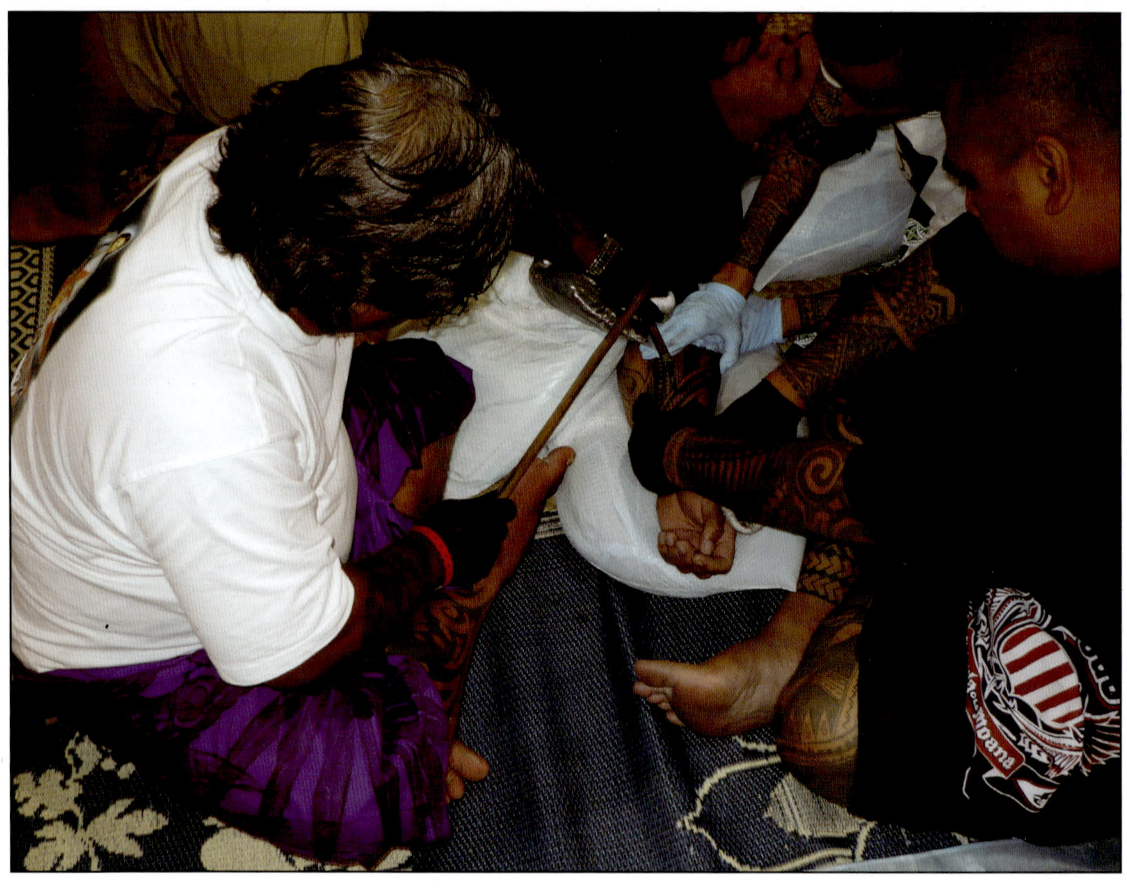

Su'a Suluape Alaiva'a Petelo tattooing a client with the au. By the author

Filipino Tattoos: Ancient to Modern

bone was used to make needled tattoo combs in the Marquesas Islands as well as some of the larger tattoo combs in Hawai'i.[19] Other materials used for these needles were the tusks of pigs and bamboo points. The needles were razor sharp and capable of executing very precise lines and designs.

After dipping the tool into the ink, the artist used another long stick as a mallet and tapped repeatedly the back of the comb to force the needles and ink into the skin. *Tek-tek* (pronounced *tük-tük*) was a word sometimes used to describe the hammer stick in the Cordillera of the Philippines. In Samoa, the word for the hammer stick is *sau-sau* or *auta*.[20] The Ilokano word *baut,* which means "a stick used for hitting," may be related (baut = auta = sau). *Patik* was another word to describe the mallet stick for tattooing.[21]

In the Visayan Islands, *batuk* or *patik* were words used to describe tattoos. The Indonesian word *batik* is used to describe textile patterns, but is similar to the word "*batek.*" Here again, we see a conceptual link in how wearing tattoos was perceived as nearly indistinguishable from wearing clothing. In the Cordillera, the actual tapping was also called *tek-tek,* which means "to hit slowly."[22] "Tek" forms the latter syllable of the common word for tattoo, "*ba-tek.*" The word *tek-tek* may be related to the Polynesian word *tiki,* which was used by Marquesan people in the word to describe tattooing, *patu-tiki. Tek-tek* is likely derived from the same concept as the word *ta-tak* in Tagalog which means "to mark." Some believe that this word came about as an imitation of the tapping sound. The word *tek-tek* may be an onomatopoeic word imitating the tapping sound of the mallet stick against the tattooing comb. This same interpretation is also used as one of the explanations for the word *tatau* or *ta-tatau* in the Polynesian languages, from which we derive the word "tattoo." If *tek-tek* or *ta-tau* were onomatopoeically translated into English, it would be "tap-tap." Most interpretation of the words "*tatau*" or "*kakau*" (in Hawaiian) comes from the words "*ta*" (*ka*) to strike, "*tau*" (*kau*) upon. *Tatau* is most often used in Polynesia as the verb to describe the act of tattooing, and the patterns are individually referred to as *Moko, Pe'a, Patu-tiki, Uhi*, etc.

To use the tattooing tool, *gisi* or Polynesian tool like the Samoan *au*, the artist first dipped the needles into the ink and position the tool a little above the skin over the area to be tattooed. The tattooing tool was braced or counterbalanced in one hand so that when it was struck with the hammer stick the needles would be driven into the epidermis and then spring back to its position above the skin. By tapping the tool repeatedly, the tool would bounce up and down, in and out of the skin, like a sewing machine.

Generally, the tattoo artist would pull the skin to stretch it and make sure the tool could accurately trace the design and insert the ink to the right depth in the skin. In some places, a tattoo artist would be accompanied by assistants who stretched the skin for the artist. This prevented the tool from becoming stuck in the skin. If the ink was not driven deep enough, the tattoo could eventually fade and disappear as the skin renewed itself.

Sometimes the tool conveyed the ink into the puncture marks and at other times the ink was rubbed into the wounds after the puncturing. This was the method among the Bontoc people of Luzon. Instead of dipping the tool into ink the artist would hammer the design into the skin before

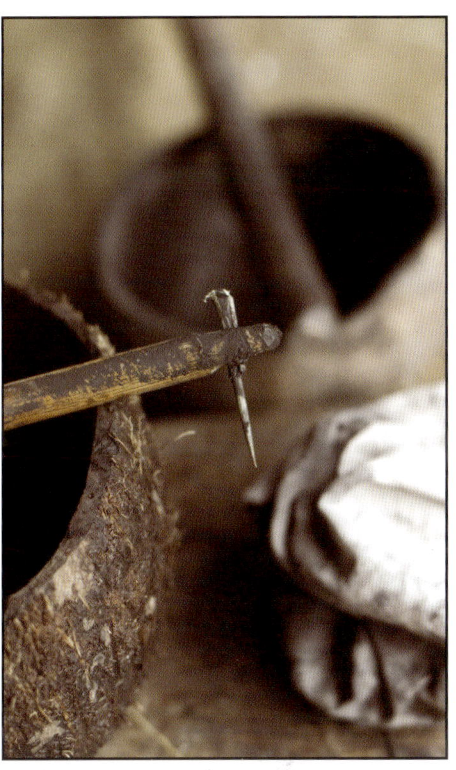

The gisi (kisi) tool of northern Luzon, made from a lemon thorn, Courtesy of Farlet Vale

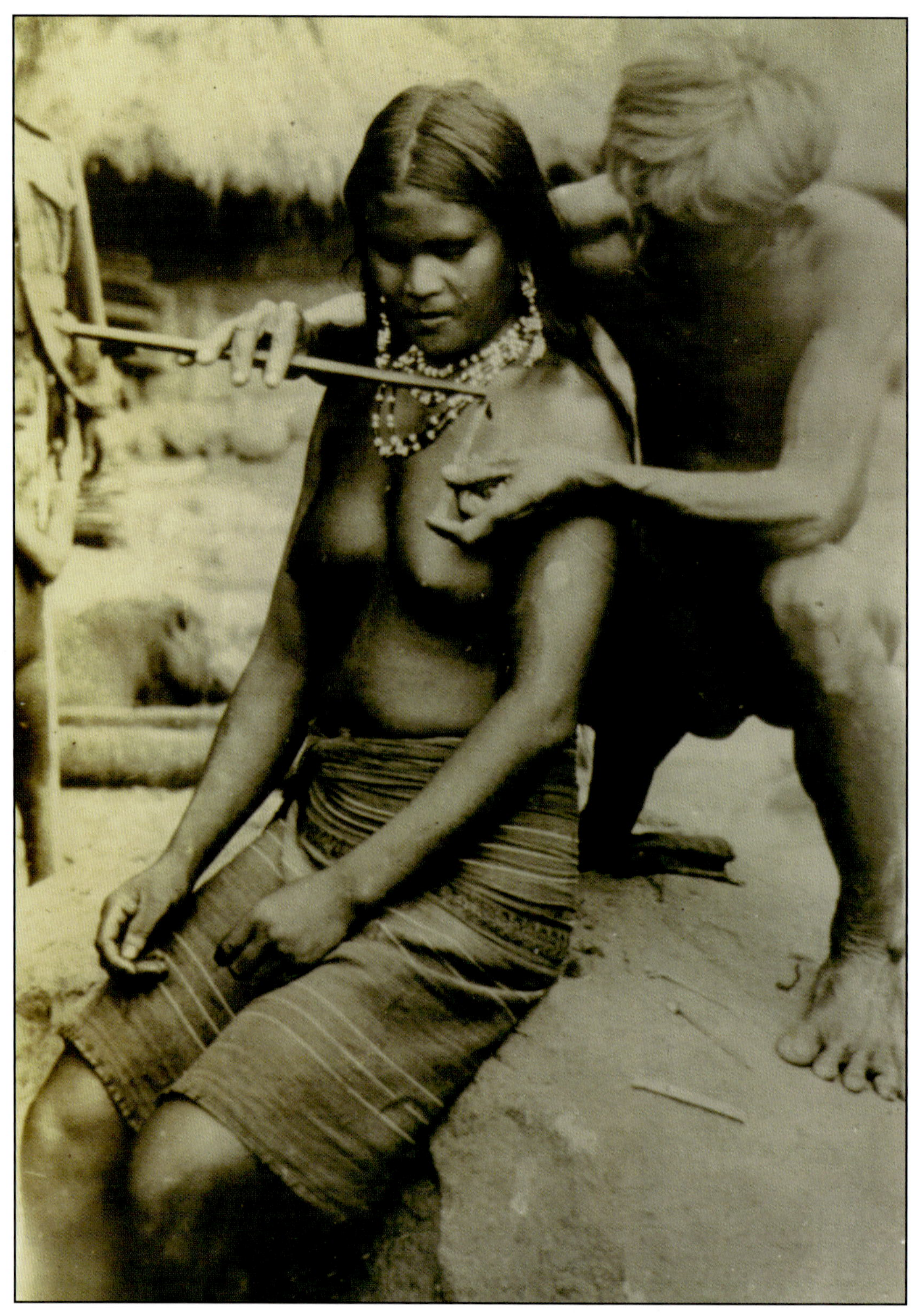

A Kalinga woman being tattooed by the manbatok (tattoo expert), circa 1900. In many early photographs, black and white film could not distinguish between brown skin and dark blue tattoos. Author's collection

Filipino Tattoos: Ancient to Modern

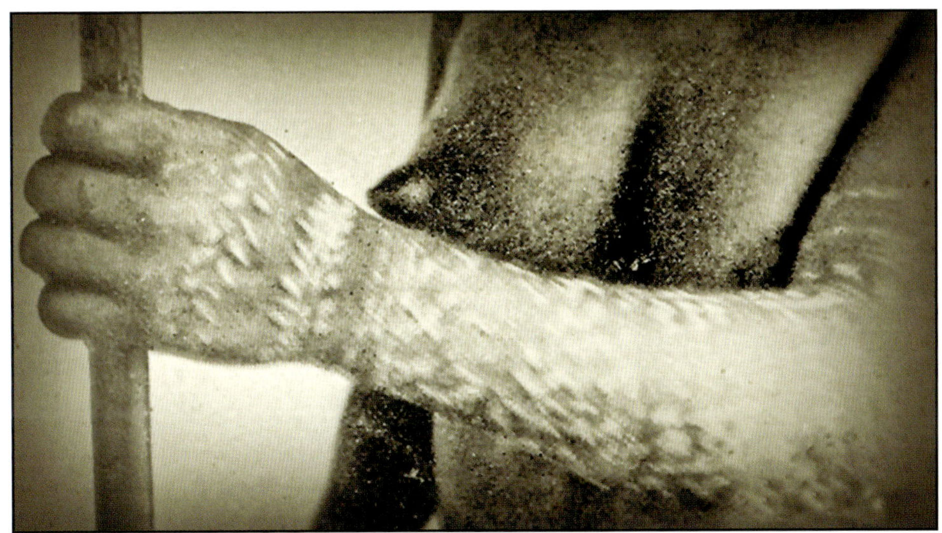

Swollen tattoo marks from Bontoc.
Photo by Dean Worcester ca. 1900

rubbing soot into the wounds.[23] Some Maori peoples of New Zealand similarly put charcoal pigment into the wounds after pricking or cutting open the skin.[24] Early chroniclers of Marquesan tattooing report the same method of rubbing in the ink after pricking the skin. Some Philippine groups would apply tattoos by pricking the skin with needles or a thorn with the ink on the comb. The tattooed designs would sometimes take months to heal afterwards. A celebration usually took place after the tattoo was complete to honor the recipient, in both the Philippines and the Pacific Isles.

The following excerpt is from a Dutch researcher and photographer, Ron Schaasberg, who traveled to villages in Bontoc and Ifugao. Apo Maria Whang-od showed him her method of tattooing:

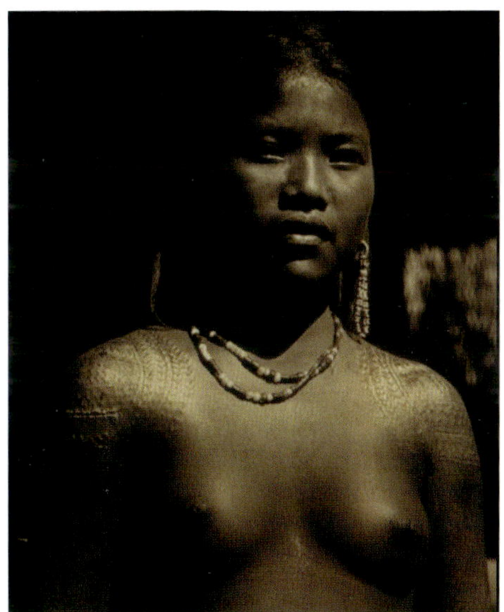

A young woman from Lubuagan in 1932 with fresh welting from the recent completion of tattooing on her shoulders. Photo courtesy of the Buchholdt Family Collection

Fang-od [Whang-od] prepares her equipment. She puts a pot on a fire, takes a sharp thorn from a shrub (tinik), a coconut shell with water, and then starts scratching the soot from the bottom of the pot and mixes it with crushed charcoal and a little water. The ink is ready. She has two sticks, one with the thorn and the other to be used to tap or hit the stick with the thorn. While tattooing, the thorn will puncture the skin and leave the ink under the skin. Fang-od uses pieces of long grass dipped in ink, and presses them firmly on the arm so she can follow the lines while tapping the thorn with ink.

She starts putting on the horizontal patterns. Then she picks up her two sticks, one with the needle and the other to tap on the stick with the needle. The first punctures are made on the skin and the first line starts to appear. Fang-od slowly but very precisely keeps working away on the upper arm. She uses a few patterns and figures that can be found in almost all tattoos: grass (inal-alam), centipede (ginay-gayaman), stars (tinat-araw) and the ladder (tey-tey). Fang-od finishes the work in two hours. Some oil is put on the tattoo to protect it from dirt." [25]

Faye Cooper-Cole relates the slightly different Itneg method of tattooing:

This tattooing is accomplished by mixing oil and the black soot from the bottom of a cooking pot, or the pulverized ashes of blue cloth. The paste is spread over the place to be treated, and is driven in with an instrument consisting of three or four needles set in a piece of bamboo. Sometimes the piercing of the skin is done before the color is applied; the latter is then rubbed in.[26]

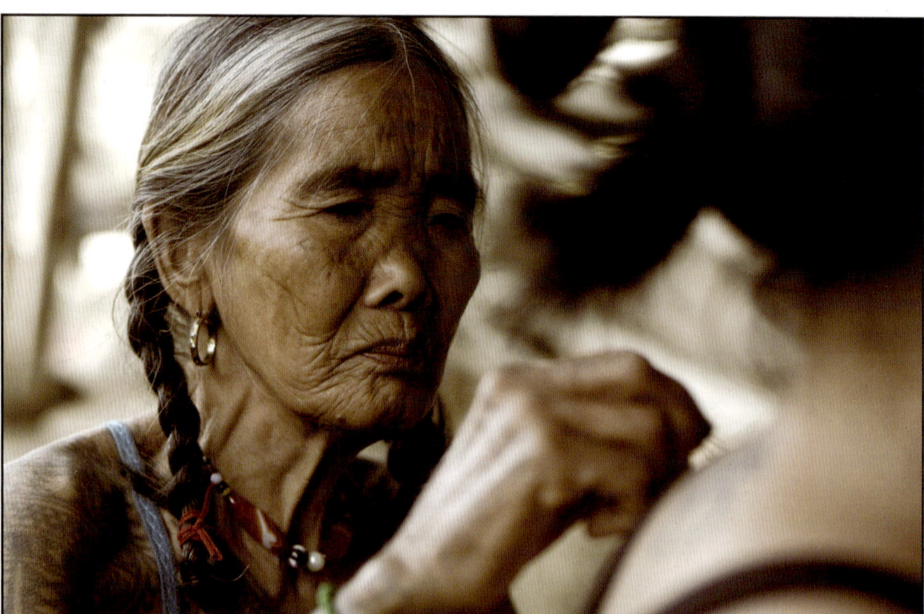

Pages 28-30
Photo series of Apo Whang-od tattooing. courtesy of Farlet Vale:

Right: Apo Whang-od tracing the design before beginning the work

Below: Setting the thorn taken from a lemon tree

Opposite: Apo Whang-od beginning the work

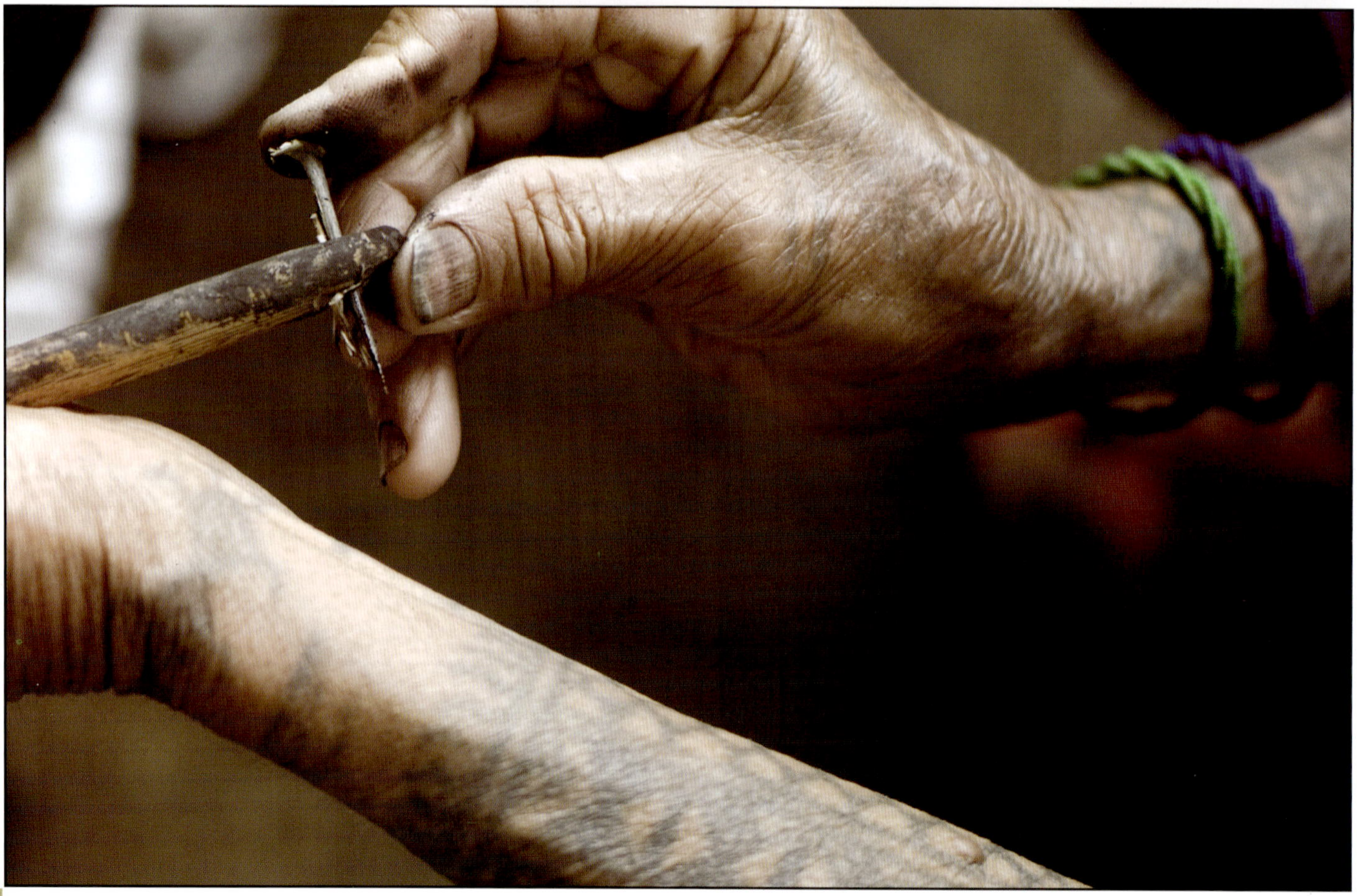

Filipino Tattoos: Ancient to Modern

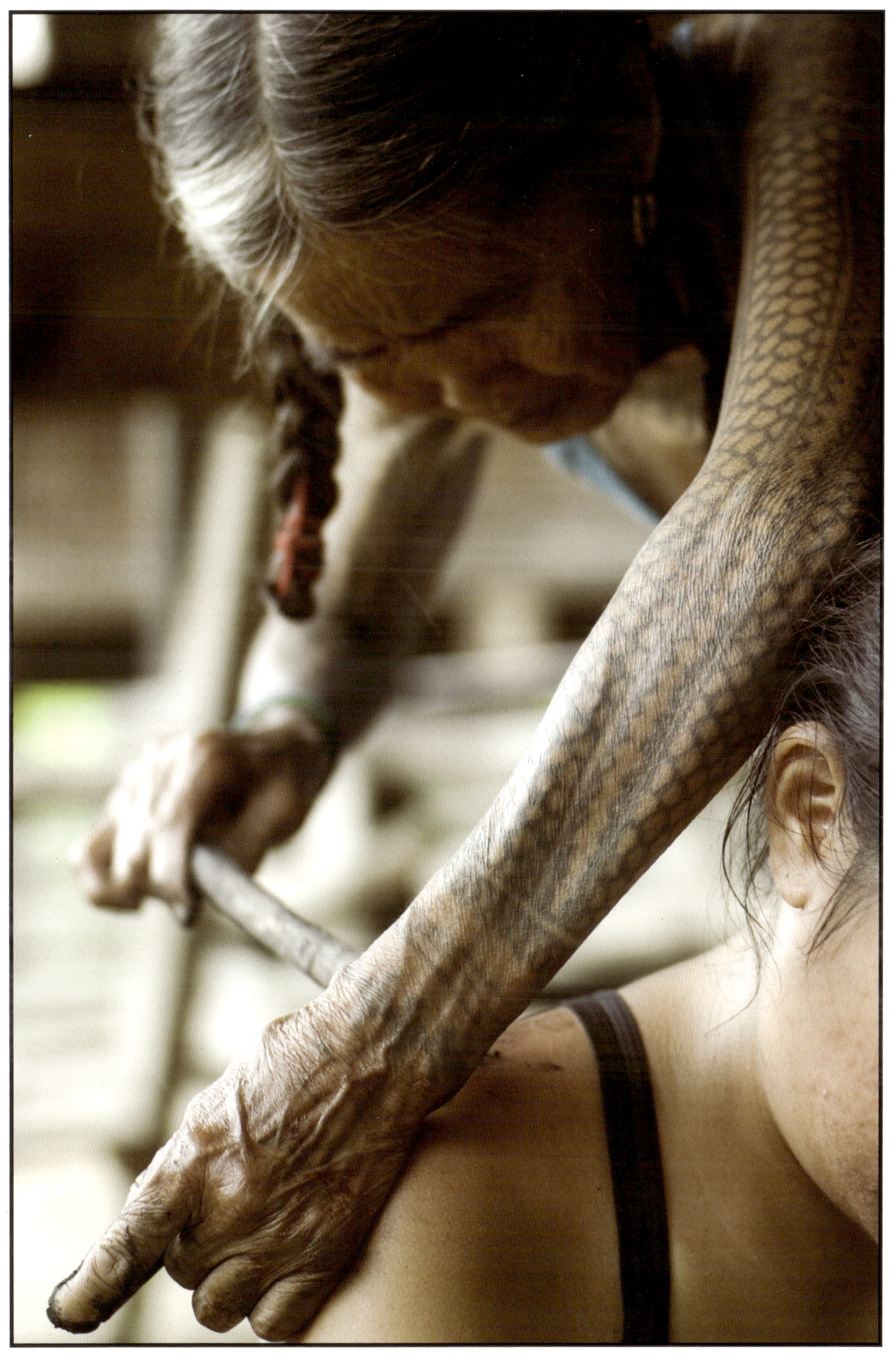

The shedding of blood as the ink is inserted

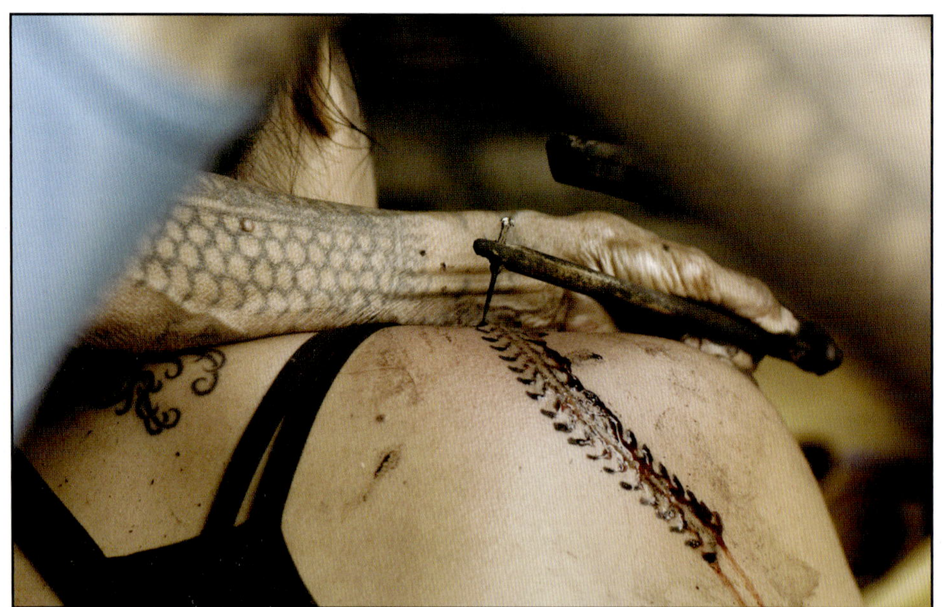

The Kalinga backhanded technique. The Kalinga hold the tattooing comb back-handed with the thumb and index finger as a counterbalance to allow the tool to move up and down as it is struck. The position of her index finger allows Apo Maria Whang-od to pivot the head of the tool without necessarily moving the entire hand

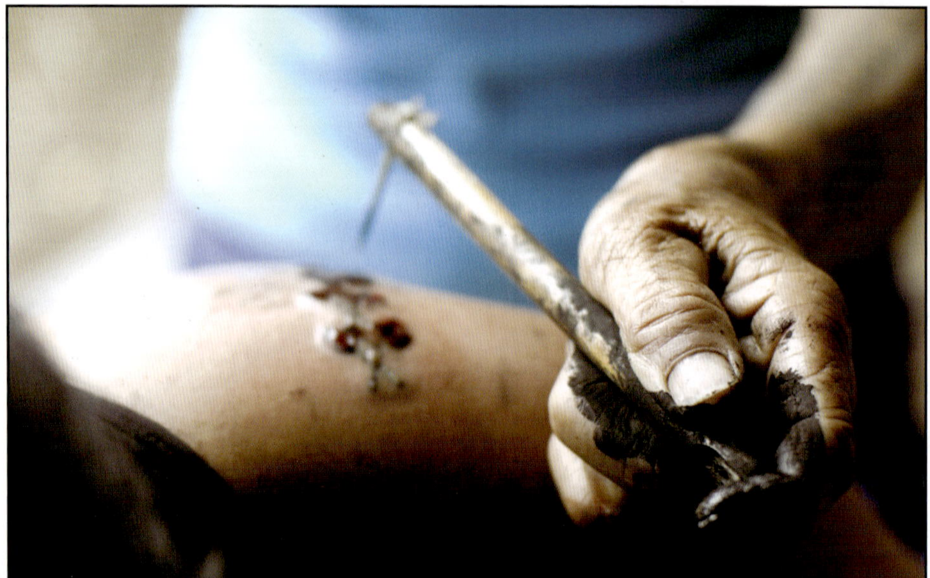

The finished tattoos of a python and centi-pede beginning to scab

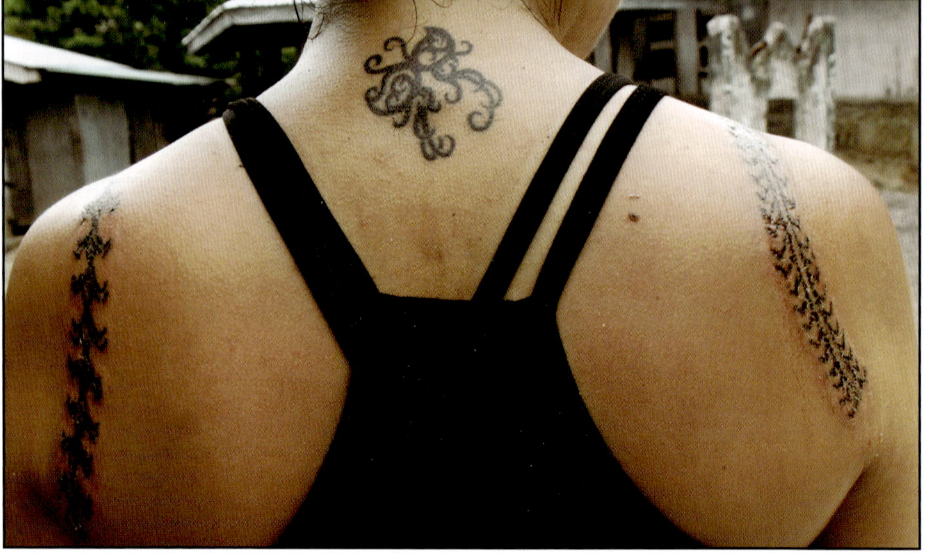

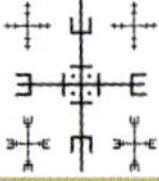

Chapter 3

Reasons for Tattooing

Why was tattooing historically such an important practice among many Austronesian peoples? Why suffer through pain and possible illness and death for these marks upon the skin? The short answers are that it was preferable to be tattooed than to be without. In the Philippines, tattoos were applied to men and women because, in general, they were considered an extension of a man's loincloth or a woman's skirt, as a form of clothing.

For example, a Kalinga woman's tattoo was called *fattong*, meaning "to put on." When the foreigners had asked the people to stop tattooing the response was, "We have to, lest we be naked." or "Why then we should be naked?"[27] Tattooing was an essential and permanent form of covering the body.

Aside from being a form of clothing, types and qualities of tattoos reflected roles in society, tribal identity, status, prestige, eligibility for marriage and, of course, personal beauty. Above these reasons were the spiritual beliefs associated with tattooing. Tattooing was part of an important rite of passage for both men and women. Certain designs recognized manhood and personal accomplishments while others conveyed a woman's attractiveness and promoted fertility and the continuity of the family or village. Still other tattoos gave or directed passage into the afterlife, while some illustrated the important link between mortals, their ancestors, gods and the intimacy of communication between them. These representational tattoos also venerated the avatars of their ancestors in the mortal world and reminded them of the knowledge and wisdom that was available from them. The same tattoos also protected them from reprisals from angry ancestors who may feel vengeful if forgotten or neglected by their mortal descendants. Other tattoos protected individuals from evil or malicious spirits by obscuring the identity of the wearer. Most often, these symbols and designs contained intertwined layers of meanings. The multitude of reasons for becoming tattooed gave a fuller life to the possessor of these symbols. With this in mind, let us explore some of the significance and reasons for tattooing.

Men's Tattoos and their Relationship to Headhunting

The Isneg Legend of the Origin of Tattoos

In the beginning the people who migrated to Apayao did not have any tattoos on their bodies. The people multiplied and scattered upon the different mountains of Apayao. As they did so the men strived to gain greater respect and prestige among themselves. There came a time when a man dreamed about tattooing his forearms.

One day a man named Halos-sab was sleeping. While he slept he dreamt of a very handsome man with tattooed forearms walking towards him. He asked Halos-sab if he would like to be admired and respected by his barriomates. Because of his wish for more respect Halos-sab answered "yes." The man told Halos-sab how he could have tattoos on his arms like his. The man told Halos-sab he must first carefully fasten five to ten needles onto the end of a curved piece of unsplit rattan. Then he must collect carbon [charcoal] from burning another piece of rattan. Then he must take the tool and use it to make the designs on his skin. Afterwards

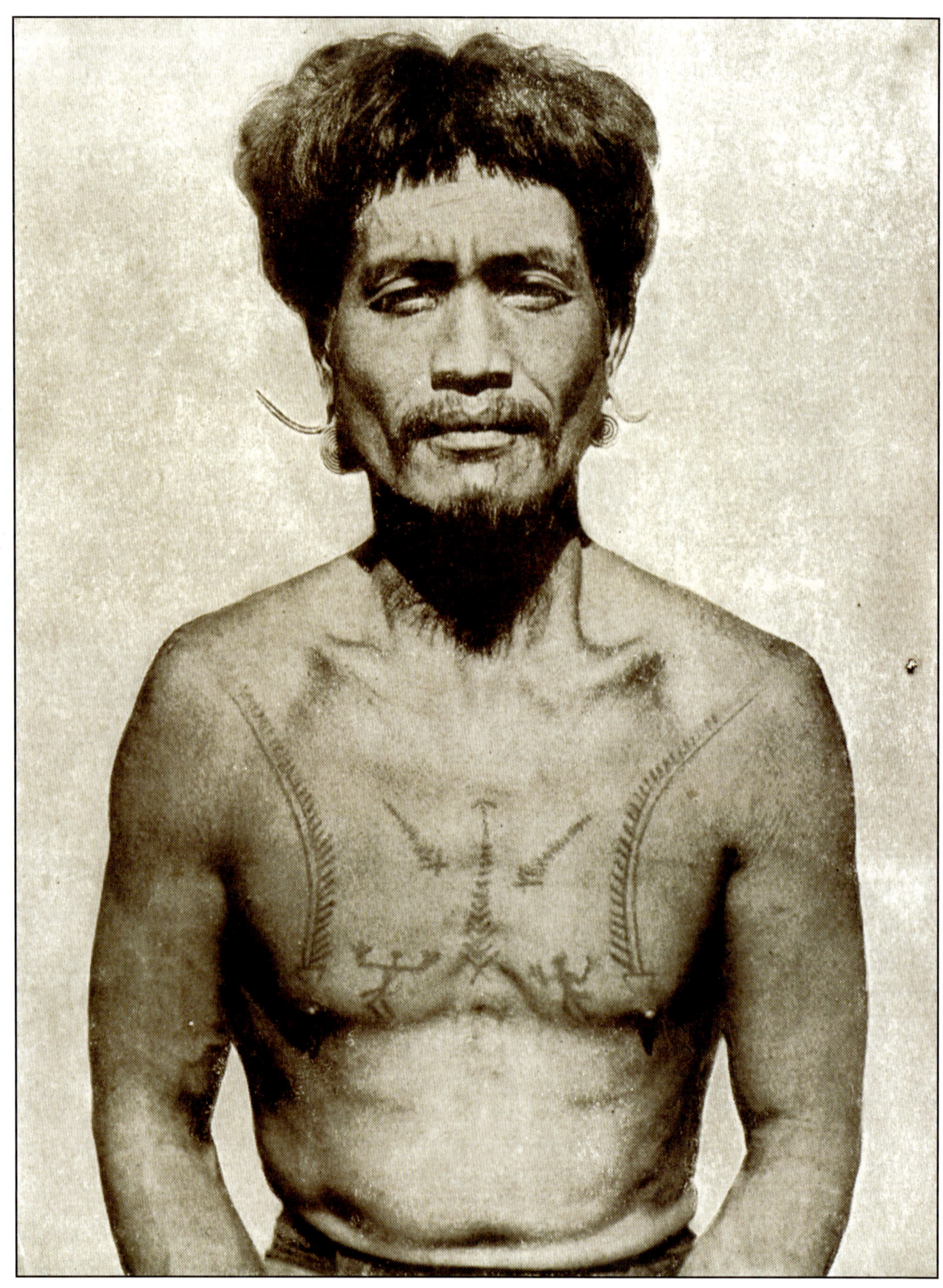

An Ifugao man with a chest tattoo called chak-lag, signifying his headhunter status.
Photo by Dean Worcester ca 1900

Filipino Tattoos: Ancient to Modern

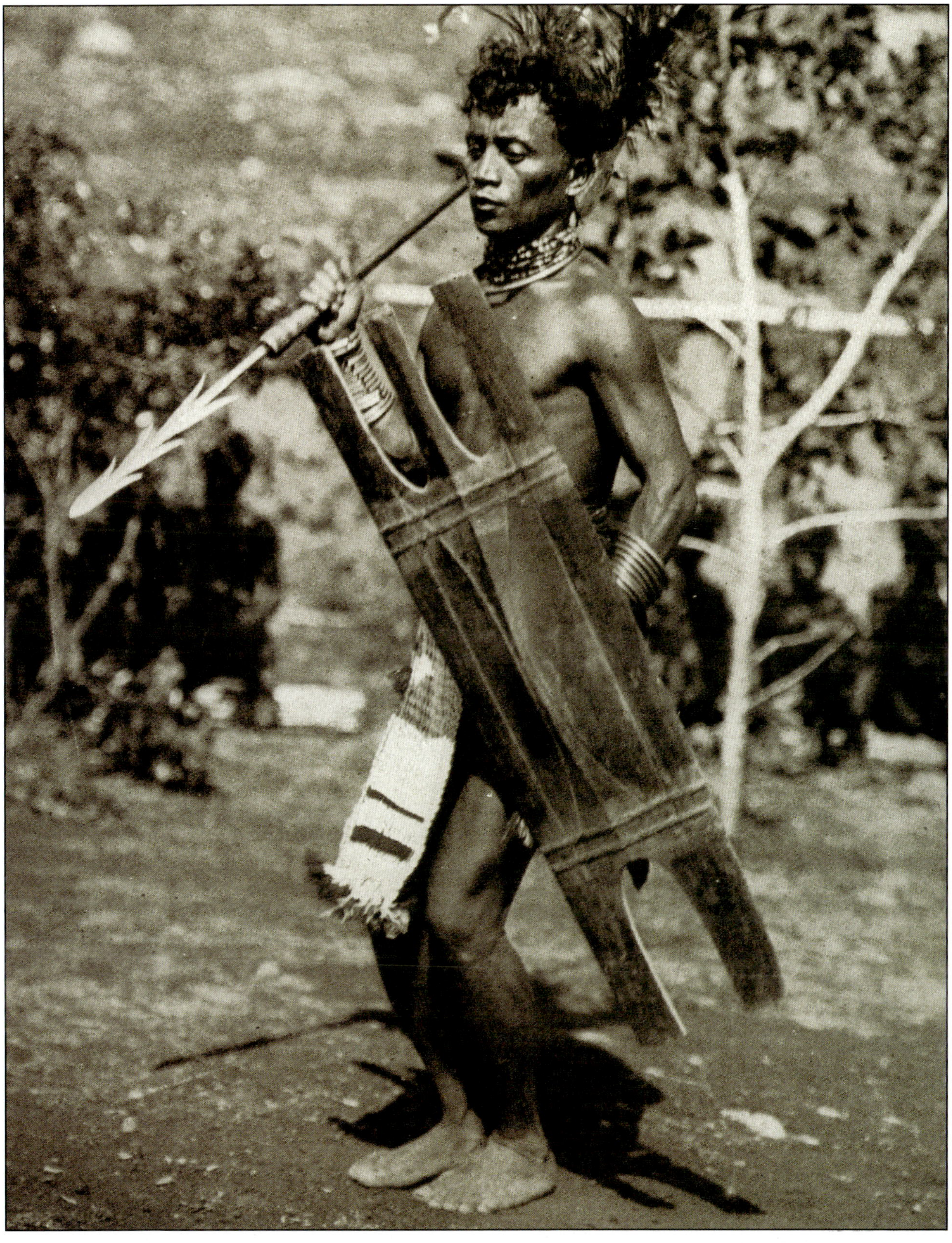

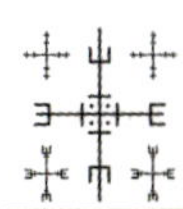

A Kalinga warrior dancing with shield and barbed spear. Photo by Dean Worcester ca. 1900

Head trophies that were provided as a sacrifice for the village. Photo by Dean Worcester ca. 1900

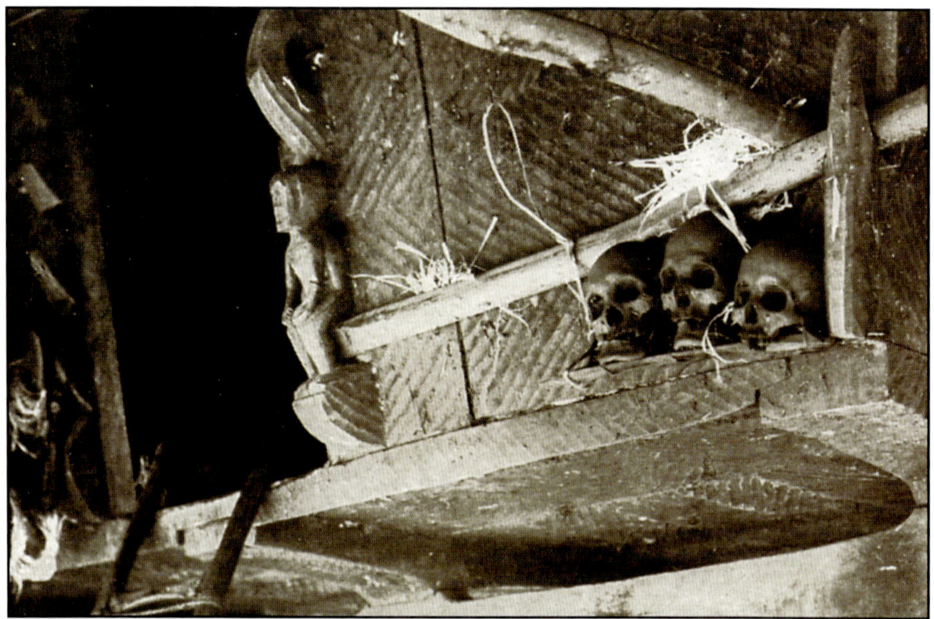

Opposite: An engraving of a partially tatto-oed man from the Benguet region. ca. 1850

he should rub the carbon onto the wounds. He explained that when it healed the tattooed portion would be black. The dream man told him it would never wash off or change. The man further told Halos-sab that he must persevere so that when Halos-sab was able to kill any man he would be well known as a brave man and as a man prepared to fight whenever provoked.[28]

Among many of the peoples of the Philippines, the majority of men's tattoos had to be earned through displays of courage in battle and the taking of lives or heads. These particular tattoos on specific parts of the body were the outward marks of valor, courage, manhood, and martial prowess. Although there were tattoos that were not associated with headhunting and warfare, such as the *babalakay* and *inangkid* motifs (which are discussed in Chapter 6), much of what is now known about tattooing in the Philippines, especially among the Cordilleran people, is understood in the context of headhunting. With this in mind let us briefly examine headhunting traditions.

Headhunting and warfare were the required activities which qualified a man for most tattoos. Early in the Spanish colonization of the Philippines, Spanish chronicler Father Francisco Antolin remarked how the Igorot men tattooed the face, hands, arms, legs and the whole of the body right down to the buttocks.[29] These men embodied the Spartan elite of the warrior class with the evidence of their bravery and character nearly covering their entire body. As Spanish friars and priests converted the people to Christianity, the warfare and headhunting activities requisite for most tattoos was lost. By the latter portion of the 1800s, full body tattooing was in decline. In 1883 doctor Hans Meyer remarked:

It struck me that I observed such complete tattooing only on older men… In the 'pacified' rancherias, the younger generation appears to be unfaithful to the old tradition. In Banaao, at any rate, the majority of the young men satisfy themselves with a little arm tattooing, a spiral or circular sun-image on the back of the hand, and a series of parallel rings about the calves.[30]

Filipino Tattoos: Ancient to Modern

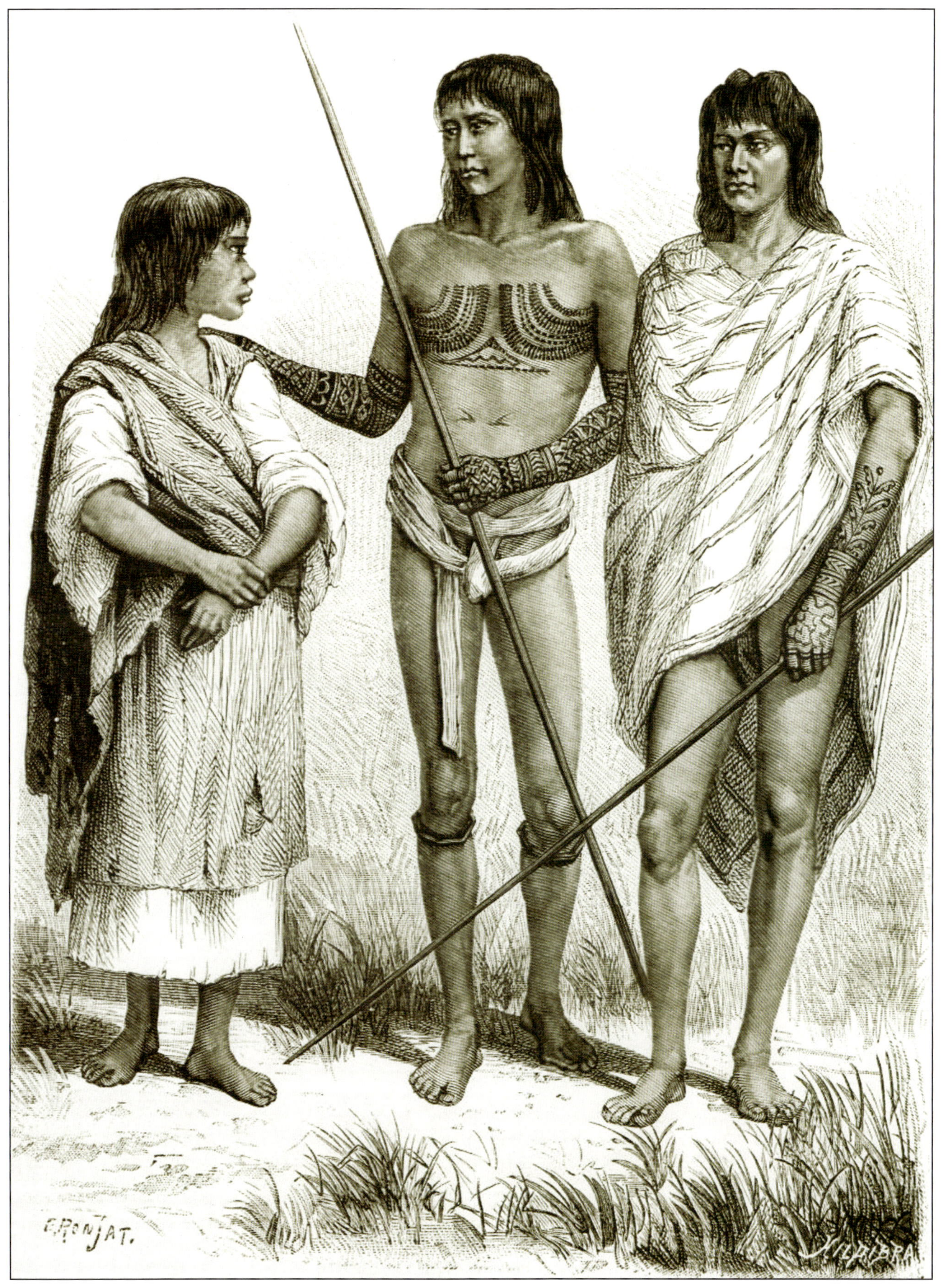

Reasons for Tattooing

By the early-1900s, tattooing became more limited among the Cordilleran peoples so that arm and chest tattoos (the mark of a headhunter) became the main focus of tattooing. With the rapid decline of headhunting in the 20th century, even these tattoos became infrequent. The last of the men who possess the headhunter's mark received their tattoos during World War II when the ban on headhunting was relaxed in regards to taking Japanese soldiers' heads. Most of the men who possess the headhunter's chest emblem earned their tattoos during World War II.

As with most of the peoples of the Cordillera mountain range of Luzon, young Kalinga males earned tattoos by participating in headhunting raids. There were different tattoos for different types of participation on the headhunt. When a boy came of age, he could merely observe a raid from a distance and be eligible for a type of tattoo identified as "*dakag*" by Edward Dozier in his book, *The Kalingas of Northern Luzon Philippines*.[31] For this a man may not necessarily have to kill an enemy to be tattooed but he must have been a part of the headhunting party that took a head. To be tattooed was a privilege and was a mark of prestige for the Kalinga men.

According to Franklin Baton, author of *The Kalingas: Their Institutions and Custom Law,* permanent marks of honor were earned in five ways:

1- wounder of a living enemy, *gimaiyang*
2- deliverer of the killing blow, *manela*
3- taker of the lower jaw before the head is severed, *sami*
4- taker of the head, *maniwat*
5- wounder of the torso, *dumagin.*

After these five levels were achieved, a man could receive any other tattoo without further killings.[32]

Men's tattoos mainly covered their chest, stomach and arms, but also their face and legs. When a man has killed another or taken a head, he received a series of lines or stripes on the back of the hands or wrists called, *gulot*, meaning "cutter of the head."[33] The men who have killed two people have tattoos put on their arms, while the man who kills more than two people is allowed to have his chest tattooed. A Kalinga chest tattoo is called *biniking* or *bikking.* A favorite tattoo for such prestigious warriors is the *khaman,* or head-axe. It was placed on the thighs, sides of the torso, cheeks of the face and back. Anthropologist Analyn Ikin Salvador-Amores states that special dakag tattoos for a man's back showed recognition for extraordinary and unsurpassed courage and represented the pinnacle of manhood, called "*Datum*" among the Ilubo Kalinga. Such a man with unsurpassed bravery was addressed by the honorific title "*mu'urmut*" and had his back nearly covered with bands of tattoos horizontally stretching across the field of his middle and upper back. The mu'urmut was looked to for leadership and typically was the peace pact holder between villages. The ascension to the Datum level correlates to other traditions in the Philippines where ruling chiefs were chosen from the warrior class and called "*Datu.*" Men of the Datu class were typically more extensively tattooed than those of lesser rank. Spanish historian Antonio de Morga records, "...the more prominent of the men, [Datu class] from their youth, tattoo their whole bodies, by pricking them wherever they are to be marked

Filipino Tattoos: Ancient to Modern

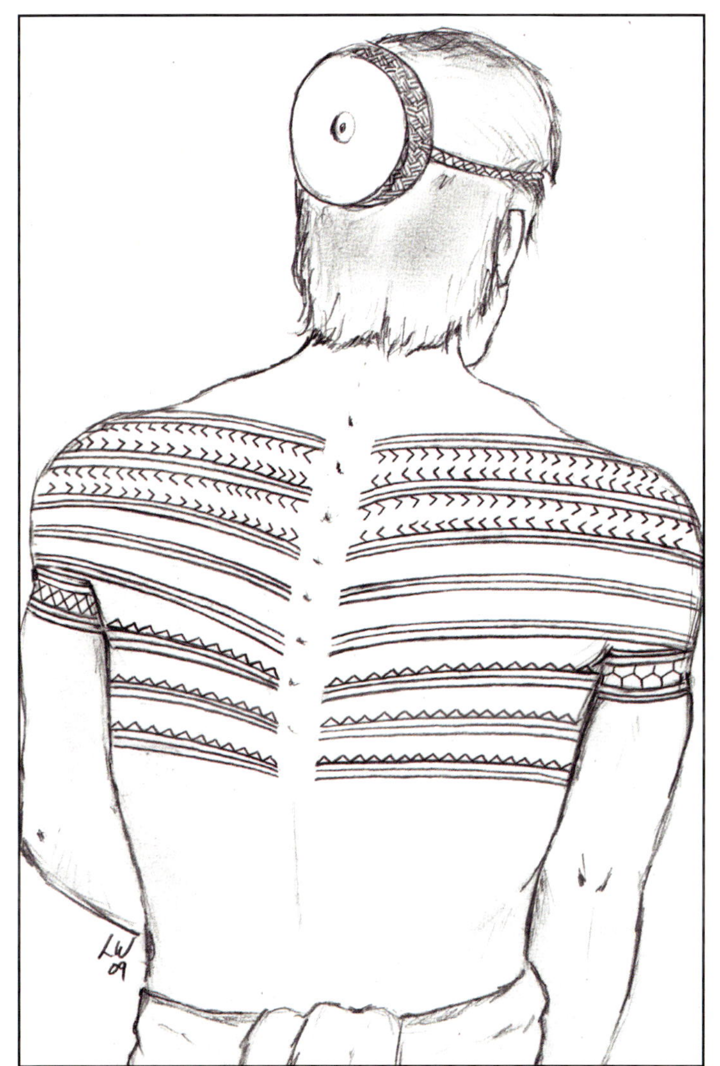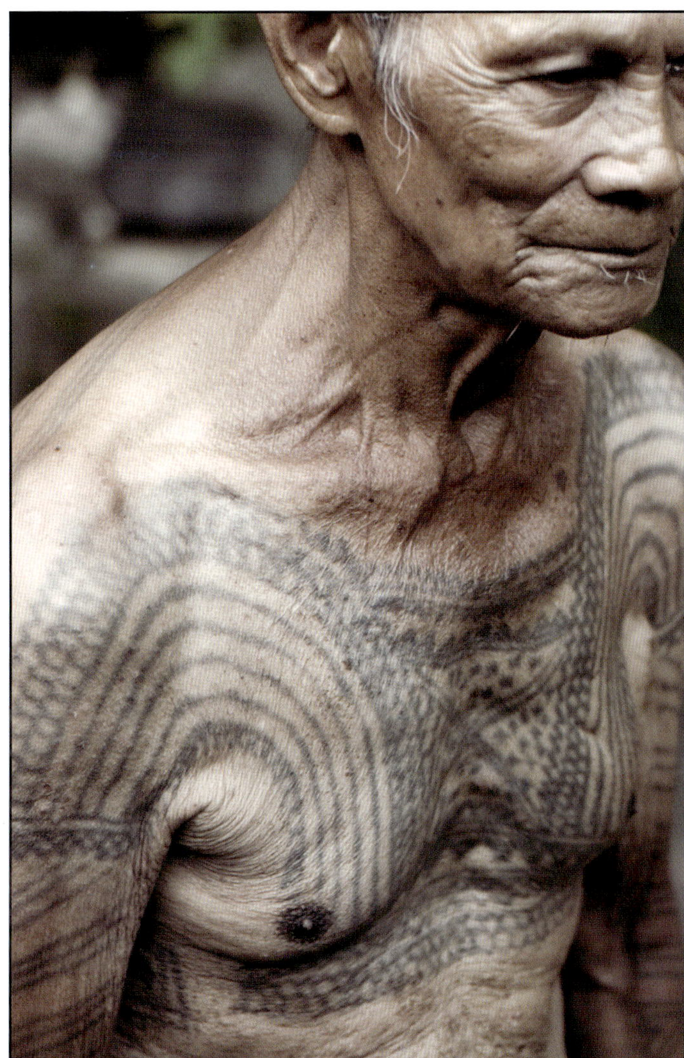

and then throwing certain black powders over the bleeding surface, the figures becoming indelible."[34]

The title and class of Datu was apparently common in many Austronesian cultures. On the island of Java, nobles and chiefs were called by a similar title, "Ratu." In Fiji, a ruling chief and governor of the people was, and still is, called by the same title, "Ratu." In the Philippines, wives of Datus or Rajahs of the muslim areas sometimes were called "Ratu," such as Ratu Triana of Limasawa. The Samoans had a similar word, "*Latu*," meaning "one in charge of work." The Maori of New Zealand retain a form of this concept in the word "*Ngarahu*," meaning "leader." On the island of Mangareva in eastern Polynesia, Mangarevan mythology names their gods prefaced with the title "Atu," meaning "Lord." Examples include "*Atu-motua*" (Lord-Father) and "*Atu-moana*" (Lord-Ocean).[35] Another cognate in Kiribati is the word "*Atu*," which means "head." Hawaiian chiefs in the past were often referred to as "*e ku'u Haku*," meaning "my master." According to Tahitian mythology, the first inhabitants of Tahiti had no aristocracy and were instead ruled by warrior-chiefs titled "*Fatu*," very similar to the Datu of the Philippines. When rival aristocracy migrated to Tahiti, headhunting was practiced in ousting the previous Fatu leadership.[36]

Left: The dakag tattoos on the back of an Ilubo man show that he has reached the highest level of manhood, called "Datum." This drawing depicts three types of Dakag tattoos. By the author

Right: A Kalinga mu'urmut of the Datum level. Photo courtesy of Farlet Vale

Headhunting in the Philippines was practiced to one degree or another throughout much of the islands at the time of the Spanish advent in 1521. Depending on the community, reasons for headhunting incorporated everything from the avenging of wrongs, the acquisition of hunting or fishing grounds, the necessary "sacrifice" for the good of the village, and finding a mate. Most of what has been written about headhunting in the Philippines comes from the Cordilleran peoples of Luzon, who practiced headhunting (and its associated tattoos) into the 20th century. Throughout Austronesia it was believed that all parts of a person's body contained part of their essence or spiritual strength, with the head being a special reservoir of spiritual power. Among many Filipinos it is still considered very bad luck to touch another person's head except in the most gentle of ways. To strike another's head was thought to be unlucky and could cause insanity or stupidity. Even the hair of the head is considered sacred and invested with power. The Maori of New Zealand believed that everything that touched a chief's head absorbed some of his *mana,* or spiritual power, and became sacred. A chief's hair had to be cut by a priest. Afterwards, the cut hair, the obsidian blades used to cut the hair and even to carved comb that held the chief's top-knot in place were secretly buried by the priest to prevent sorcerers from stealing them. [37] (I recall as a young boy watching my grandmother brushing out her long graying hair. After she was finished brushing it out, she would gather all the hair that clung to the brush and hide it, or bury it, "to keep it safe from the *mangmangkik*" [evil spirits]. She explained to me that this was to prevent the mangmangkik from using the hair to make her sick.)

Among the Cordilleran peoples of the Philippines, when a man took the head of another, the spiritual power of the head could be ritually applied to the fertility of the people, the crops and animals of the village. In many areas a celebratory feast, generally called "*cañao,*" was held to honor not only the warriors of the headhunt but also to appease the spirit of the victim. The head was sometimes placed in a bamboo basket cushioned by beautiful red hibiscus flowers. The *cañao* and its related ceremonies, in effect, made the spirit of the victim a benevolent member of the community. In other places only the spiritual power of the head was ceremonially distributed among the members of the village.[38] Other times the sacrifice was to appease the spirit of an actual *anito* who was malevolent due to some offense or to prevent such spirits from becoming incensed and causing misfortune. In general, the successful headhunt assured the fertility of animals, crops and people, all of which were intertwined.[39] Skulls were kept as talismans of power by the shaman of the village. Men who contributed to the prosperity of the village through head-hunting proved themselves to be of a higher character than other men, and their victory was usually forecast prior to the headhunt by the village spiritual leader through sacrifice and the observing of omens. The men themselves watched and obeyed any spiritual signs along the path to the enemy village. The combination of spirituality, sacrifice and bravery qualified them for special chest tattoos that both honored them as head-takers and blessed them. Chest tattoos were composed of sweeping decorated lines that came from each nipple on the chest and arched over the shoulders and down the arms, with a "V"-shape spread over the chest.

A headhunter's chest tattoo of the Cordilleran peoples was called by different names. The Kalinga generally called these elaborate chest tattoos *bikking* or *binibiking*. According to Apo Maria Fang-Od, the last traditional Kalinga tattoo artist, in an interview with Lars Krutak, these chest tattoos when looked at as a whole represent the *gayang* or eagle. The *gayang* was the "Lord of Birds" and the messenger of creator god *Kabunian*. In other areas such as in Bontoc these headhunter emblems were called *chak-lag*[40] and are said to represent steps of the rice terraces. Among the Ifugao, although the chest tattoo was much simpler, it still arched up from the nipple over the shoulder. The designs used in its composition represented the "*ginay-gayaman*," or centipede.

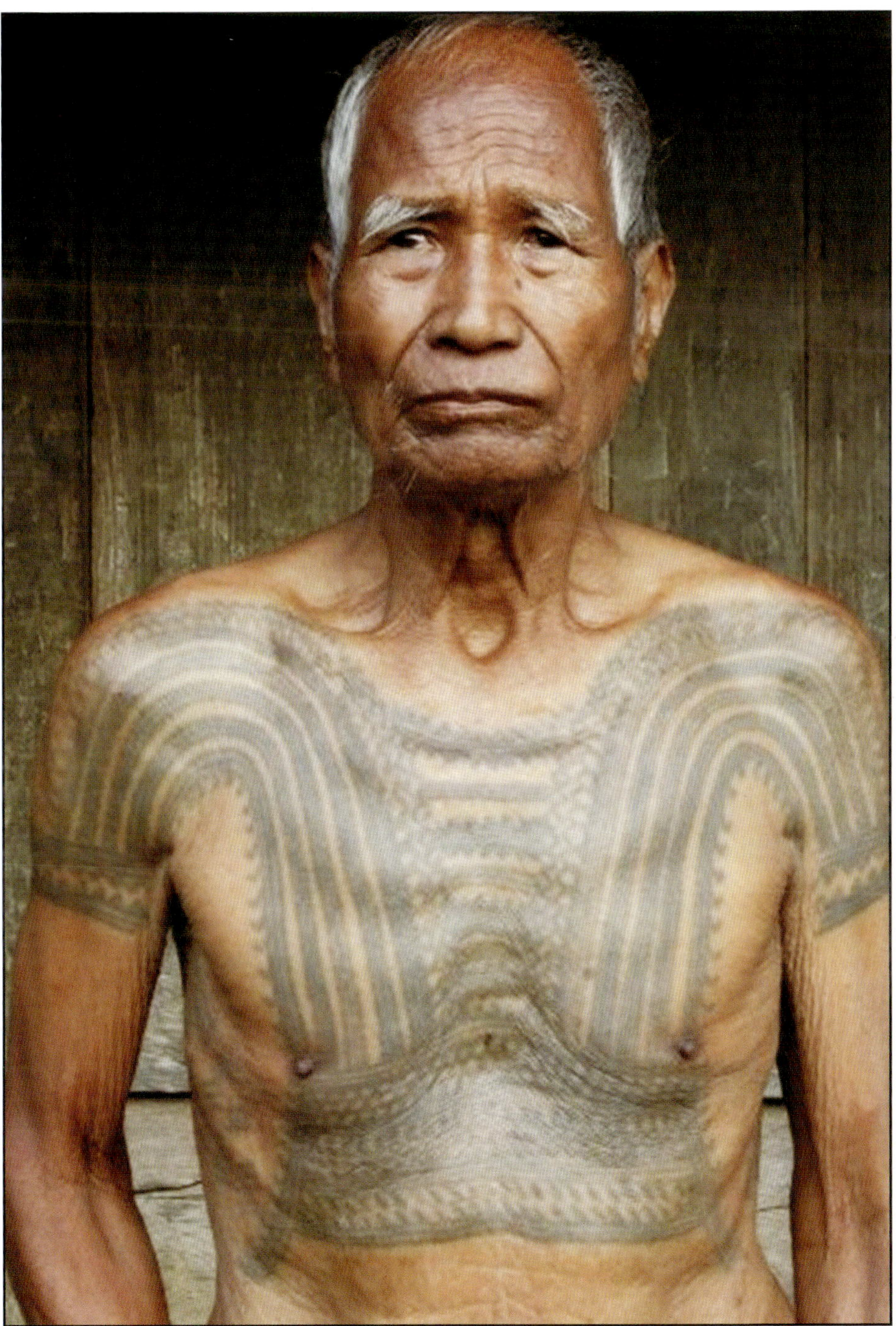

Lakay Ollasic of Kalinga with his binibiking chest tattoo. Lakay Ollasic earned his tattoos by taking Japanese heads during World War II when the Japanese invaded the Philippines. He is also a cultural activist who has spoken on several occasions to preserve Kalinga traditions and culture. Photo courtesy of Edward Adrian-Vallance

Similar beliefs existed among Polynesians and other Pacific Islanders. Head-hunting was also practiced in the Pacific Isles. Heads were taken as trophies in Samoa in the late 1800's in warfare. Carl Marquardt states in his book, *Die Tatowierung bieder Geschlecher,* in Samoa in 1899, that individualized tattoos of points and lines upon the forearms of Samoan men were made so their bodies could be identified if they lost their heads in battle.[41] The Maori warriors of New Zealand and warriors of the Marquesas Islands also took heads has trophies in battle. Skulls were kept by various peoples in the Pacific as remembrances of dead family members, such as in the Kiribati Islands. Skulls were also kept for spiritual and ritual purposes at Tahitian *marae,* or sacred temple enclosures. Tahitians believed that *mana* (spiritual power) could be passed to another person through violence, from the slain person to the victor. When a man died, his skull retained his power and was kept in the eaves of the house to bless the house with its power. English Captian James Cook, when traveling through Tahiti, remarked about the many skulls that were within Tahitian *maraes.* From clues left within the Polynesian languages, we find even more understanding of the headhunt.

The word for head, throughout much of the Austronesian world, is usually a form of the word *ulu* (commonly spelled *ulo* in the Philippines). However, in Hawaiian the word *ulu* is not commonly used to describe the head, but usually means "to be possessed by a spirit; to be inspired by a spirit or god; to enter into and inspire."[42] Hawaiians believed that the spirits of their ancestors hovered about the heads of their descendents. Ancient Filipino beliefs about the head seem to confirm this. In the ancient Philippines, the *ulo* (head) was the most concentrated reservoir of spiritual power. Hawaiians typically use another word, *po'o,* for head instead of *ulu. Po'o* in Samoan is a less formal way of saying "head," while *ulu* can mean "to enter into" as well as "head." In the Tongan language, *ulupoko* means "skull." The Hawaiian word *po'o,* when coupled with *iwi* ("bone"), can also be used for the word "skull" (*iwi po'o*). But *po'o* in Hawaiian can also suggest a cavity or a depression, which alludes to the fontanel, or soft spot, at the top of the head. *Lulunan* in Ilokano is the fontanel, or soft spot, in a baby's skull. Among Tahitians, the head is called *upo'o.* Among the Marquesans and New Zealand Maori, the word for "head" is *upoko.* These words seem to be a compound of the words *uru* (*ulu*) and *po'o. Ulupoko* must have been the original word that the words *upo'o, upoko, ulu* and *po'o* came from. Therefore, *ulupoko* conveyed the concept that "inspiration from the spirit world came through the fontanel of the head or skull."

When Tahaki (a Tahitian folk hero) was a boy, his goddess mother, Hina, conferred all her magical powers upon him by having him open his mouth over the crown of her head. It was then that Tahaki felt inspired to do great deeds and to travel. Hina conferred her ability through the crown, or fontanel, to her son. In essence, she taught him through the source of her own inspiration, the *ulu.* Variations of the word *ulo* (*ulu*) are found in the Ilokano words *isuro* (to teach) and *mannuro* (teacher.) Similar use is found in the Tagalog and Cebuano word for "to teach", *magturo.*

In Polynesia Hina, or Sina, who was the mother of Tahaki in some Polynesian traditions, is the moon goddess. The moon (feminine) itself is known as *mahina* or *masina.* Interestingly, it is the moon goddess that

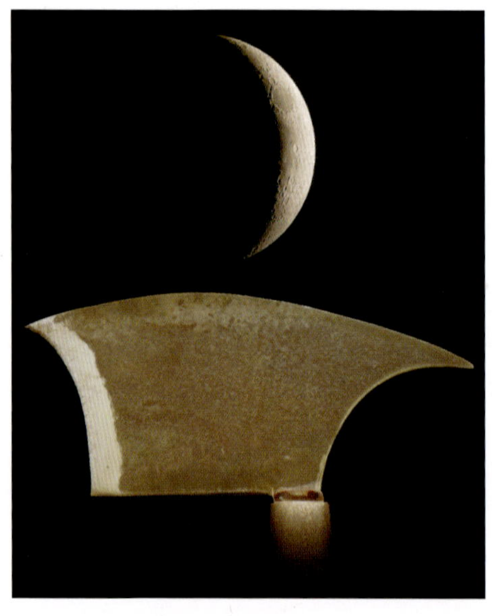

A headaxe blade compared to the Signa'ana phase of the moon. By the author

Filipino Tattoos: Ancient to Modern

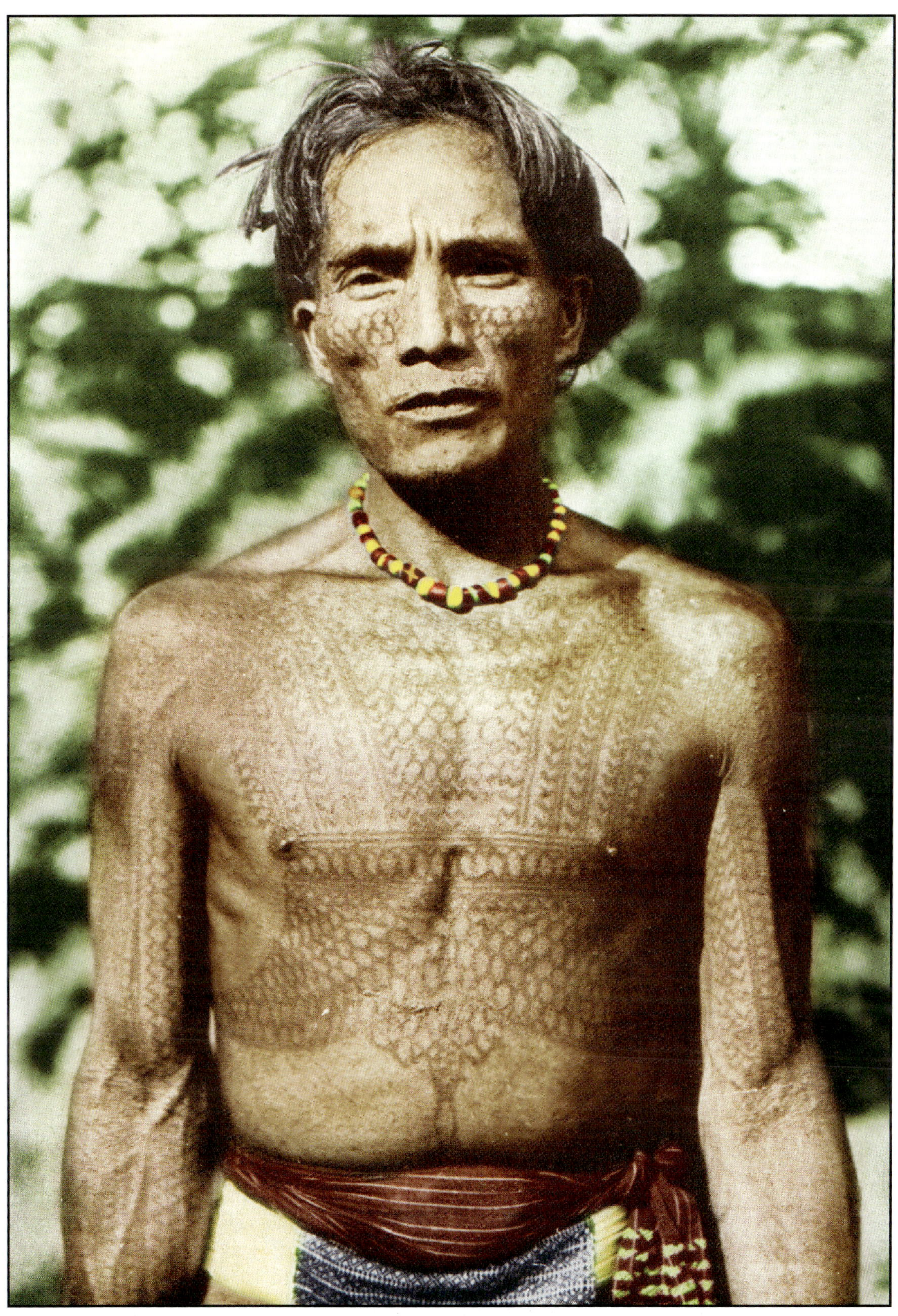

Kalinga warrior with extensive chest and face tattoos attesting to the many heads he has taken. Circa 1905

Reasons for Tattooing

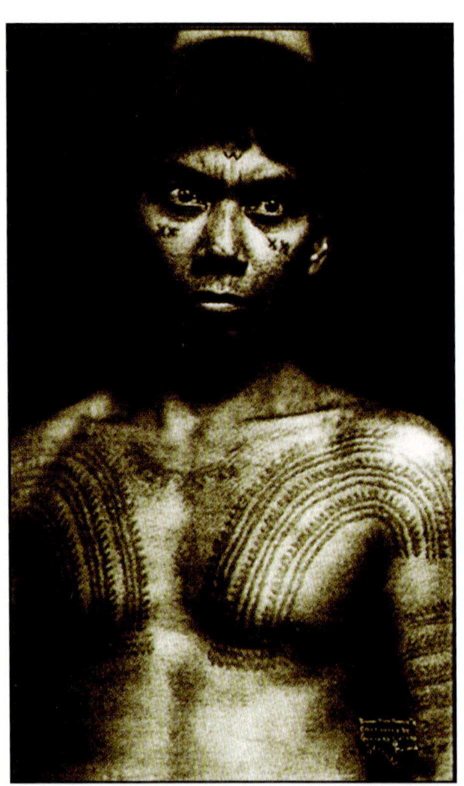

A Bontoc man with the "chak-lag" or chest tattoos marking him as a successful headhunter. Circa 1905

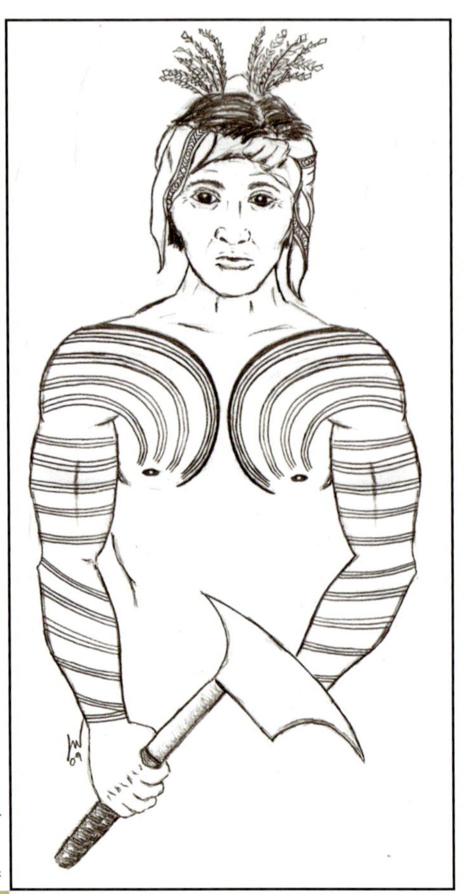

The burik of the Gaddang men earned through headhunting. The three parallel lines granted passage to the afterlife. Women had similar three-lined tattoos on their hands radiating from the wrist to each of the knuckles. By the author

is the originator of headhunting in the Philippines. According to Bontoc tradition, the moon became annoyed with one of the sons of the sun (masculine) while he watched her making a pot, so she beheaded the little boy. The sun quickly reattached the boy's head and brought him back to life. The sun said that because of the example of the moon's actions, the people of the earth world would also cut off each others' heads.[43] In Itneg tradition, the moon or moon goddess was called Sinag, similar to the Polynesian Sina or Hina. The moon goddess Sinag is thought to be an ancient progenitor of the Itneg people.[44] In the Bontoc region, the when the moon is one quarter waning it is called *Signa'ana* and resembles the curved form of the headaxe. Therefore, when a head is taken with the curved *signa-ana*-shaped head axe, the story of the moon goddess taking the first head is re-enacted. This phase of the moon is sometimes tattooed on the ribs of Kalinga males and called *sorag* (*sinag*). The word "*sorag*" denotes specifically the radiance of the moon. Salvador-Amores explains that the *sorag,* or moon light, was a headhunter's light when caught in the darkness of the night.[45] In Tagalog the word "*sinag*" describes the radiance of light.

Herein lies the origin of beliefs about the sacredness of the head and its relationship to headhunting. The head was the nexus of the spirit world to the mortal realm. It was the sacred point at which the ancestors inspired their descendants and conveyed upon them spiritual power. It was the procurement of this intense concentration of spiritual power and abundance of spiritual nexus (*ulu*) that granted men the privilege of being tattooed with the headhunter's chest emblem.

Tattoos on the Legs

Similar requirements for men to be tattooed existed in the ancient Visayan islands of the Philippines. To be recognized as a warrior, Visayan men had to kill an enemy or perform some brave deed to receive their first tattoo. Unlike the Cordilleran peoples of Luzon, whose arm or chest tattoos marked them as successful headhunters, the Visayan male's *batuk* (tattoo) that marked him as a *bayani* (heroic warrior) extended from the ankles to the waist.[46] While it is highly probable that different regions had their own variations of men's tattoos, generally the male's tattoo was characterized by long bold lines up the legs to the waist. According to early accounts, these lines, both straight and zigzagged, were called *labid* and were about an inch thick.[47] In interpreting the meaning of "*labid*," three possible explanations of this design can be made, all of which may have been used in the past.

The first explanation is that *labid,* as recorded by the Spanish, may have been a dialectal variation of the Cebuano word *labi*, which means "coconut tree". The logs made from the coconut tree were used as pillars to support raised houses in the Philippines. In this context, a *labid* design described how the legs are the support of the body, just as *labi* pillars support a house. It could also infer how the bayani warrior was the support of the village or the Datu. In the old Philippines, the sons of a Datu, from his secondary wives of high caste, were called by the chiefly title, *tumao.*

Filipino Tattoos: Ancient to Modern

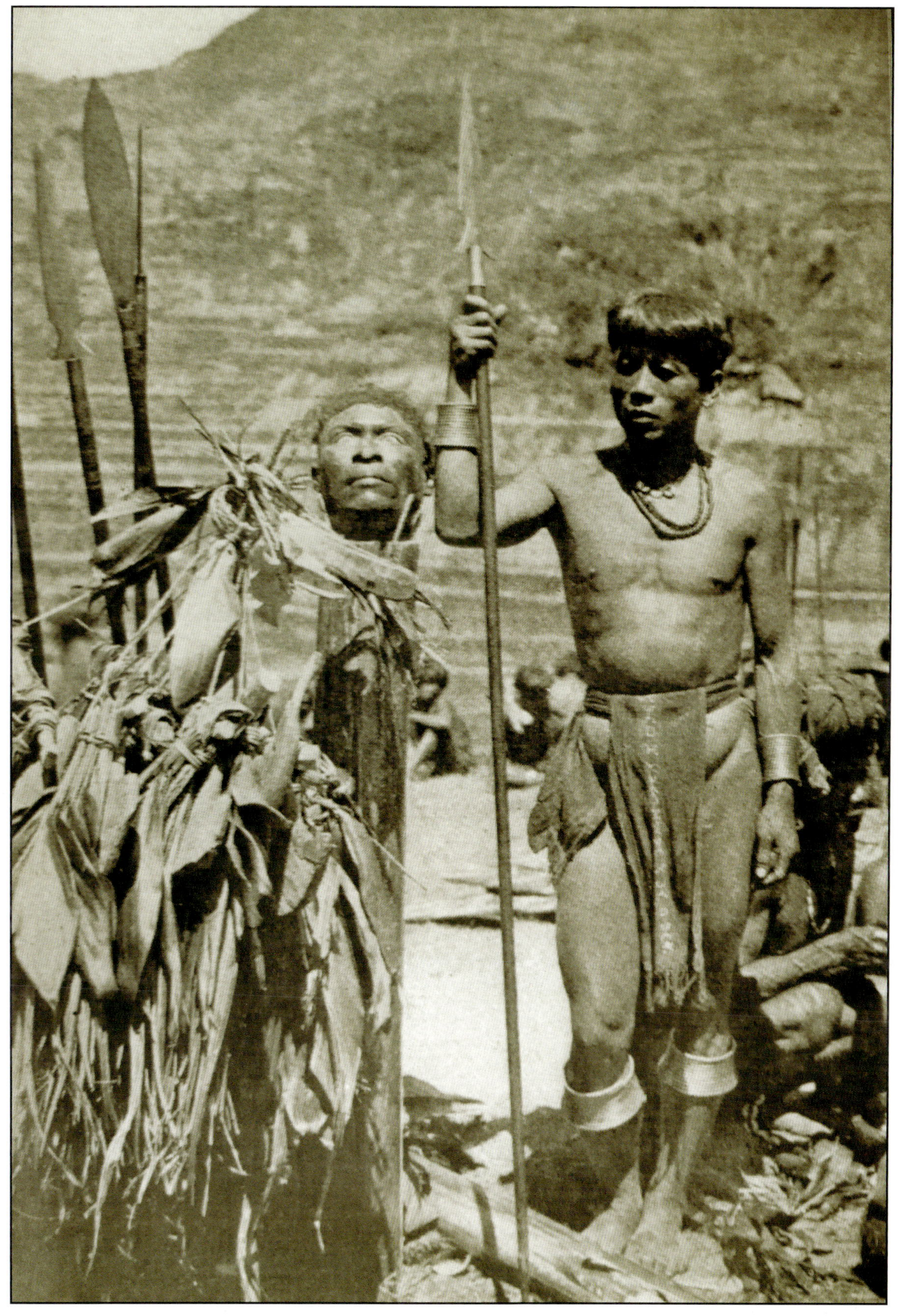

An Ifugao warrior with a freshly taken head, ca. 1900

These men were described as *sandig sa dato* or the <u>support</u> of the Datu[48] which may correlate to the concept of the labi being the <u>support</u> of the house. These men along with other freemen comprised a Datu's military force. It was in military action that men earned the labid tattoos on their legs. A possible correlation to this is in French Polynesia where a tattoo of the coconut tree up the legs of a man was reserved for those of a chiefly blood-line.[49]

The second explanation is that *labid* is related to the word in Cebuano, *lapad,* a type of fan palm that is commonly called *anahaw* in Tagalog. The *anahaw* is actually known as *labid* in Ilokano. These trees were also used for pillars for house posts, spear shafts and axe handles. Therefore, the *labid* could represent spear shafts, which figuratively describe the valor in which the tattoos were earned through warfare. The large leaves of this tree are also used for rain capes. Protection from the rain was important, especially when it rained while the sun was shining and the sky was reddish. This event was thought to be the mark of the *anitos* at war with mortals. Women and children were expressly kept indoors during such a rain.[50] As such, the *labid* tattoos could represent protection from malignant spiritual forces.

A third possible cognate of *labid* is *lapid,* which describes an old and large outrigger canoe used for carrying cargo.[51] In the Philippines, most canoes had double outrigger floats, one outrigger on each side of the canoe. In a similar context as the *labi* or *lapad* being used as pillars or posts to support a house, the *lapid* outriggers carried, or <u>supported</u> on the water, people and cargo being transported. When observing *labid* tattoos recorded in the Boxer Codex, there is one, large, inch-wide stripe with a thinner line on each side of it. As a whole, the three lines on the legs are grouped together. The design may be symbolic of the *lapid* canoe, with the thick, inch-wide stripe representing the canoe's hull and the thinner lines next to it as the *katig,* or outriggers. In relation to this, the term *labid* may have been derived from the same source as the Kalinga term *binulibud,* which describes the three parallel tattooed lines on the arms of warriors of the past.[52]

Throughout Luzon, lines of tattooing were often grouped in threes. Three parallel lines were mandatory tattoos for the Gad'dang people to travel into the afterlife. In ancient Visayan beliefs, a dead person's soul, or *kalag,* would travel into the underworld where it met a ghostly boatman named *Magwayen,* who ferried the soul across a body of water to *Sulad,* or *Sa'ad,* the land where the ancestors dwell.[53] It is possible that if the *labid* of the Visayas and the *binulibud* are related, that the concept of gaining passage into the afterlife may have accompanied these important leg tattoos.

Although Spanish chroniclers reported that both straight and zigzagged lines were called *labid,* this is unlikely. In many places throughout the Philippines and Pacific Islands, zigzag tattoos represented water. Among the Ilubo people of Kalinga, the zigzagged lines of their tattoos represent water on women but snakes on men.[54] The snake was symbolic to the Kalinga as a warrior symbol, but also as a symbol of ancestor spirits, or *anito.* To the Visayans, pythons were thought to be messengers or the physical embodiment of the *anito.* Often on ocean journeys by canoe and especially on sea raids, Visayan men believed that having a python

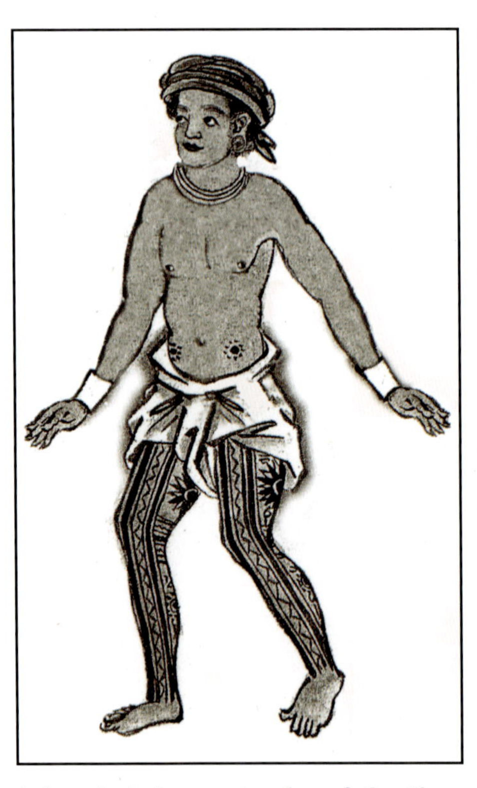

A hypothetical reconstruction of the Visayan male's first tattoos including the labid leg stripes and water or python designs. By the author

Filipino Tattoos: Ancient to Modern

on board was to have their ancestor's spirit participate with them in the raid.[55] It is therefore likely that the zigzagged lines of the *bayani batuk* represented travel over water, and/or the python *anito* that traveled with them.

A Visayan *bayani,* in gaining his first tattoos, discovered that tattooing itself was a difficult rite of passage. The body would be swollen and prone to infection afterwards. As a man went through life, with each successful victory in battle, he received tattoos like badges of honor to the arms, chest, back, neck and, for the fiercest and bravest warriors, his face. [56] Hence, more tattoos demanded the more honor you were accorded.

The tattooed legs became a mark of distinction, especially in Luzon where tattooing the upper body was more popular and generally tattooed first. Legs were tattooed only after much accomplishment. Prior to 1905, Albert Jenks, an American ethnographer, observed a Bontoc tattoo specialist, named Finumti, who was distinguished from other tattoo artists by being tattooed from the hips to the knees with a large, double-scallop design.[57] Prestige in tattooing legs is found among other Austronesian peoples. It appears in oral traditions of the Austronesian Atayal people of Taiwan who originally tattooed legs first, and later applied dense designs to the face. Dense tattooing always turned the faces of their ancestors black, and gradually facial tattoos became more limited in application.[58]

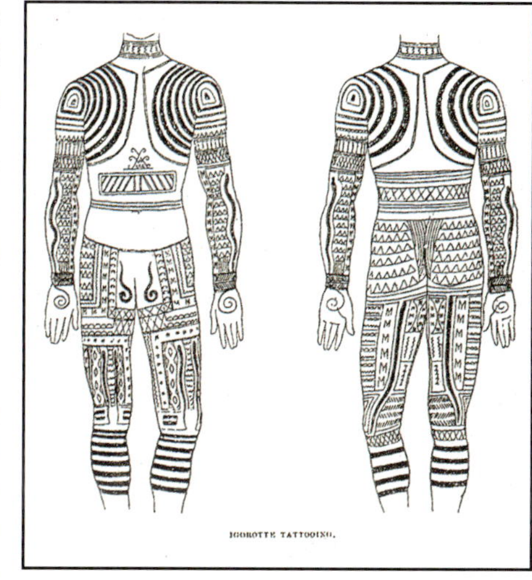

An illustration of the Benguet body suit tat-too by Hans Meyer 1880

A Kabayan mummy showing the tattoos on the lower legs. Courtesy of Alexis Duclos

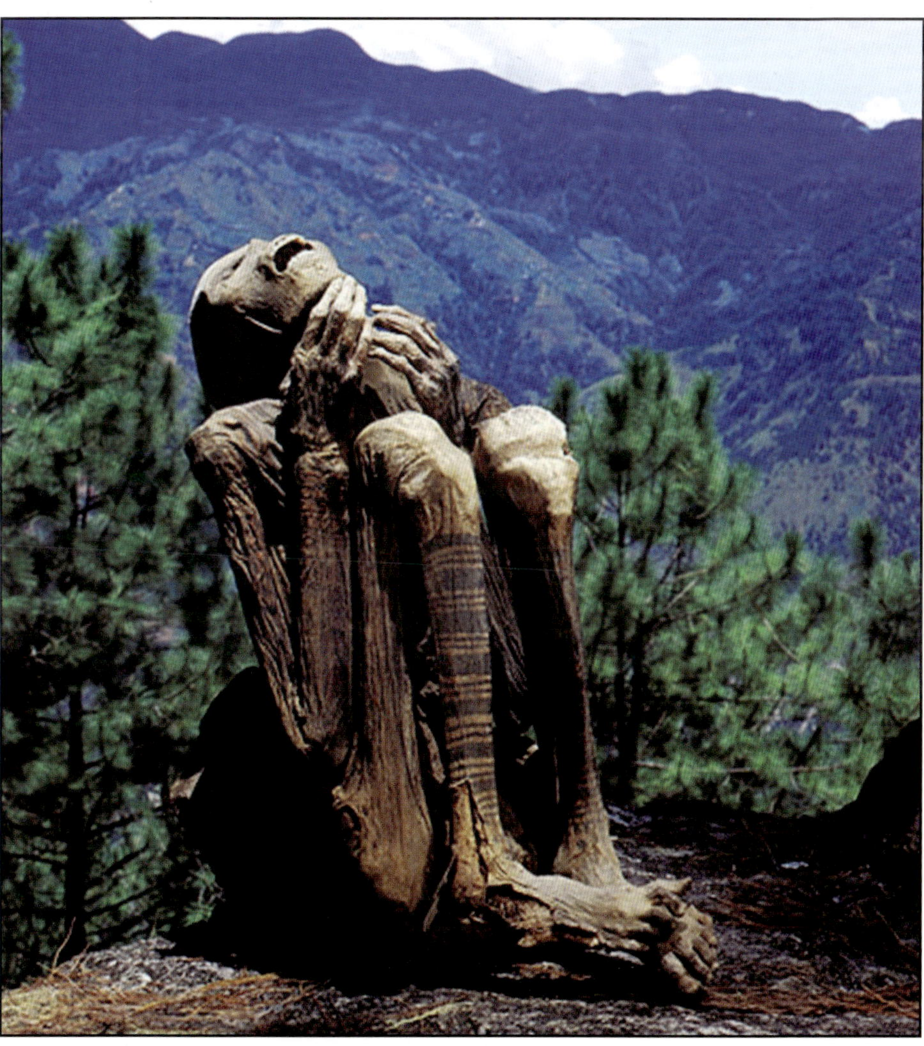

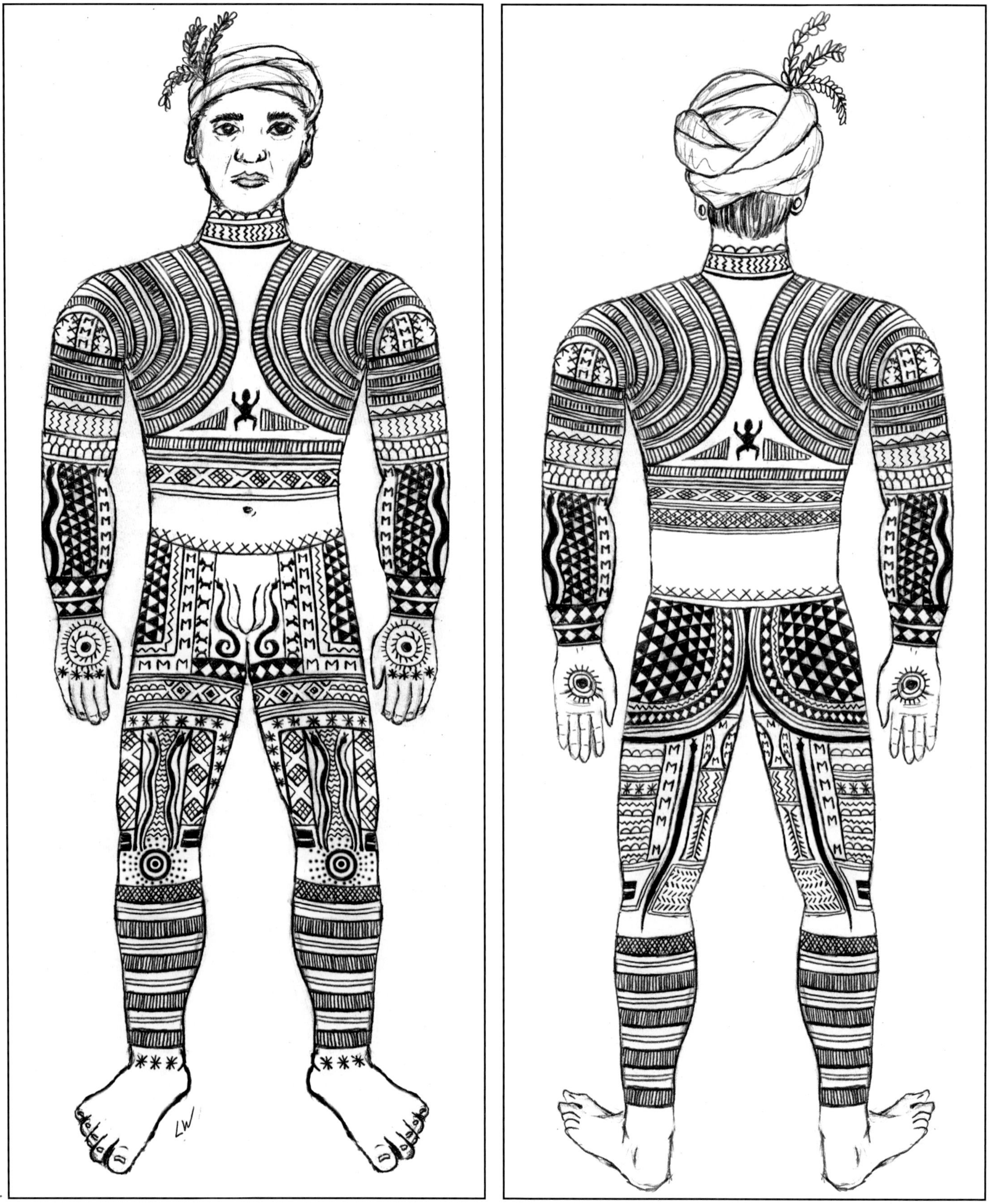

A reconstruction of the Benguet body suit tattoo both front and back based on the drawings of Hans Meyer and the tattoos seen on exhumed mummies from the Benguet area.

Filipino Tattoos: Ancient to Modern

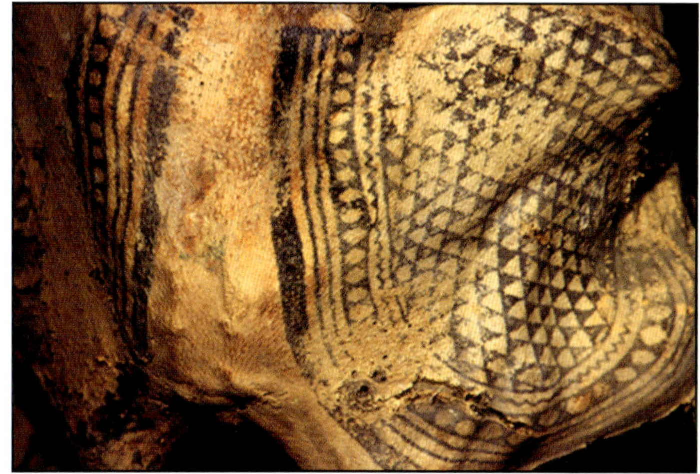

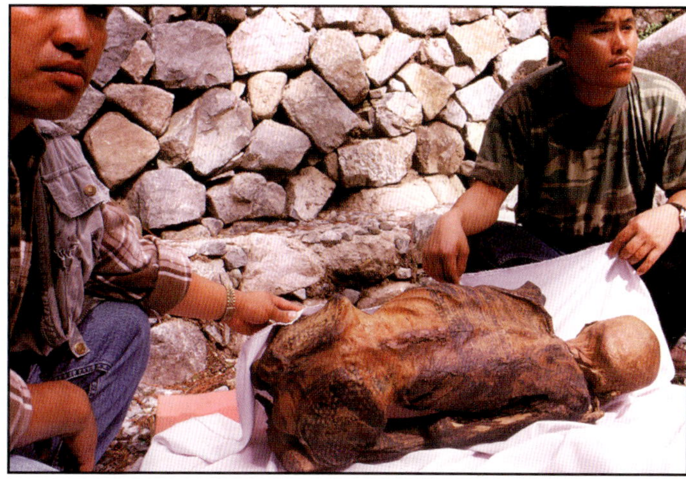

There is a striking similarity in lower body tattoos worn by the ancient Benguet region's men and Samoan and Tongan men of Polynesia. The framing or arrangement of the Benguet men's lower body tattoos, as seen on mummies from the region and illustrations by Hans Meyer, is similar to the framing of Samoan and Tongan tattoos.

Some of the motifs within the Benguet, Samoan, and Tongan designs are nearly identical. The tattoos of the Samoans and Tongans contain much more dense black areas than the Benguet lower body tattoos, but like the Benguet region tattoos extended from the knee area to above the hips. The Visayan men's initial tattoo into manhood also bears a resemblance to the Samoan and Tongan tattoos. The Maori men of New Zealand wore a type of "pants" tattoo that extended from the knees to the waist, called *puhoro*. Maori chiefs, subordinate chiefs and even men of the lower classes had facial tattoos, but the leg tattoos set the wearer apart with greater honor. The leg tattoo was worn by men who had completed studies in the *Whare Wonanga*, a specialized house of sacred learning and also by chiefly warriors of great distinction of the northern region of New Zealand.[59] Leg tattoos have also been observed among Dayak peoples of Borneo on warriors who were accomplished headhunters, but also upon chiefly women. The men and women of the island of Rotuma, near in the Fijian main islands, both possessed tattoos upon the hips and thighs, similar to the Samoan *Pe'a* tattoo that were recorded in 1826 by Isadore Duperrey in a book about his travels, *Voyage Autour du Monde*.[60]

Similar tattoos have been observed throughout Oceania in various forms. Abbreviated hip and thigh tattoos were found on the women of Fiji, where it was restricted to the buttocks. In some places the men are the wearers of this type of tattooing, in other areas the women are the wearers, and in other places both men and women wore them. For example, some of the ancestor carvings found in New Zealand show male and female figures with the *puhoro* leg and buttocks tattoos. In Tahiti, both men and women wore abbreviated lower body tattoos that were restricted to the hips and buttocks, with the women blackening nearly the entire buttocks.[61] Hip and buttock tattoos were called *taomaru*, literally meaning "girdle

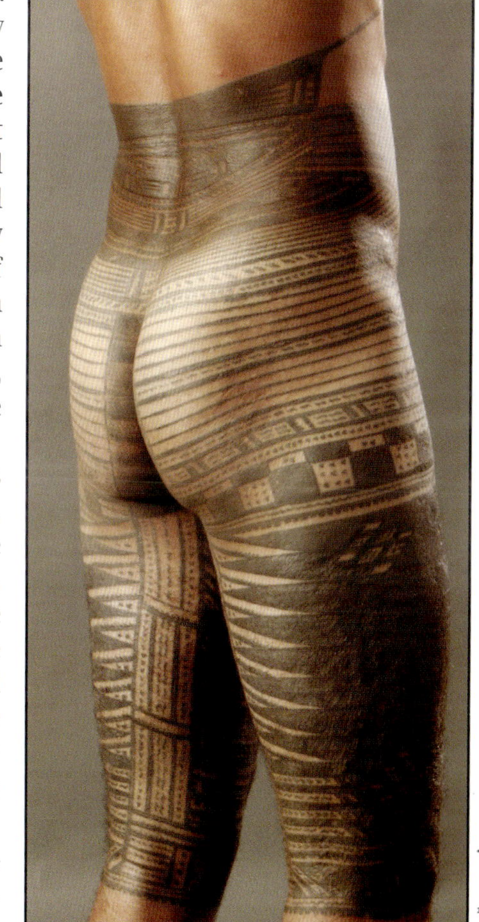

The Samoan Pe'a or body suit. Photo by Cloud Surfer. http://commons.wikimedia.org/wiki/File:Traditional_Samoan_Tattoo_-_back.jpg Used under GNU licence. http://commons.wikimedia.org/wiki/Commons:GNU_Free_Documentation_License

Reasons for Tattooing

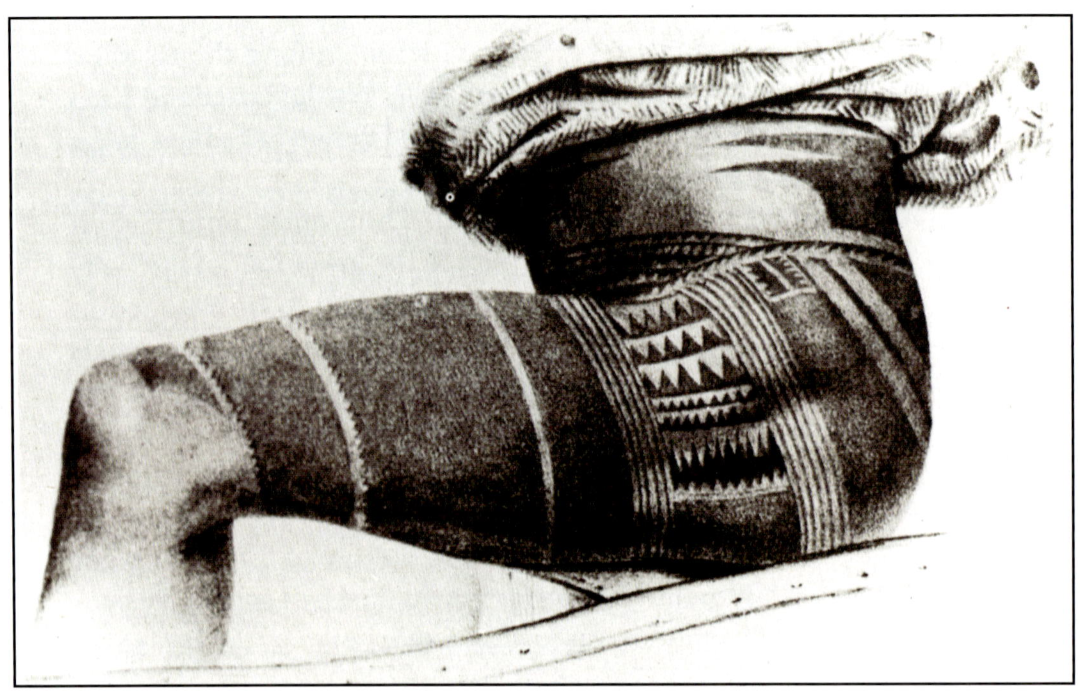

The lower body tattoos seen in Tonga. After D'Urville

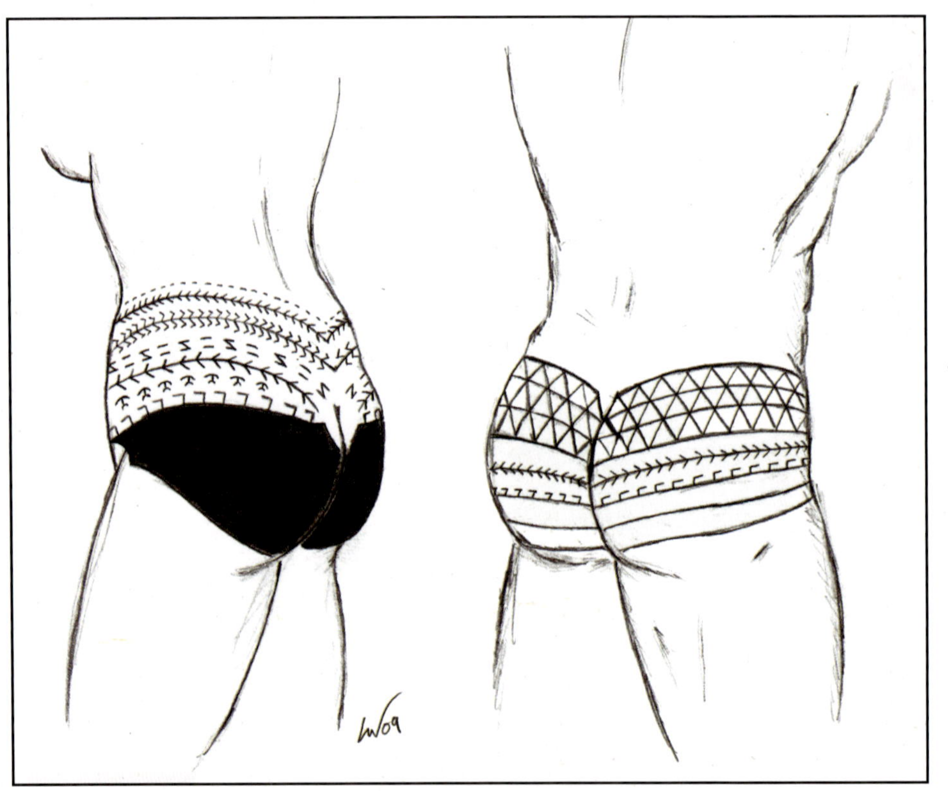

The Tahitian male and female buttocks tattoos called taomaru appear to be abbreviated versions of the Samoan tatau. The tattoo on the left was worn by both men and women in Tahiti. The tattoo on the right was likely from the island of Ra'iatea. Drawings after Sydney Parkinson, 1769. by the author

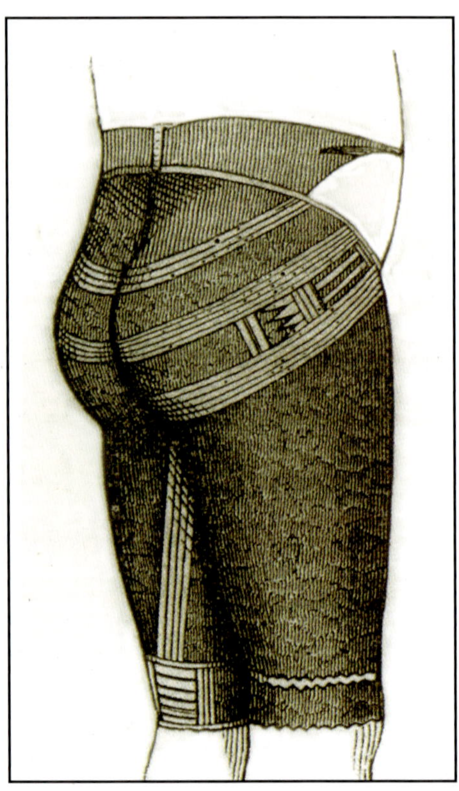

The first published illustration of the Samoan Pe'a or tatau. This depiction is very similar to the tattoos found on Tongan men. After A.T. Agate 1845

Filipino Tattoos: Ancient to Modern

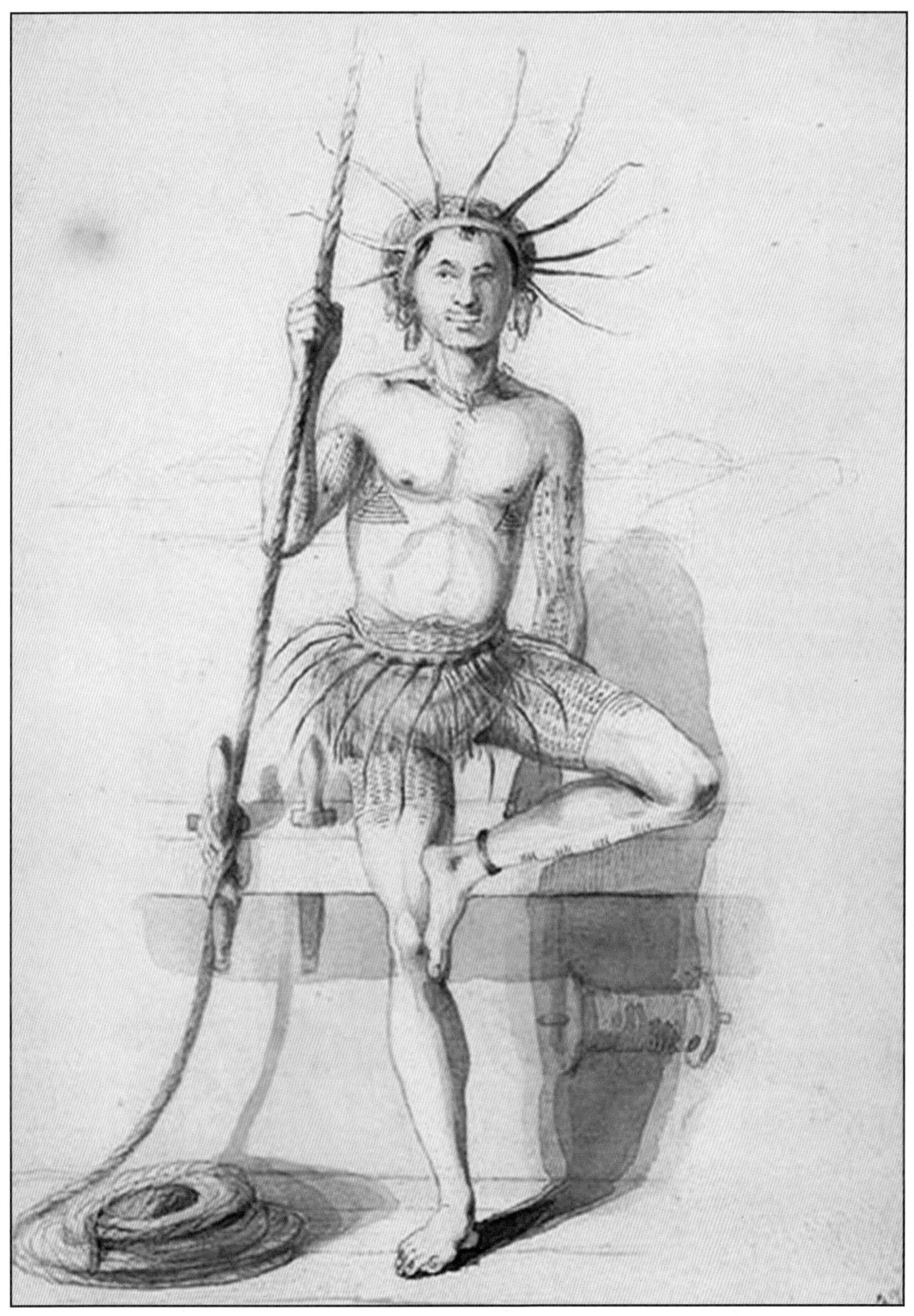

A rare depiction of a Tuvalu man's leg tattoos by Alfred T. Agate in 1841. Tattooing of the legs must have come from a very early time in Austronesian history because it has been found in various forms throughout much of the Pacific.

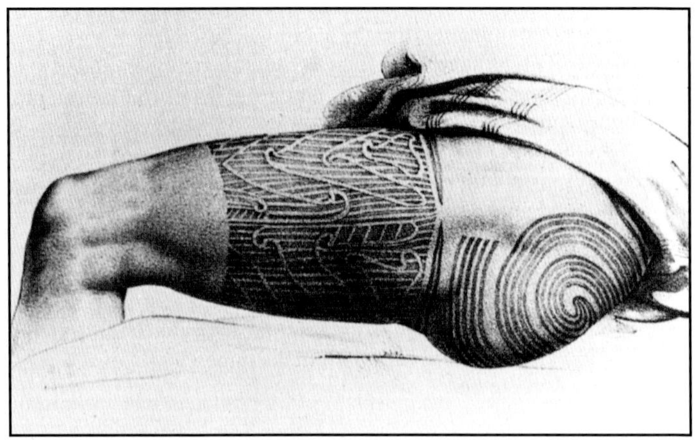

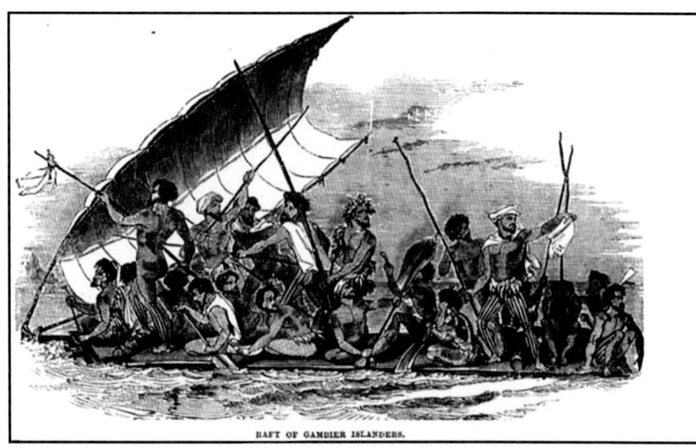

Left: The Maori Puhoro leg tattoo. Drawing by Sydney Parkinson, 1769

Right: Raft of the Gambier (Mangareva) Islanders from A Narrative of a Voyage to the Pacific and Bering's Straits, 1831. There are a few men on the raft with tattoos on their legs in various stages of completion. The man holding a cloth appears to have complete leg tattoos resembling striped pants.

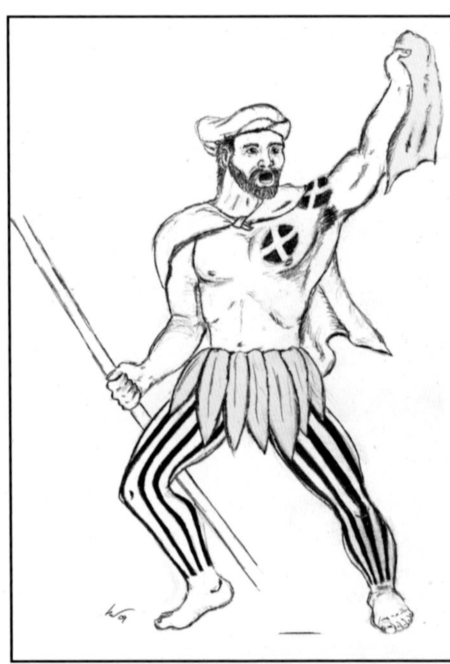

Detail of the poupou leg tattoos of the men of Mangareva. By the author after an illustration from: A Narrative of a Voyage to the Pacific and Bering's Straits. Note the similarity of the leg stripes to the Visayan labid tattoos.

of spears".[62] On the island of Mangareva in Eastern Polynesia, leg tattoos took the form of vertical stripes down the legs from the hips to the ankles. These tattoos were called *poupou*, in general meaning "pillars."[63] This is similar in appearance and context to the possible interpretations of the *labid* leg tattoos on Visayan males. These leg tattoos must have come from a very early time in Austronesian history, for it has been found in various forms throughout much of the Pacific region.

Tattooing among ancient Filipino and Pacific Islander men was important for recognition as an adult or to achieve chiefly status. The pain of the tattooing itself was the rite of passage. Often, in ancient times, men of the Philippines and places such as Samoa, Tonga and the Marquesas islands in French Polynesia were not allowed to be married until they were fully tattooed.[64] It was not just the tattooing that qualified a man as a possible mate, but the deeds he had done to qualify for tattoos.

Also, the amount of tattooing and quality of the tattoos denoted a man's status. This was common in many groups in the Philippines and in other island groups of the Pacific. Until to modern times, sons of a Samoan chief, called *manaia* (mah-nigh-ah), were required to be tattooed with the traditional tattoo (*Pe'a*) from the bottom of the knee cap to the top of the hip to be recognized as a chief. Only the most skilled tattooing artists created *manaia*. In parts of Luzon, men who had taken heads were also called by a similar title, called *maingal* (mah-ee-ngal), *maingel, maingor,* or *mingor* depending on the location. It is possible that the titles *manaia* and *maingal* could have stemmed from the same root word in the Austronesian past.

Women's Tattoos

Women's tattoos are most commonly explained as being for the beautification of the body and to increase attractiveness to men. While this was true, tattooing was also considered an essential form of clothing, or took the place of clothing. The Itneg women, for example, wore strings of beads wrapped highly around their forearms. Fine lines were tattooed underneath the beads so that when the beads were removed the arms would not appear naked. These tattoos covered all the areas where beads were normally placed, and they resembled the tattooing of the Southern Kalinga, but with more space between the lines.[65]

Filipino Tattoos: Ancient to Modern

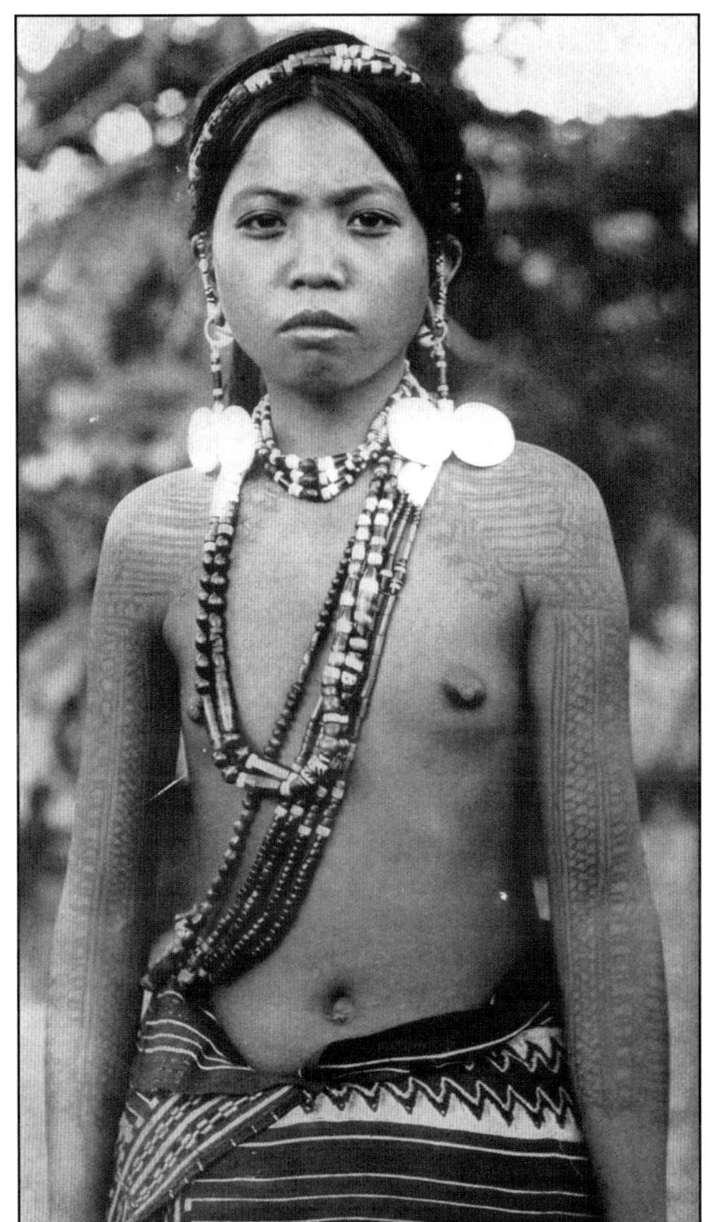

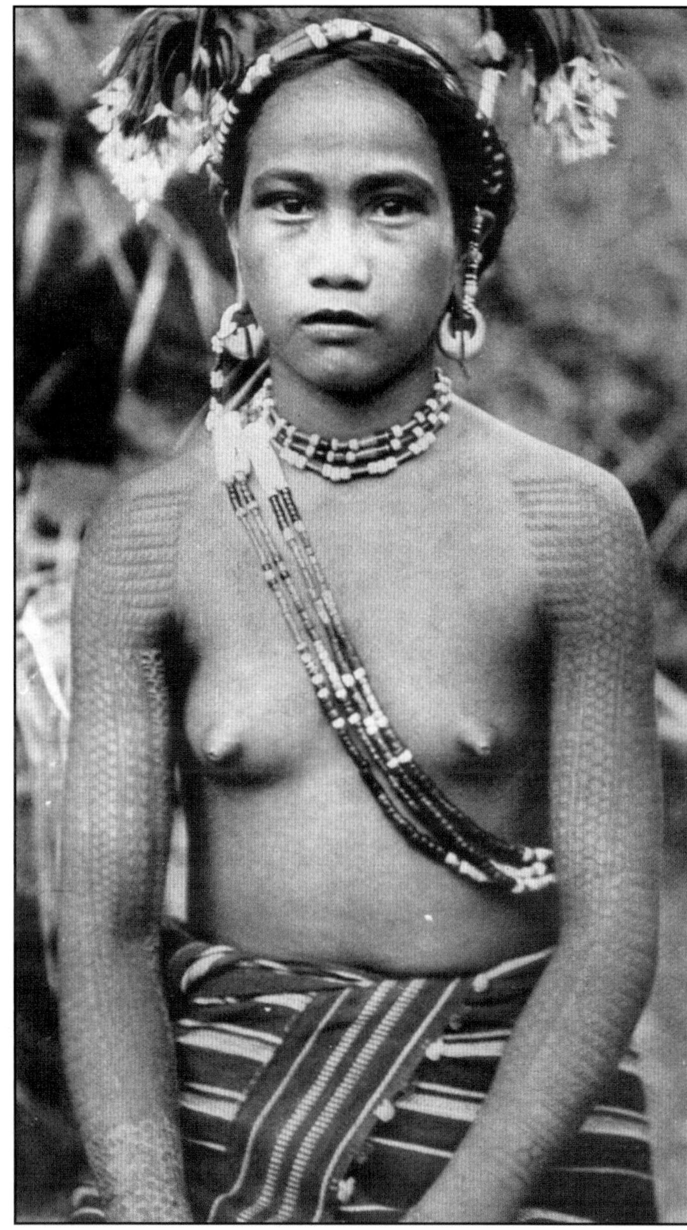

Some of these tattoos themselves were thought to be a type of charm to the men. Tattoo anthropologist Analyn "Ikin" Salvador-Amores recorded that these tattoos were thought to help prevent skin from sagging as a woman aged. Women's tattoos were often placed on the shoulders, arms and hands, or even just the hands. Much like the women of Palau, certain Dayak tribes of Borneo, the Marshall Islands, Ponape, and Samoa had finer lines and tattoos were more sparsely placed on the same parts of the body. The Manobo women of Mindanao wore elaborate tattoos on their breasts and calves, similar to the designs embroidered on their clothes.

Women often received their tattoos at puberty to proclaim their coming-of-age as a mature and marriageable woman. Tattoos for women also signified fertility and the bravery and strength needed to endure childbearing. Being able to endure hammering needles into your flesh would certainly display physical fortitude. According to Salvadore-Amores, the Ilubo people of Kalinga reported that a woman who refused

Left: A tattooed young woman from Kalinga with arm tattoos and mother of pearl earrings, ca. 1905

Right: A tattooed young woman from the Kalinga borders with lingling-o earrings, ca. 1905

Reasons for Tattooing

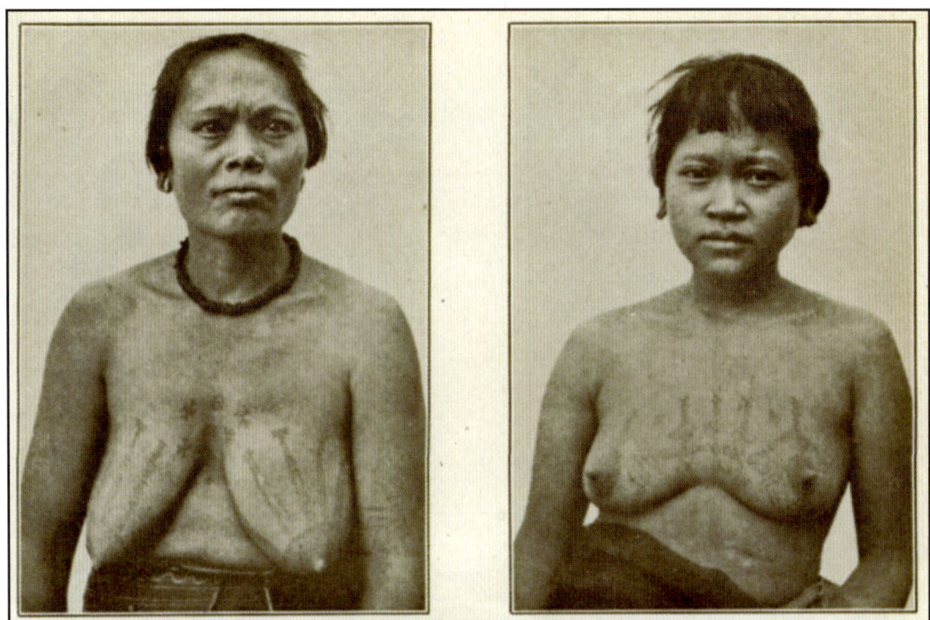

Manobo women with breast tattoos, ca. 1900

to be tattooed was barren. Tattoo motifs for women included items from their life and role in society, such as rice mortars, seeds, rice plants and symbols of the community. Agricultural symbols extended not only to their work in the fields but also were symbolic and spiritually intertwined with fertility and childbearing.

Among the Kalinga, a young woman who reached puberty would have one arm tattooed one day and the other arm the next day. Salvador-Amores relates that young Kalinga women received small x-shaped tattoos or dashes similar to an equal sign (=) on the face, that were identified as *lin-lingao.* These were placed on their cheeks, the tip of the nose, chin and on the forehead. *Lin-lingao* tattoos marked them as a marriageable woman and were also used to confuse malicious spirits of beheaded or killed individuals, called *alam-alam.* These spirits were believed to exacted revenge by taking away the spirits of unborn infants.[66] All illnesses were thought to be spiritual in nature, due to machinations of evil spirits or sorcery. Therefore, the protective nature of ancestral spirits expressed in tattoos was thought to be effective prevention of disease. Tattoos were also applied as a form of medicinal treatment, such as on goiter or other swellings to reduce inflammation.[67] Similar medicinal tattoos have been found on natural mummies in various parts of the world.

Women's tattoos also served a spiritual function. Among the Ibanag and the Isneg, any woman whose hands were not tattooed would not be accepted into the underworld for the dead.[68] Among some ancient Visayan and Ibanag women, only the hands were tattooed.[69] According to Father Francisco Colin, who lived in the 17th century, women of the Visayan Islands limited their tattooing to one hand and part of the other.[70] But his account may not be entirely accurate, because having "part of the other " [hand] suggests an incomplete tattoo. Other sources state that the Visayan women also tattooed the arms, chest and a portion of the thighs.[71] Ibanag hand tattoos were called *appaku,* because of their resemblance to the *paku* fern. These tattoos were likely similar to the *fungana* fern tattoos of the Kalinga, which look like a row of diagonal dashes attached to a single

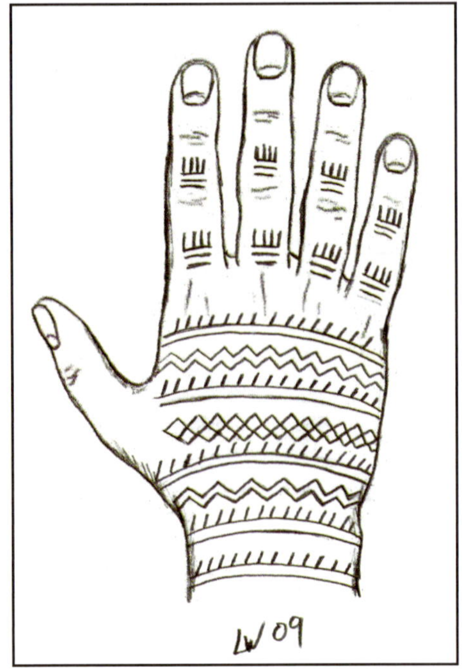

A hypothetical reconstruction of the ap-paku hand tattoos of the Ibanag people. By the author

Filipino Tattoos: Ancient to Modern

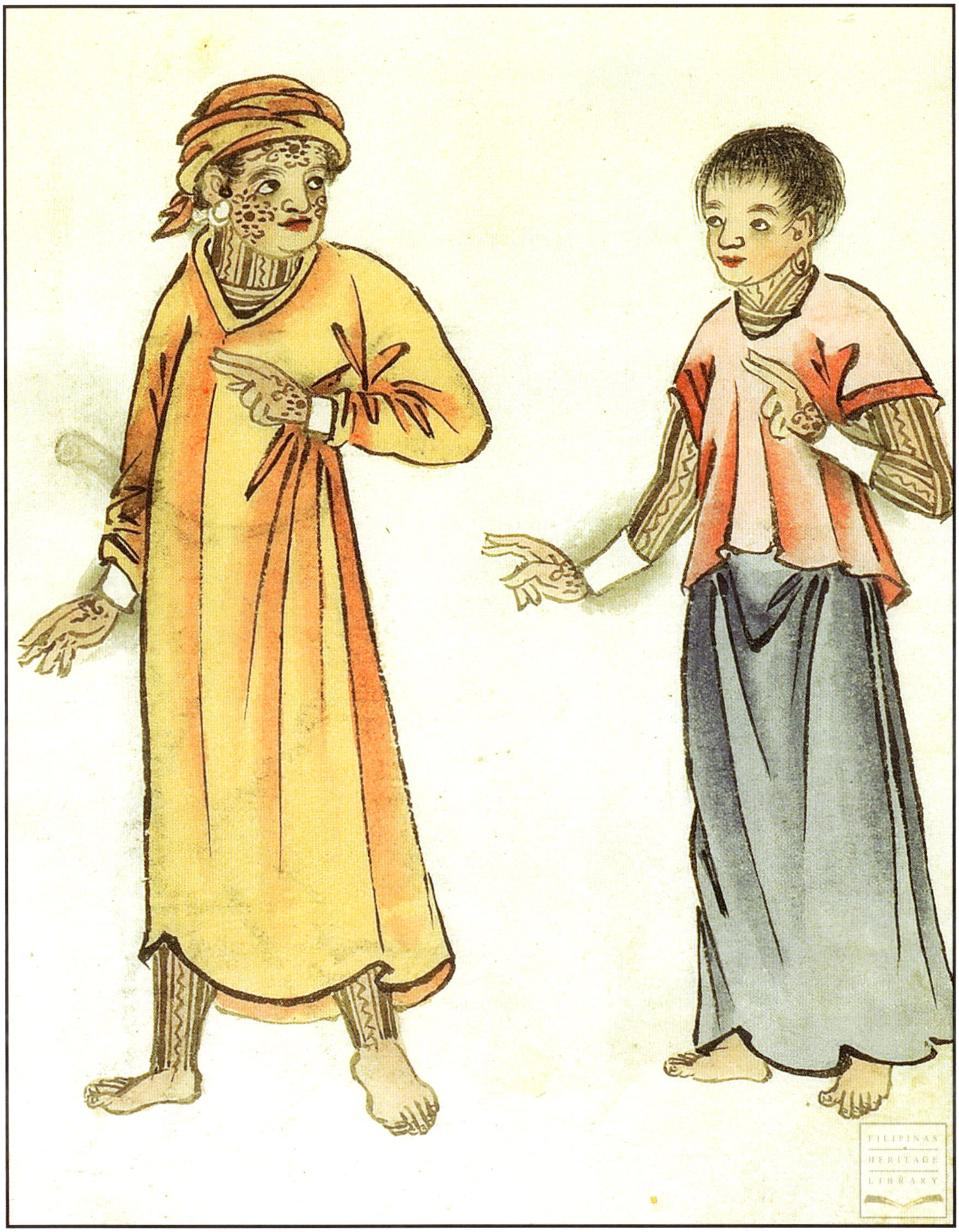

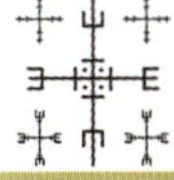

A Visayan man and woman with tattoos, Boxer Codex 1590 courtesy of the Filipinas Heritage Library. The man on the left is wearing a garment called "saob" used for formal occasions but should have been depicted as being open like a robe. The woman on the right is in mourning as seen by her lack of ear ornaments and short hair. In ancient Visayan society men and women kept their hair long although men usually braided and bunched their hair under their pudong or tuban. In the past men and women would sometimes shave off the hair of their heads and eyebrows at the death of a loved one. Because of the sacredness of the head and the hair, this expression displayed a profound grief. This woman's short hair shows that it has been some time since the death of her loved one although she still does not wear any ear jewelry. Her arm tattoos resemble the man's tattoos but from what is visible of her tattoos near the neckline they differ from the man's.

Reasons for Tattooing

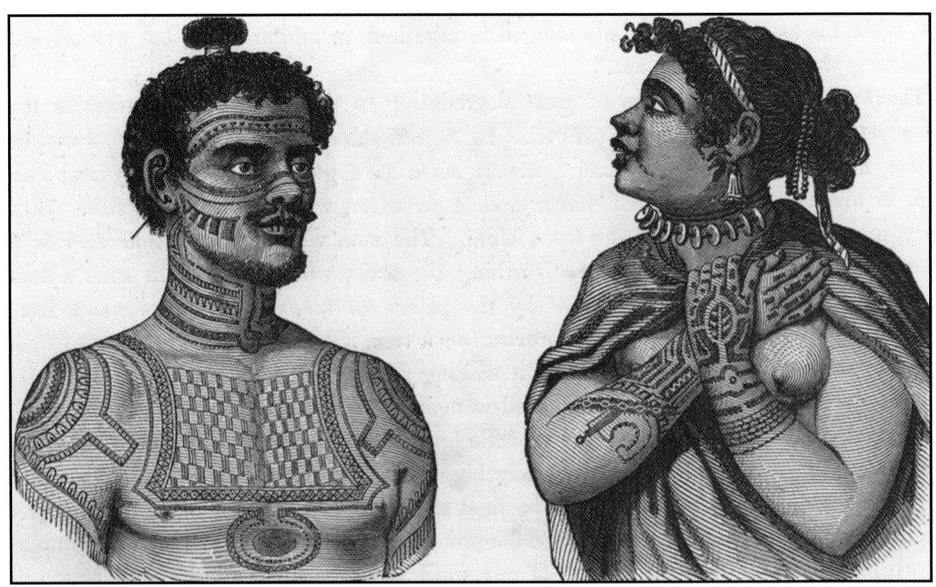

or double line, like a feather. These designs signified the fertility of the land but symbolically represented the women's fertility as well. *Appaku* tattoos were required to pass into the land of the ancestors in the afterlife. Other peoples of the Philippines have similar beliefs. It is possible that belief in the necessity of tattoos to gain admittance to the afterlife existed throughout the islands in the past.

It is possible that tattooing the hands of women served another purpose, once more associated with the underworld of the dead. Among many Austronesian peoples, the ceremony of secondary burial was performed for the body of a loved one. It was the highest form of affection for the deceased. Secondary burial was usually performed a year after the death of a person and involved either letting the corpse rot in a temporary structure or burying it until most of the flesh had rotted away. Then the corpse was exhumed and stripped of its remaining flesh. In the Visayas and in Hawai'i the remaining flesh would be cast into the ocean.[72] The bones would be washed, ceremonies were performed, and celebrations recounting the deeds of the deceased would be told. Then the bones would be lovingly wrapped and reburied. In excavations of burial jars found in ancient Palawan, human bones were painted with red hematite before being hidden in caves.[73] The Maori of New Zealand similarly painted the bones with red ochre before hiding them.[74] In the Marquesas Islands of French Polynesia, only women with tattooed hands could prepare food. In addition, Marquesan women with tattooed hands were the ones who performed the rite of cleaning the bones during secondary burial.[75] Similarly, it was the *babaylan* (women shamans) of the Visayas who are recorded with performing this function of ritual cleaning of the bones.[76] A similar rite was performed by Kalinga women. At the end of a year of long mourning, a ceremony was held called *Kolias* that lasted for twenty-four hours and entailed feasting, stories of war exploits, songs and dances. This officially ended the spouse's grieving and taboo restrictions. However, if the wife continued to mourn or cry after the *Kolias*, it was considered bad luck. Then the woman was often asked to exhume the body, wash and clean the bones and rebury them because this would resolve any remaining grief and prevent further bad luck from falling upon the mourner.[77]

Filipino Tattoos: Ancient to Modern

Although secondary burial no longer takes place in the majority of Austronesia and the Philippines, customs that stem from this ancient practice remain. Although the deceased's bones are not exhumed today, families will gather together on the anniversary of the death of a loved one and visit the grave site. Stories of their lives are remembered and retold by their loved ones.

The function of women in secondary burial was based on their role as life bearers. While some scholars have been tempted to associate a woman's tattooed hands with protection from defilement with the dead, this seems to be a Western paradigm. In the old Austronesian belief system, ancestors (many of whom were elevated to godhood) were the foundation and source of life. At death, the soul returned to the ancestors in the homeland of the underworld. Therefore, death was a sort of reverse birth. It is only natural that women, who are the source of life in this world, would be the ones who performed this function. Being tattooed on the hands was a visual reminder of the connection to ancestors in the underworld who were the source of all life.

In a similar manner, as life bearers, it was the responsibility of women to prepare food to sustain and continue the posterity that originated with the ancestors.

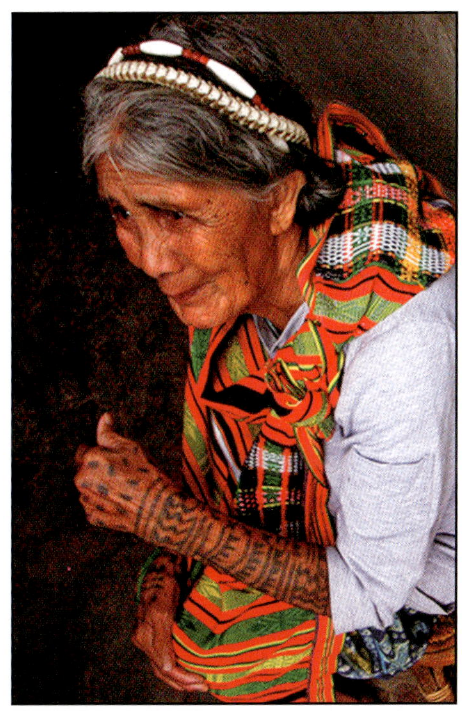

A Bontoc woman with stars, ladder, fern leaves and lightning tattoo motifs. Courtesy of Ayeona Langfia

Tattoos were also performed on women to set them apart, as being of a special caste, wealth status or privilege. Tattoos could show ownership of property, such as rice fields. Women of the Marshall Islands were similarly set apart by their tattoos to show their chiefly rank. In Samoa, young women, usually the daughters of a village chief known as *Taupou*, wore special tattoos on the legs, called *Malu,* to show their sacred status. These women were considered clean enough to chew the sacred 'ava plant that was used to make a ceremonial drink known in many places as *kava*. In the Philippines, the quality of a woman's tattoos also showed her rank or wealth in the village by indicating that a woman's family could pay for a fine tattooist. Naturally, a more expensive artist did better work. In the Bontoc region, a woman's tattoos were described as *kala-kalawang* (crude tattoos) or *kagawisi* (beautiful tattoos).[78]

Unlike men who had to earn their tattoos through requisite bravery, character and knowledge, generally women were entitled to their tattoos at puberty. Women of the Philippines, unlike other parts of Southeast Asia and the Asian mainland, were not necessarily considered subordinate or subservient to men. The roles of the genders were different, but one not considered more important than the other. Both partners in a marriage performed important, complimentary functions to take care of each other and their family. To illustrate this, both partners in a marriage could divorce at will. A man would sometimes even have to pay fines to his wife's family if she left him. Then why were women entitled to their tattoos while men had to earn them? This probably stems from the ancient perception of women in Austronesia who were perceived as powerful and inherently spiritual. They were joint creators of life with the gods.

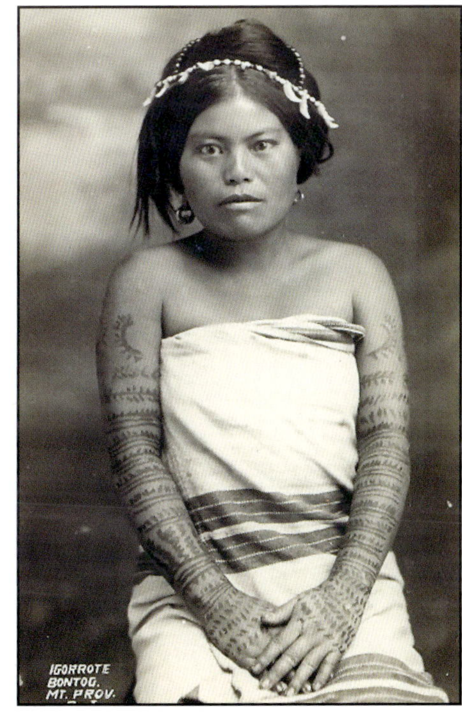

A young woman of Bontoc, 1904

In the kingdom of Tonga in Polynesia, evidence has been found of an old Austronesian perception of women. Here, a person calls their mother and all of her sisters *fa'e,* but the paternal aunt is called by the title *mehekitanga*. As *mehekitanga*, she has ultimate rights over her brother and her brother's children to control the paternal line. To demonstrate

Reasons for Tattooing

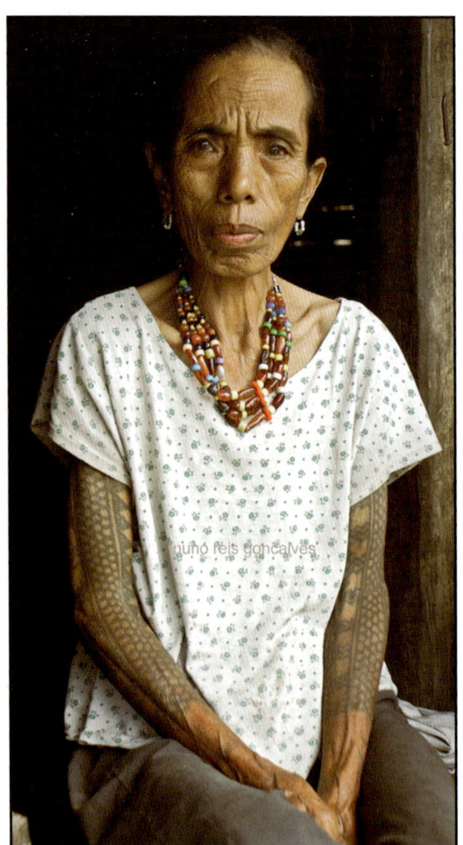

A Kalinga matriarch. Courtesy of Nuno Reis Goncalves

Below
Left: A young Kalinga girl being tattooed. Note the fresh tattoos of womanhood, called lin-lingao, covered with daubs of ink on her face.

Center: Her friends watch in support while her tattooing continues.

Right: The young woman's slight smile displays her pride and strength in spite of her pain. Photos by Kip Moore, 1920, Kalinga

the influence of the *mehekitanga*, no person, however high their rank (including the king), may be called *eiki* (chief) in the presence of their *mehekitanga*.

In ancient Hawai'i, women's *mana,* or spiritual power, was viewed as powerful and had to be protected. Consequently, Hawaiians had specific taboos to protect a woman's *mana*. Some taboos, seen through Western eyes, are seen as restrictive or repressive prohibitions – such as certain food taboos like eating pork or bananas. In actuality, they were to preserve the health of the woman or her children. For example, eating certain bananas during pregnancy and nursing causes thrush in babies.[79] Among the Iban of Borneo, women performed important spiritual warfare with evil spirits through their weaving of magical symbols into cloth. These powerful cloth talismans protected the people of the village, as well as the men, when they conducted warfare. In most places of the Philippines, people capitalized on inherent spiritual power of women by their role as liaisons with the spirit world. These women were called *babaylan,* or variations of the title such as *baglan* in Ilokano. They interpreted omens and dreams, divined the outcome of events, and communicated with members of the spirit world. In some places, the *babaylan* even led the men to battle and ceremonially threw the first spear![80] In these ways a woman's tattoos were constant, visual affirmation of her strength, procreative power and spiritual receptivity that she brought into this world.

In addition to their inherent tattoos, women of the Philippines were also tattooed after having participated on an attack on the enemy with men. In some regions, such as in Kalinga and Apayao, women were tattooed any time a male relative took a head or was tattooed.[81] Among the Isneg, a man may elect to have his daughters tattooed with the marks of his headhunting valor instead of him.[82] These tattoos served as a warning to those who may have intentions of harming these women or taking their heads. These tattoos showed that the girls had able-bodied warrior relatives who would avenge them if the girls were harmed.

For example, often headhunting forays were conducted by ambush as warriors infiltrated the outskirts of a village and lie in wait to take the heads of men, women or even children. Upon seeing women with the symbols of their male relatives' valor, headhunters would have to consider whether the violence that would be returned upon their own families or village would be worth their efforts. In a similar way, the portion of a

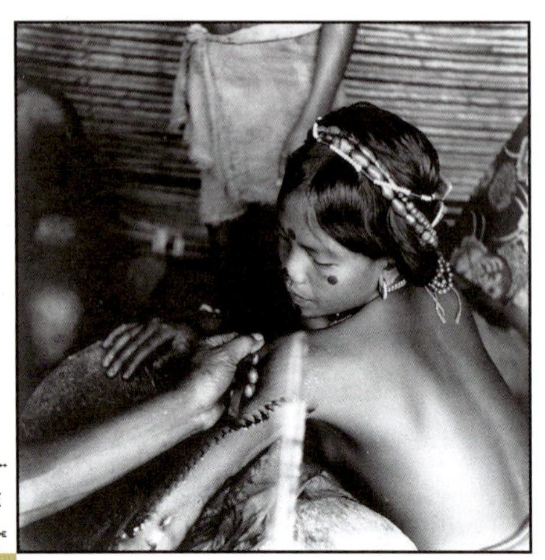

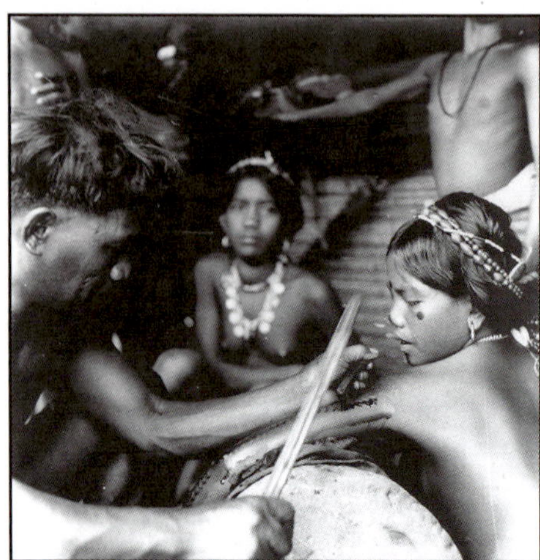

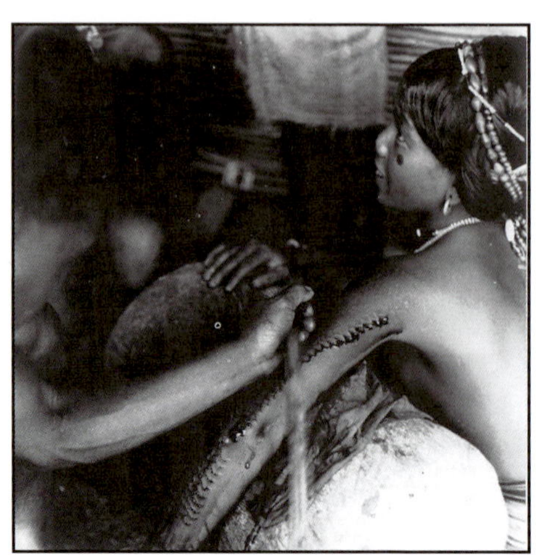

Filipino Tattoos: Ancient to Modern

man's facial tattoo – on the upper lip (*raurau*) of high ranking Maori males in New Zealand – contained specific motifs which indicated that they were protected individuals. These visual warnings related to all that any harm done to them would be avenged. Although normally these tattoos were reserved as a portion of a man's *moko* (facial tattoo), this protective piece was also extended to high-ranking women, such as in the case of the chieftess Niapo of Kiahari, Hawkes Bay.[83] In wearing a man's tattoo in addition to the woman's tattoo denoted the extremely high status of these women.

From these examples we learn what tattooing meant for these women. They were seen as not only more beautiful, but also possessing emotional and physical fortitude to endure pain and hardship, including the pain of childbirth. A woman's tattooing was an affirmation of her strength and inherent spiritual power, procreative endowment, and as a form of clothing, an enhancement of beauty and a proclamation of her status. Finally, the tattoos were a form of recognition that allowed the soul of a woman to pass into the afterlife and join the glorious chain of her ancestors.

Chapter 4

Facial Tattooing

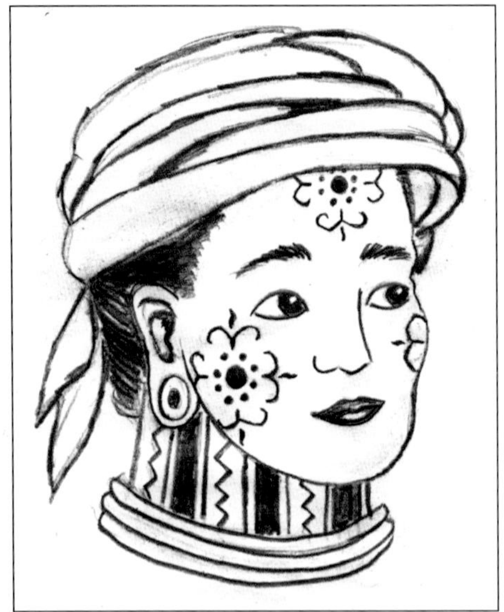

Detail of Visayan face tattoos. After the Boxer Codex by the author

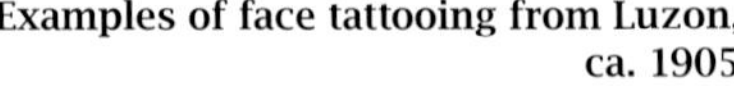

Examples of face tattooing from Luzon, ca. 1905

Facial tattooing occurred among both men and women in the Philippines, although women's facial tattoos (lin-lingao) appear to be only practiced in the Cordillera of Luzon and much more limited than the men's facial tattoos. Those warriors who were the bravest and had gained a great number of victories in battle were honored to receive tattoos on the face. *The Boxer Codex* illustrates ancient Visayan men's facial tattoos as floral-looking motifs. We do not know if the artist of the Boxer Codex took any liberties with this depiction of the facial tattoos, as we do not have any supporting record of their use on the face. These floral-looking tattoo designs are, however, found in other areas. It is possible that these designs may have been tattooed on the face, perhaps as recognition for exceptional seamanship. (A more detailed explanation for these designs will be discussed in the section titled Crab and Canoe Designs and Motifs, in Chapter 6.) From the written records we find that Father Francisco Colin recorded that the Visayan men tattooed the chins and about the eyes (*barbas y cejas*),[84] so as to appear masked. In the Visayas, facial tattoos were thought to make a man more fearsome looking but also may have alluded to a warrior's proven prowess as well. This type of facial tattoo described by Father Francisco Colin was called *langi*, which means "gaping," like the open mouth of a crocodile or bird of prey. The crocodile was revered and feared in its powerful ability to mete out death in the waters. Few escaped their jaws once grasped. In a similar way when these men worthy of the langi tattoos fought in ship-to-ship battles, they were such skillful and powerful warriors that very few escaped their strength. These facial tattoos were also called *bangut* meaning muzzle or halter.[85] However, *bangut* or *bangot* also refers to fishing hawks in whose nests was found an herb or root that was a talisman of sorts that contained the secret of their fishing skill.[86] This tattoo may have translated into how the warrior, like the hawk, was able to swiftly swoop down and capture his prey. The victim was all but helpless before them like a fish is to the hawk. As such these Visayan facial tattoos from chin to eyes were restricted to the very bravest and most proven of warriors. As both the crocodile and hawk were animal representatives of ancestral spirits who were looked to as omen bringers, these tattoos on the face may have also conveyed an affinity or closeness to these spirits. The implication here is that these men were not only the bravest and most physically fit of warriors but

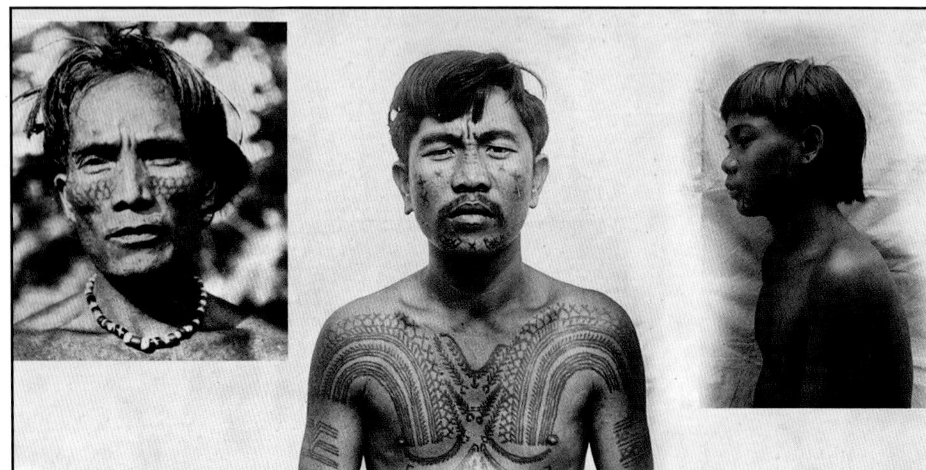

Filipino Tattoos: Ancient to Modern

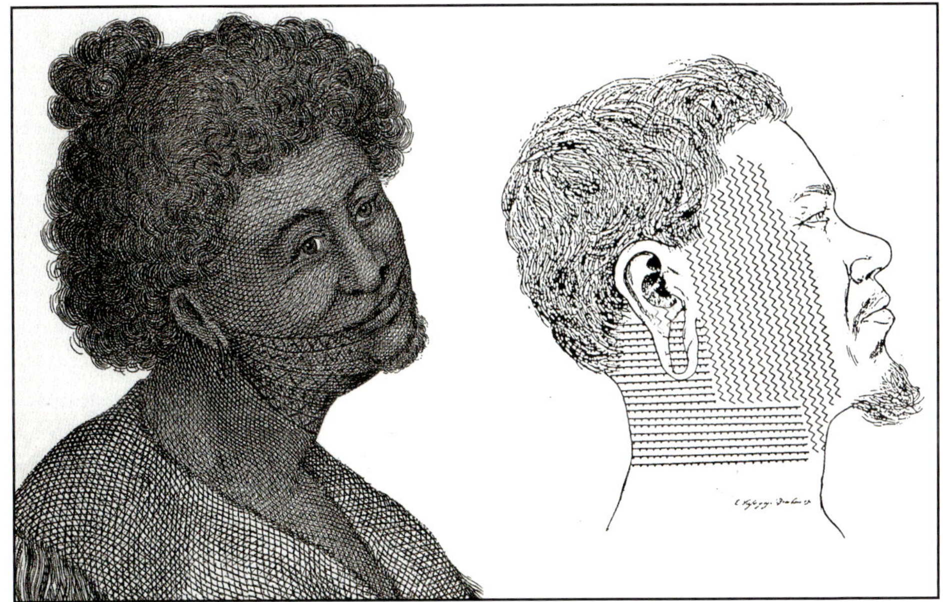

On the left is a Tahitian man with a jaw tattoo similar to the jaw tattoos of Bontoc. By Sydney Parkinson, 1769. On the right is an example of a Marshallese face tattoo. Hawaiian men had similar tattoos although usually on only one side of the face. Courtesy of Dirk R. Spennemann

also spiritually proven warriors. Young warriors would be very uneasy of challenging men possessing this form of tattooing!

From more recent examples of facial tattooing from the Cordillera region, similar facial tattoos among the Kalinga were constructed of rows of hexagons arranged horizontally across the face or in diagonal bands moving away from the nose and bridge to the jaw. These tattoos generally represent snake scales which is a warrior's symbol. Among the Bontoc facial tattoos have been observed as geometric designs in bands along the jaw-line which are similar to the designs on the mother of pearl ornaments worn by men called *tikam* or *fikum*. These jaw-line tattoos are also thought to be crocodile's teeth to create a fearsome look. Other examples of facial tattooing among other groups seem to demonstrate a

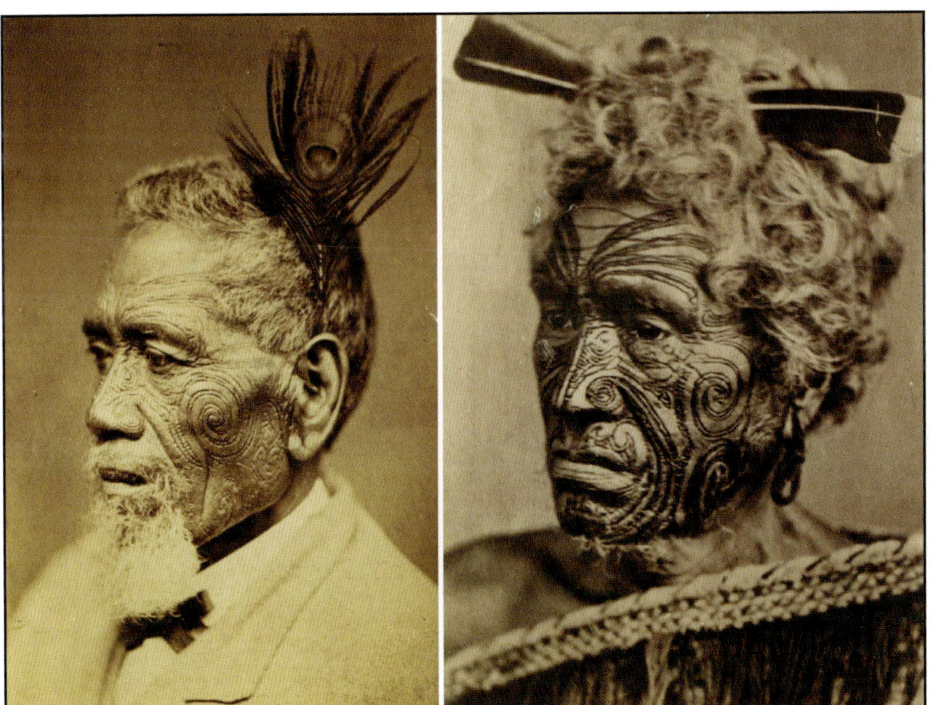

Two examples of the complex Maori face tattoos called Moko, ca. 1870

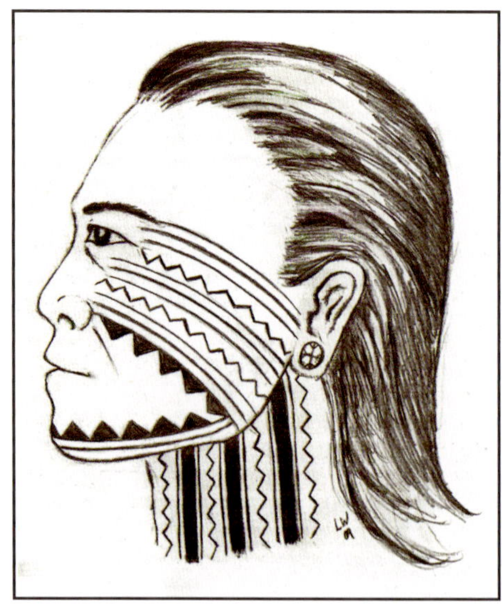

A reconstruction of the Visayan Langi face tattoo by the Author. Father Francisco Colin in his book Labor Evangelica 1663 wrote of the Visayans, "...they did tattoo the chins and about the eyes [barbas y cejas]. "Langi" was recorded by the Spanish as meaning gaping like a crocodile or bird of prey. Another word for this ttype of tattoo was "Bangut" meaning muzzle or halter. Face tattoos from ear to chin to eyes were limited to the boldest and toughest of men.

less formal arrangement and more creative license by the tattoo artist. Some Ifugao and Bontoc facial tattoos are "Xs" arranged on the face and other simple line art. Manong Hugo Prill, the President of the Hawaiian B.I.B.A.K. chapter explained that each "X" symbol tattooed on a man's face represented a head taken by the warrior.

Facial tattooing also existed in the Pacific Islands with the facial tattoos of the Maori of New Zealand called "moko" being the most elaborate. The term "moko" is also the word for lizards or reptiles in Maori which bears a parallel to the gaping (langi) crocodile facial tattoos of the Visayans. Maori moko facial tattoos denoted rank and ancestry. The ancient Marquesan warriors also heavily tattooed the face in broad black bands across the face. Hiva Oa natives in the Marquesas Islands reported that lizard motifs were anciently tattooed on the face.[87] Most early depictions of Hawaiians in the early ninetieth century show that they were much more limited in their facial tattoos which usually consisted of free floating motifs such as circles enclosing "X" or cross designs, chevrons and crescent shapes near the eyes. There is even a record of a Hawaiian man named Keawe'ai who had tattoos of *mo'o* (lizards) on his cheeks and eyebrows. A wooden idol with similar lizard tattoos painted on it was found in a cave above Waimea Valley on O'ahu.[88] In contrast to these sparse, free floating tattoos, there is a drawing done by John Webber, an artist on Captain James Cook's third voyage, that shows a Hawaiian man with the right side of his face covered in zigzag tattooing designs. Although most men of the Marshall Islands had chest and shoulder tattoos, neck and head tattoos were reserved for men of the chiefly rank. Facial tattooing among the Marshallese consisted of zigzag lines running vertically down the sides of the face, sometimes leaving the front of the face and forehead free of tattooing, but other times not.

Zigzag tattoo designs in many Austronesian cultures represent water, but in parts of the Kalinga province of the Philippines these designs can also represent snakes, especially when tattooed on men. Snakes were another reptile associated with ancestor spirits. As such, facial tattooing composed of reptile designs was likely tied to the sacred nature of the head that was the nexus of communication with the spirit world and ancestors.

The face as part of the head was the most sacred part of the body. To be tattooed on certain parts of the face, such as the eyelids, tip of the nose, eyebrows, the tip of the chin and top of the head were extremely painful.[89] A great deal of respect was accorded those who possessed this form of tattooing in the past. However, most respect for this tattooing was due to the extremely sacred nature of the head, not because of the pain. As mentioned earlier, the head was the reservoir of spiritual power and its connection to the ancestral spirits made men with facial tattoos especially honorable.

Filipino Tattoos: Ancient to Modern

Chapter 5

Spiritual Aspects of Tattooing

Many people have written about indigenous tattooing practices around the world. Often these tattoos are seen from a Western perspective and the spiritual qualities of the designs are condescendingly explained as simply being *magical*. The same has been said of the tattooing of the Philippines. But what is it about these designs and motifs that make them special, powerful or in other words magic? The following sections will explore the spiritual aspects of the tattoos as they relate to our native beliefs.

Passage to the Afterlife

Some tattoos were important tokens that allowed passage into the afterlife. But in discussing tattoos associated with the afterlife, it is important to understand the concept of death and the underworld in the Philippines. To do so we need to have a basic understanding of the ancient cosmology of the Philippines. In much of Austronesia creation myths are poetic descriptions of migration from an ancestral homeland to the islands. The mythology of today was the history of yesterday told in euphemisms and figures of speech no longer used. When read at face value, ignorant of the old poetic descriptions, these stories seem too fantastic to believe. Many creation accounts of the Pacific including those of the Philippines are remarkably similar. These tales of origin share common themes of only the sky and ocean existing which illustrates the only thing one sees when traveling on the open ocean. In the next event land is created, fished up from the ocean or dropped out of the sky. Here too is an illustration of sighting land in the distant horizon and as the canoe approaches, the land appears to rise out of the ocean due to the curvature of the earth. Figuratively it has been fished up out of the ocean. In some tales the sky or sky god drops down stones to become islands. Large clouds often gather above islands that are not yet visible on the horizon. When over lagoons, clouds will have a light green underside from the light reflected up from the distant lagoon.[90] A navigator can follow these cloud signs to an unseen island. At night navigators were guided to islands by the celestial bodies. So figuratively a stone (island) was *dropped* by the heavens. Logically the ancestors did not spontaneously emerge from the islands. They traveled there from somewhere else, an ancestral homeland. As they voyaged away from this homeland, this land mass appeared to sink into the ocean as they traveled away from it. Sometimes the underworld of the dead is spoken of as on the flip-side of this world. In terms of the sphere of the earth, distant locations are figuratively upside-down. A location a great distance from a person is still spoken of as being "on the other side of the planet." Thus death was viewed as cyclical event, the soul's return trip to where we originated. The underworld of the dead was simply a poetic description illustrating travel across the curvature of the earth from another place. With this concept in mind let us examine some of the tattoos associated with death and the underworld.

Several groups in the Philippines believed that the tattoos survived after death and were marked upon the soul itself. The tattoos were necessary to gain passage to the afterlife. This was true of the Gaddang people of northeastern Luzon. Both men and women tattooed among the Gaddang, with designs placed on their arms, legs, and fingers. Tattoos were called *burik*. The men's tattoos were mainly on the chest and arms.

These consisted of rows of three parallel lines running from the shoulders down over the pectoral muscles of the man. The framework was similar to the Kalinga *bikking* and the Bontoc *chak-lag*. Bars of three lines would also be placed diagonally down the arms. Women had a similar type of tattoo consisting of rows of three parallel lines on their hands, radiating from the wrist to each of the knuckles. These tattoos were important because they assured the wearer passage into the next life.

The Isneg of Luzon also believed tattoos were marked upon the soul. Although there were other tattoos the Isneg wore, the most important tattoos were the canoe motifs that granted them not only great status but also passage or transport into the afterlife for the dead. *Hisi* was the general term for tattoos of no specific design. But the *Andori* tattoo was the more elaborate, stylized canoe tattoos that ran from the wrist to the shoulders, according to Morice Vanoverbergh in his book, *Dress and Adornment in the Mountain Province of Luzon, Philippine Islands*.[91]

According to Isneg belief, at death the soul made its way through the underworld to an impassible body of water. There it was met by a ghostly boatman, named Kutao or Kitao, who looked for tattoos. If the soul had tattoos, he would ferry them across the water to the land of the dead where they were met by their ancestors. Similar traditions are found throughout the Philippines, especially in the lowlands near the ocean. The Andori symbolizes the canoe in which Kutao ferries souls across the waters to the underworld.

In life, the Andori also represents the status of an Isneg warrior who has killed any number of enemies. The Andori on his arms is longer in proportion to the number of enemies he has killed.[92] As discussed earlier, an Isneg woman is allowed to have the Andori on her arms if her father has killed any number of enemies in battle. Smaller versions of the Andori were also placed on the hands of women. The word *andori* is related to the word *andur* in Ilokano, which means to persevere or endure. It was a reflection of the character of the person who persevered to provide for his village, avenging wrongs and developing himself as a powerful man. It also conveys the idea of enduring or continuing the family or village. This kind of tattooing is not practiced today, due to its relationship to

A Marianas Islands outrigger canoe show-ing its asymmetric hull. The canoe of the ghostly boatman Kutao who ferried the soul across the water to the land of the ancestors was said to travel in a canoe that was split in half yet did not sink. This could well be a reference to an outrigger with an asymmetric hull.

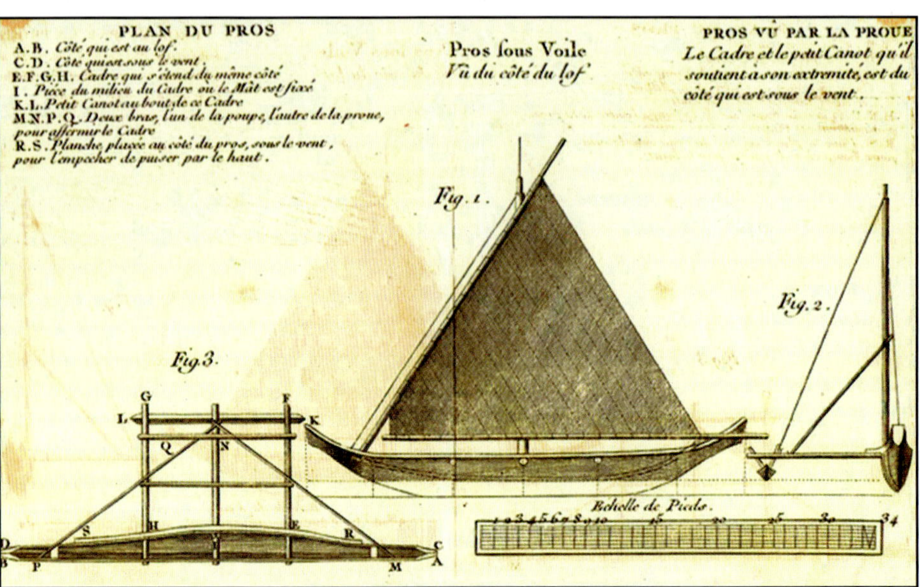

Filipino Tattoos: Ancient to Modern

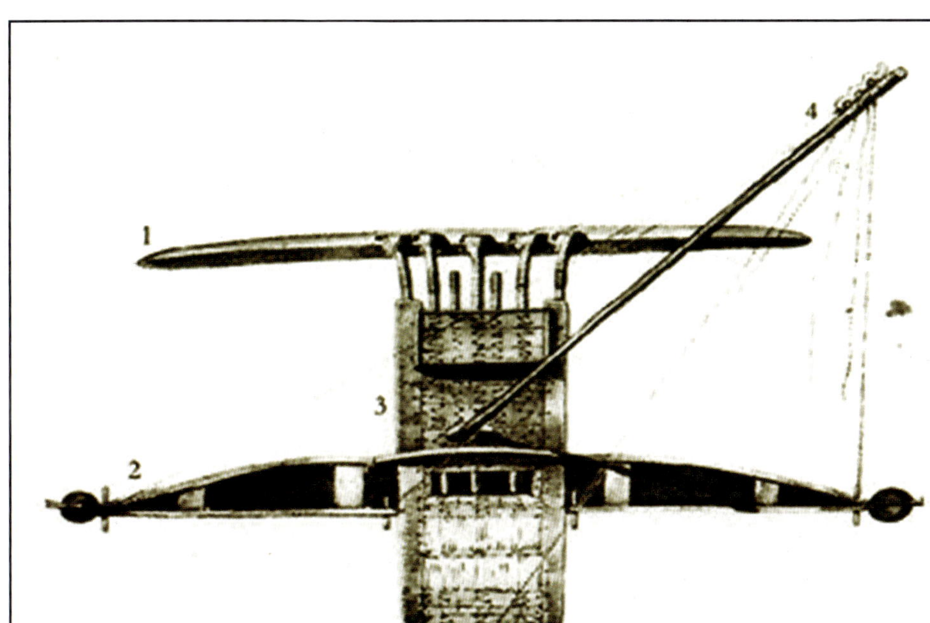

A top view of a Marshall Islands outrigger canoe called Wa lap with its asymmetric hull

headhunting that has been abandoned by the Isneg. The andori canoe tattoo and its relationship to the afterlife is derived from the canoe of the demigod Kutao and is described as only being half a canoe. It was split in half from front to back and so was missing one side, yet it did not sink.

Most Philippine *bangka* (canoes) have double outriggers with one float on each side. A canoe split in half would make it a single outrigger. In Micronesia nearly all canoes are single outriggers and many of the canoe hulls are often distinctly asymmetrical as though they were cut in half from front to back and the missing side was boarded up. This design created a type of hydrofoil out of the hull and was used to increase sailing efficiency by compensating for the offset of the single outrigger. Consequently, these canoes are extremely fast. Polynesians took the single outrigger design and created the double-hulled canoe. When looking at the andori canoe tattoo there is a double row of diamonds representing the hull, with the water design flowing over the outside of both. This may be an allusion to the type of canoe Kutao used to take souls back to the land of the ancestors. In this light, the Andori tattoo not only granted passage across the waters to the land of the ancestors, but also may have described the specific vehicle of transportation to the afterlife.

Related to the concept of the Andori being the symbol of the spirit's transport to the afterlife is the tattoo's resemblance to a tree. The Andori resembles a tree with branch-like extensions at the top, like palm fronds. Trees were revered in the Philippines because they were believed to be the housing or vessel of spirits. In some parts of the Pacific, such as in Hawai'i, canoes were perceived as modified trees whose *mana* was transformed. Thus, the Andori is the vessel that transports the soul to the underworld.

Allusions to canoes are also found in other Filipino tattoo designs where motifs are symbolic representations of reptiles and snakes. But this is just the surface meaning of the design. The underlying meaning is that they reference one's ancestors, *anito*, who make their will known through scaled creatures. A similar concept exists in Polynesia. Samoans believed

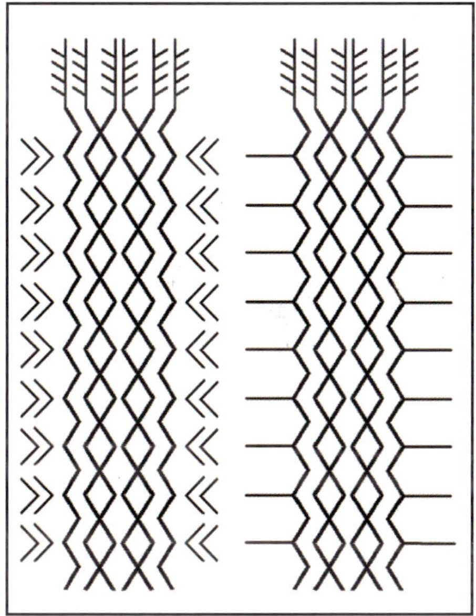

Andori tattoos after Vanoverbergh which granted passage across the waters in the afterlife back to the land of the ancestors.

that their ancestors called *aitu*, made their will known through animal avatars. In Hawaii ancestors took the form of elements of nature, including animals called `aumakua, one of which was the *Mo'o,* a large, dragon-like lizard that inhabited lakes, ponds and even the ocean. This belief bears strong resemblance to the crocodile *anito* of the Philippines who is called by a similar name, *Nuno* or *Nono,* which means "grandfather."[93] The Maori have similar lizard-like water deities, called *Taniwha* who dwelt in harbors, rivers, and lakes. Collectively, they were called *atua,* or gods, and sometimes assumed the form of a floating log.[94] Crocodiles are often mistaken for floating logs in the water. These perhaps dragon-like water gods stemmed from old memories of crocodile gods that existed in the Austronesian homeland. In the Philippines, all reptiles, especially crocodiles and snakes, symbolized canoes in myths as well as textile and tattoo motifs and the daily spiritual life of ancient Filipinos.

The link between reptiles and canoes is prevalent in much of Southeast Asia. In the Philippines and Indonesia, canoe prows were made into stylized crocodile heads. Also, Austronesian Kayan people of Borneo believed that old pythons turn into dragons called *langunan.*[95] Symbols of these dragons were carved on coffins and especially on both symbolic and real boats. In the Visayas, pythons were taken on sailing voyages and raids to secure the blessings of the ancestors.[96] Back tattoos of the Visayan Pintados depicted in the Boxer Codex bear strong resemblance of scale patterns on the backs of reticulated pythons in the Philippines. The centipede design may also have evolved from a canoe concept. A canoe with several people paddling in unison on each side resembles a centipede traveling over the ground. Each design that incorporates crocodiles, serpents and possibly even the centipede is reference to a maritime heritage and homage to ancestors who sailed the seas.

The Boxer Codex back tattoo as compared to the scale pattern of the reticulated python. Photo of python by Tim Vickers

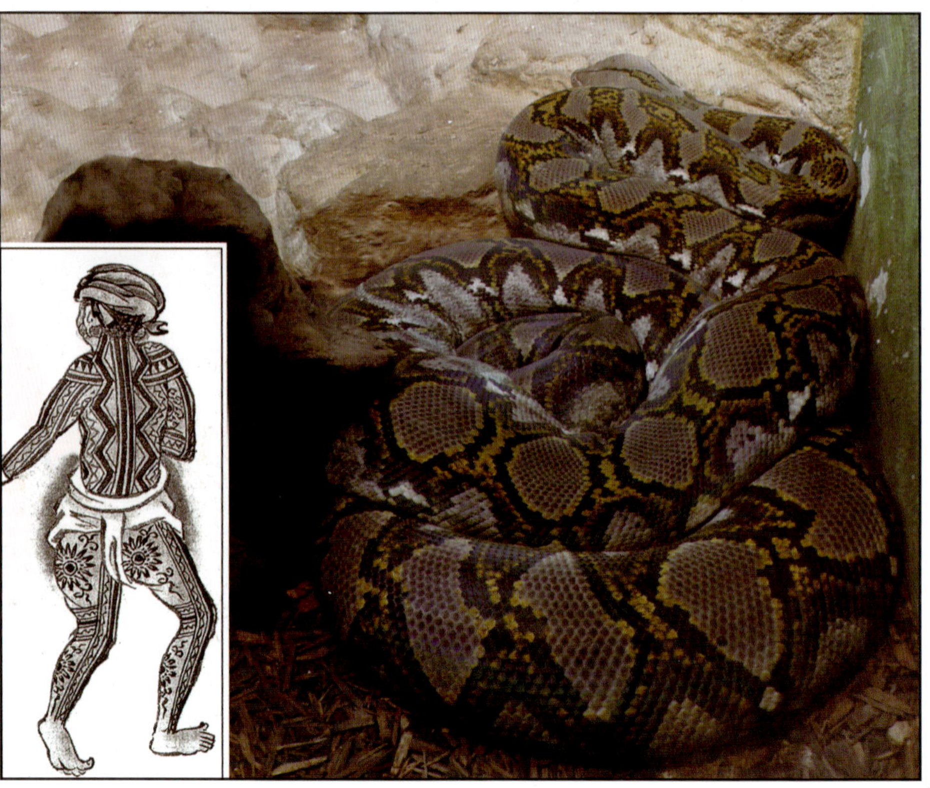

Filipino Tattoos: Ancient to Modern

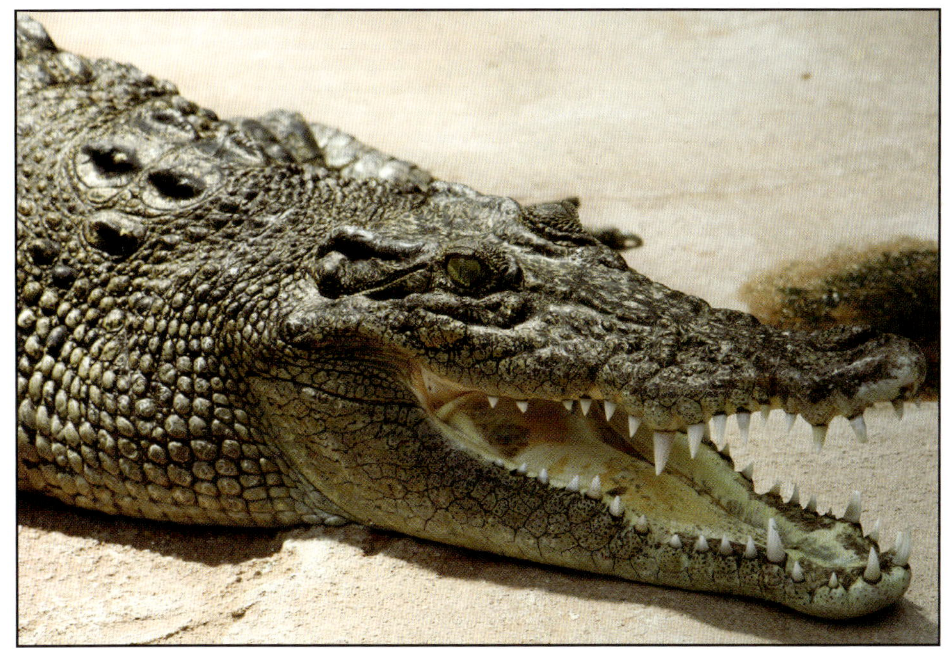

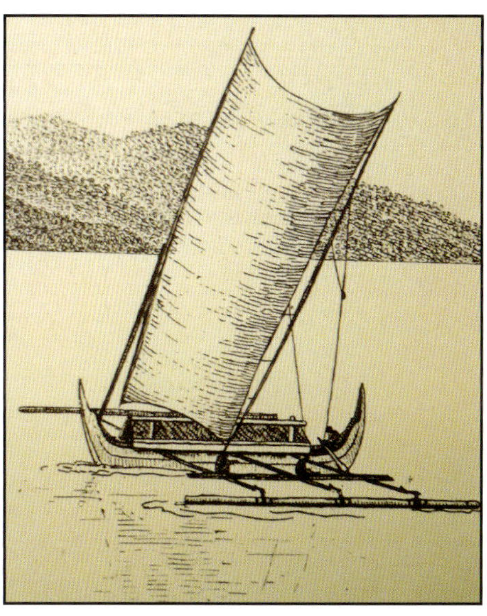

The gaping mouth of the crocodile was the inspiration of the prows of canoes in the Philippines and Indonesia. The crocodile held special significance in the past as the animal representative of the ancestor spirits. It was called Nuno, meaning grandfather and given offerings when crossing rivers. It may well have been the inspiration for dragon or gigantic water-dwelling lizard deities in the Pacific Islands. Photo by Matthias Trischler. http://commons.wikimedia.org/wiki/File:Crocodile_Crocodylus-porosus_amk2.jpg Used under licence of creative commons share and share alike 2.5 http://creativecommons.org/licenses/by-sa/2.5/

The Karakoa man-o-war canoe of the Philippines and Indonesia with a highly stylized crocodile head, ca. 1840

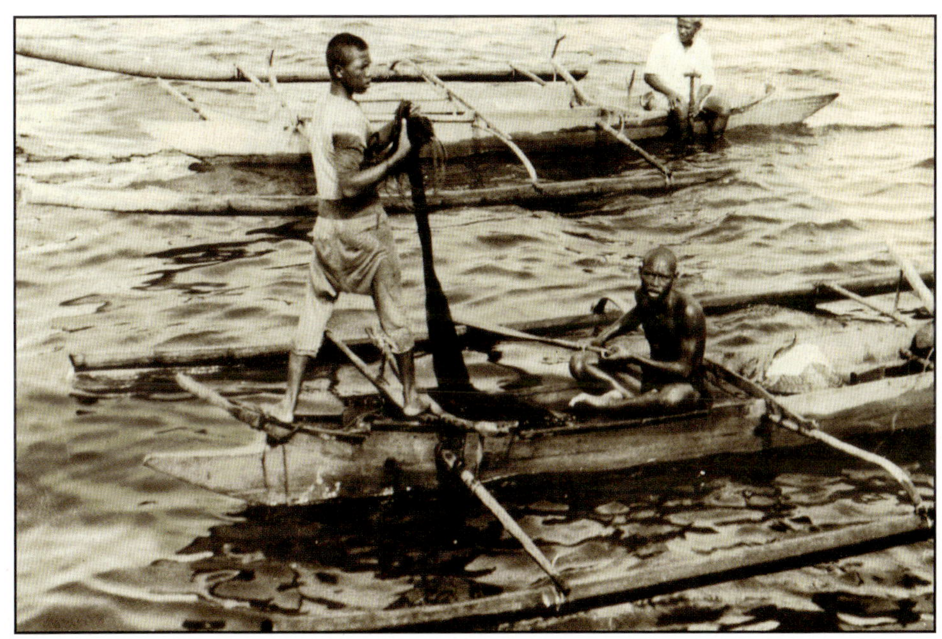

An outrigger canoe from the Sulu area of the Philippines, with a crocodile prow with its open mouth

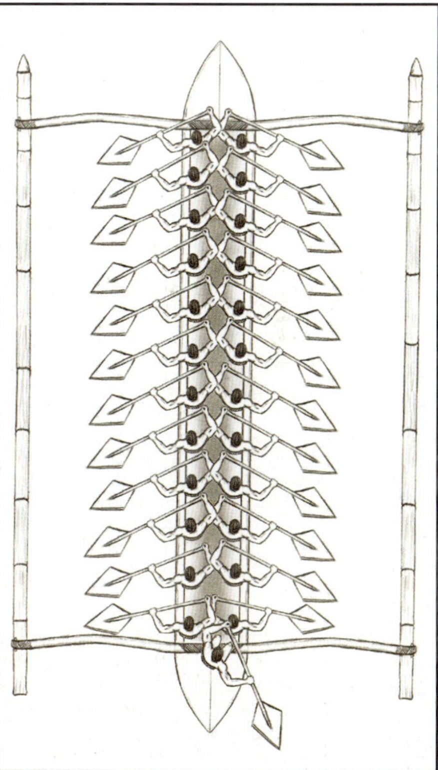

A drawing of an outrigger canoe showing the resemblance to the Gayaman or centi-pede. By the Author

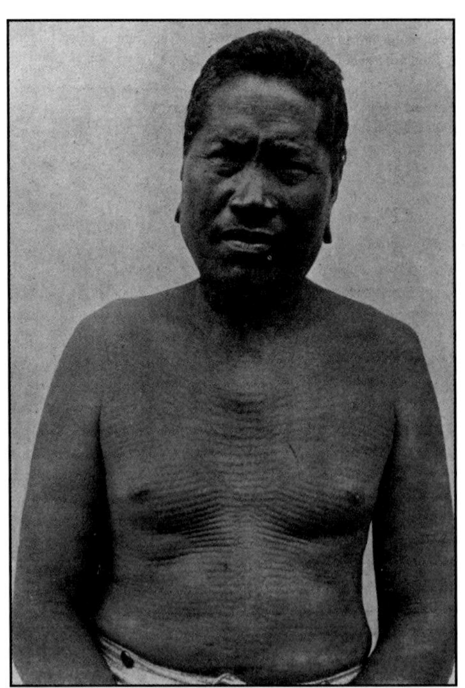

A tattooed Chief from Milé in the Marshall Islands, ca. 1890

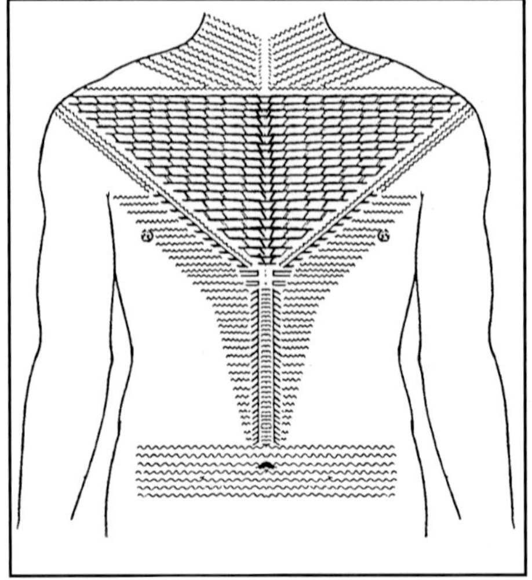

A drawing of the Marshallese chest tattoo of the Milé Chief, representing the prow of a canoe cutting through the water. Drawing courtesy of Dirk R. Spennemann

Tattoos of Samoans and Tongans not only reflected the chiefly status of the wearer but also were a visual reminder of the migratory origins of their people to the islands. According to author Sua Sulu'ape Aisea Toetu'u, the *va'a* or *vaka,* or canoe tattoo, across the lower back of Samoan and Tongan men represents canoes that brought the first kings to their islands. Samoan and Tongan leg tattoos have repetitive bands around the legs that look like stacked *vaka* tattoos.

In Micronesia, Marshallese men's chest tattoos also represent a canoe with a mast, waves of water reflecting off of the prow and cloud designs.[97] It is possible that the chest tattoo also alludes to the migration of Marshallese to their islands. Their v-shaped chest tattoo also bears resemblance to *bikking* tattoos of the Luzon highlands in the Philippines. The tattoos of origin and afterlife may be one and the same, for it was by canoe that people came to the islands, and it is by canoe that they return to the land of the ancestors after death. Caskets for the dead in the Philippines were sometimes constructed in the same way as canoes and ruling chiefs (*datu*) were sometimes buried in full-sized man-of-war canoes called *karakoa.*

It has been said that the canoe is the great metaphor for the culture of the Pacific Isles. This is no exception in the Philippines. In creation myths the canoe is spoken of figuratively as a piece of bamboo that brought our ancestors to the islands. In Polynesia the myths of the creator god Tangaloa or the demi-god Maui fishing up islands out of the sea is actually a figure of speech describing sailing towards an island and seeing that land seemingly rise up out of the ocean. Again it is a reference to their knowledge of the curvature of the earth. In Ilokano tradition it was the god Angalo (sometimes spelled Angngalo) who sealed the first ancestors up in the bamboo and cast it into the ocean to make landfall in the Philippines. In the Visayan islands Angalo figuratively gives birth to the islands and is the source of the seas very similar to his Tahitian variation "Ta'aroa."

The god Angalo appears to be the Philippine variant of Tangaloa of Polynesia. The creator god "Loa" of the Marshall Islands also caused islands to rise out of ocean. In Polynesian tattooing the stories of these and other gods were figuratively represented in tattooing. Some of the tattoos of the Philippines which closely resemble these tattoos may have at one time borne similar meanings. Understanding oral traditions or myths grants even deeper insight into the symbolism behind the tattoos and the relationship of the wearer to the gods. Most often this god Tangaloa/Angalo is the distant progenitor of these peoples and venerated as an ancestor through the wearing specific motifs.

The Anito (The Ancestors)

Representational tattoos of birds, snakes, reptiles and centipedes were constant reminders to be aware of omen events. These prominent symbols of the ancestor spirits were a visual prompt of a person's responsibility to consult the spiritual world for guidance. By so doing, they were blessed in their efforts and protected from harm and danger. The blessing of the tattoo came from these practices, not from simply having the tattoo. It was the possession of the knowledge associated with the tattoo and acting upon that knowledge that brought blessings into the life of the wearer.

The spiritual world was made up of different spiritual entities. Above all, these were usually a supreme being called by various names: Bathala,

Filipino Tattoos: Ancient to Modern

Laon, Apo Namarsua, Kabunian, etc. The supreme being was appealed to in cases of geat misfortune and disaster. Below this being were lesser gods or disembodied spirits made up of ancestral spirits who had been deified. Throughout the Philippines, these spirits are generally called anito, who were mainly interactive with their living descendants. Below them were humans, who were embodied spirits, and also selfish or malevolent non-human spirits, called *mangmangkik*. (This spiritual world was taught to me by my grandmother, Catalina Coloma Rivera, who was a *mangngilut*, or midwife and healer.) The last groups of spirits belonged to animals, plants, rocks and the natural world. In the ancient Philippines, people believed that each individual person had their own unique soul that lived through the mortal life and continued to exist after death. The *anito* was the ante-mortal (or post-mortal) mind, essence, individuality, and center of a person. After death, a person's spirit was still conscious and aware of the physical world. They still felt love, anger, compassion, and friendship with those still living. In many places throughout Austronesia the concept of family extended beyond the veil of death. The spirits who had passed on were still interested in the lives of their living relatives and descendants. These ancestor spirits were called "*anitu*" or "*anito.*" Similarly, Samoans called their ancestor gods or spirits *aitu*; Chamorro people of Guam called them *aniti;* and the people of the Tuamotu Archipelago in French Polynesia called ancestor gods *vaitu.* Although there were many other spirits, generally the spirits you wanted to interact with were the anito, because they were family who cared for their posterity and had a vested interest in your success. But just like families today, you could have good and benevolent people or selfish people in a family. Therefore, care was exercised when interacting with these spirits.

In certain ceremonies, anitos were encouraged to care for their posterity and were appeased with sacrifices and offerings. Children were named after ancestors to invoke their blessings.[98] It was believed that deceased ancestors interact with their living descendants and communicate with them. Communication could come in the form of inspiration to the mind and by what some may call a "gut feeling." A good or bad feeling would indicate whether or not one was to pursue their course of action. Chills up the spine could be the indication of the presence of an anito. Dreams were also a medium of communication, as the mortal mind tried to put into context and interpret what it learned from the spiritual world. Other types of communication could come as spiritual manifestations, apparitions or forceful possession (as was the case with my great-great grandmother, Honorata Esmerelda Eslabra, who was a spirit medium, called a *mangnganito* in Ilokano).

In addition to direct forms of communication, anitos could make their will known indirectly by influencing behaviors of animal avatars or representatives. Signs and omens initiated by the ancestors through the actions of birds, centipedes, snakes, crocodiles and other reptiles, as well as other animals, reminded one to open oneself spiritually so they could be advised by the ancestors who could see beyond mortal limitations. It was these animals that made up much of tattoo designs. Submission to the advice or council of one's elders or ancestors ensured success. Those who lost their heads were careless of these signs and omens from their ancestors who would have warned them of the danger.[99] Consequently,

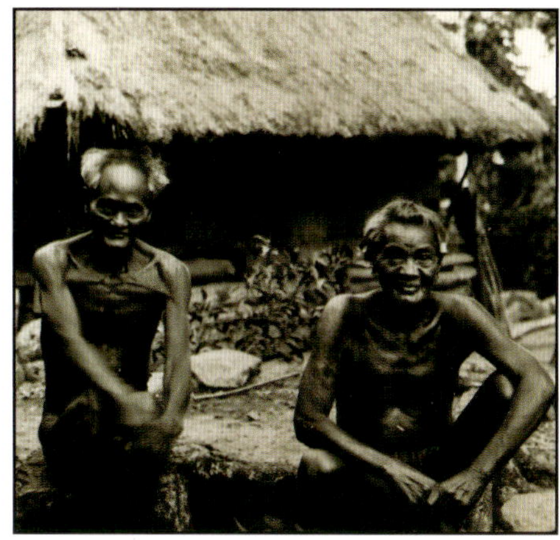

Two old men sitting outside a house from Lubuagan, Kalinga 1932. Photo courtesy of the Buchholdt Family Collection

there were traditions to appease *anitos* and make them feel both honored and amiable toward their descendants.[100]

In some respects tattooing in the Philippines was a form of ancestor veneration, though not necessarily ancestor worship. It may be compared to the Ilokano tradition of *atang*. When preparing and serving food, some choice pieces are set aside for the dead as an *atang* offering. For example, my deceased grandmother liked to eat the crispy ears of roasted pig, so a portion of the ear was set aside as *atang* to honor her. According to Aurelio Agcaoili, head of the Ilokano Department at University of Hawaii, Manoa, the *anito* eat the *ugaw*, which is the spiritual substance of the food.

Atang beliefs vary a little from place to place. Some Ilokanos believe that as the food dehydrates and shrinks, it is viewed as the physical consumption of the food offering. In my family, it was not thought that *anito* actually consumed food nor consumed the spiritual essence of the food. What we believe is that by setting aside those favorite parts for them, we showed that we honor, revere and remember them. We believe that by offering *atang* we show them we still love them as they love us, even though they are unseen. In other places the *atang* was seen as a way to appease the *anito* so that they do not feel neglected, and so inflict bad luck on their descendants.

In Ilokano and Itneg weaving traditions, certain symbols are woven into cloth, such as the *sinan gik-gik* that represents the white, yellow-legged rooster called *karurayan,* who was the messenger of the *anitos*. By incorporating the *sinan gik-gik* image into the cloth, the *anitos* are pleased and satisfied.

So it is also with tattooing in the Philippines. Being tattooed with the representations of the messengers of the ancestors, such as centipedes, reptiles, and birds, shows respect for their knowledge, wisdom and obedience to their whisperings. At the same time, it is a visual reminder not only to be in tune to their warnings and impressions but to follow the example of their character. For example, the snake or python was considered the physical manifestation of the *anito* or ancestor spirit. If a person encountered a snake while traveling, they were to pause, speak with the snake, and re-evaluate their journey. The practice of pausing and speaking with the snake (*anito*) was actually an opportunity to be spiritually receptive whether to be enlightened or warned by the spirit world. The various snake designs that occur in many tattoo motifs that accompany headhunter status are not only visual evidence of a man's war record but also of his communion and relationship with his ancestors that enabled him to achieve his victory. As he wore these designs throughout his life, the designs reminded him and those who saw him of his ancestors' interest in his success. It was also a reminder of his responsibility to maintain his relationship with them by conducting himself honorably so that communication between them would remain open.

In connection with this concept, the natural world was regularly observed for omens as communication or warnings from ancestor spirits or gods. For example, in many places in the Philippines and the Pacific, flights of birds were observed for signs and omens. Birds also appear often in many tattooing traditions among Austronesian peoples. Generally, a bird calling on the right side of a path, flying from the left to right side of

Filipino Tattoos: Ancient to Modern

a road, and then calling on the right side and then flying to the left,[101] or flying in the direction one was heading were all good omens. This meant that one's journey would be successful or prosperous.

People of the Benguet province (Ibaloy & Kankana-ey) believed that birds, such as the cuckoo, eagle, pitpit, crow, and other blackbirds, were messengers of misfortune, depending on the circumstance. If the pitpit bird chirps fast and long, then a traveler would be welcome wherever he was going. If the pitpit's chirps were slow, it was a warning to be cautious on his journey. Two birds chirping on both sides of the road was an alarmingly bad omen. The Itneg people of Luzon paid attention to the small bird called the *labeg*, that was thought to be a messenger of the spirits, especially *Kaboniyan*, one of their paramount gods. The flight of the labeg was observed as well. If its flight accompanied the warriors on a raid, its calls could warn or encourage the men.

When men of the pre-Hispanic Visayan Islands made a journey of any kind, they listened for the call of the limokon or koro-koro bird, a kind of turtledove with green and white feathers and a red beak and feet. Special attention was given to it when going on war raids, expeditions and even marriage proposals. Its call was thought to be a warning of failure, misfortune or doom. The Mandaya of Davao also paid heed to the limokon's calls and regarded it as a messenger from the spirit world. If the limokon cooed from the right on a journey, it was a sign of good fortune. If the limokon cooed from the left, back or front, it was regarded as a bad sign and a person's plans needed to be changed.[102] The kingfisher is also an omen bringer of death in Ilokano beliefs. It is called the *salaksak* and its call signals the death of a friend or family member.

Similar beliefs existed in ancient Samoa where different types of birds were seen as messengers or the physical embodiment of gods. Similar to Ilokano beliefs, the kingfisher was thought to be an omen bird in Samoa. According to George Turner, in his book, *Samoa, A Hundred Years Ago and Long Ago,* the kingfisher was believed to be the incarnation of the war god, *Taema,* who is also, incidentally, one of the goddesses who introduced tattooing to Samoa. If the Kingfisher flew on before the warriors going to battle without returning, it was a good sign. The owl was also especially revered in ancient Samoa. Owls were called *aitu langi,* or gods of heaven. As in the Philippines, Turner states that Samoans watched the flights of owls because they were seen as omens. If, when going to war, an owl flew toward their destination, it was a sign of success. If the owl flew away from their destination or across their path, it was a sign to return home immediately. Similarly, the god *Matuu* was represented by the heron on the island of Manono. It, too, gave troops a positive sign by flying before them into battle, but if it crossed their path it was a bad omen. Similarly, in the Northland of New Zealand the owl was called *Hine-ruru* or "Owl Woman." If the owl is seen flying ahead of someone or walking on the road it is a sign of protection. If the owl flies straight along one's path, there is nothing to fear; but if an owl flies across the path, it is a sign that something is wrong.[103] Hawaiians also looked to the owl, or *pueo,* for guidance. Pueo was thought to be the avatar of a specific genealogical line of ancestor spirits. Ancestor spirits in Hawai'i are called `*aumakua,* and in function are similar to anito. Many personal stories from Hawaiians relate that when lost, they followed an owl to safety. In Hawai'i, roosters that crowed at night were thought to be messengers from the ancestor god Kane-ulu-po (literally, "Kane who stirs awake or inspires at night"). Their crowing was a sign that a person needed to prepare for illness or the arrival of visitors. If illness was already in the household, it meant that the person needed to meditate for inspiration on the cause of the illness.[104] (Having had roosters myself, I know they often behave like watch dogs and crow on the approach of strangers.)

Placement of Tattoos

The placement of tattoos is nearly as important as the tattoo motifs themselves. Some tattoos are to be seen from the perspective of the wearer, while other designs are meant to be seen from the perspective of the viewer. Because the human body is a moving canvas, tattoo motifs appear to change shape; depending on the angle they are viewed they can take on different or additional meanings.

An important aspect in the placement of tattoos is whether they are on the left or right side of the body. Generally speaking, in Polynesian and Filipino beliefs, the left was thought to be the weaker or feminine side, while the right was thought of as the stronger, masculine side of the body. This concept applied to being right-handed and to the right side of the body in general. The right side was the side of the father and the left side was the side of the mother. With the exception of the Te Arawa and Ngoi Tahu tribes, this idea was reversed among most of the Maori tribes in New Zealand, in displaying one's heritage through moko or tattooing.[105]

Although the names for the left side of the body are different from culture to culture, the meanings are usually associated with being the weaker or profane side. For example the word for the left side in Samoan is *agavale* (anga-va-lay), which in addition to being the "left side" also means "to treat unkindly." This also corresponds to the flight of omen birds traveling from right to left or calling from the left as a bad omen or warning that the spirits would treat them "unkindly." The components of *agavale* also appear to convey this belief about bad omens in terms of travel: *aga* (to set forth) and *vale* (in vain.) Although some Austronesian

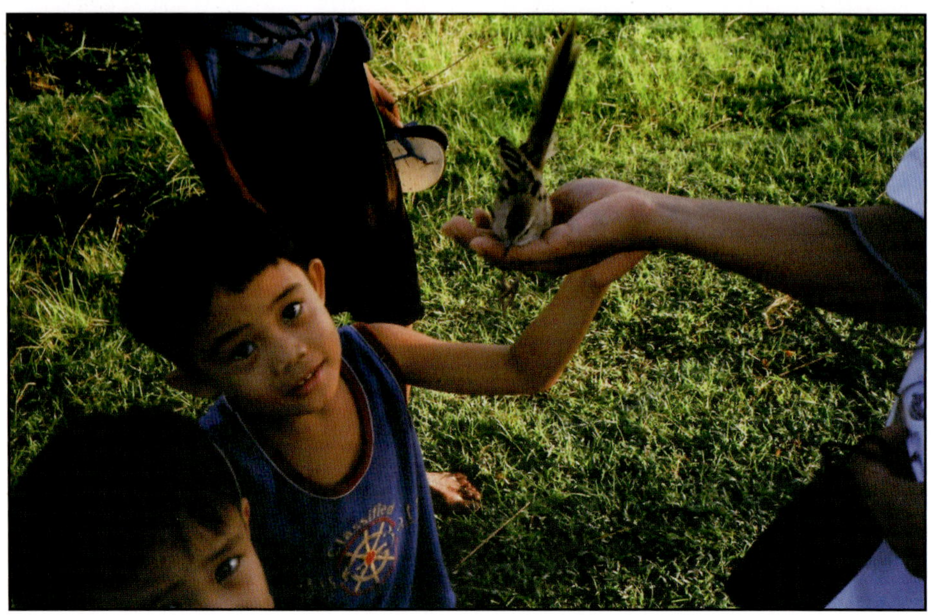

The pit-pit omen bird, also known as the pitit in Tagalog and pipi-it in Ilokano. Caught by the author's young cousin. Photo by the author

Filipino Tattoos: Ancient to Modern

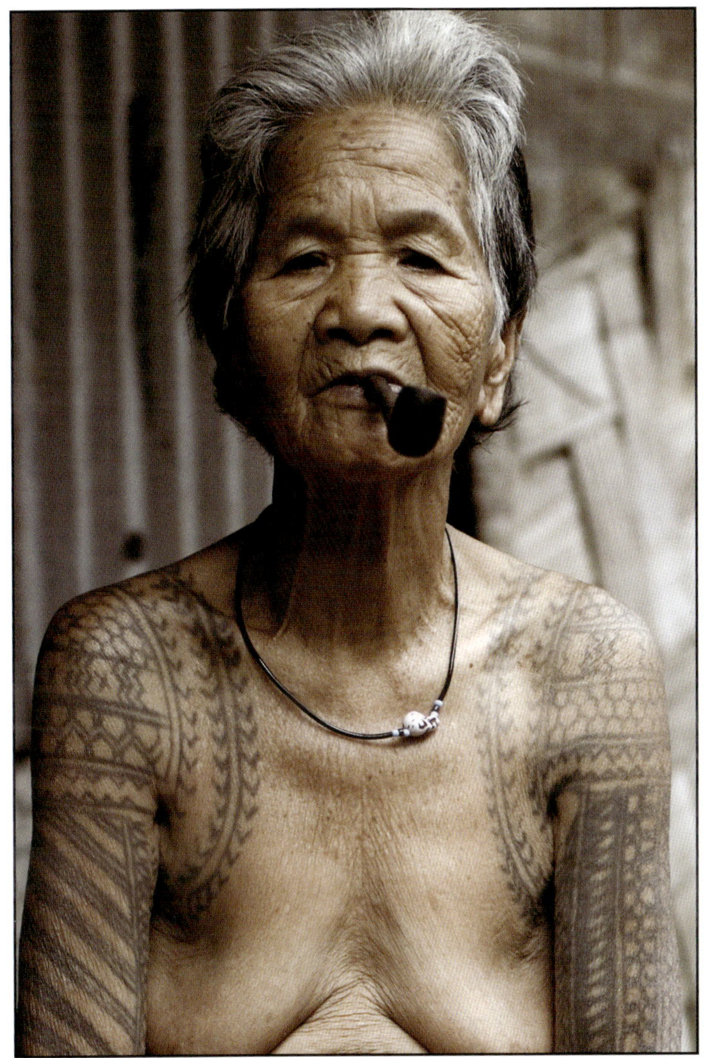

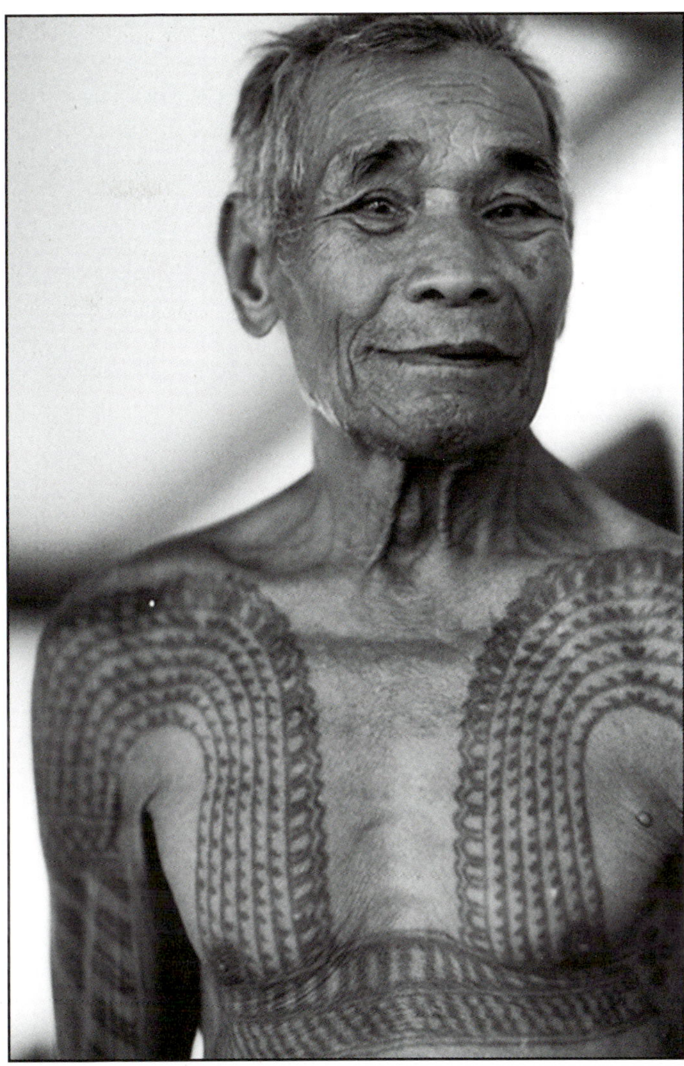

Left: Kalinga Elder Apo Leg-leg, with differing tattoos on the right and left arms and shoulders. Note the binulibud tattoos on her right arm. Photo by Farlet Vale

Right: A Tinglayan man with fungana (fronds of the tree fern) tattoos on his chest. The grass-like tips along the edge of the fronds are oriented so that as they follow the curve from moving up the chest and down onto his arms. The tips of the fronds are pointed downwards as though the wind is blowing from above. Photo by Tetsu

cultures tattooed symmetrical tattoos on both sides of the body, in the Philippines this was not always so. Among some Kalinga groups, although superficially a *binibikking* chest tattoo may look symmetrical, the motifs may be slightly different on each side to convey a meaning or a blessing on the wearer. At other times the tattoos on the left and right arms or hands are different.

The Ilokano term for the right side is *kanawan* (ka-naw-ahn), which relates to the stronger side of the body. A similar word exists in Tagalog: *kanan*. The term "*kanawan*" is a derivative of the word *kanawa* (ka-now-ah), which means "to defend, guard or protect."[106] This coincides with the belief in the travel of birds from the left or the weaker side to the right, which is the stronger and "protected" side (kanawa). In Maori, the right side is called by similar words, *kātau* (ka-taw) or *mātau* (ma-taw) In Samoan, the word for the right side is similar as well, *itō taumatau* (ee-too tah-ow-mah-tah-oo). Similar beliefs exist in Judeo-Christian traditions such as in the *Bible's* "Book of Psalms," psalm 118 verse 16 reads, "*The right hand of the Lord is exalted: the right hand of the Lord doeth valiantly.*"

The positioning of tattoo motifs and their orientation upwards or downwards was also a likely important aspect in how the tattoos are read. For example, in the ancient days of the Philippines, the orientation of a

Spiritual Aspects of Tattooing

man's weapon was an indicator of his mood or intentions. If the weapon such as a spear was held with the blade facing forwards and upwards, he was on the hunt or going to war. If a man's sword or bladed weapon was held with the sharpened blade facing up or if his spear was carried point down, he was in mourning or of a non-aggressive disposition.[107] In Ifugao tradition, the hero *Balitok* goes in search of powerful sorcery by journeying to an underworld village of ghouls by diving into a lake in the downstream lands. Before diving into the lake Balitok and his companions turn their spears around the opposite way to show their friendly intentions.[108] It is possible that the orientation of tattoos also conveyed these same attitudes of an aggressive or peaceful disposition.

Often the application of the orientation of tattoo motifs can differ from one location to another. How these tattoos are read largely depends on whether the tattoos are meant to be seen from the perspective of the wearer or of the viewer. Similarly, tattoos facing towards the head or towards the feet play a role in how they are read. The head in most Austronesian cultures, including the Philippines, is taboo or sacred, due to the belief that it acts as a conduit through which the ancestors inspire their descendants. The head is also associated with the heavens or sky-world, while the lower portion of the body is associated with the earthworld and the underworld or the ancestral homeland. For example, a man may have star motifs tattooed around his ankle representing the opposite nature of the underworld's skies – but from his perspective looking down at his feet, the stars are right-side up.

An Ifugao tradition of the divided child is that the child of a heavenly being and an earthly parent is divided in half. The halves are made whole (and restored to life) with the upper portion for the heavenly world and the lower portion for the earthworld.[109]

The perspective of a tattoo changes as the human body moves. Hands were especial parts of the body to be tattooed because they traveled between the earthly and heavenly worlds (upper body) and the underworld (lower body) depending on what task they performed. This was especially significant for women, who brought new life into the world through childbirth. Giving birth was symbolic of life, originating from ancestors in the dark underworld (the womb) moving into the earthly and heavenly worlds of light. Similarly, hands symbolically transverse from the underworld to the earth world.

Conversely, a Kalinga male with the *gulot* head-taker's tattoo on the wrist or hand represented dispatching people from the world of the living to the afterlife, with the weapon raised in hand above the head then striking downward below the waist. Understanding this belief becomes especially significant in the observation of traditional dances. Many Bontoc women are tattooed with a series of dots or dashes on the backs of their hands. A native of this area, Manang Ayeona Langfia, has stated that the dot patterns represent stars. Another informant states that these dots are seeds. It is likely that both interpretations are used. A Bontoc woman with seed/stars motifs tattooed on her wrists and hands normally sees them below her as she works, reminding her of her role in planting crops. But when she dances with her arms stretched out and upward, the same tattoos can represent the heavenly world (stars) above and the gods who watch her from above. It may be implied, therefore, that through their

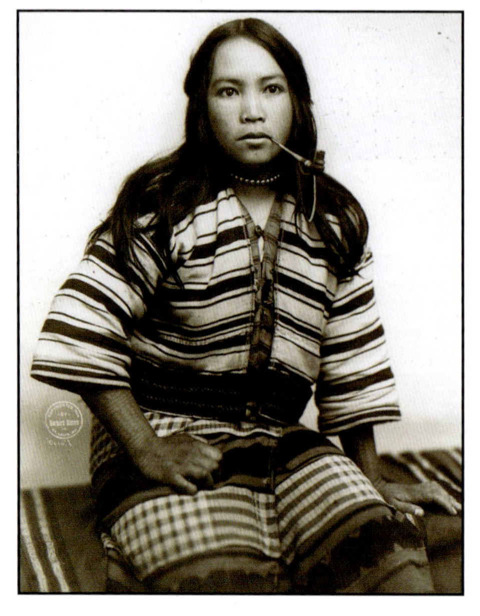

The Ibaloi woman from the opposite photograph sitting, 1904

Filipino Tattoos: Ancient to Modern

blessings her "seeds" [figuratively children or posterity] will be multiplied like the stars in the heavens.

The names of tattoo designs could vary from village to village, even in the same region. Therefore, specific tattoo variations identified the wearer as being from a certain village or family, and this idea applied to earthly life and the spiritual realm as well. The T'boli people of Mindanao became tattooed to increase their personal attractiveness and because they believed the tattoos would glow after they died. Light from their tattoos would illuminate the way through darkness of the underworld to the afterlife. The tattoos also made them recognizable to their ancestors in the afterlife. Men had their forearms and chests tattooed with *bakong* (stylized animal) and *hakang* (human) designs, or *blata* (fern) and *ligo bed* (zigzag) patterns. Women had their forearms, calves and breasts tattooed in a similar manner.[110] The patterns can be seen also in their intricate cloth weaving.

Related beliefs existed in Borneo among the Iban people whose tattoos were thought to glow in darkness of the afterlife to guide their souls through to their ancestors. A similar concept exists in Eastern Polynesia

An Ibaloi woman dancing with her arms outstretched with a Bontoc and Ibaloi man, 1904

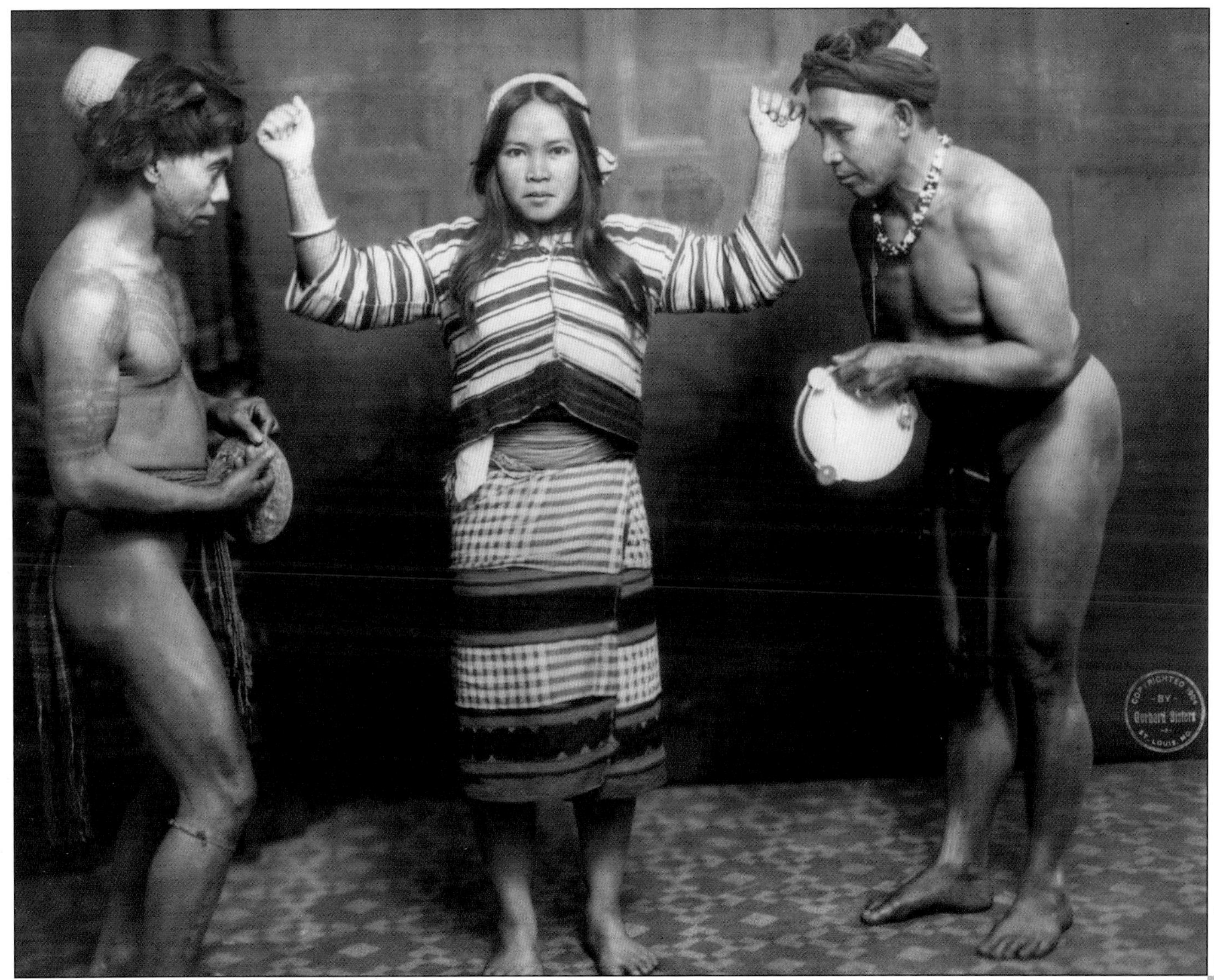

where tattooed triangles around an ankle represented shark's teeth. In Hawaiian and Tahitian tradition, an `aumakua ancestor spirit in the form of a shark bit a descendant while they were swimming and the descendant cried out his name so the shark ancestor could recognize the mistake. The shark stated that the person with those marks on its ankle would not be bitten. This began a tradition of tattooing an ankle with rows of dots as a form of recognition between the shark `aumakua and his descendants.[111] Keone Nunes, Kahuna Ka Uhi (traditional tattoo expert) of Hawai'i, confirms that in designing a tattoo special consideration must be given to ensure that the design is *pono,* or spiritually correct, regarding one's ancestry.[112]

Beyond a sense of tribal identity, personal adornment or status, tattoos also conveyed guidance and knowledge. For example, an old word in Ilokano to describe tattooed people is *burikan,* taken from the word *burik,* which in modern Ilokano means "engraved" or "spotted." It has similar cognates in other parts of the Philippines, such as *kulit* in Cebuano and *ukit* in Tagalog, both of which mean "to carve." A similar cognate in Cebuano, *buling,* also means "spotted." From these examples we learn that the root word is "*uri*" or "*uli,* depending on the language. By comparing several cognates throughout the Pacific region, more revealing ideas come to light.

In Hawaiian the word *púliki* means to gird on or a vest. Its root word "*uli*" means a dark color or deep blue, in both Samoan and Hawaiian. The Hawaiian word for tattoo "*uhi*" may also be conceptually derived from *uli. Põuri* means "dark" and *tawauri* means "black" in Maori. These descriptions are allusions to the color of tattoos. Also in Maori, a similar cognate, *ko<u>pure</u>,* also means "spotted." In Tongan, `uli means "a spot such as a mark," just as the modern use of the word "*burik*" means "spotted" in modern Ilokano. But the word "*uri,*" or its variant "*uli,*" in several Austronesian languages also means "to steer or guide," specifically in the context of sailing a canoe. The word "*uli/uri*" is also incorporated into the names for rudders or steering paddles of canoes throughout Austronesian-speaking peoples. In Samoan, "*uli*" means "to steer," such as in steering a car. In Ilokano, the word for steering paddle is *pangy<u>urit</u>.* In Tongan, the steering paddle is called *fohe 'uli,* and the Hawaiians called it *hoe'uli.* In Indonesia, the rudder of a boat is called *kem<u>udi</u> kapal* and in Tarawa, a language of Kiribati, the word for rudder is a shorted form, *bui.* Again we see a close tie to the ancient maritime culture. We can infer that "*burik*" denotes that there is some kind of *steering* or guidance contained within the tattoo. The concept of guidance is further confirmed when cross-referencing the root word for "soot" or "tattooing ink" *(iro/biro)* with similar Polynesian words. Herein we also see how tattooing was perceived in ancient times.

Edward Tregear wrote, in an article for the *Transactions and Proceedings of the New Zealand Institute,* the following about the origins of the word "*iro:*"

> Whaka-iro, to carve; to adorn with carving; tattooed. I have remarked in former papers that there is a high probability that the Maori or Polynesian people have formerly known a much higher state of civilization than at present, and that evidence to that effect was to be found in the manner in which some of their words are used. Expressions relating to tattooing

Filipino Tattoos: Ancient to Modern

(forms of ta and tau) also mean to print, to paint or mark on the skin; to make letters, to count, to designate; "to print upon native cloth as in former [times] "to put down for remembrance, to reckon descent, genealogy, to give publicity, to rehearse in the hearing of another that he may learn, to appoint boundaries, &c.; the obvious inference being that the tattooing or printing was not for mere ornament, but was at some time an actual writing. Whaka-iro, to carve, is generally applied to wood-carving, but is, in an obsolete sense, used for tattooing. I will give as an example the line in Sir George Grey's *Polynesian Mythology* referring to the strife between Manaia and Ngatoro-i-rangi, when Ngatoro destroyed the host of his enemies in a storm raised by his incantations. Among the corpses of the drowned the body of Manaia was recognized by the tattooing (whaka-iro) on his arm. In Polynesia, whaka-iro is not used in any way to denote carving; it has a far higher value. Samoan, fa'a-ilo, to show, to make known. Hawaiian, hoo-iloilo, to predict, to guess. Tongan, ilo, knowledge, understanding: ilonga, a sign, a mark: faka-iloilo, to distinguish, to call to mind: ilohele, cunning, as a bird that knows the snare: tairo, to mark, to point out, to select: tairoiro, a soothsayer; to foretell. Mangaian, tairo, to mark, to take notice. Mangarevan, aka-iroga, a sign, a mark; to mark, to make a sign. Aniwan, iro, to know. Paumotan, tairo, to mark, to stamp. It is evident that these references to knowledge, marking, distinguishing, foretelling, &c., do not refer to ornamentation by carving, but have a far more subtle bearing on the real meaning of whaka-iro. It may be that our word whairo (whairo), imperfectly understood, dimly seen, may have been coined (or shortened) from whakairo, at a time when the true signification of the word was becoming obscured and dying down, until the writing assumed the appearance of mere unmeaning ornament and fanciful design.[113]

The Samoan word "*fa'ailo*" is defined "to signal, a navigational aid," while "*fa'ailoga*" means "to mark, sign, evidence, symbol." This calls to mind the tattoos of the T'boli who believed that their tattoos upon death glowed upon the soul and illuminated their way through the underworld to the afterlife like a navigational aid through the darkness of the underworld. Identical beliefs exist with the Iban people of Borneo. Within the Iban rosette tattoos on the fronts of the shoulders is a small spiral that represents the belly of a tadpole that is, in turn, symbolic of the beginning of life. Conversely, these tattoos were believed to glow upon the soul after death and serve to light the soul's way through the underworld of the dead.[114] Similarly, canoe tattoos of the Isneg were evidence or a symbol of the spirit's worthiness to be granted passage to the afterlife.

The deeper meanings of "*uri*" as part of the word "burik" and Tregear's explanation of the different layers of "*iro*" and its relationship to tattooing brings to light the profound meaning behind tattooing. It was to mark and infuse the wearer with distinction, knowledge, understanding and guidance in how one should manage their life, in concert with the community and spiritual world. Sulu'ape Uili Tasi, a traditional Samoan tattoo artist, confirms that the tatau of the Samoans, "… is like a manual on how to live your life."[115] This information, honor and guidance (*iro*) once placed into the skin became symbolically, spiritually and literally a part of the wearer.

Spiritual Aspects of Tattooing

Chapter 6

Shared Tattooing Motifs with Pacific Isles

Tattooing was apparently a common practice among ancient Austronesian speaking peoples from a very early time. The geometric icons and framing similarities among Filipino tattooing and Pacific Islander tattooing were similar enough for Doctor Rudolf Virchow, in speaking of the remaining examples of Filipino tattooing prior to 1917, to state:

> Those [tattoos] known show conclusively that in the matter of tattooing the Filipinos are not differentiated from the islanders of the Pacific; they form, moreover, an important link in the chain of knowledge which demonstrates the genetic homogeneity of the inhabitants.[116]

Throughout the majority of islands where ancient Austronesians migrated, tattooing was perpetuated and practiced, and similar tattoo designs are found throughout the region. Sometimes the designs were made larger, smaller, altered or known by other names, and interpretations varied from village to village, but commonalities exist in which one can see relationships with each other.

Many designs and symbols were taken from nature, to be stylized into more basic geometric shapes, such as rows of triangles, hexagons, straight and zigzagged lines. The designs were similar throughout the Pacific region, but adapted to represent different meanings according to each island's particular culture; but the concept remained the same. With this in mind, we shall examine a common tattoo motif used throughout Austronesian groups, the triangle.

In the Philippines, rows of triangles represented crocodile teeth, crocodile spines or mountains. According to Lars Krutak, some Kalinga groups identify unfilled rows of triangles as steps of rice terraces. In other Pacific Islander groups, such as in Tahiti, Hawaii and the Marshall Islands, rows of triangles represented shark's teeth or islands, depending on the context or placement of the tattoos. Triangle tattoos held a similar concept but were adapted locally.

Of course the orientations of the triangles influenced their interpretation. Triangles with the apex pointing downwards may represent islands of the underworld, depending on the island group or village. Although tattoos often followed specific patterns depending on the community, each tattoo was unique and personal to the wearer, with each symbol or component having specific meaning or representation. A symbol could be placed alone, but was usually placed in combination with other symbols to represent a deeper meaning or power. The *chak-lag*, or chest tattoo, of the Bontoc represented rice terraces that are a figurative ladder to the sky-world. Yet many different symbols can be incorporated within the *chak-lag*.

The same can be said of tattooing in the Pacific Islands. Some islands, such as Samoa, the Marshall Islands, New Zealand and Yap, had organized and traditional frameworks in which tattooing motifs were arranged. In other islands tattooing traditions were more focused on the aesthetic placement of the tattoo designs. Some motifs were tied in meaning to deities or were representations of the deities.

A few of the common and similar tattooing motifs found among Pacific Islanders and Filipinos are presented here, based on interpretations

Filipino Tattoos: Ancient to Modern

learned. Some people may understand the motifs differently, as the same tattoo motif in one village may represent a specific concept while in a neighboring community or family it may mean something completely different.

Al-alam/Fungana

Al-alam is the Bontoc term for this tattoo, meaning "fern", according to Manang Julia Bete. These tattoo motifs are common in many areas of Luzon and also in other Pacific Islands. According to Manong Jotoc, these designs are called *al-alam* in Bontoc and they symbolize young rice plants of the terraces, like blades of grass. In a context among the Kalinga, each row of this design represented a head taken, and the number of rows designated for each head varied from place to place. In this context, the design is a warrior's symbol.

Sometimes the whole design composed of rows of *al-alam* was considered to be rows of rice terraces or even fronds of the tree fern called *fungana*. Interpretations largely depend on the region. In Bontoc, the design with plants standing erect represents the fields owned by the wearer of the tattoo. In a larger context, the design also represents the multiplying of crops, livestock and children. Their multiplication was completely dependent to the success of the headhunt and subsequent application of the head's spiritual power to win the favor of the gods or spirits. These motifs were tattooed on both men and women, with the designs generally being placed on the chest and shoulders for men and restricted to the shoulders and upper arms for women.

The Ifugao also used this pattern to represent centipedes in a man's chest tattoo (*chak-lag*) for the successful headhunter, and the Samoans, Tongans and Tahitians tattooed an identical motif. According to Sua Sulu'ape Aisea Toetu'u, the name for this tattoo is "*Tala-tala*" and it represents the barbed tail of a stingray. *Talatala* can also mean to "talk,

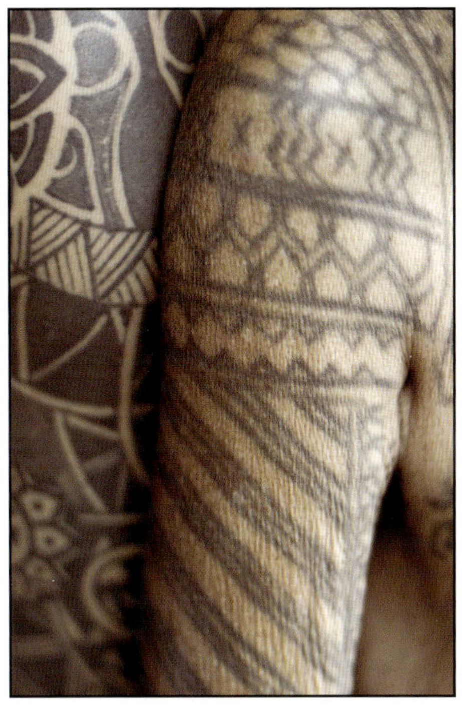

Close-up of Apo Legleg's shoulder tattoo, showing the rows of triangles identified as "steps of the rice terraces" by Lars Krutak. Photo courtesy of Farlet Vale

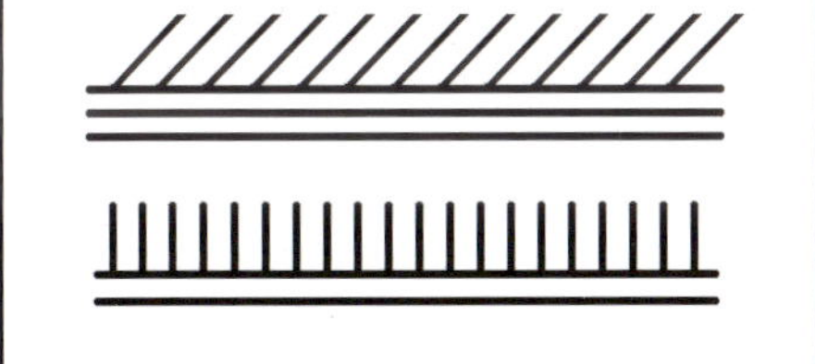

The al-alam or fungana design

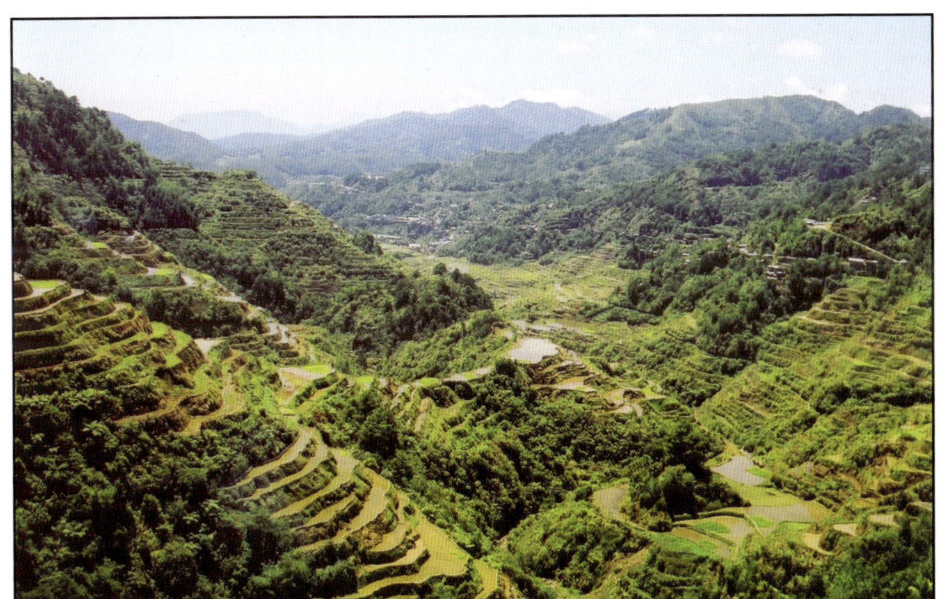

The Banaue rice terraces of the Philippines. Rows of al-alam curved on the chest resem-ble the terraced mountains. Photo by Magalhães

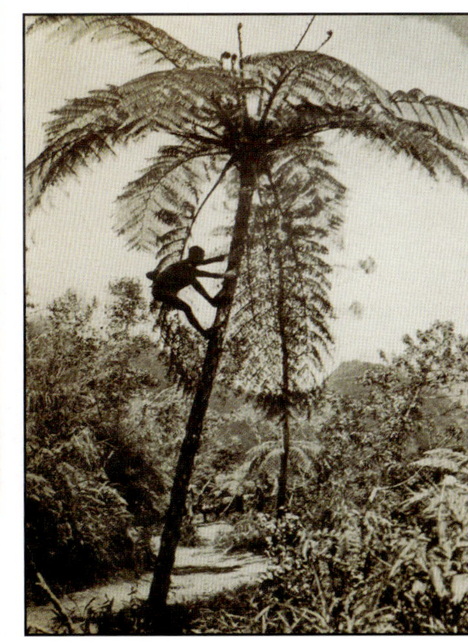

A large tree fern from the Philippines, circa 1900. Photo by Dean Worcester

Shared Tattooing Motifs with Pacific Isles

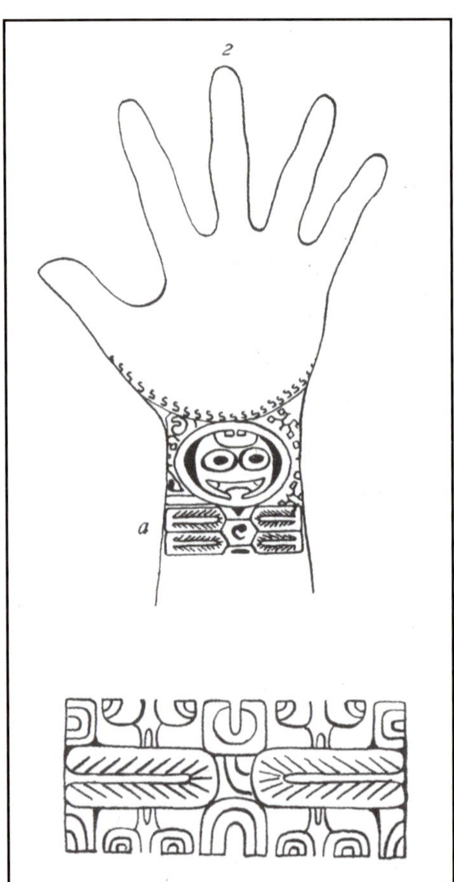

Marquesan tattoo patterns from Polynesia with the koua'ehi or coconut leaf designs incorporated within it. The koua'ehi design is similar to the fungana [al-alam] fern tree fronds tattoos of the Kalinga. By Willowdean Chatterson Handy 1922.

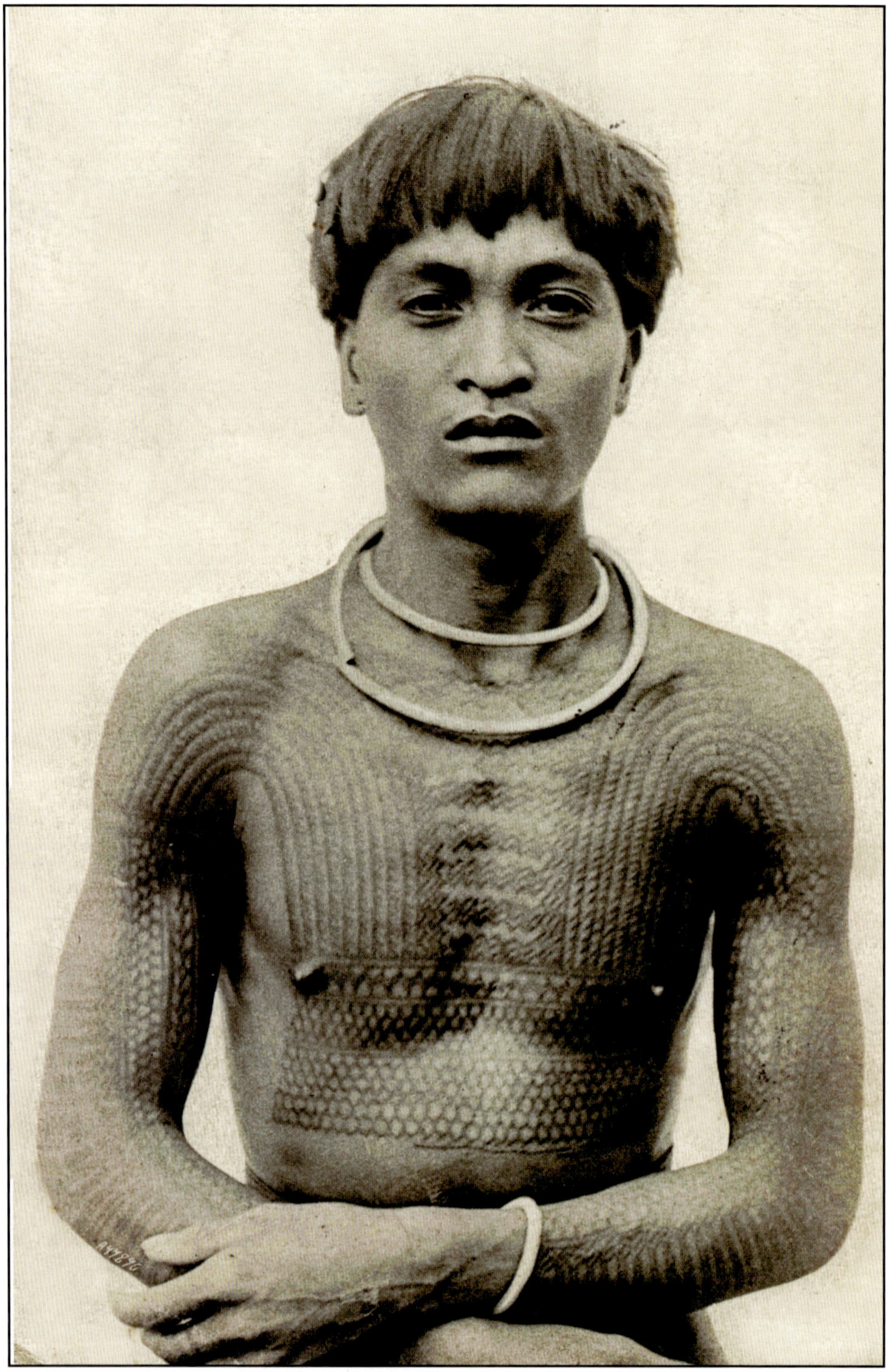

discuss, confer, and be reported," all rights conferred upon a fully tattooed *manaia* to be able to speak in the assembly of chiefs. Despite differences in interpretations, the names "*tala-tala*" and "*al-alam*" appear to have been derived from a common source: (tALa – tALA(m). According to Samoan tattooist Michael Fatutoa, this design also is called the "*fala*" or leaves of the pandanus tree. This interpretation is similar to the Kalinga "*fungana*" interpretation and name. In the Marquesas Islands in French Polynesia, similar designs, called "*koua'ehi*," are said to represent coconut leaves,[117] again drawing a parallel to fungana tree fern frond tattoos of the

Filipino Tattoos: Ancient to Modern

Kalinga. Hawaiians wore a tattoo of coconut trees on their shoulders with fronds constructed similarly to the fungana design. The Marshallese also have a tattoo motif identical to the *al-alam* called "*Lonjak.*" It is normally found as part of the prow portion of a Marshallese canoe chest tattoo. The meaning of the *Lonjak* has not been recorded, although its placement shows similarity to *al-alam*-like finals on the top or prow of the *andori* canoe tattoo, which had these *al-alam*-like motifs that could represent the ornate prow carving or feathered plumes that once adorned canoes in the Philippines.

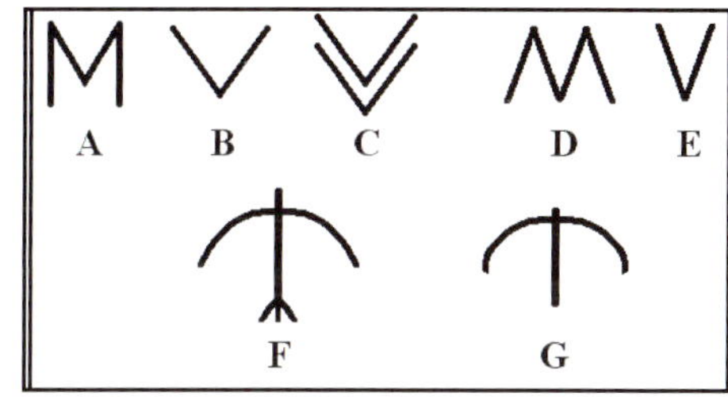

Various bird motifs from the Philippines and Pacific Islands

Bird Motifs

Many types of bird motifs appear in Filipino tattooing, as birds played an important role in the creation of the world and were thought of as messengers from the spiritual world. In some places birds were the physical manifestation of spirits. Tattoos of birds served to remind the wearer of their connection to the spiritual realm. These beliefs are mirrored throughout the Pacific, as bird messengers and harbingers seem to play a part in so many islands across the Pacific. They figure in mythology, worship and other art forms besides tattoos.

In many islands birds are a part of their creation myths. In the Philippines a kite, a hawk-like bird, flew to the first land. In the Samoan version *Tuli,* in the form of a plover, descends to look for the first land. In Tonga this bird was the son of *Tangaloa,* named *Tangaloa ʻAtulongolongo.* The last part of his name "longolongo" itself suggests a messenger. As the ancestors sailed to the islands, they used sea-going birds like frigate birds, terns, and boobies as guides to the islands that were out of their line of sight. These messengers from the skies flew away from their island homes in the morning and back to their nests on land at dusk. Carefully observing the flights of these sea birds gave the ancient ones successful guidance to new islands. When looking for landfall, seeing a familiar bird flying in the same direction of the canoe's travel must have been a good sign. But if the bird was flying away from their intended landfall, this was probably seen as disturbing, especially if it was unusual for that time of day or season. For example, frigate birds flew back towards land at dusk but also retreated to islands when storms approached. Seeing a frigate bird flying in the opposite direction of a fisherman who is heading out to sea was an obvious sign of trouble. For this reason the frigate bird is sometimes called the lightning bird by some Filipino peoples because of its association with storms.

After the ancestors colonized their new lands, their reverence for birds continued and inland birds were looked to for guidance as well. Just as the sea birds gave the ancestors the ability to *see beyond their own eyes* to find islands and avoid trouble on the seas, the inland birds served a similar function. For example, birds by their very nature are easily startled into flight. In the Philippines a man going on a headhunting raid or war expedition would often pursue his prey with the utmost stealth. While approaching an enemy, a spooked bird might give the warrior clues to where his enemy lay. Even if he was the one who startled the bird, the bird would not intentionally fly towards another human.

If a warrior was not the one who spooked the bird, but it came flying towards him in spite of his presence, that may have been a clue that a

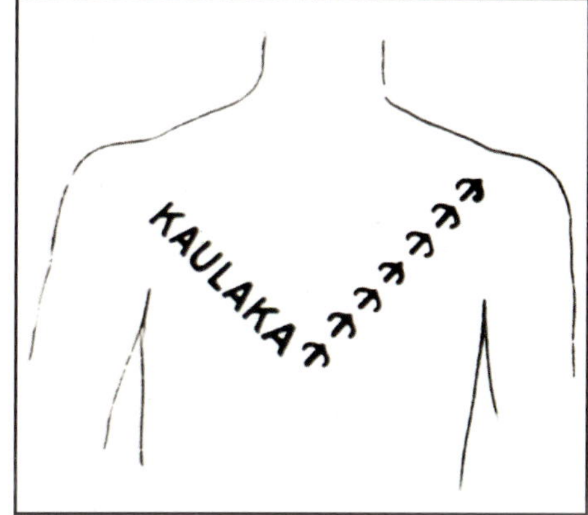

Hawaiian bird motifs on a man from Kaua'i with the name of his deceased wife on one side of his chest and koa'e birds on the other side. After Agustin Kramer, 1899

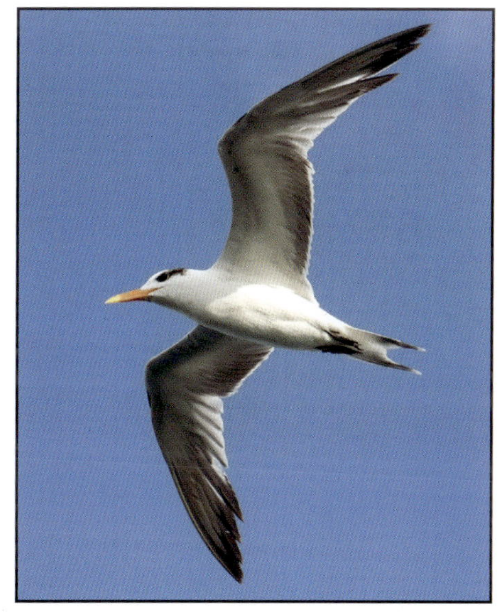

A Tern in flight displaying a m-shaped silhouette, which is the inspiration of the m-shaped tattoo motifs. Photo by Ianaré Sévi. http://commons.wikimedia.org/wiki/File:Thalasseus_maximus_flight.jpg Used under licence of creative commons share and share alike 3.0. http://creativecommons.org/licenses/by-sa/3.0/

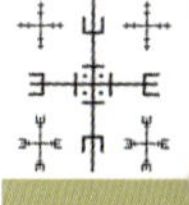

Shared Tattooing Motifs with Pacific Isles

larger group of enemy warriors were concealed nearby. Certain birds make specific types of chirps or cries when danger is near to warn each other. Hearing and understanding different calls gave the ancestors another form of awareness beyond their own senses. Paying attention to the calls and flights of birds was practical in nature as well as reminders to be attuned spiritually. The ancestors' traditional beliefs about birds were not the simple superstitions of primitives that many would like us to believe. Rather, their traditions illustrated intelligence and wisdom of the ancient ones. Not only are the tattooed figures of birds nearly identical in Samoa as the Philippines, but not surprisingly similar beliefs about the flights of certain omen birds also existed in Samoa.

Three major bird tattoos that occur in the Philippines have nearly identical counterparts in Samoa and other parts of the Pacific. It is unknown what specific bird the V-shaped bird tattoos represent in the Philippines. It is found as part of the overall design of some versions of the canoe tattoo of the Isneg people, called "*Andori,*" as a reduplicated motif (*figure C*). In the Andori design, bird motifs are a widened V-shaped motif. It may represent the Serpent Eagle, *Spilornis holospilus,* that has a widened V-shaped silhouette in flight. In Samoa the "V" shaped bird tattoos are called "*fa'avaetuli,*" meaning "like the leg of "*Tuli*" (*figure E*). Tuli was the son of Tagaloa who, in the form or a golden plover, flew over the primeval ocean. The V-shaped motif, turned on its side, resembles the bent leg of a bird. Another interpretation of this motif in Samoa is that it represents the *Pe'a* or flying fox. The flying fox was also an *aitu* to some Samoan families. The *Ginawang,* or hawk tattoo of the Ifuago people, is also a spiritual messenger. Although figure F is a common representation of the *ginawang* tattoo, there is another version shown in the next section.

Hawaiian people had in the past a similar tattoo identified as "*Koa'e*" birds[118] (*figure G*). The bird tattoos seen on mummies found in the Benguet region which have a distinctive M-shape (figure A) and are similar to Samoan bird tattoos called "*Gogo*" (*figure D*), which represent the Brown Noddy, a seabird of the tern family. According to Michael Fatutoa, this motif is sometimes called the *Manusina,* White or Fairy Tern. This same M-shaped bird motif was found running up the inner arm of a mummified Hawaiian woman, as recorded by Kenneth Emory, author of *Hawaiian Tattooing.* M- shaped bird motifs are said to represent the *Noio* (Hawaiian Tern), *Manu o Ku* (White or Fairy Tern), *Kolea* (Pacific Golden Plover), or *Moli* (Laysan Albatross) depending on the area and lineage of the individual.[119] Seabirds of the tern family often have an M-shaped silhouette when flying, which was the inspiration for M-shaped tattoos of the Samoans and Hawaiians. It is not known which bird the M-shaped tattoos represent on Benguet mummies. Nor do we know their specific meaning, since these tattoos are no longer practiced. According toManong Benicio Sokkong, a traditional music instrument maker from the lower Chico River village of Tanglag in Kalinga, figure D was a tatoo design used in his area that represented mountains and was called "*pinay-pay-jiu-jiu.*" The name for their paramount omen bird in this area is "*i-jiu*", which composes the last two syllables of pinay-pay-jiu-jiu. Perhaps the design more directly represented to the i-jiu omen bird in the past.

The designs are always placed traveling upward on the body, towards the head, from what has been seen on mummies and from a drawing done

Filipino Tattoos: Ancient to Modern

by Hans Meyer, a German cartographer in the Philippines in 1880. This implies an upward movement, toward the head or the heavens, both of which are considered sacred. It also implies communication towards the heavenly realm or a connection to the supreme or higher gods, who in many Philippine belief systems spoke through the actions and flights of birds. According to Chief Sielu Avea, the *Gogo* tattoo represents beauty and venturing into the unknown "without fear".[120] This certainly correlates to Samoan and Philippine beliefs that if a bird messenger goes before you, you may proceed without fear of harm and expect success.

Centipede Designs

The centipede is a tattooing motif shared by Philippine peoples of northern Luzon and Polynesian peoples. In the Philippines, the centipede, generally called *gayaman*, represents protection from poisons and harm in general. According to Lars Krutak, a tattoo anthropologist, centipedes were called *bulbulun di mangayaw,* or friends of the headhunters, by the Kalinga people. They were seen as messengers by the ancestors and omen bringers when pursuing the headhunt. Krutak explains that the centipede

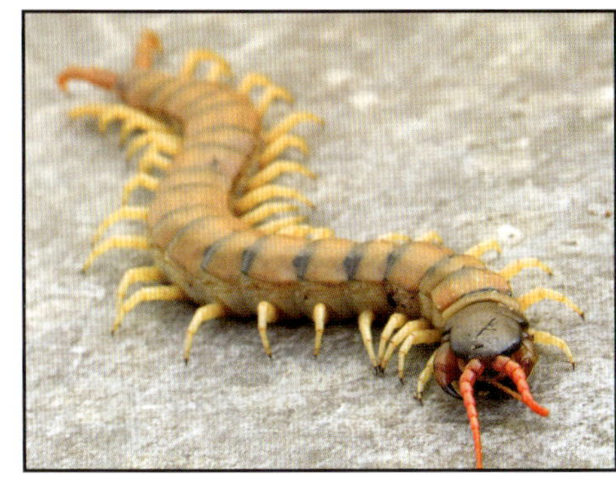

The centipede has been the inspiration for not only the fighting prowess of warriors but its segmented body is a powerful visual symbol of the continuity of life. Photo by Eran Finkle. http://commons.wikimedia.org/wiki/File:Scolopendra_cingulata_-_D7-08-2291.JPG Used under licence of creative commons share and share alike 3.0. http://creativecommons.org/licenses/by-sa/3.0

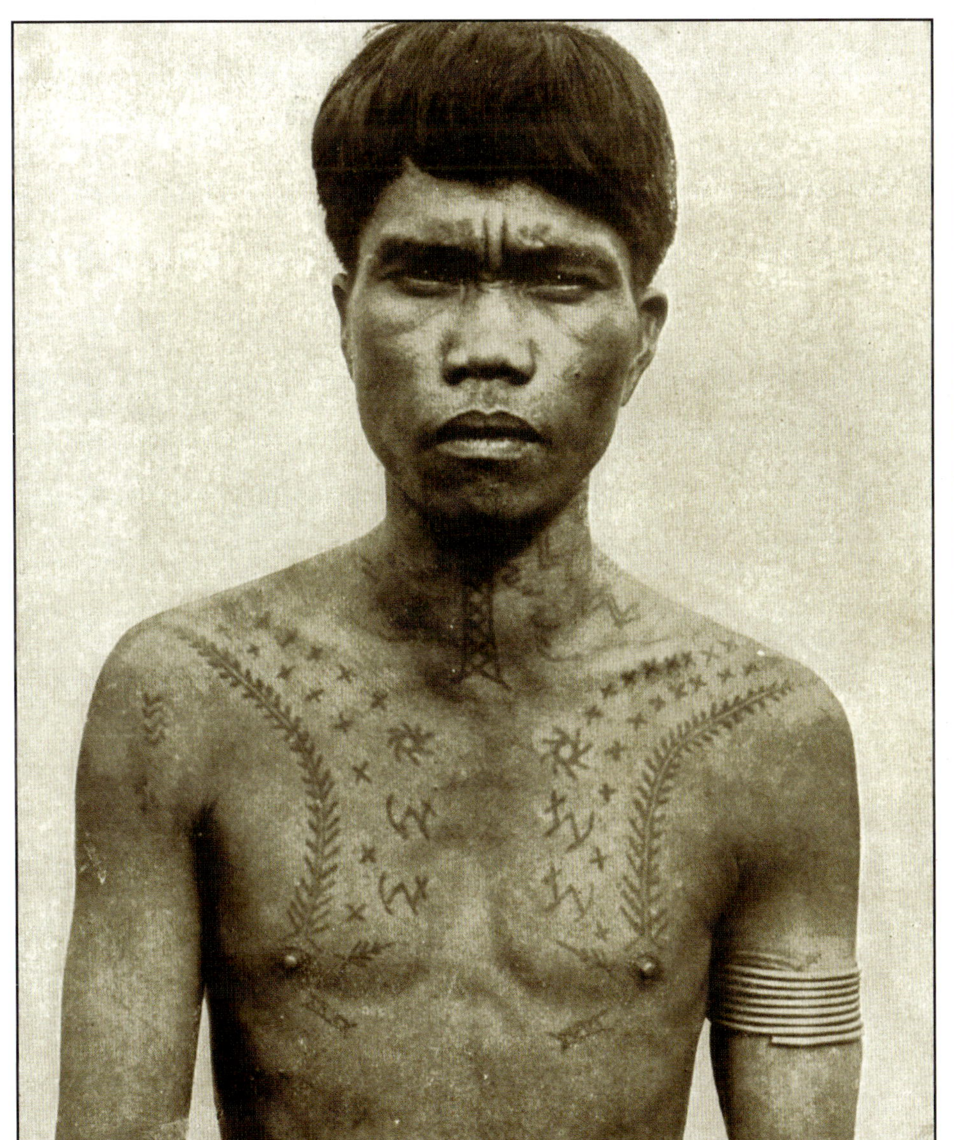

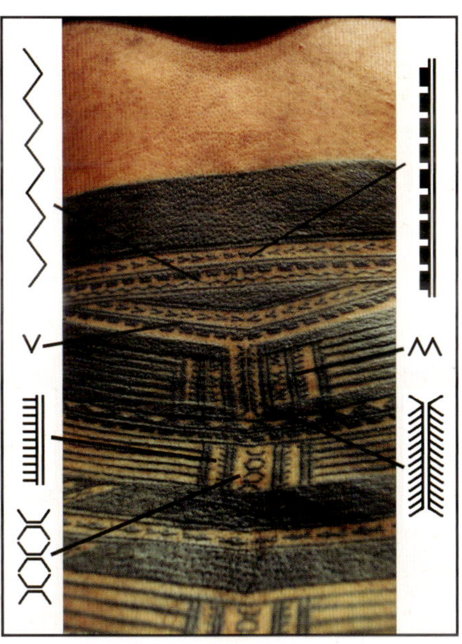

The similar Samoan centipede tattoo in the small of a man's back. The other motifs are the fe'e (octopus), the gogo (brown noddy in flight), vae o Tuli (the leg of the snipe), the fala or tala-tala (pandanus leaves or stingray tail) and aoao (cloud structures). Tattoo by Su'a Keli. Photo courtesy of Michael Fatutoa

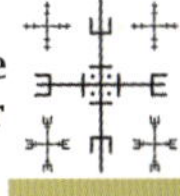

Centipede tattoos on an Ifugao man from the Philippines, ca. 1905. Photo by Dean Worcester

Shared Tattooing Motifs with Pacific Isles

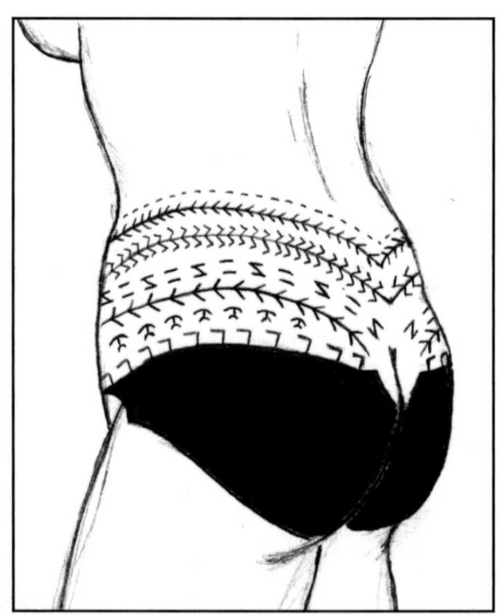
Centipede-like tattoos from Tahiti. Detail from a drawing after Sydney Parkinson

for the Ifugao people represented the warrior and his ability to bite or sting his victims[121] (*figures A, B, C*). It is more likely that the centipede represents the war party in this context, because men almost never went on headhunting expeditions alone. Traveling to an enemy village single file through the forests to disguise their numbers, each member of the war party was figuratively a segment of the centipede. In effect, the war party was a macrocosm of the aggressive centipede. Other forms of centipede tattoos exist in the Philippines but are composed differently.

The Samoans also include the centipede in their tattooing of the *Pe'a*; generally the Samoan centipede tattoo represents a person's ability to endure pain.[122] It is a mark of character for the bearer that shows they can endure all forms of pain. This meaning is similar to the Philippine concept of protection from poisons and harm. Although tattooed smaller in scale, the Samoan centipede is identical in form to the Philippine version (*figures A and C*).

The name for centipede in Samoan is *"atualoa;"* In Samoan *"atua"* means "god" or "gods" and *"loa"* means "long." Together the name means *"the long god."* But the word *loa* also means "from a long time since." So another interpretation of *atualoa* can be *"the gods from a long time since."* It could imply that the centipede's segments represented generations of gods stretching back through time. This generational concept would be similar to the idea of the war party members making up a line of people.

Other centipede-like designs occur in the Pacific Islands and one such tattoo motif is worn by Hawaiians. This barbed design is identified by Tricia Allen, in her book *Tattoo Traditions of Hawai'i,* as the *"ihe"* or spear tattoo[123] (*figure D*). Early European visitors to Hawai'i illustrated their depictions of Hawaiians with variations of the *ihe-ihe* design on different parts of the body. Sometimes the design is shown running up the inside of the legs of both men and women, from the ankle to the genital area. As Allen points out in her writing, when Europeans illustrated the native peoples of Hawai'i, sometimes the placement of tattoo designs were done at the artist's whim or were added on later from copied renditions by other artists. In this light, old depictions of tattooing designs should be viewed in context with the whole of the native culture.

Given the importance of genitals as the connection to one's posterity, in Hawaiian beliefs, one wonders, "Why would *spears* be pointed toward this sacred part of the body?" The placement and repetitive nature of this design suggests generations and procreation, similar to Philippine and Samoan centipede designs and meanings. Native Hawaiian P.F. Kwiatkowski, author of *The Hawaiian Tattoo,* has identified this design as *Puahala,*[124] meaning "flowers of the pandanus tree." The word *"pua"* in Hawaiian commonly means "flower," but also carries the meaning of "child" or "descendent." The word *"hala"* is the name for the screw-pine, *pandanus tectorius*, but also means "to pass, as time; to pass by; to die."

According to Keone Nunes, designs that went up the outside of a man's thigh were called *"ala-niho,"* meaning "the path of teeth" or "biting path," consistent with male aggressiveness and valor. (This correlates to the Ifugao concept of the centipede representing the warrior's ability to "bite" his enemies.) Figure D is identified by Nunes as *"maka-ihe"* (spear points) or *"lei-hala"* (garland or string of *hala*), similar to Kwiatkowski's description.

Filipino Tattoos: Ancient to Modern

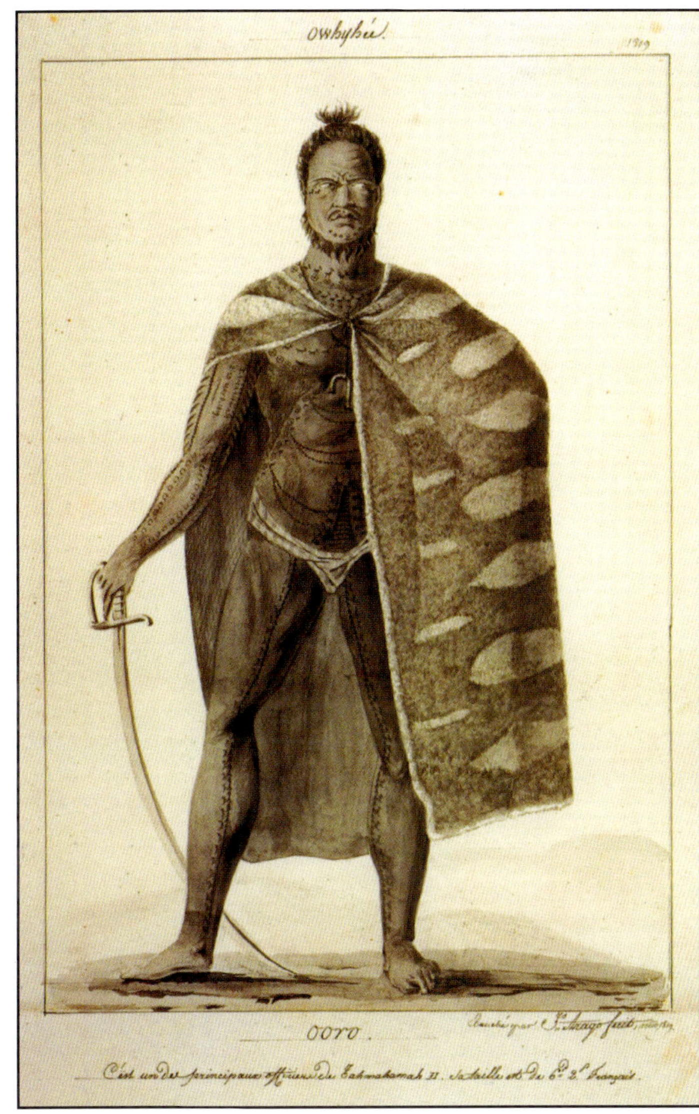

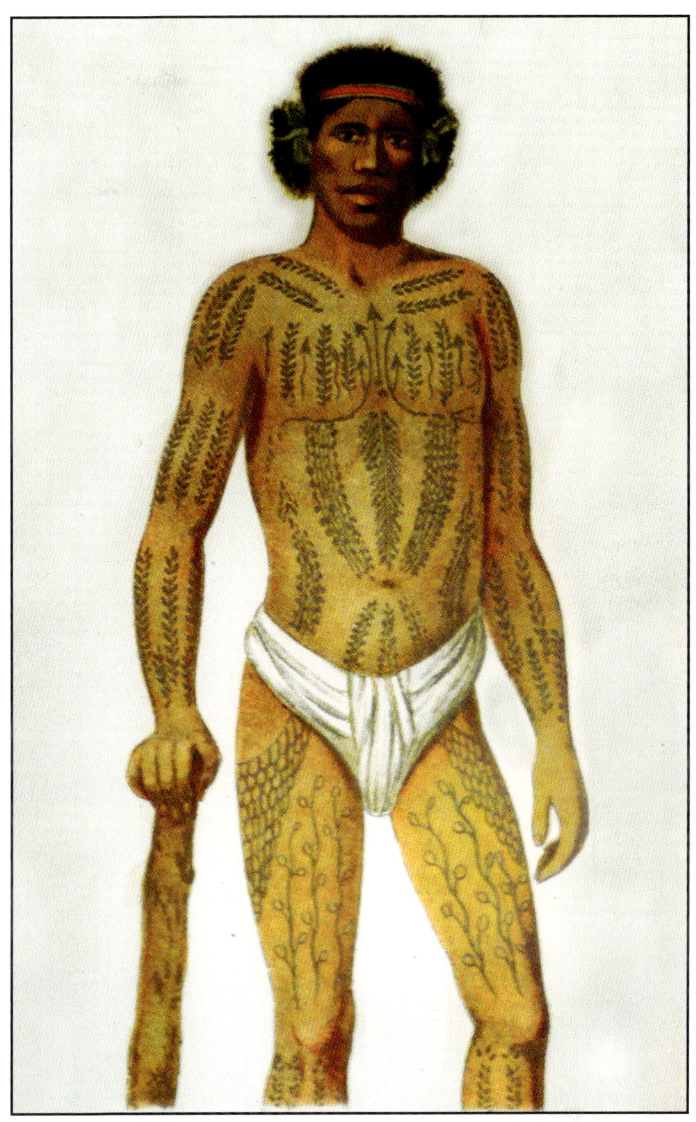

Another design, repetitive triangles representing shark's teeth, were also placed on the thighs as *ala-niho*. According to Nunes, when the *maka-ihe* was placed on the inner thigh of women, these designs were called "*ala-ma'i*," literally "genital path," but figuratively "the path of birth." In this context the design seems to allude to the continuity of the family. This additional meaning suggests a reproduction and genealogical continuity more consistent with the tattoo's placement. Adrienne Kaeppler, author of *Hawaiian Tattoo: A Conjunction of Geneology and Aesthetics*, hypothesizes that the stepped triangle and stacked chevron designs appear to be symbolic of the backbone, which is associated with a person's genealogy in Hawaiian beliefs.[125] The stacked chevron design is also reminiscent of the centipede (*figure E*). Similar stacked chevrons have been observed among the Kalinga and Ifugao but are oriented with the points upward. They resemble unfinished centipede designs (see *figure 133*). Likewise, in Maori beliefs the backbone represents the main line of descent genealogically.[126] Perhaps this Hawaiian design is a form of the centipede tattoo found in the Philippines and Samoa that lost its original name over time.

Left: A Hawaiian chief, Ooro, drawn by Jacques Argo in 1819 with repetitive centipede-like designs running up his legs and arms. Courtesy of the Honolulu Academy of Arts

Right: An illustration made circa 1900 of a Caroline Islander from Micronesia with centipede-like designs on his arms and legs as well as in the center of his chest. Note the hexagon patterns on his upper thighs.

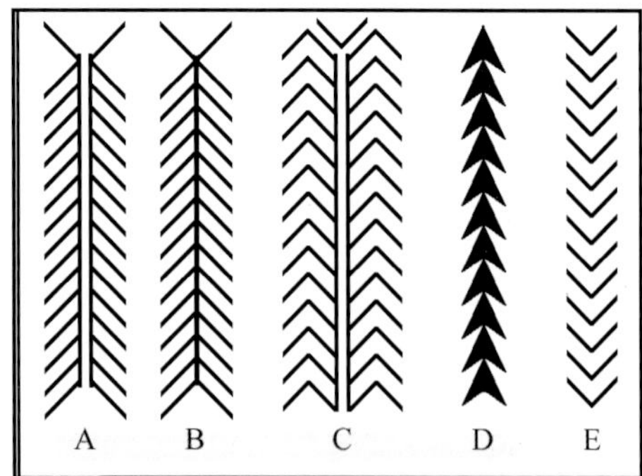

Centipede and centipede-like tattoos

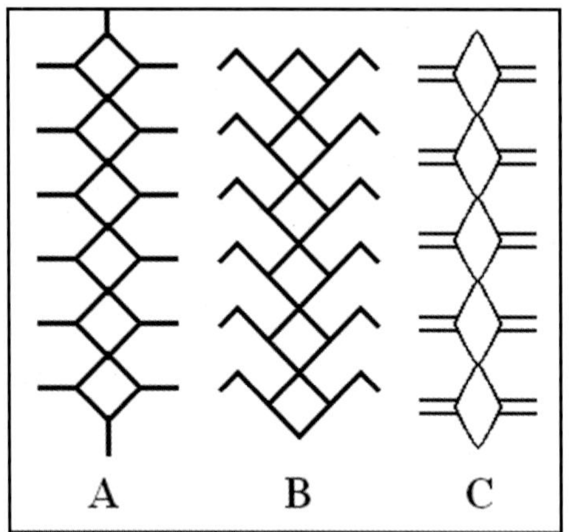

The centipede-like designs come from various Kalinga groups of Luzon and are interpreted by some as python designs. These designs are reminiscent of the backbone vertebrae which is a symbolic representation of genealogical lines in parts of the Pacific.

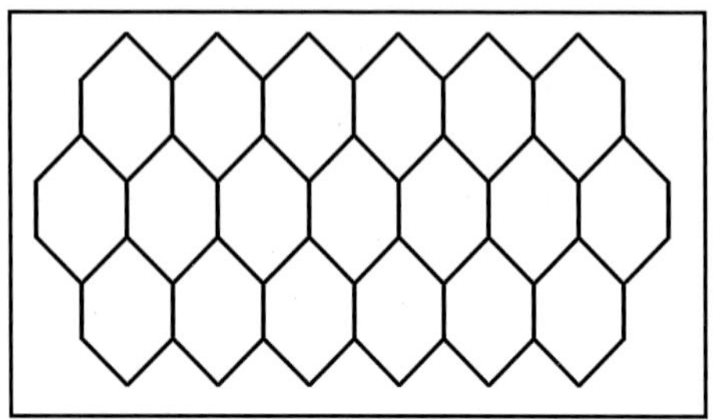

The hexagonal inufu-ufug design found primarily among the Kalinga people of Luzon

Other centipede and centipede–like tattoos are described in other parts of the Pacific, such as Guam, the Caroline Islands, Tahiti, Tikopia and the Cook Islands. In ancient Tahiti, men and women wore tattoos on the buttock and arched designs over the hips to the pubic area. This design was called "taomaru" or girdle of spears (*tao* = spear, *maru* = girdle). However, designs that could be inferred as spears are distinctly centipede-like. Interestingly, the word "*tao*" in the Philippines means "person or people." If thought of with this meaning, the <u>taomaru</u> would be the "girdle of people" or figuratively "girdle of ancestors."

Long ago in the Cook Islands, the centipede tattoo stretched up the back with legs along each side of the spine of chiefly men. These tattoos were called *tuata'iti* on the island of Mangaia and *manuta'i* on the island of Aitutaki.[127] The interpretation of the Cook Island names can mean "the gods walking in a row" or "animal that walks in a row" respectively. Similarly, the *atualoa* (centipede) design of Samoa is often placed in the center of the small of the back, although it does not extend up the entire spine as the Cook Island tattoo does. In some respects the centipede resembles the backbone vertebrae linked together. In Kiribati tradition, the end of the spine of the ancestor *Nareau* the elder was planted in Samoa, where it grew into the ancestral tree "*Kai-n-tiku-aba*." From the limbs of this tree the first people emerged and are poetically described as *flowers* (similar to *puahala*) that spread throughout the world.[128] If these concepts are linked, the centipede once again can be a symbolic reference to origins of the ancestors.

From these examples, it is possible that the segmented centipede originally represented each of these concepts, especially male valor and courage. The motif reminded the wearer of the generations that came from sacred, procreative power of women. The centipede also represented the chain or generations of ancestors and gods that look on from the spirit world to watch over and protect you. Each leg or segment of the centipede body may have represented an ancestor or god. Perhaps each segment, with two legs, symbolized a father and mother pair stretching not only back through time but also into the future, reminding the wearer that their heritage and posterity would continue forever.

Hexagonal Tattoos

Commonly thought of as honeycomb patterns, hexagonal tattoos, the Kalinga people say, represent woven mats. It is called "*nirafa-rafat*", "*inufu-ufug*" or simply "*ufug*" by Kalinga people.[129] Among the Itneg, carrying baskets are woven with this type of hexagonal pattern, which they call *minmináta*, meaning "many eyes."[130] In the past, woven rectangular fish traps, called *bobo,* were made of bamboo strips in a hexagon pattern. (Now these types of fish traps are made from chicken-wire.) According to Manong Benicio Sokkong, these designs are called in his area "*tinab-batab-bad*" and represent python scales.

The *inufu-ufug* design is also said to represent the scales of the centipede among the Ilubo Kalinga, and to people of the Benguet region they are the scales of a snake or centipede. Yet this stylized design may actually be human figures interlocked. Nearly identical patterns have been incised into Bontoc shields and *fikum* (large mother-of-pearl ornaments). Sometimes within each hexagon, is a dot which makes the design resemble

Filipino Tattoos: Ancient to Modern

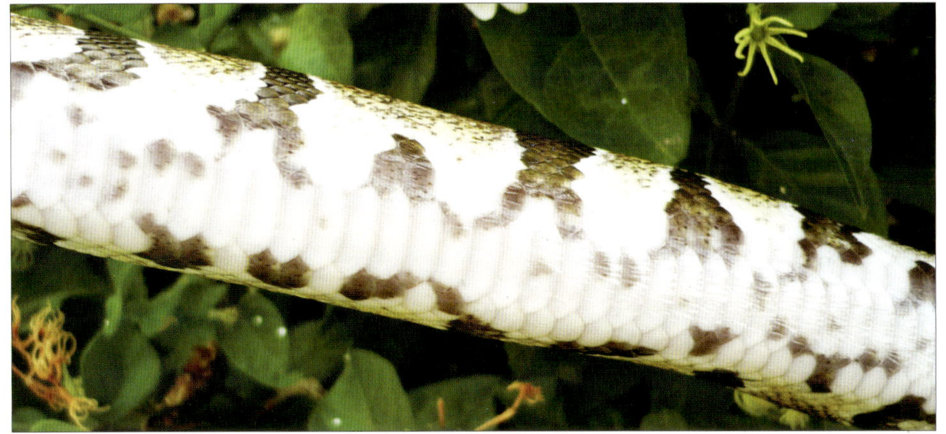

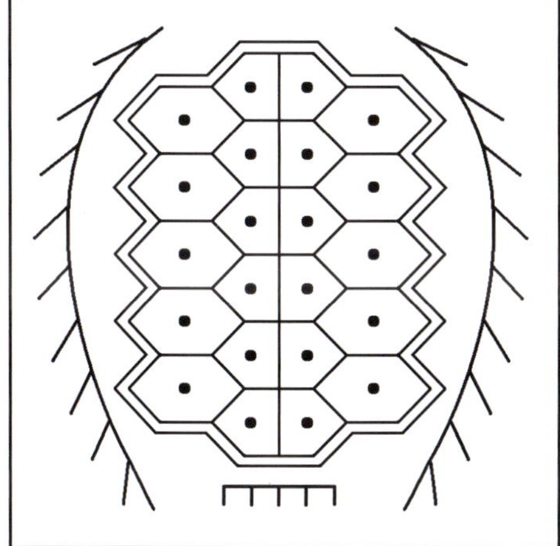

The belly scales of a python showing the inspiration of the inufu-ufug design. By the Author

The Roti Island thigh design that resembles the shell of a turtle. Drawing by the author after Van Dinter

many eyes, as described in the name "*minminata.*" This interpretation may imply the eyes of many ancestors watching over a person or additional spiritual awareness due to the seeing-eyes of ancestors. The dots also seem to transform the hexagons into stick figures of human beings. As a protective tattoo, this design is likened to the multitude of ancestors, family members and children interlocked or woven together through the past, the present and into the future.

In much of Luzon and other parts of the Philippines, snakes, lizards, crocodiles and other reptiles were also thought to be avatars of the ancestral spirits (*anito*). From this perspective, the snake scale design calls to mind the multitude of one's ancestors.

Another interpretation of this design is that it represents the skin of rattan fruit, which is also hexagonal. This might symbolize fruitfulness or fertility, which is a common theme in tattooing throughout Austronesia. There is considerable variation of interpretation, depending on the location.

Like scales of a snake, hexagonal designs symbolize stealth and prowess of the warrior or snake, as an omen-bringer of the ancestors. When encountering a snake, a person was to stop and re-evaluate their plans, in effect open themselves to spiritual insight. People of the Marshall Islands tattoo this same design and call it "*bõd,*" and they equate the design with a reptile. To the Marshallese, hexagon designs symbolize dermal plates of a turtle's shell, which represents "strength and intellectual power and cunning."[131] A large sea turtle is in a Marshallese legend of a girl named *Wõt Kileplep* who flees her abusive family and travels to other islands on the back of a sea turtle named *Lijebake,* who is her grandmother.[132] The *bõd* turtle pattern may have a similar connection to ancestors as *ufug* designs from the Philippines. Another similar tattoo, from the island of Roti in Indonesia southwest of Timor, was placed on the thighs and bears strong resemblance to a turtle's shell. It incorporates the center dot within each hexagon that seems to be missing in Kalinga and Marshallese tattoos.

In Samoa, another similar tattoo resembles one row of stacked hexagons placed in the small of the back. This design, called "*aoao,*" looks like a cloud formation. According to Avea, this design allows a man to speak to the heavenly world, like an antenna that gives the wearer "*the*

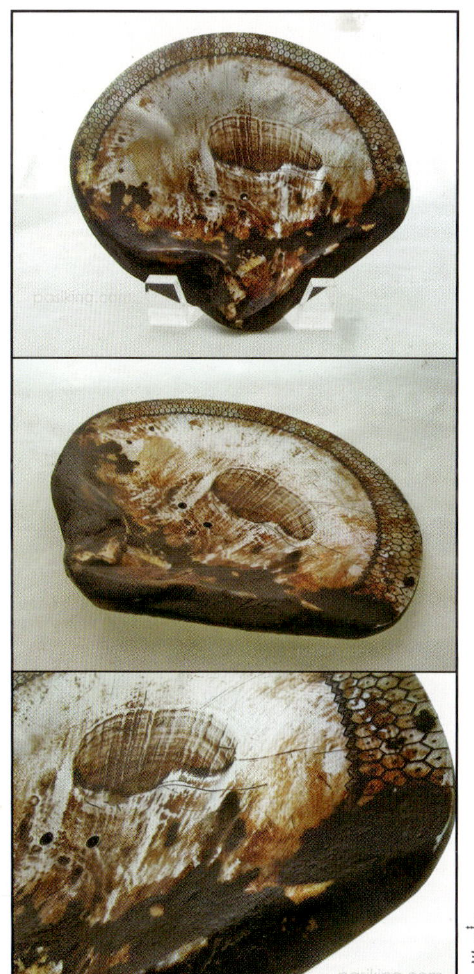

A Bontoc mother-of-pearl fikum ornament, with hexagonal patterns. Photo courtesy of Pasiking.com

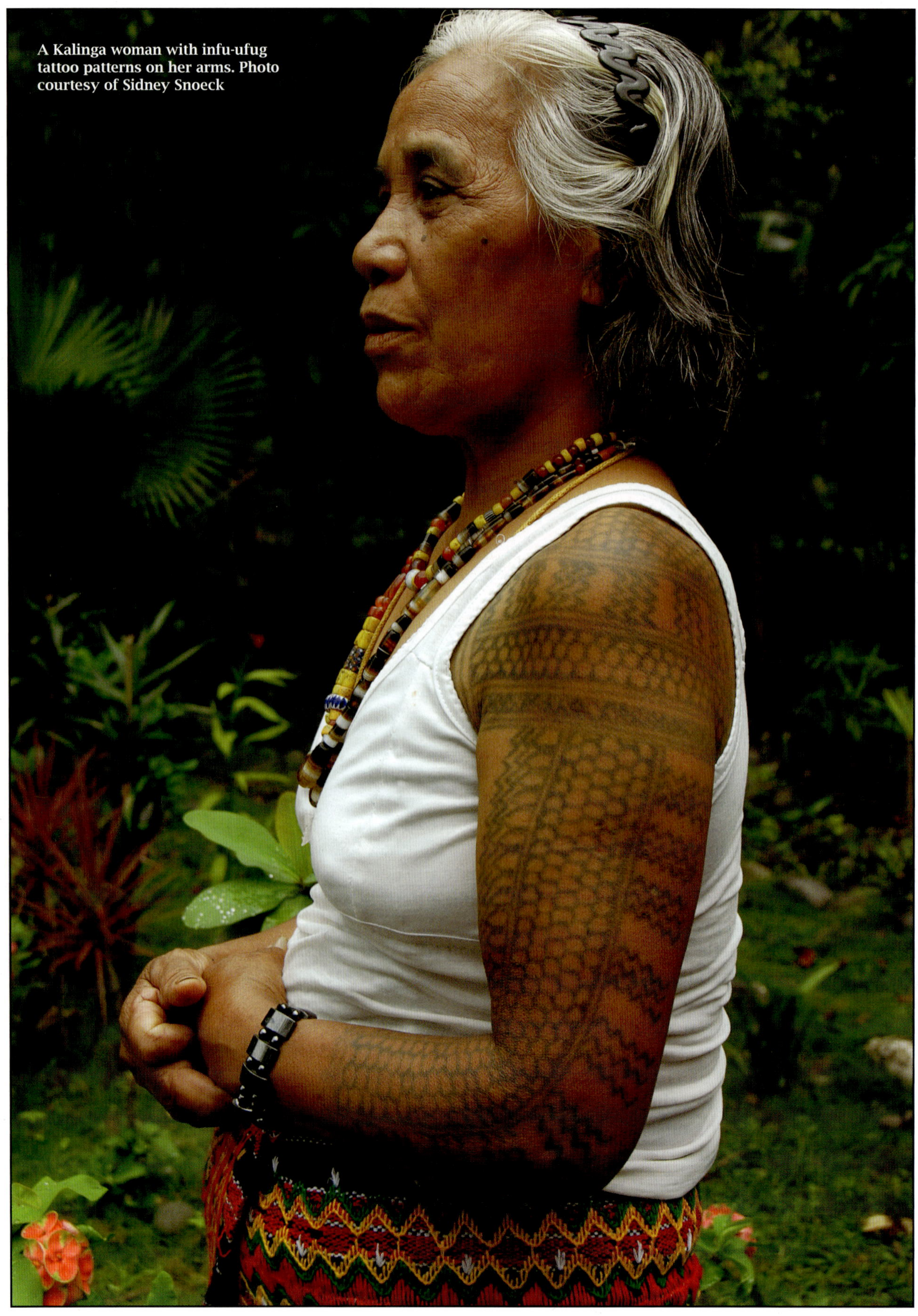

A Kalinga woman with infu-ufug tattoo patterns on her arms. Photo courtesy of Sidney Snoeck

Filipino Tattoos: Ancient to Modern

Inangkid and Hook Designs

A motif (figure A) was identified by Vanoverbergh as *inangkid*.[134] It was tattooed mainly on the arms of men and women; the women ususally receiving the tattoo at puberty. This design is commonly thought of as a fern leaf, the connection having first been proposed by Albert Jenks in his book *The Bontoc Igorot*.[135] Giant tree ferns grow like palm trees in many parts of the Mountain Province. As a fern frond grows, it slowly uncurls and resembles a hook. According to Manang Gabie M. Buduhan, the word *inangkid* is taken from the words *hakid, pakid* or *akid*, all of which describe an implement used for "hooking" an object (usually fruits) not within arms' reach. A *hakid* is a long wooden pole made from the Y-section of a branch, with one extension of the Y left long and the other extension cut short to form a hook at the end. Small *hakid* are used in rice fields to parry grass and cut it while clearing a parcel of land. The Inangkid motif most resembles this activity with the curved portion representing the *hakid* and the straight extensions representing grass that is being cleared. The Ifugao are famous for their extensive and massive rice terraces. Much of their traditional lifestyle revolves around the construction, repair and maintenance of terraced plots of land. In this context, the Inangkid convey industriousness and preparation of land for planting. Men and women alike shared this activity. There is a metaphor here as well. In ancient time, the fertility of women was associated with the fruitfulness of crops and fruits. Tattooing a young woman ready for marriage with the Inangkid prepared her "soil" to have a "seed" planted within her. In a similar context, the *kowit,* or hook, tattoos on the calves of the Iban of Borneo mark the wearer as having reached puberty. The *hakid* is also used to reach fruit on trees. Placing this tattoo on arms conveys being able to obtain items that are out of reach, and this idea is related to harvesting crops. Since it is a highly visible tattoo, it can also imply the ability *to hook* the attention of the opposite sex. As the *hakid* allows one to partake of the "fruits" normally out of reach, thus there is implied spiritual context behind this design. It also implies being able to obtain things beyond the limits of the mortal body.

Similar tattoos among Marshall Islanders include one that is called *tokrak (figure C)*, which represents a curved stick used as a fire hook to spread hot stones on the earth oven.[136] Although more angular in its application, it closely resembles the curved portion of the *inangkid* minus the grass. Again, the context is being able to manipulate outside limitations of the physical body.

It has been said that the zigzag design, called *kein kom*, evolved from a similar, hook-like motif *(figure B)* which, when tattooed in horizontal rows, became blended into a zigzag line.[137] The *kein kom* resembles a hooked stick used to pick breadfruit out of a tree. The context is the same as the *inangkid.* The Marshallese *tokrak* motif is similar to the Bontoc *yûp-yûp* or lightning motif *(figure D)*, as identified by Ayeona Langfia, a native of Barlig in the Mountain Province. In conjunction with this symbol being a force of nature, Keone Nunes proposes that the design in figure C,

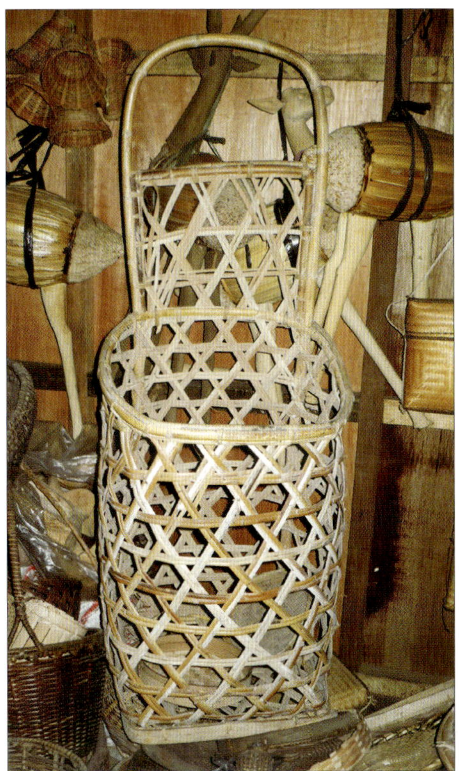

The hexagonal minmináta weaving pattern that means "many eyes"

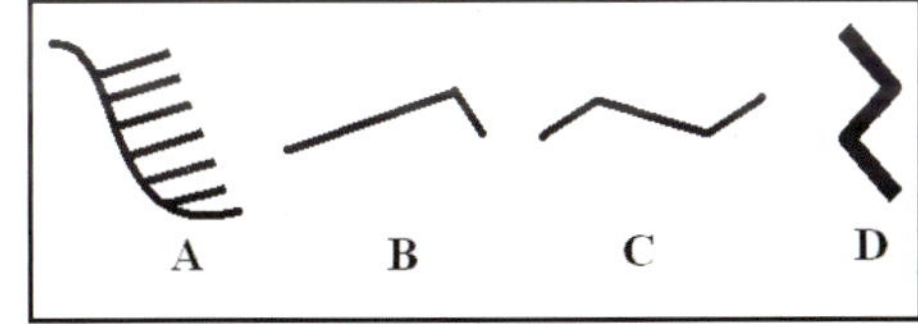

Inangkid and other hook designs

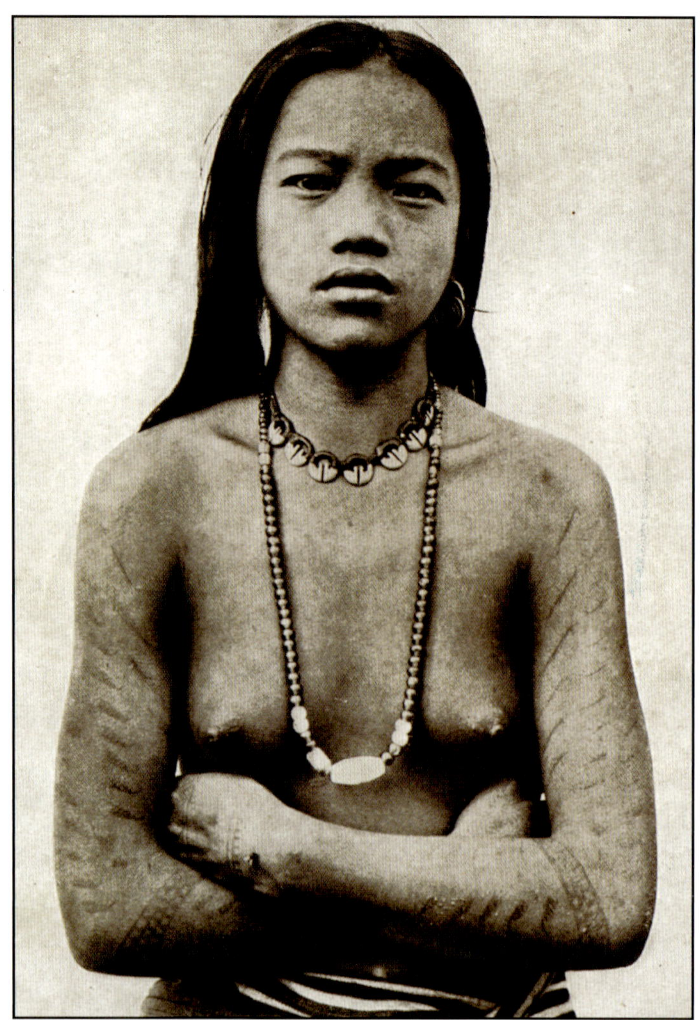

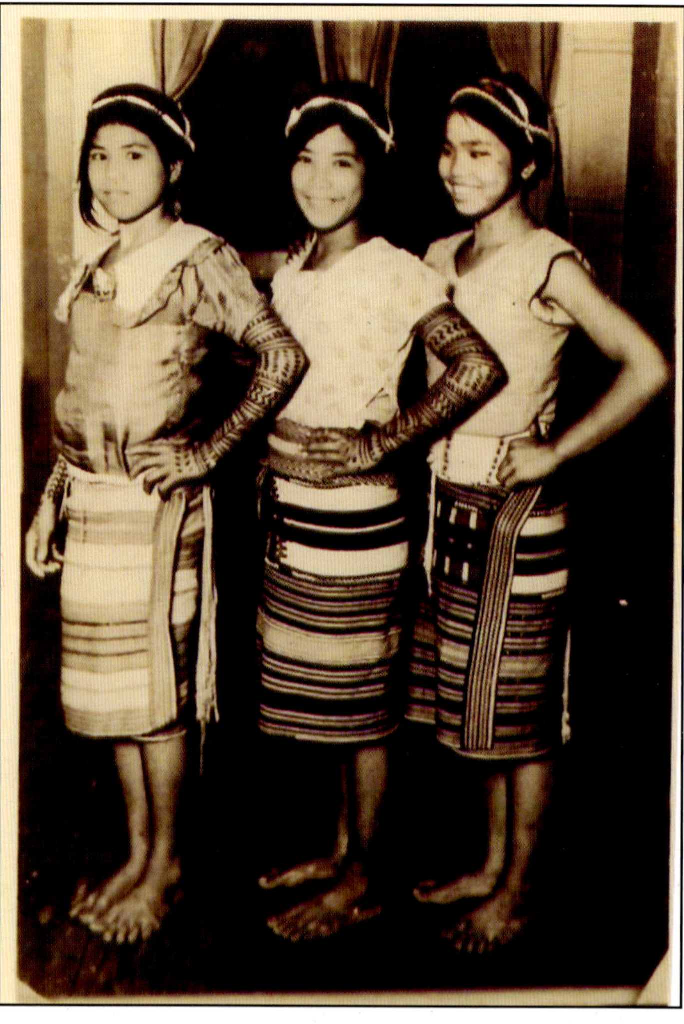

Left: An Ifugao young woman with Inangkid tattoos on her arms. She also has pongo bracelet tattoo bands of triangles around her forearms and triangle motifs on her fingers and an al-alam design on the back of her hand. Photo by Dean Worchester, ca. 1905

Right: Bontoc young women, one of which bears the yûp-yûp lightning tattoos. circa 1950. Photo courtesy of Edward Walters

when the base is done in pairs placed parallel to each other with each end having an oblique line, is a type of *makani* or wind design in Hawai'i.

According to Michael Fatutoa, a nearly identical motif to figures C and D in Samoa is called *fa'a anufe*, and it is normally found in the *pula tele* and *pula laiti* portions of a Samoan *tatau*.

The word *fa'aanufe*, meaning "worm" or "caterpillar-like," describes a fertility symbol that must be tattooed on men but is occasionally tattooed on women. It represents a worm that is symbolic of the phallus. Comparing the worm or caterpillar with fertility in Samoa derives from the creation myth of the Samoans. It is said that when the world was newly formed there existed only ocean and sky. Tagaloa's son, Tuli, in the form of the plover bird, flew between the sky and ocean with no land to rest upon. Growing tired, he complained to his father who threw down (or fished up) a stone, from which land was created. Eventually a vine grew upon the land but then became rotten. The god Tuli pulled up the vine from the primeval earth and on its roots were worms or grubs. Tagaloa sent his servants and fashioned these grubs into men; these were ancestors of the Samoans. This creation story bears strong similarity to a Visayan creation myth. (*See Appendix*)

Filipino Tattoos: Ancient to Modern

Crab and Canoe Designs

The Philippine design (*figure SE4*) and variations of it are no longer tattooed in most of the Philippines, but it is found on textiles. Variations of these designs are sometimes used in embroidered designs on the *barong* Tagalog, which are derived from tattoos of Manobo people of Mindanao.[138] The motifs (*figure SE3 and SE4*) have a few variations and were found throughout many parts of the Philippines (see *figures M1 and M2, page 92*). Figures SE1 and SE2 are similar woven motifs from Indonesia. Variations of this design are also found in Borneo and other parts of Southeast Asia where it is usually identified as a crab motif. The Visayan buttocks and facial tattoos appear to be variations of this design. Figure SE4 usually represents the *kappi* (also known as *kippi*) or the small blue edible river crab depicted in Ilokano and Itneg woven textiles. It is also identified as "fishhooks" or *lawig* by Faye Cooper Cole[139] (*figure B*). It is possibly a symbolic representation of *Apo-ni-Tolao,* the demigod hero from Itneg mythology who possessed a magic fishhooks, the god *Angalo* of the Ilokanos who was not only the creator of the world but also spoken of as a traveling fisherman,[140] or the god Lumauig, whose name in some languages of the Philippines is the conjugated form of lawig, meaning "the one who hooks." (figuratively "the one who fishes"). Another meaning of his name would be "the traveler." When placed in vertical rows, the Kappi design is called *kinarkarayan* conveying a sense of rivers but was also called, *binekbeklat*, which means "resembling a python."[141]

Pythons in the Philippines were associated with ancestor spirits and canoes. Great care was taken not to harm snakes so as to not inadvertently harm or offend one's own ancestor. Often on sea voyages ancient Visayans would take pythons with them to secure their ancestors' blessing as they traveled. The kappi motif, when incorporated into the *binekbeklat* python design, can also imply canoe travel.

The Samoan woman's tattoo incorporates a design very similar to this on the back of the knees, called "*malu*" (*figure 113*). The meaning of the

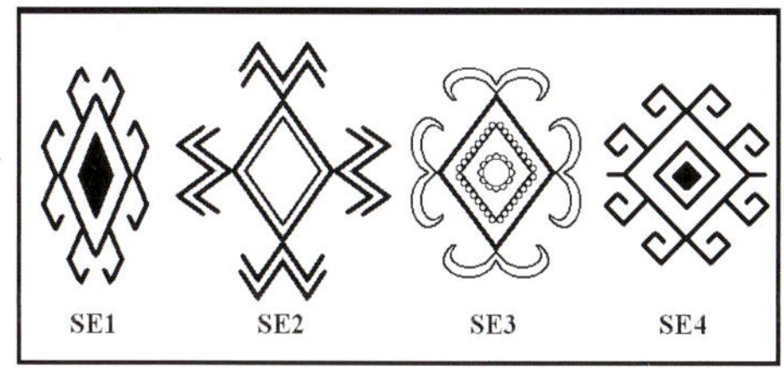

Figure SE4 is an Ilokano / Itneg woven design; SE3 is a tattoo and woven design of the Manobo people of Mindanao; SE2 is from Sulawesi; SE1 is a similar Batik design from Timor

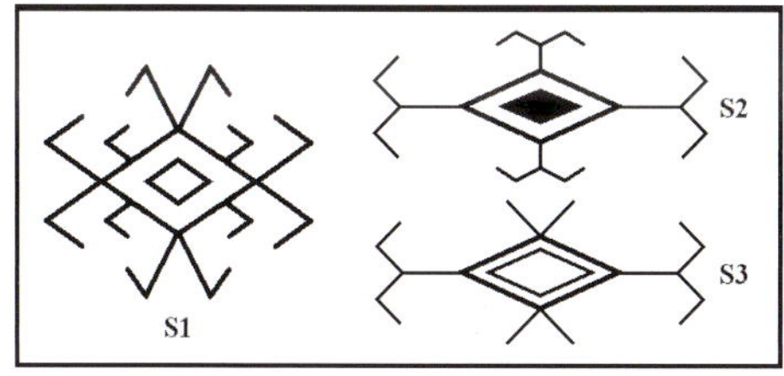

Old Samoan Malu tattoo designs: S1 after Marquardt, 1899; S2 after Te Rangi Hiroa, 1930; S3 after Marquardt, 1899

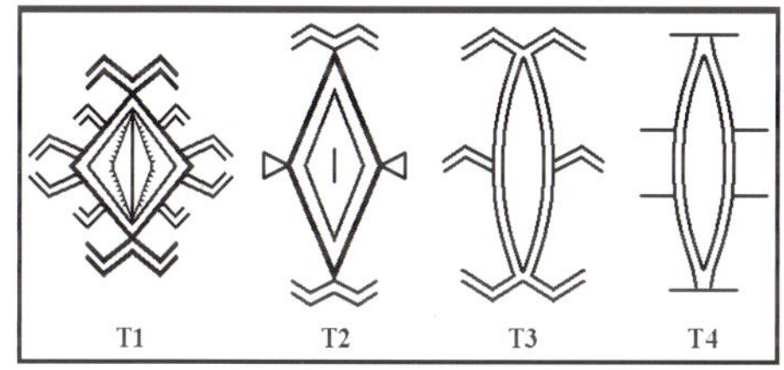

Tikopia carved canoe and tattoo designs called fakafoiika: T1 and T2 are carved faka-foiika designs from the canoe Sapiniakau (after Firth 1960). T3 and T4 are fakafoiika tattoo motifs on the upper arms of the men of Tikopia.

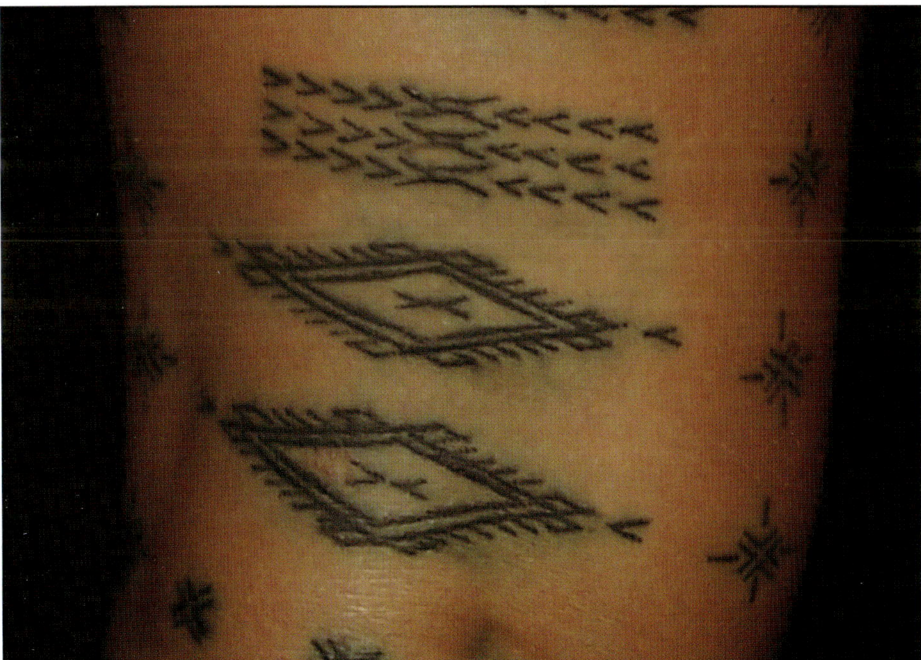

Malu tattoo design of Samoa.
Photo by Runningtoddler

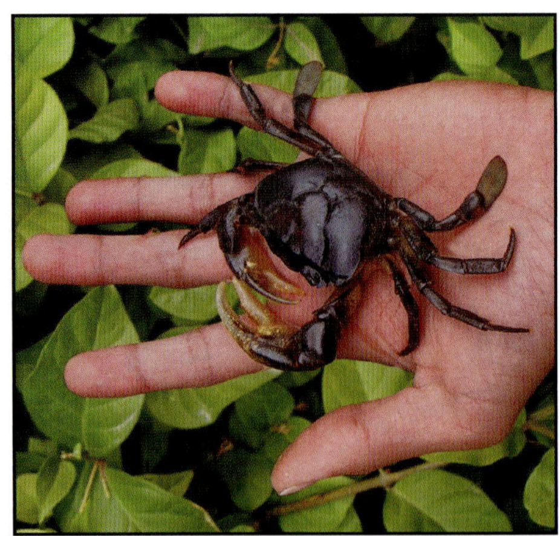

The Kappi crab, also known as Talangka bukid in Tagalog

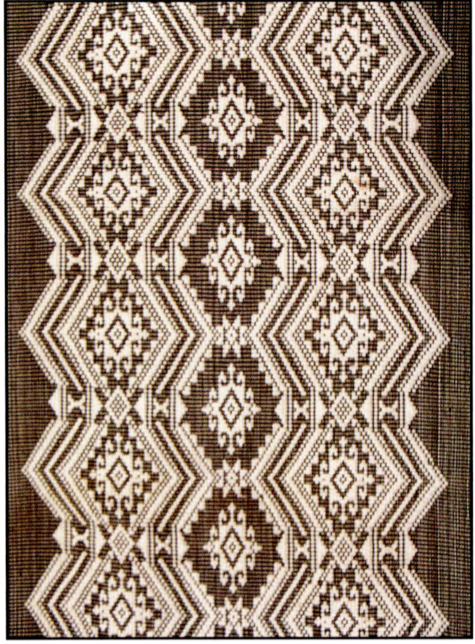

Abel (woven cloth) with Binekbeklat design

word "*malu*" is "shelter" and implies protection, such as when used in the context of *fa'amalumaluga*. The *malu* motif may have a deeper meaning that is related to ocean travel and fishing. When emphasis is placed on the final vowel (*malú*) it means "to be soft" and "calm," but also means "fish-basket." In the Tongan language, *malu* also means "security" and "safety." But another version, "*malú*" adds further clarification to the Samoan definition meaning "calm ocean." This variation of the word "*malú*," with its references to the marine environment "fish-basket" and "calm ocean," coupled with the first definition implying "security" and "protection" comes into further clarification when examining the similar tattoos from the Polynesian island of Tikopia, called *fakafoiika* (*figures T1-T4*).

The *fakafoiika* was tattooed on the body, but it was also "tattooed" or carved on canoes. The *fakafoiika* is said not to represent any particular fish, nor is one end thought to be a tail or head, and the appendages do not represent fins.[142] *Fakafoiika* translates as "to come back or return [with] fish" or "the fish that returns." This is what a fisherman does. He travels out into the ocean, hoping for a calm sea and returns with fish for his family's fish basket. (Fishing is generally not very good when the weather is rough at sea.) So the meanings of the *malú* tattoo and the *kappi* design of the Ilokano and Itneg people coincide with each other. These designs are clearly related to the ocean environment and are fishing motifs. Some of the Tikopian variations of the *fakafoiika* are also canoe-like in appearance (*figure T3 and T4*), which further suggest canoe travel and fishing.

In Itneg and Ilokano textiles there is another motif called *inik-ikan* (*figure A*). It is very similar to some of the variations of the *fakafoiika* motifs (*figures T2 and T3*) and resembles a fish with another tail where the head should be. The *inik-ikan* appears to be a composite motif that incorporates the morning star motif, called *sinan-baggak* or *sinan-bagbagak*. *Sinan-bag-bagak* is represented by concentric diamonds. In old Iteng beliefs, Bag-bagak was the morning star and the husband of Sinag the moon goddess. Their daughter married a mortal and her subsequent son, Takyayen, became a progenitor of the Itneg peoples.[143] The morning star, or the planet Venus, lies low in the horizon and does not follow the course of the stars across the sky from east to west because it is a planet. Depending on the time of year, Venus appears above either the western or eastern horizon. When Venus appears in the east it is visible before dawn and heralds the morning. When it appears in the west it is visible at dusk to begin the evening. Over a six-month span, the planet Venus travels up from the eastern or western horizon and then narrowly turns and returns back to the horizon. The word "*bag-bagak*" translates as "*I advise*" in Ilokano. The morning star was used by many cultures as an orientation star to find direction. In a sense it advised a traveler which way was east. Although the *sinan-bag-bagak* is a standalone motif, it is also incorporated as part of the *inik-ikan* motif. Perhaps the *fakafoiika* motif (the returning fish) is related to the *inik-ikan* with its morning star motif, which describes the strange star (or figurative fish) that traveled up and returned back to the horizon. Because of its directional nature, this motif may be related to periods of the year when ocean currents and winds were favorable for travel over the ocean.

The *kappi/lawig* design appears to be a more elaborate *inik-ikan* design and represents fishhooks. Figure A is the *inik-ikan* woven design

Filipino Tattoos: Ancient to Modern

as found in cloth, and figure B is the theoretical tattoo design based on the woven motif. When duplicated in tattooing, the *inik-ikan* resembles the *Laga* design, which will be discussed later.

Similar designs to the *kappi/lawig* motifs in Indonesian tattooing illustrate correlations between these tattoos and the *babalakay* tattoo of the Isneg people of Luzon. One theory is that the *babalakay* tattoo stems back to the primal ancestor and brings a greater depth of understanding to the *Kappi/ Lawig, Malu* and *Fakafoiika* tattoos. The *babalakay* tattoo is a cross with three finger-like extensions coming from each end of the cross. Generally it is described as being a "spider."[144] However the term "babalakay" does not mean spider. Its components are "*baba*," meaning "low" or "base," and *lakay*, meaning "grandfather" or "venerated old man." "Baba" in Ilokano also means "underneath," such as in describing the underworld for the dead, *idiay baba*. *Babalakay* implies "the old man from underneath" or the grandfather (*Lakay*) from the underworld (*baba*). The *Babalakay* figure is likely a reference to the Isneg peoples' founding ancestor(s).

If the Isneg and Ilokano shared a common ancestry, who was the original ancestor? The Ilokano creation myth revolves around Angalo, the giant who is traditionally hailed as the progenitor of the Ilokano people. He is also a creator god among some Visayan peoples. He is known throughout the Pacific as the creator god or sometimes as a sea god, under the most commonly used name of Tangaloa. In Hawai'i he is known as Kanaloa, one of the primal gods where he is the god of the ocean. He is known as Tangaroa in New Zealand and is the sea god there as well. In French Polynesia he is called Ta'aroa or Tanaoa, and he is the source of all creation. In Samoa and Tonga he is the creator god Tangaloa, who fished islands up out of the sea. On the island of Rotuma, north of Fiji, he is called Tagroa sir'ia. In New Hebrides he is called Tagaro or Takaro and is the creator of mankind and the world.

In the Marshall Islands there is another incarnation of Tangaloa as the god Loa, who created man and the world. Here again he raised islands out of the sea. In Ilokano myth, Angalo dug holes in the earth for the expanse of the oceans. He formed the islands and the sea, and the mountains and valleys on them. It was Angalo who formed the first man and woman from his spit (i.e. fathered). He placed them inside a bamboo tube and set them out on the waves of the sea to reach Luzon. Other traditions say that Angalo was also a traveling fisherman, which would explain how in other Austronesian cultures he is the god of the sea. His association with the spider may have been due to his fisherman abilities. (Both spiders and fishermen make and mend nets.)

"Fishing up islands" is a figure of speech, for that is what a navigator does on an ocean voyage: bring islands up out of the sea. As one sails closer to an island from a distance, it does appear to rise out of the water. To illustrate this point and a spider's association with fishing, there is a creation myth from Borneo among the Kayan people. According to the Kayan, originally the world only existed as ocean and sky. A spider descended from the sky and spun a web. In his web he caught a stone that began to grow and it filled the horizon and became the world. In Micronesia many of the creator gods are spiders or have spider forms. The name of the creator god Areop-Enap, of the island of Nauru in Micronesia,

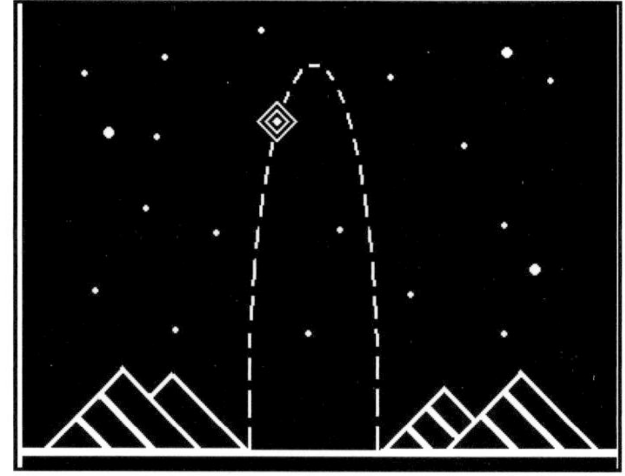

The path of Bag-bagak (Venus) in the sky over a 6-month period:

Malú (Samoan) - Soft, calm, fish-basket
Malú (Tongan) - Security, safety, calm ocean
Fakafoiika (Tikopia) - To return with fish
Kappi / Lawig, (Ilokano / Itneg) - Crab, fishhooks
Babalakay (Isneg) - Spider [figurative fisherman]

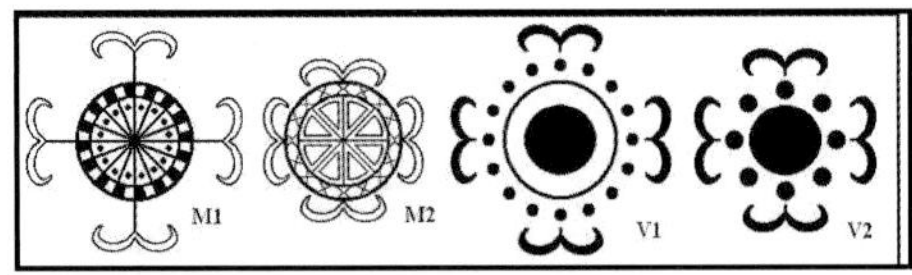

M1 and M2 are textile designs derived from the tattoos of the Manobo people of Mindanao. V1 and V2 are similar designs seen on the Visayan warriors of the Boxer Codex.

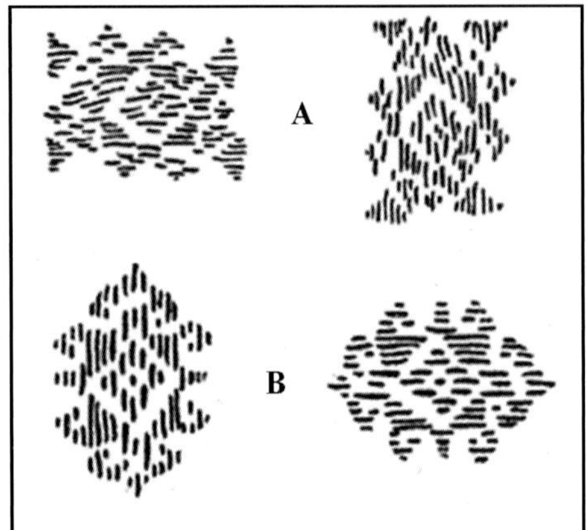

The inik-ikan (fish) motif [A] and the lawig (fishhook) motif [B], as found in woven textiles

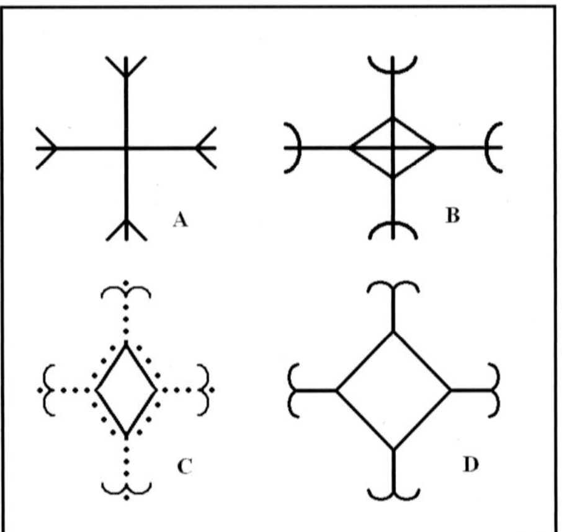

The babalakay tattoo (figure A). Figures B to D are headhunter tattoos from Ceram in Indonesia that bear similarities to both babalakay and kappi designs.

The babalakay tattoo motif as compared to similar Mangyan cross designs from Mindoro found on clothing and basketry called pakudus. These designs were believed to keep evil spirits away.

translates as *"old person spider,"* similar to the meaning of *babalakay.* The Kiribati god Nareau is described as a human god but also possesses a spider form. Nareau is possibly a variant of the Polynesian god Tangaloa under another name. The Micronesian creation myths involving Nareau forming the world from the shell of a giant mussel in which he was is similar to the creation account of Ta'aroa (Tangaloa) of the Tahitians and the Visayan version of Angalo creating the world. In the Tahitian and Visayan creation myths, the god raises up the shell of the sky, lets light into the world, and with the shell creates the heavens.[145] Nareau, the spider god in Micronesia, performs the very same tasks. As he emerges from the mollusk shell as a spider, an interesting visual symbol occurs. If one were to imagine a spider emerging from inside a clam or mussel with its legs protruding first, the combinations of the legs and shell would resemble a crab. This may have been the origin of the *kappi* design. When looking at one of the variations of the *babalakay* tattoo, which is supposed to represent a spider, and compare it with some of the other variations of the design from Ceram in Indonesia, one can see how the design may have been derived from a common design sometime in the past. Figure A is the *babalakay* and figures B, C, D are designs from Ceram in Indonesia. Figure D especially resembles the *kappi* or fishhook design. What is interesting about the crab design is that it only possesses eight "limbs," like a spider. The missing pinchers would bring the count of limbs to ten. It is likely that this design may have originally represented a spider, as the designs in figure SE4 do illustrate. In the Philippines and Micronesia, the creator god was represented by the spider or the crab (the spider emerging from the shell of the earth), but in Polynesia Tangaloa was represented by the octopus.

Ta'aroa in Tahiti and Kanaloa in Hawai'i are both identified with the octopus, which is commonly called "squid" in Hawai'i. In Samoa the demi-god "Tae-o-Tagaloa" (feces of Tagaloa) was born from a human mother as part human and part *"fe'e"* or octopus. Magic in southern Polynesia has many associations to the number eight, probably due to the eight limbs of the octopus. In Hawai'i, a kahuna who was performing a healing blessing on a sick person invoked the god Kanaloa as the god of the octopus saying, *"E Kanaloa , ke akua o ka he'e!"* ("O Kanaloa, the god of the octopus!") The association of the octopus with the spider is obvious. Both have eight legs. What was the spider to the ancient Austronesian mind but a diminutive land version of an octopus? Or what was the octopus but the ocean dwelling version of the spider? The Samoan people do not represent Tagaloa with an eight-limbed motif, but they do tattoo representations of the octopus in the men's *tatau.* This design, called the *"fe'e"* or octopus, is an abstraction of the tentacles of the octopus. It is made by making a straight line with small blackened-in rectangles along its edge, like the suckers on the tentacles (*see page 81*).

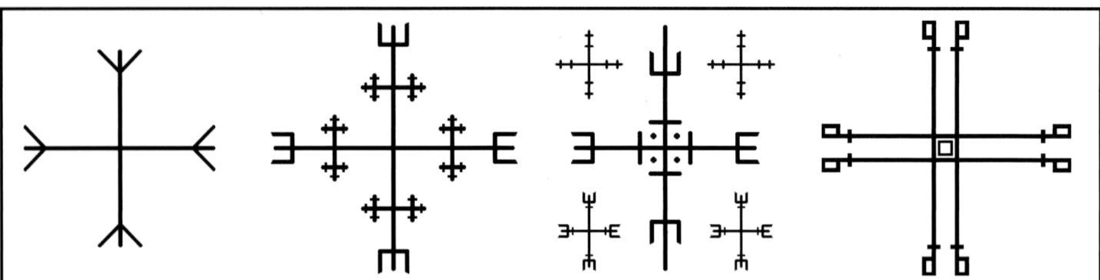

Filipino Tattoos: Ancient to Modern

The crab, spider, and octopus appear to be interconnected as interpretations of the same concept. It is possible that this old tattoo design, relating to the fishing culture of the past, commemorated a deity or progenitor of the people of the Pacific.

Malú (Samoan)	Soft, calm, fish-basket
Malú (Tongan)	Security, safety, calm ocean
Fakafoiika (Tikopia)	To return with fish
Kappi/Lawig (Ilokano/Itneg)	Crab, fishhooks
Babalakay (Isneg)	Spider, figurative fisherman

Karayan/Tiniku

There are several versions of the Karayan/Tiniku designs used as a symbol for water found throughout the Philippines and the Pacific, in both tattoos and textiles. Shown are the two most common versions of this design typically tattooed on the arms, hands and legs of both men and women in the Philippines. This motif is tattooed on Kalinga men on the chest and the abdomen and is found tattooed on similar parts of the body in the Pacific regions.

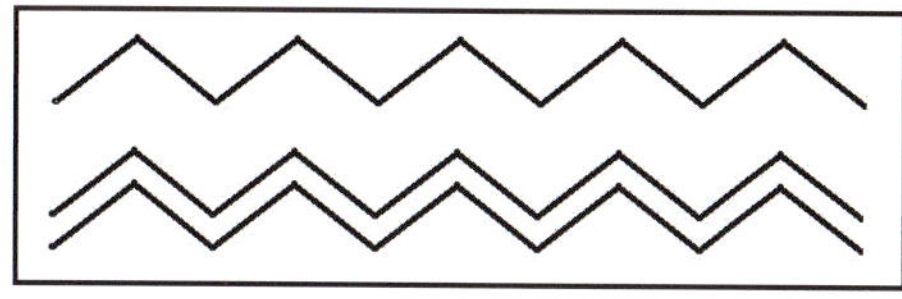

Karayan/Tiniku motifs

One name for this motif in the Philippines is *karayan*. The word "*karayan*" means "river" in Ilokano. On a very basic level the *karayan* is a water symbol showing constant movement. The higher meaning is the waters of life feeding the land and people. It represents travel of all streams and rivers down the mountains and hills to the ocean abyss which, in Itneg belief, is the entrance to the underworld of the dead. The *karayan* design is also seen on much of the woven cloth of northern Luzon, especially among the Itneg and Ilokano people. According to Virgil Mayor Apostol, author of *Way of the Ancient Healer*, the zigzag lines of the *karayan* design represent *surong* (upstream) and *puyupuyan* (downstream) elements of indigenous cosmological beliefs. *Surong* symbolizes birth and new life, while *puyupuyan* (literally, where the river meets the sea) symbolizes the afterlife. *Surong* is the upstream region of the cosmos where an important ritual altar is located and the origin of all flowing water, in other words, of *life*. Apostol elaborates that *puyupuyan* represents the downstream region of the cosmos of death and the afterlife, where all flowing waters (life) return to the vast ocean. The ocean is the source of our ancestors who sailed from distant lands and returned at death. The root word of *puyupuyan* is *puyo*, which means "a small breath or puff of air," or it can mean "a gentle breeze." It calls to mind how, in some Philippine creation myths, humanity's first vessel of life was bamboo, formed from a marriage between the land breeze and the sea breeze. Bamboo sailed across the waters and was pecked open by a hawk, and the first man and woman came forth from it. This story is a metaphor of the first people's migration to the islands. Bamboo represents the outrigger canoe (which in the Philippines has bamboo outriggers) that sailed across the waters by a blowing breeze. To them, traveling *puyupuyan* (downstream) to the afterlife was a return to the breath of life or ancestral ocean that spawned humans. This is not unlike the Polynesian belief that the afterlife of the dead is located under or in the ocean. The afterlife is called *Pulotu* in western Polynesian traditions and *Po* in eastern Polynesian beliefs. Indeed, the word *puyupuyan*, with its

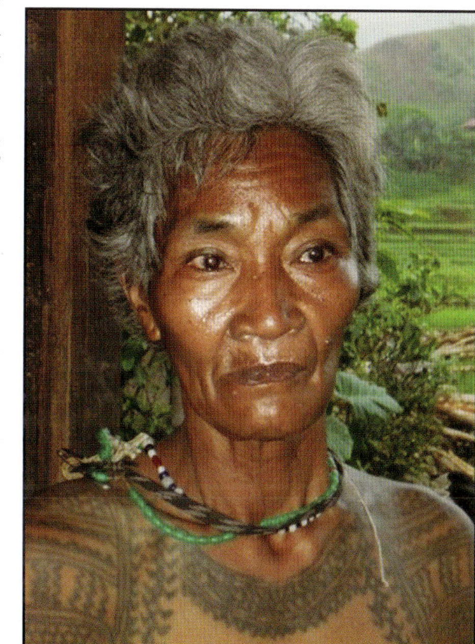

A woman from the village of Gaan with water designs on her shoulders. Photo courtesy of Edward Adrian-Vallance

root word *puyo,* seems to be related or distant cognates of the Polynesian terms *pulotu* and *po.* (Puyupuyan=Pulotu/Puyo=Po)

Another name for these designs is "*tiniku.*" According to Manang Gabie M. Buduhan, a native Ifugao from the Ifugao word "*pikuwon,*" which means "to bend." Adding "*tini*" and abbreviating the root word "*piku*" to "*ku*" converts it into past tense, thus the word means "bent." It refers to the path of the headhunt, going over switchbacks on the mountain trails. Anyone who has traveled in the Cordillera of Luzon understands how the roads and trails are "bent" back and forth up and down the mountains. This motif's meaning may be a remnant of an older meaning found in the Pacific Islands where the same motif is called "*Aso pi'o*" in Samoan and represents the bent path of a sailing canoe, tacking back and forth into the wind. A similar design with a similar name, called *binakuko,* is found among the Kalinga. The design is done in the negative, as a black band with the zigzag portion being left untattooed and forming opposing alternating black triangles.[146] It also represents the paths a warrior has traveled on his expeditions.

In Samoan tattooing, this design is usually placed under the canoe design on the back, and speaks of the travels of the chiefs in a canoe from their original homeland *Pulotu* (the underworld) to *Savai'i.* This interpretation confirms and correlates to the Ilokano/Itneg karayan design interpretation given by Apostol, where all streams and rivers travel to the underworld. The two root words of this design are cognates as well, and both mean "bent" (*pi'o* = *piku*). A Marquesan tattoo with a similar name, "*kopiko*"[147] meaning "zigzag," incorporates a zigzag line, but more closely resembles the Kalinga mountain design (see Filig). The Marshallese also tattooed this motif and called it "*Jalili*" or "*Dannin wot,*" which mean "rain water."[148] The word "*dannin*" is similar to the Ilokano word for water, "*danum.*" In Marshallese tattooing, the *Dannin wot* was found on chest tattoos of the men. The entire composition of the chest tattoo of the Marshallese depicts the prow of a canoe with the *Dannin wot* design flowing over the body of the canoe as it travels. It may be implied that this representational canoe was a reminder of the community's first migration.

Laga

Laga designs were used by the Itneg in their tattooing and are still used in both Ilokano and Itneg weaving patterns. According to Fay Cooper-Cole, author of *The Tinguian: Social, Religious, and Economic Life or a Philippine Tribe,* these designs represent the woven pattern on the backing of Spanish chairs.[149] However, since this design also is found in tattooing, it is more likely to represent woven mat patterns, similar to the Kalinga "*ufug*" designs. Similar designs were also worn by the Benguet peoples in the past and are seen on mummies from Kabayan caves. Like the double meaning of the *ufug* design, this pattern also is related to snakes and perhaps eyes. In the Benguet region, this design was related to python or snake scales, so it possibly conveys the relationship of the wearer to their ancestors whose will was made known through the behaviors of snakes. The snake also symbolized prowess of the warrior. The *laga* design may also be related to the *Ikan* design resembling several fish joined together or caught in a net. There is a resemblance of the *laga* design to the net design of the Samoans, called *fa'a upega.* This design is worn just above

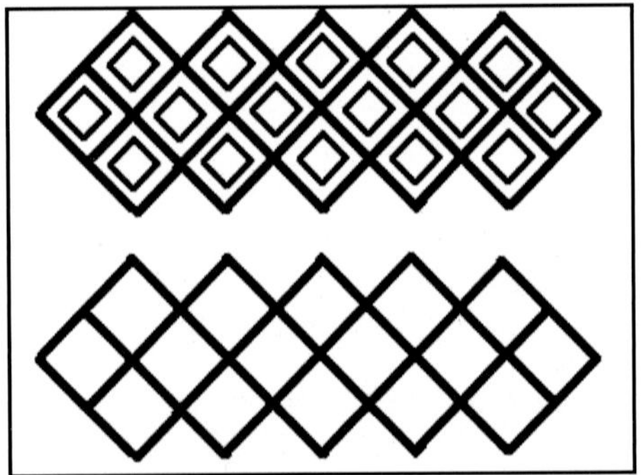

The laga or woven design

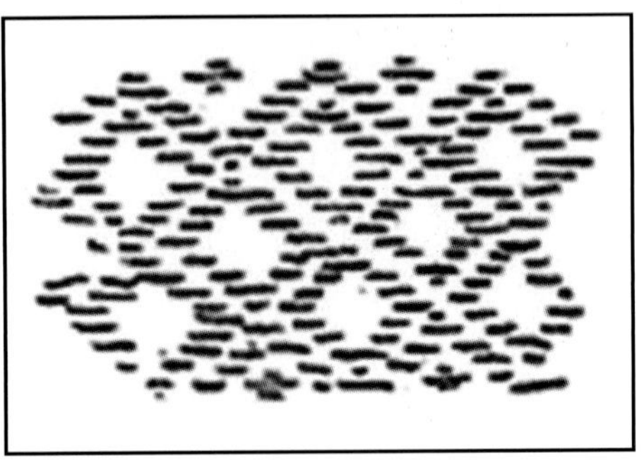

The laga pattern, as illustrated in Fay-Cooper Cole's book, The Tinguian: Social, Religious, and Economic Life of a Philippine Tribe

Filipino Tattoos: Ancient to Modern

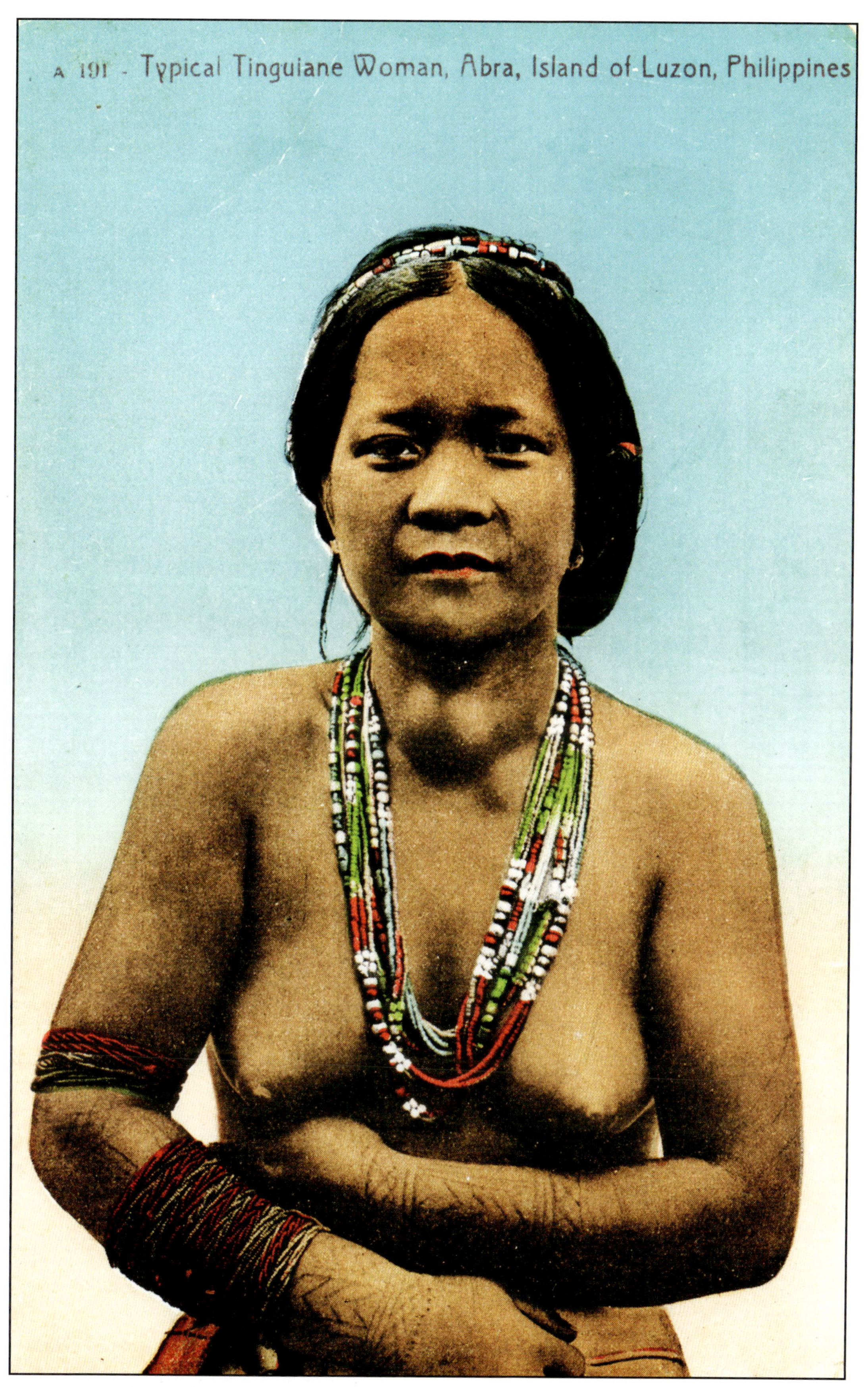

An Itneg woman with tattooed forearms, ca. 1900. The laga design faintly appears just below the elbow. Author's collection

Shared Tattooing Motifs with Pacific Isles

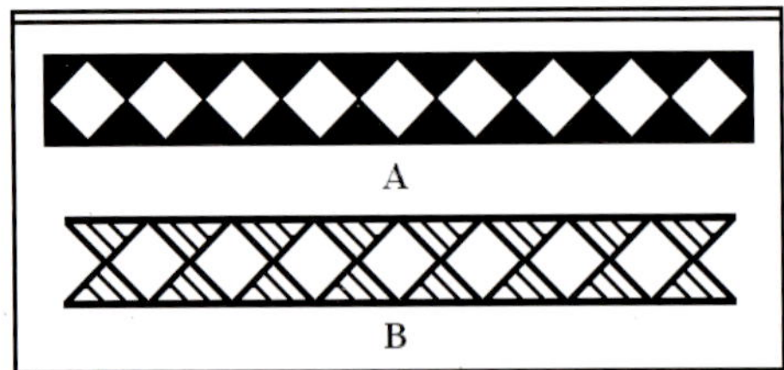

Mata and panyat designs.

the pubic area as part of the *Pe'a* and generally is covered when wearing a *lavalava*, a sarong-like wrap. It is called in Hawai'i "maka `upena," meaning "net mesh," but literally "eyes net" or figuratively a "net of eyes." In Hawai'i, if alternate squares were filled in it would be a *Mo'o* or *Kiha* design, which is a reference to scales of the supernatural lizard `aumakua, discussed earlier.[150]

Mata/Panyat

Mata is the universal word for "eye," throughout most of the Pacific region and is found in both tattooing and textiles. In Ilokano weaving traditions, patterns like this, and diamonds in general, are called "*sinan-mata*." In Itneg this pattern is called "*minat-mata*." The Kalinga, who still have living representatives with tattoos of this design, call it "*inata-ata*."[151] All these terms incorporate the word "mata," or eye. This design represents the many eyes of your ancestors watching over you and implies additional sight beyond your own, a spiritual awareness.

Some groups in the Philippines such as the Kalinga use this design to symbolize the vigil of days and nights "watching" for the return of those who were on the headhunt or the number of days and nights the warriors spent on the headhunt. In this context it suggests patience and perseverance. This was worn by both men and women on the arms. It is also seen in the center of the chest designs for Kalinga men. Lars Krutak also identifies this design as "*panyat*" or "rice bundles." (*figure B*) A very similar design is seen on the leg and buttocks tattoos for men anciently from the Benguet region. (*figure A*) According to Su'a Suluape Aisea Toetu'u, Samoans use this tattoo design as part of the tatau of the *sogo-imiti* or *pe'a* to represent the eyes of their ancestors. Samoans also call the name of the design *mata*. (eyes) It is a design that marks the wearer as a *matai* or chief. Georg Heinrich von Langsdorff, an early German ethnologist, recorded in 1804 an identical design among the people of Nuku Hiva in the Marquesas Islands in French Polynesia. In Hawai'i the pattern is part of the "*Maka Akua*" (eyes of gods) design often with a diagonal square design in the white areas.[152]

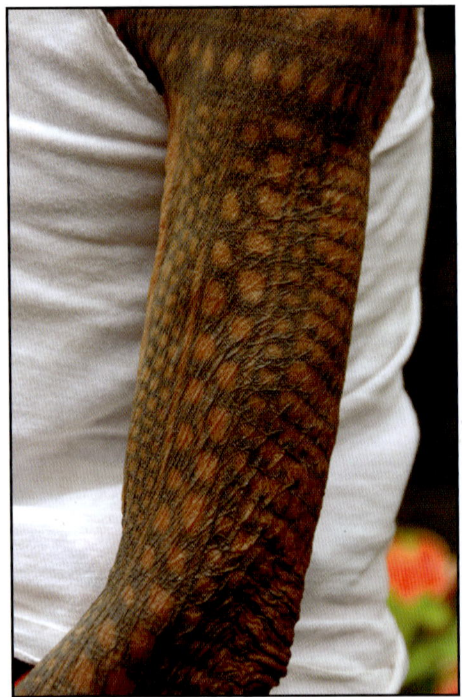

Panyat designs on an elderly woman from Kalinga. Photo courtesy of Sidney Snoeck

Minat-mata or eye designs in woven cloth

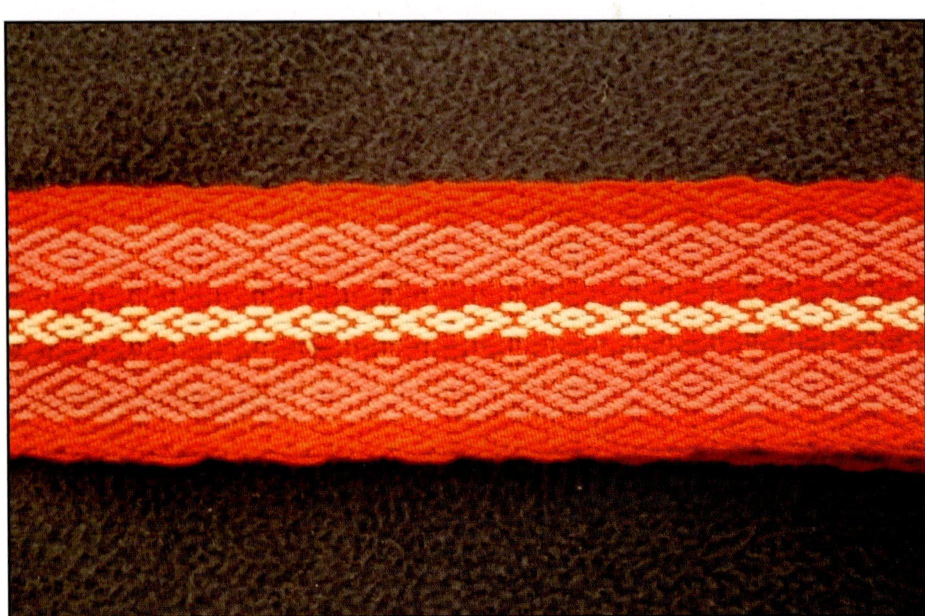

Filipino Tattoos: Ancient to Modern

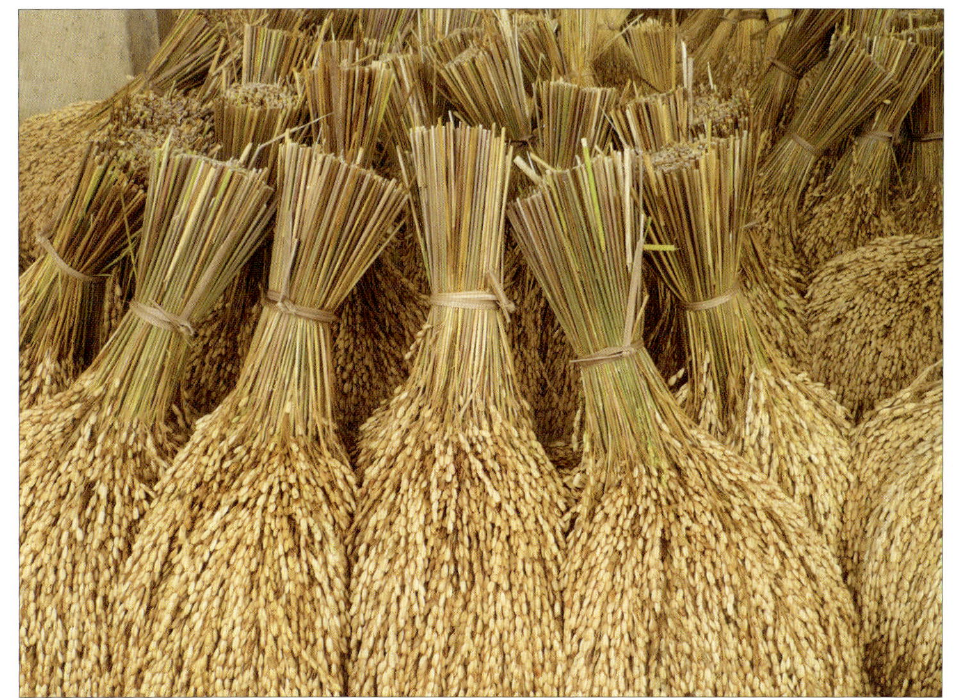

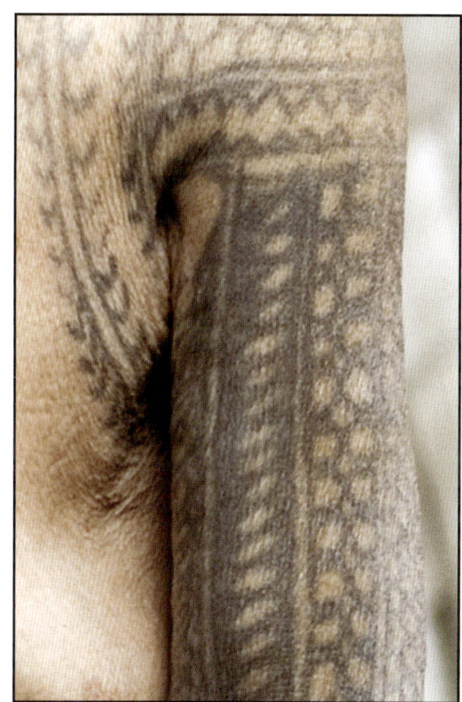

Pinulikawkaw

A design was worn by the Ifugao people of the Mountain Province and identifed as *pinulikawkaw* by Morice Vanoverbergh. According to him, this design could be placed anywhere on the body.[153] The word "pinulikawkaw" is the past tense of the word, "*malikawkaw*" which means, "to go around." Semantically it refers to getting lost such as a hunter who loses his way home in a thick forest. Obviously the tattoo does not imply that the wearer of the tattoo was lost or should get lost. Rather in the context of headhunting it records how the enemies of the wearer of this tattoo were lost while pursuing them after the headhunting raid. This tattoo can also be a protection piece for the wearer so that enemies or evil spirits that pursue them will be lost while trying to follow them. In other contexts pinulikawkaw refers to having traveled to a destination in a roundabout way, having taken a less traveled or obvious route.

In Samoan tattooing this same design is called *fa'aanufe ele'ele* meaning "earthworm" or "caterpillar like" and is a variation of the *fa'a anufe* discussed in the section about the Inangkid and its variations. Sometimes it is applied in a more angular form like the tiniku design. Here again the *fa'aanufe ele'ele* is a fertility symbol and implies the phallus. It is only used in women's tattoos. The Marshallese call this design *kõdo;* it is said to represent clouds.

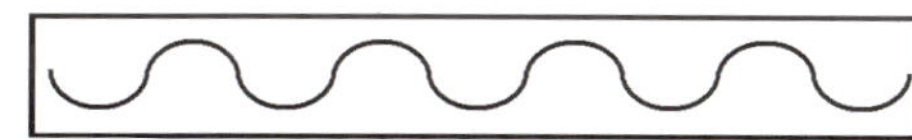

The pinulikawkaw design

Chapter 7

A Selection of Filipino Tattoo Motifs

Although there are many tattoo motifs that are shared or similar between the Philippines and Pacific Islands, there are some designs which are more distinctly Filipino. The following selection of a few of the motifs from the Philippines should be more commonly recognized as Filipino.

Aso/Kinahho

Dogs were typically called variations of the word *aso* in the Philippines. Tattoos representing dogs were tattooed by the Ifugao and people of the Benguet region. **Figure A** is the dog tattoo of the Ifugao. It was placed on the chest. In the past dogs were used for hunting and as a ceremonial food for certain celebrations and ceremonies. To be able to provide dogs for celebrations was a sign of wealth. More recently the dog has become a delicacy and eaten for any occasion in many places of Luzon.

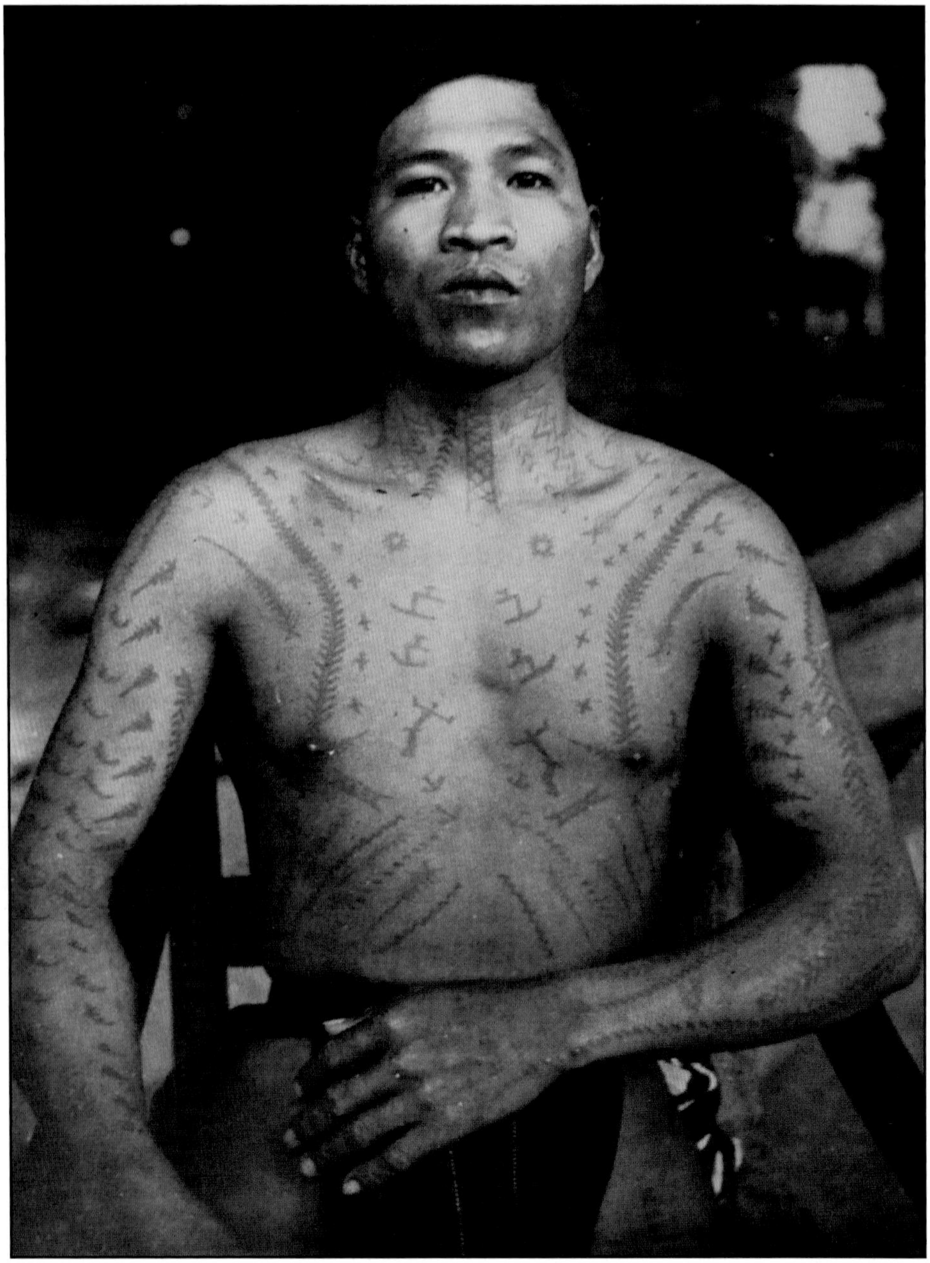

An Ifugao man with various tattoo motifs, including centipedes, dogs, scorpions, Inangkid, Hingahangal hawk and Pinuli-kawkaw eagle tattoos

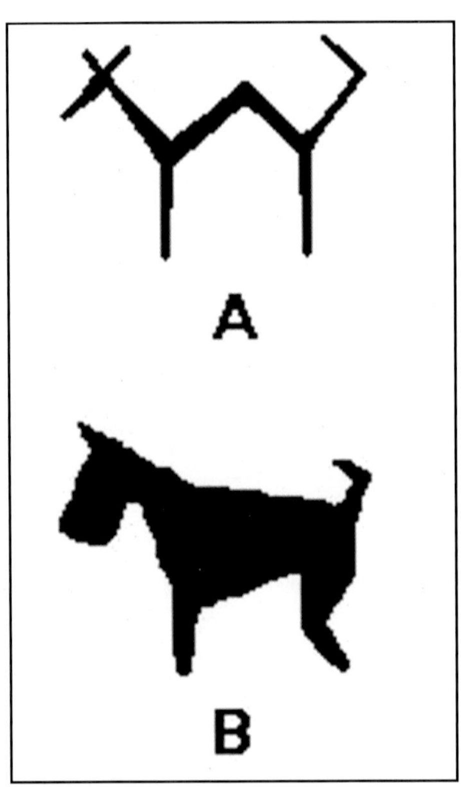

Aso or Dog tattoo motifs

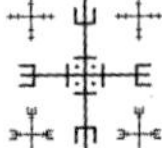

According to Manong Hospicio Binlingan Dulnuan, son of Buwaya, an Ifugao cultural teacher and advocate, the Ifugao offered dogs as sacrifices for only two ceremonies, the Hinagoho, which was a rite of protection, and the Dallung, which was a victory celebration after a successful headhunt. Ifugao people believed that by offering dogs in the Dallung they could ask for favor from the spirits and protection for a warrior with security. The rite is also done to appease the spirit of the enemy. During the Dallung, a special talisman was constructed called Pinnokla, which was made from the victim's skull and was bound to a specially shaped board called *kinahho,* that means "like a dog." The Pinnokla was made to protect the warrior from the distress, bad feelings or bad dreams that may have been associated with headhunting. It also protected him from the effects of sorcery that were likely used by relatives of the victim. Dulnuan further explained that the psychological effect of the *kinahho* tattoo was to instill fear upon any would-be killers of the person wearing the tattoo. A killer would have to think twice about attacking a person with a *kinahho* tattoo who had protected himself through the Dallung rite. Manong Hospicio also has explained that *kahho* (dogs) also served as guardians. When strangers approach a house or village, dogs would bark. The elders state that dogs are able to perceive spirits, so in a real way dogs provided protection by forewarning people of possible physical and spiritual danger. With the Dallung ceremony and construction of the Pinnokla, according to Manong Hospicio, the *kinahho* tattoo symbolized spiritual forewarning of danger that often presented itself in a person's dreams.

Figure B is a more naturalistic dog tattoo, as seen in a horizontal row across the back of the mummy of Apo Anno from the Benguet region. Apo Anno was known for being a great hunter. Dogs are still used in the Philippines for hunting, chasing down and cornering prey. While hunting through thick forests or jungles, a hunter cannot always see his prey, but hearing the chasing dogs' barking enabled the hunter to adjust his pursuit and home in on his quarry. In effect, dogs extended the hunter's awareness in the way dogs make villagers aware when strangers approach. The Aso design across the lower back most likely represents Apo Anno's great hunting prowess and perhaps his extension of awareness.

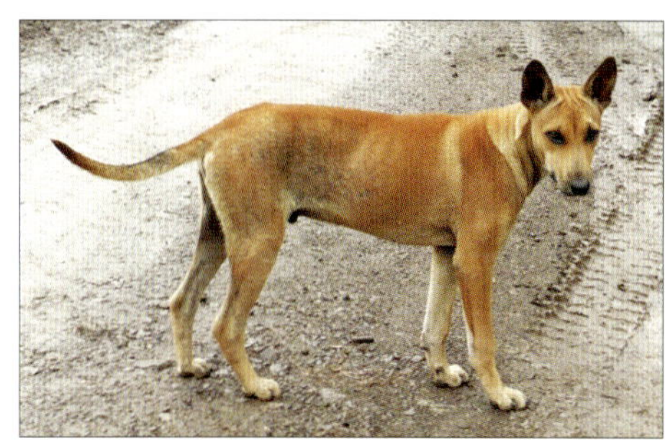

The Philippine dog. Photo by the Author

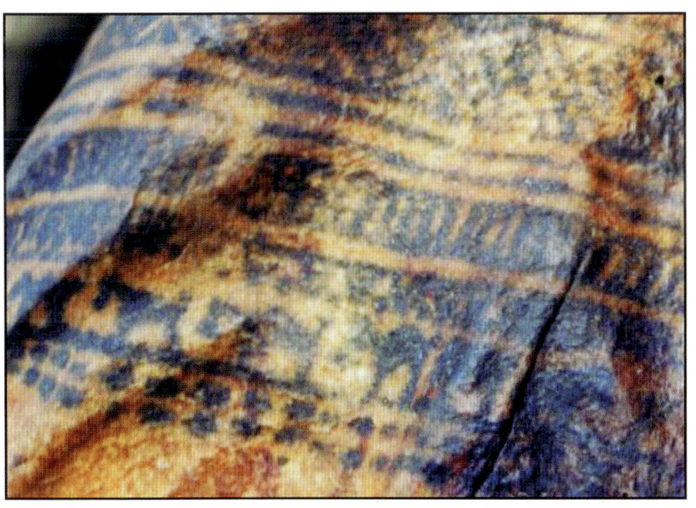

Left: Dog tattoos on the mummified back of Apo Anno. Detail from a photo by Art Tibaldo

Right: Dog tattoos on an Ifugao man. Photo by Worcester

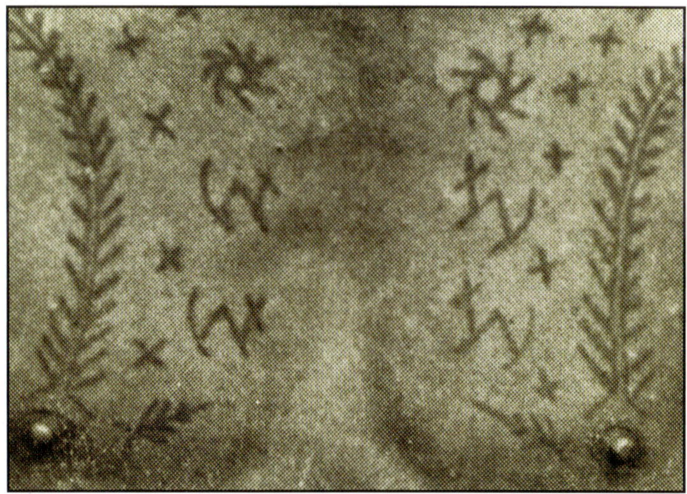

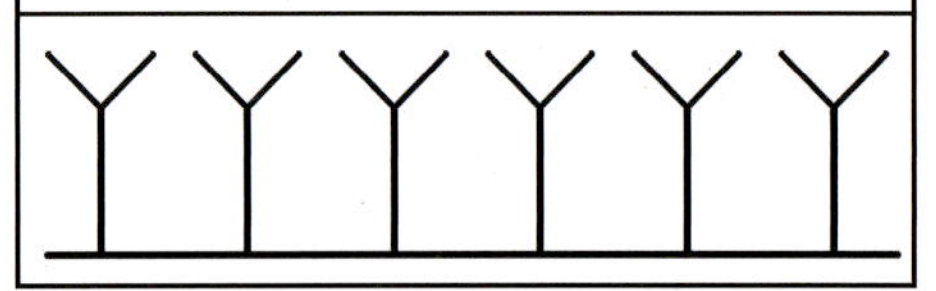

The chila na urog or tongue of the snake design

Chila na Urog

The forked-tongue-of-the-snake design, or *chila na urog,* is found in Southern Kalinga. Because snakes and other reptiles were thought to be physical avatars of the ancestors' will, their hissing tongues represents the whispering voices of ancestors. The design tells us that to hear the voices from the spiritual world we must be calm and quiet. As with other snake and reptile designs, this was also a symbol suggesting the stealth and prowess of a warrior. More importantly it was the warrior's submissiveness to the council given by the snake (*anito*) that made him a successful warrior. This rare tattoo motif has been seen in the Kalinga and Bontoc regions, while other areas have similar motifs or have incorporated this design into other motifs, not only for tattooing but in other decorative arts as well. Another interpretation is that this design represents plants growing, representing fruitfulness and fertility.

Right: Bontoc shield decorated with Chila na Urog design. Courtesy of Tribalmania.com

Far right: Detail of chila na urog on the shield. Photo courtesy of Tribalmania.com

Opposite
Top: A Kalinga woman with the chila na urog design as part of her sinokray, or collar tattoo. Photo courtesy of Sidney Snoeck

Bottom: Detail of the showing the chila na urog. Photo courtesy of Sidney Snoeck

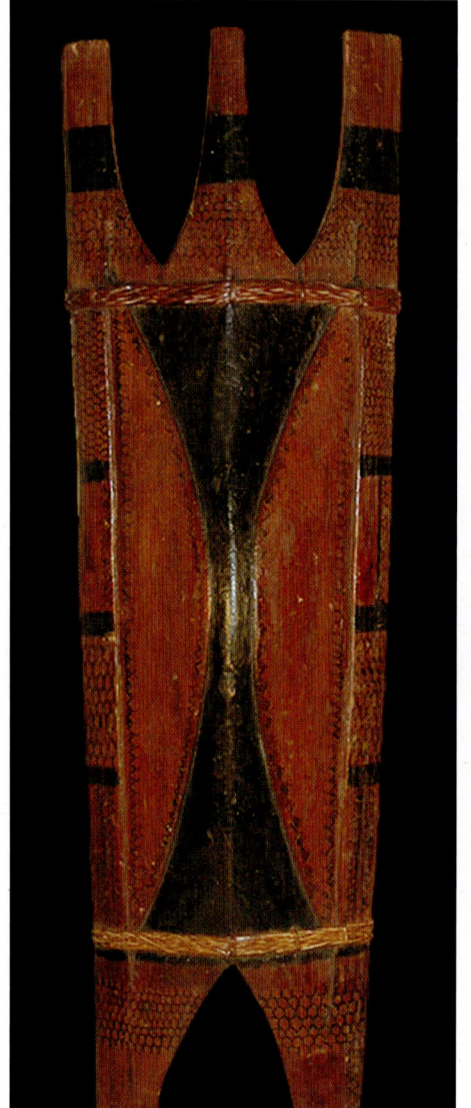

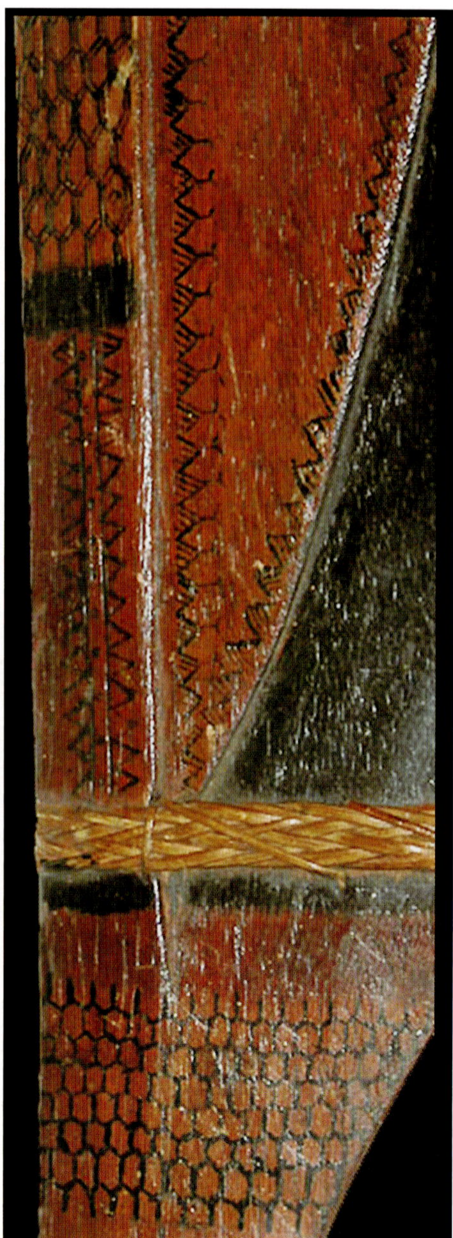

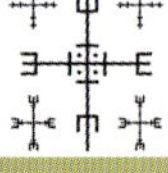

Filipino Tattoos: Ancient to Modern

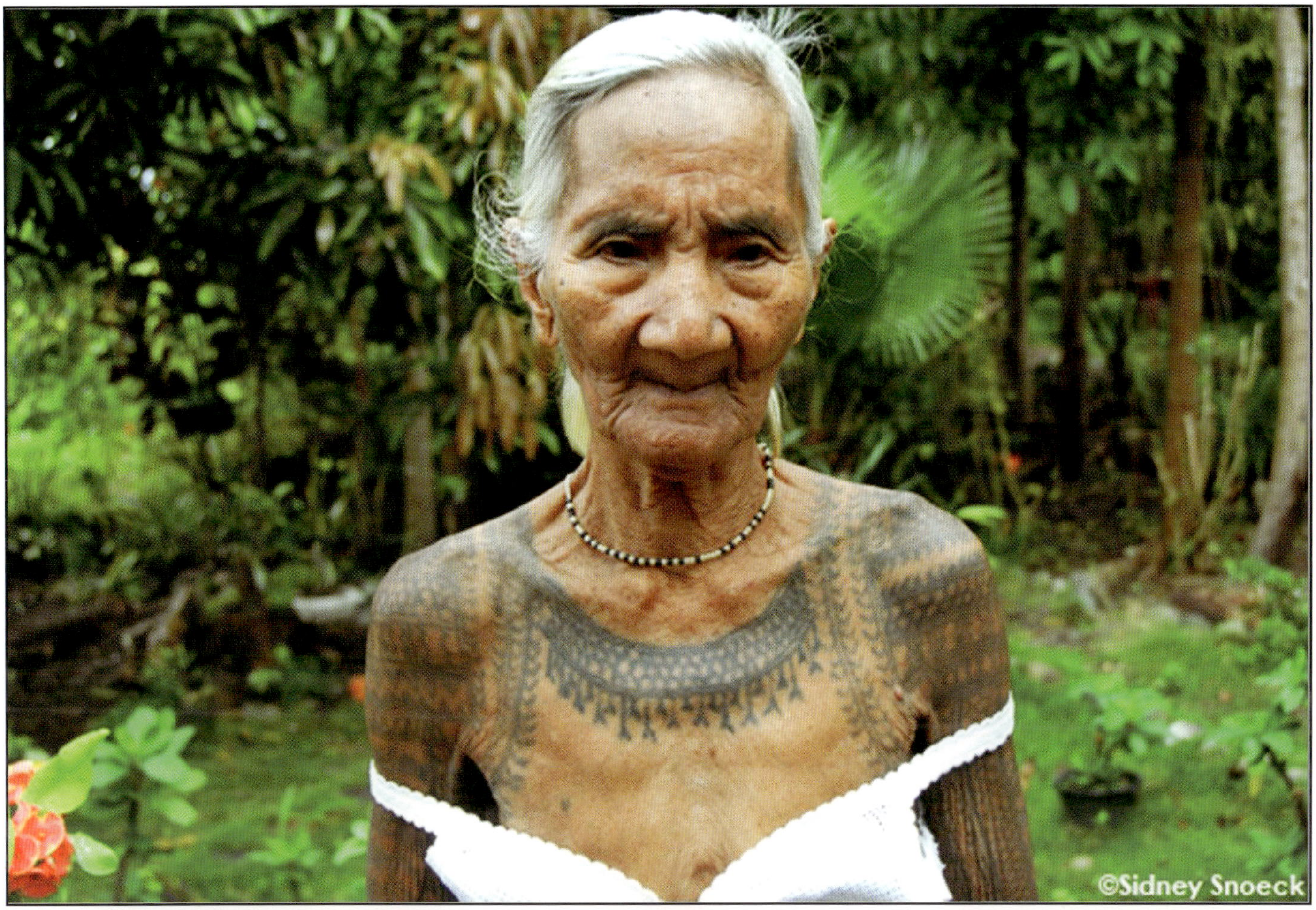

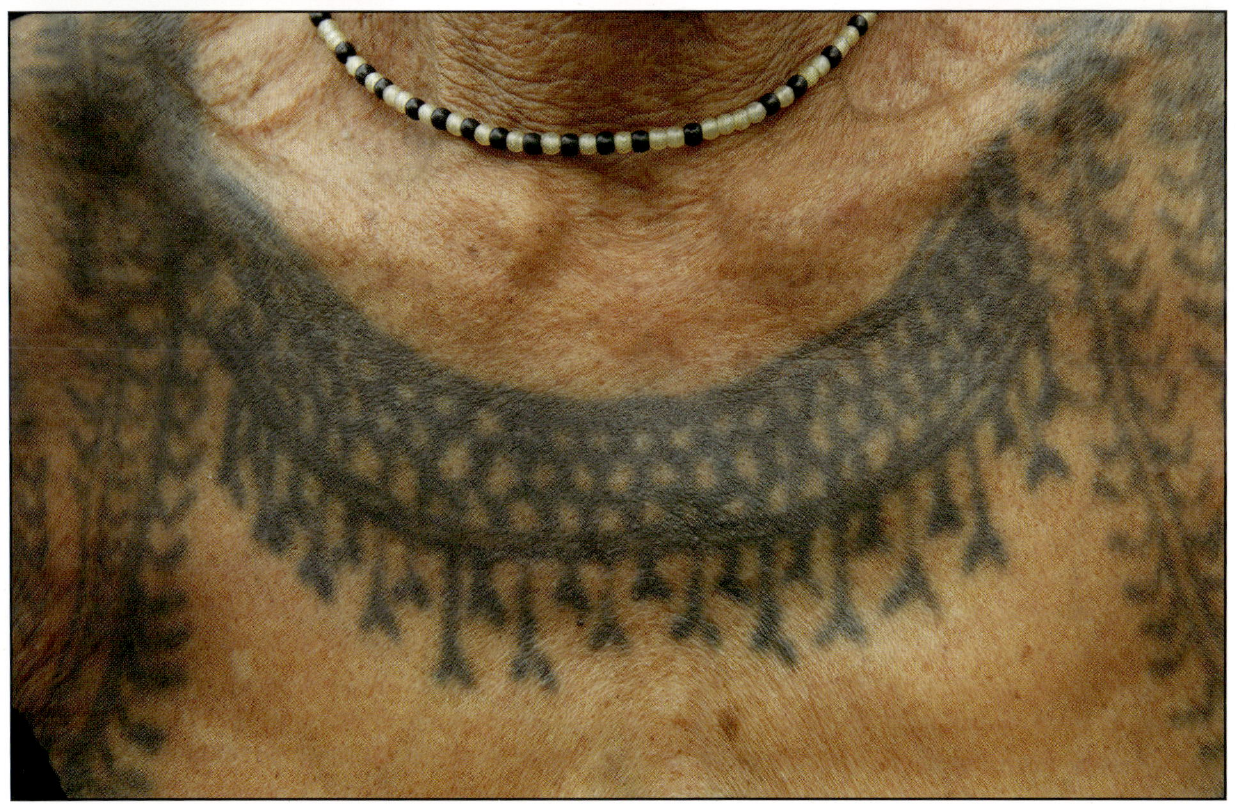

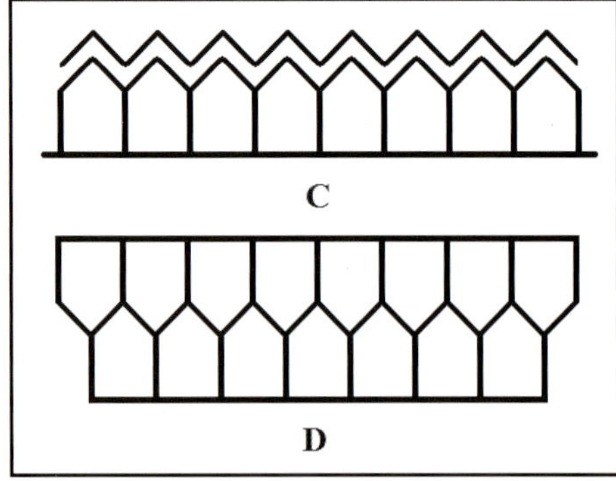

Filig or mountain designs

An old, colorized image of a Lubuagan woman with filig designs, 1913. Photo by Worcester for National Geographic Magazine

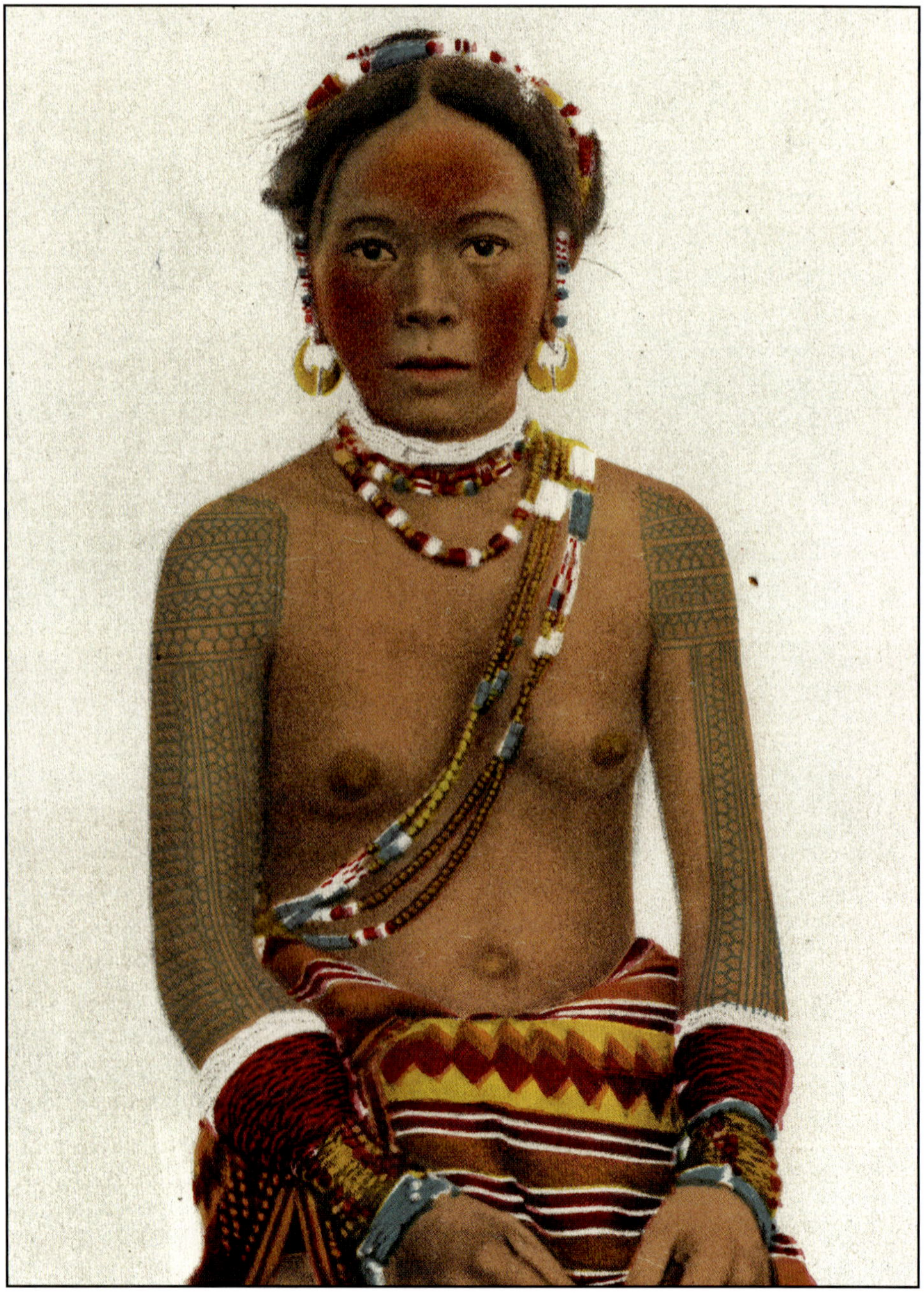

Filig

Filig designs were identified by Professor Ikin Salvadore-Amores as representing mountains.[154] The word for mountains is "*filig*" in the Southern Kalinga dialect, and sometimes this design is doubled with a row of mountains on the top facing down as well as from the bottom. Other times all the lines are doubled or an extra line is placed zigzagged across the top, similar to the *tiniku* or *binakuko* designs that represent pathways of travel through the mountains. The Cordillera of Luzon or old Mountain Province contains many switchback trails and roads. In the old days, travel on foot on these paths up and down mountains was difficult, requiring perseverance and endurance. Depending on interpretation, the zigzag portion of the design could also represent rivers of water flowing through the mountains.

Filipino Tattoos: Ancient to Modern

Ginawang

Ginawang is an Ifugao tattoo identified by Morice Vanoverbergh and typically seen on chests and shoulders of the men.[155] Although Vanoverbergh records the *ginawang* as a motif representing an eagle, it is, in fact, a hawk. (In Kalinga the word *gayang* does refer to an eagle.) The word *ginawang* actually means "like a hawk," being derived from the Ifugao word for hawk (*gayang*). The *gayang* was an omen bird watched for its patterns of flight in headhunting expeditions. In a larger context it represents all omen birds in general and the message of good fortune or blessing of the anitos or ancestors for a particular task. The "*Ginawang*" or hawk tattoo of the Ifuago people is also a spiritual messenger. The *Ginawang* tattoo is usually oriented with the head up or angled to the right or left, but generally in an upward direction. Like other bird motifs, it implies communication to the heavenly realm or a connection to higher ancestral gods who, in many Philippine belief systems, "spoke" through the actions and flights of birds.

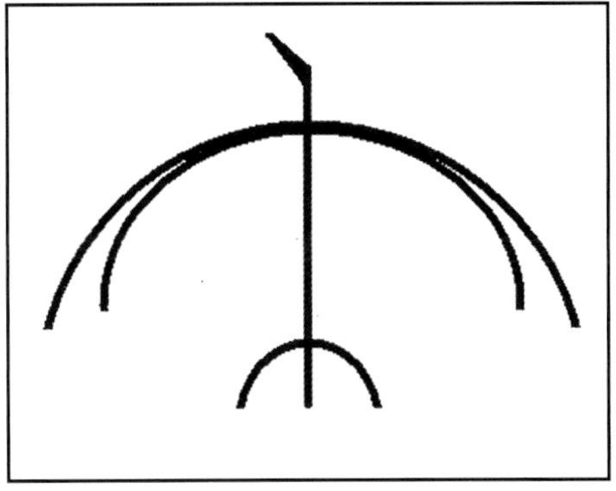

Ginawang or hawk tattoo motif

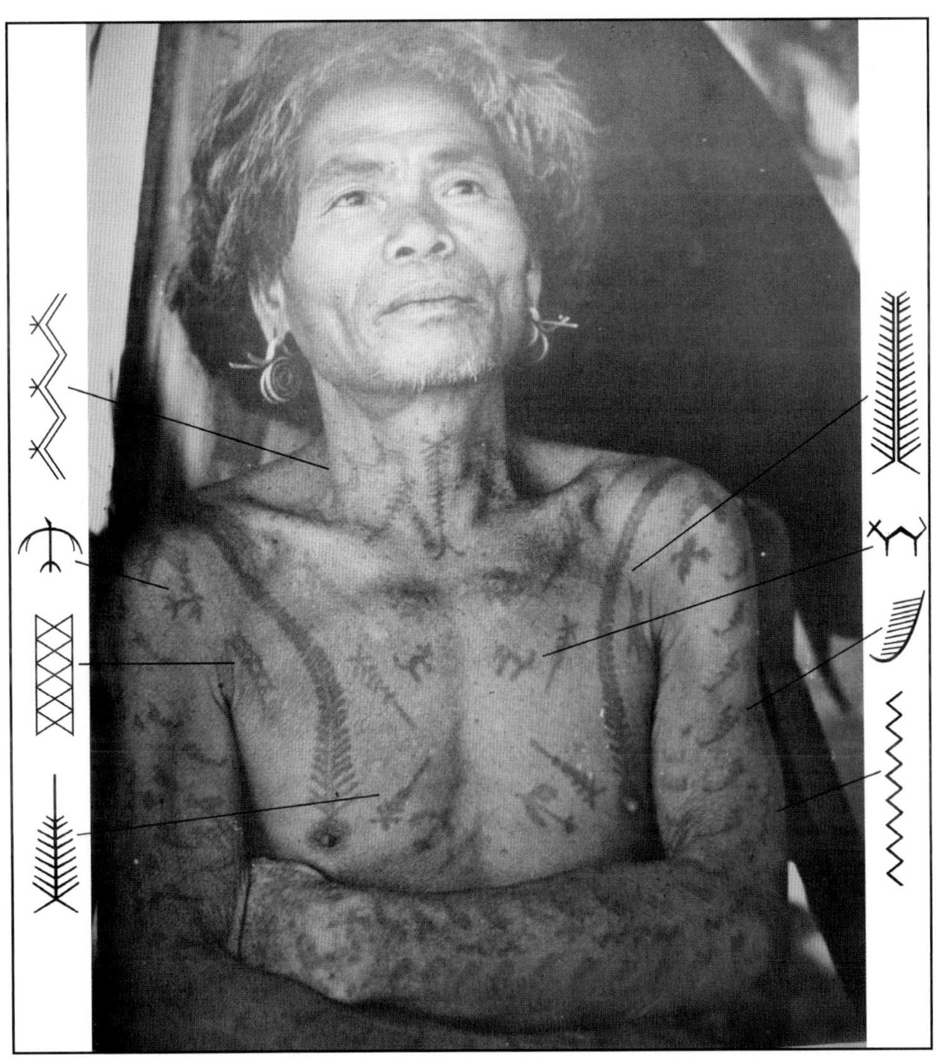

An Ifugao man with the ginawang hawk motifs as well as lightning, dog, pinulikawkaw, inangkid hook designs, scorpions, centipedes, and ladder motifs, ca. 1910

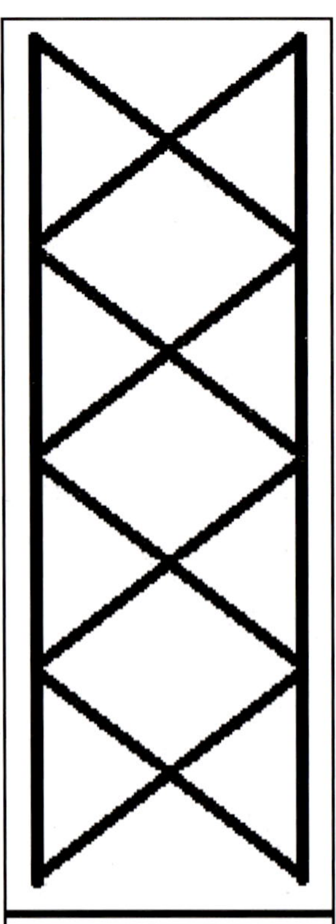
The Hinanghangal tattoo design

Hinanghangal

The *hinanghangal* tattoo was placed on Ifugao men's throats and occasionally on the chest according to Vanoverbergh. Manong Jaime Buyayo, a native Ifugao, has said *hinanghangal* comes from the word "*munhangal*," which literally means "to sing," specifically in the context of the Honga portion of the Baki prayers of the Ifugao Mumbaki or shaman. Honga are rites of thanksgiving or well-being that are performed for the attainment of social prestige. According to Manong Hospicio Dulnuan, in a specific part of the Honga the participant chants the Honga while inside his house. The Mumbaki then takes a ladder to poke and try to force him out of the house. To this the participant inside the house proclaims, "I am a *kadangyan!*", meaning a person of wealth and status.

Oration among the Cordilleran peoples and the ancient Filipinos was an important way for a man to convey his genealogy, share his past exploits, convey his opinions and show his mastery of the language. The Hinanghangal tattoo conveyed an abundant building of complex oral structures in bundles of thoughts and phrases. Perhaps in the past this tattoo gave a man the right to participate in various ceremonies, village councils and other public forums.

Anthropologist Lars Krutak identifies this tattoo as "*Ardan*," or neck-ladder, that symbolized the movement of a young warrior to a higher level. This may be a reference to Manong Hospicio's description of the participant in the Honga proclaiming he is now a person of wealth, in effect moving up the social "ladder."

Ladders in the Philippines were sometimes made by taking a log of wood and cutting gouges out of them to form steps. The Hinanghangal/Ardan design resembles this type of ladder with the diamonds of the design being the gouges in the wood. This design was sometimes found on the chest as well and sometimes is described as being a shield.

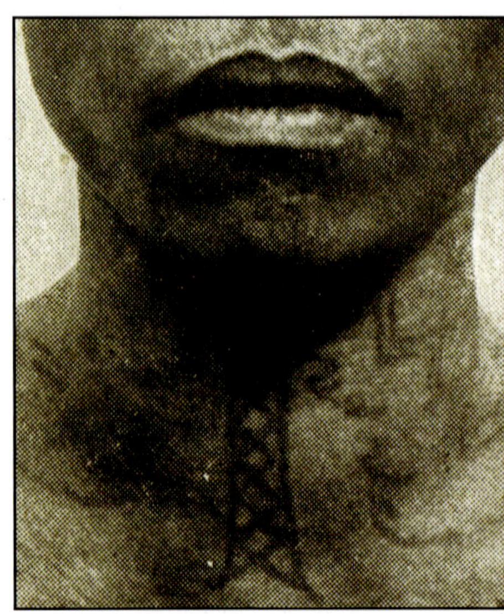
Detail of an Ifugao man's hinanghangal tattoo on his throat.

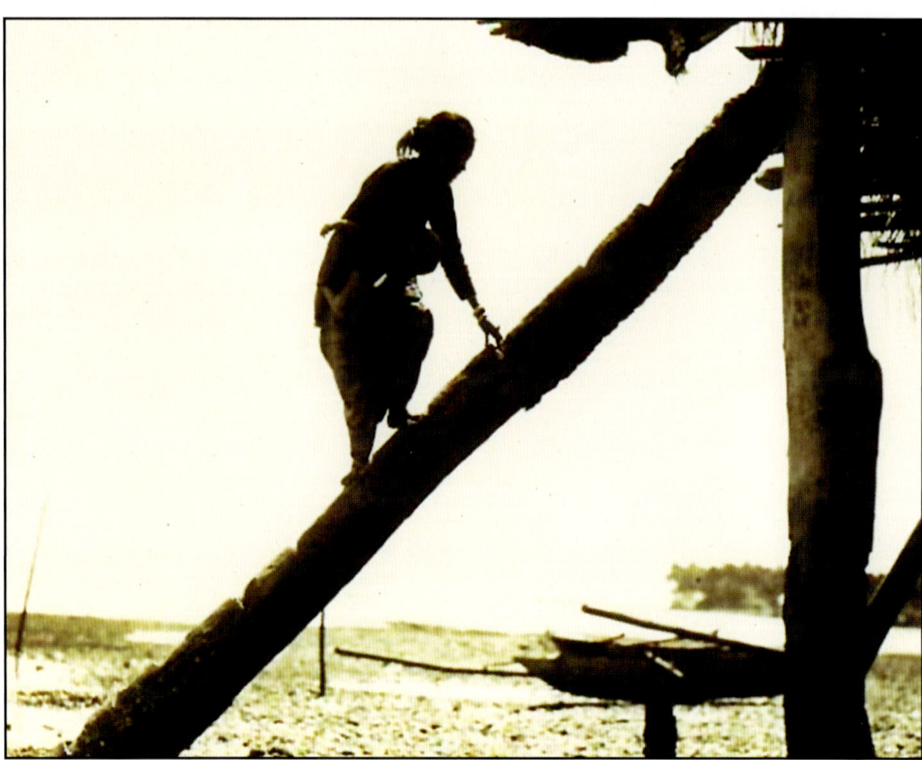
A simple log ladder, which may be the inspiration of the Hinang-hangal or Ardan tattoo, ca.1890

Filipino Tattoos: Ancient to Modern

Hinuliab

The Hinuliab tattoo design was rare to find in the early-1900s, primarily among the Ifugao and peoples of the Benguet region, and variations of it were found among other peoples of Luzon. According to Manong Jaime Buyayo, the Hinuliab in Ifugao are human figures, with their hands in a prayer position, that are attached to the front of a house. *Gansa* (gongs) are hung from their hands. Their heads support shelves that the rice wine jars are kept on. In this context, the tattoo represents the ability to hold or support sacred items. It may also represent the figures holding these sacred items, which in turn represent ancestor spirits. The design itself resembles upside-down anthropomorphic figures, again implying the ancestors, especially if seen from the perspective of the wearer looking downwards. (From this perspective the figures would be right side up.) The word "*hinuliab*" also refers to sharpened stakes of bamboo that are used as weapons for hunting or are driven into the ground for protection from enemies, especially when camping on headhunting trips. In other places, these sharpened stakes are called *pua* or *suga*. A variation of the word *Himuliab* means "a fire that is flaring up," symbolic of the spirit. According to Manong Hospicio Dulnuan, "The word '*hinuliab*' comes from the word '*huliab*,' which means 'to cover, bless, to accept and to be given strength by the elders or by the mumbaki.'" He also states that it was used on both clothing and tattoos in the past. This design may have conveyed a multitude of meanings. The tattoo was placed on the shoulders, neck, arms and thighs, according to Vanoverbergh.[156]

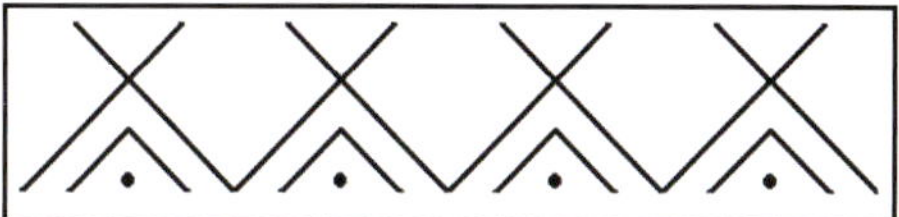

The Hinuliab design

Sharpened bamboo stakes (hinuliab) driven into the ground for protection against enemies. Other names for the hinuliab are pua and suga.

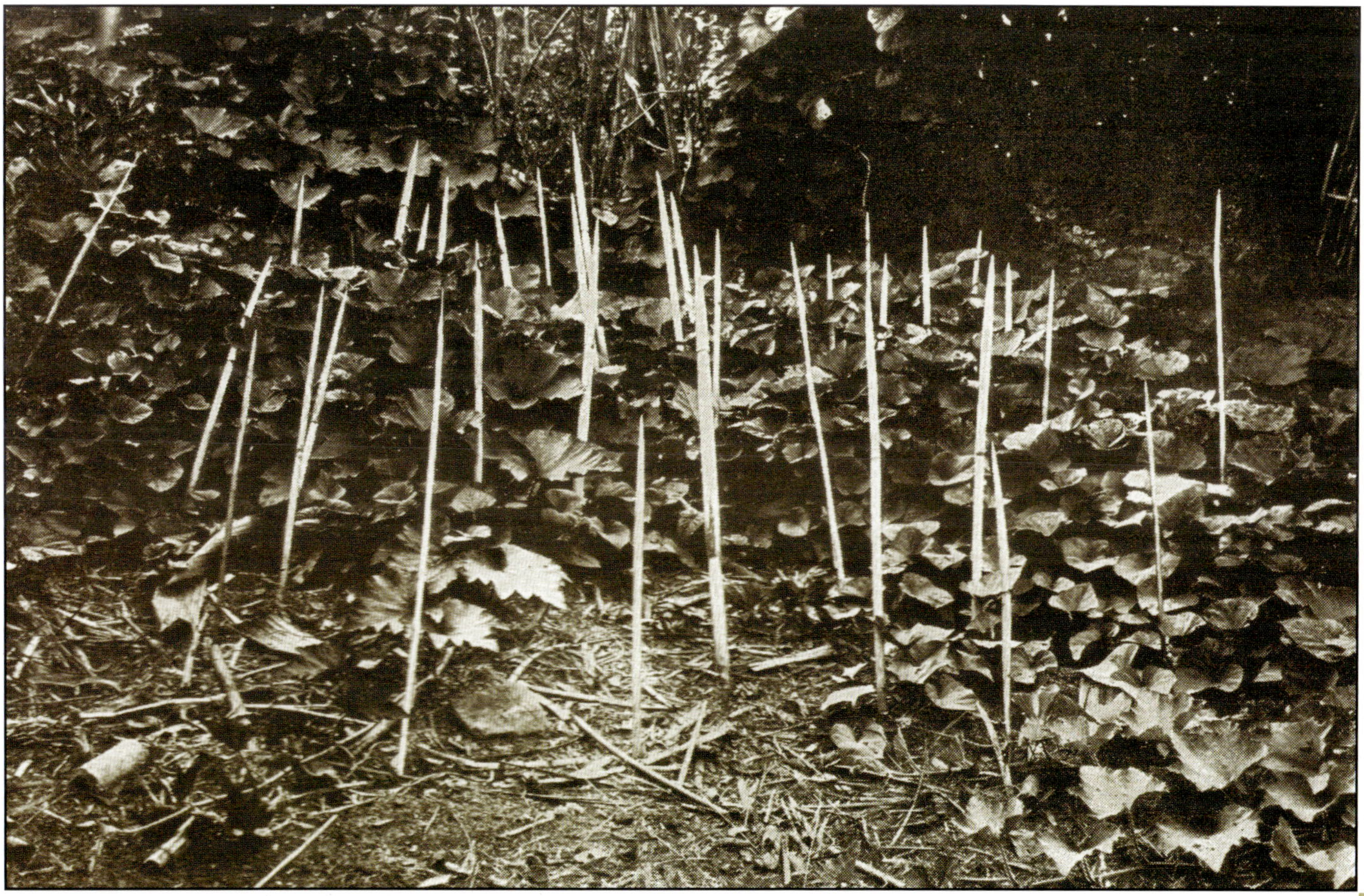

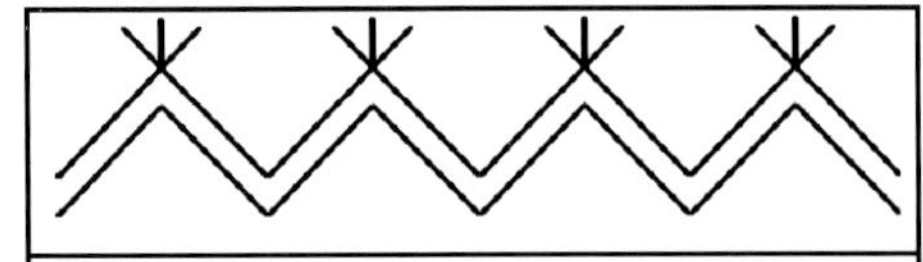

The Kinilat, lightning design.

Kinilat

Kinilat is an Ifugao design that represents lightning, the word meaning "lightning-like." In the Ifugao language, lightning is called "*ilat*." In other places, lightning is known as "*kimat*" or "*kilat*" and is represented with zigzag lines without the three extensions at the top of one side of the angles. It is usually represented by double zigzag lines.

Depending on the ethnic group, lightning can represent different things: the Ifugao tattooed this design mainly on the neck, and to them lightning is the representation of Ovug, the divided child.

In an Ifugao myth, the god Dumagid had a son with a mortal woman, Dugai. One day, when Dumagid was to return to the sky, he was going to take his son, Ovug, with him, but the mother's people did not want to part with the child, so the god divided the child in two parts, one part for the heavens and one part for the earth. The two halves each were brought to life and had their missing sides restored, creating twins. One twin became the lightning and the other became the thunder.[157]

This tattoo symbolizes the common concept in the ancient Philippines that people possessed dual souls. The lightning, which travels down to earth, represents a connection to the earth world and the thunder, which rumbles in the sky, represents the heavenly world. The *kinilat* tattoo can symbolize the nature of man being a mixture of both the heavenly and earthly worlds.

A variation of this myth of the divided child is found among the Kankana-ey people. In their version of the story, Lumauig [Dumagid] descended from heaven and married a human girl. Soon they had a child together, but the girl's sisters were jealous of her and put garlic under the couple's bed. Lumauig did not like the smell, so he told his wife that he was going to return to the sky and would take half of their child with him. He divided the head from the body, but upon returning to the sky the head was angry that it did not have a body. So Lumauig made it a body and legs, and it became the thunder. The body left on earth also was unhappy because it could not talk, so Lumauig returned and created a head for it. This child became the lightning. The lightning married the thunder, and so thunder and lightning, as husband and wife, are always found together.[158]

The interpretation of this story is that men and women are two parts of one person. The two lines in the *kinilat* tattoo represent this union. The *kinilat* looks similar to the *Karayan/Tiniku* tattoo for this very reason. The plain zigzag line represents water flowing along a riverbank and is the male aspect. The other line, with the three extensions on each of the outside corners, is the bank of the river and the female aspect. Water nourishes or "fertilizes" the soil of the bank, and together the lines produce life, which is represented by the plants growing out from the bank (the three extensions). The extensions also are a representation of a woman's vulva.

In other Ifugao tradtions, the earthbound parent is the husband of the relationship, named Kinngaowan. The goddess from the skyworld is Bugan. They live in the lower world with their child, but the people eat forbidden foods, such as ginger, with the game that the father, Kinngaowan, traps. Consequently, Kinngaowan and his people are cursed with skin eruptions. The cursed people blame him and his family and they avenge themselves by smearing pounded ginger on the wall of the couple's house. Kinngaowan and Bugan move their family from the valley

Filipino Tattoos: Ancient to Modern

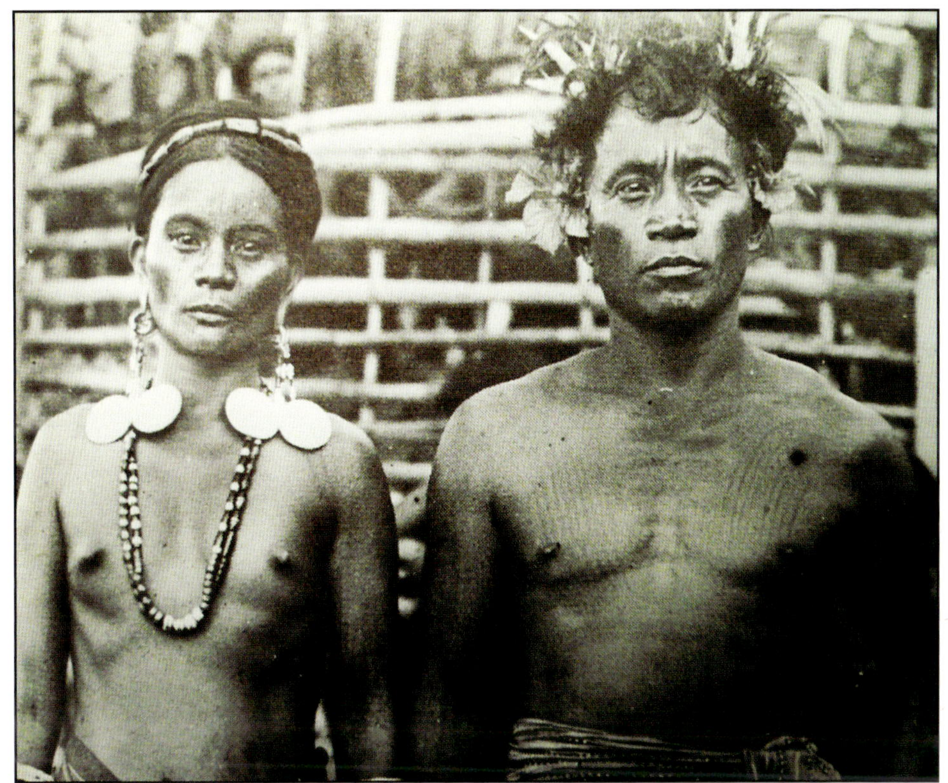

A Kalinga couple from about 1900. The husband wears red hibiscus flowers behind his ears, showing that he is a successful warrior.

to a place high in the mountains, but the people follow them and continue to smear their house with pounded ginger. Bugan proposes they move to the skyworld, but Kinngaowan is unable to make the ascent. Bugan then suggests that they divide their child, the lower half for Kinngaowan in the lower world and the upper half for her in the skyworld. Bugan instructs him to reanimate and make whole his half of the child. But Kinngaowan is unable to do so, and the body begins to rot. The heavenly Bugan, upon smelling the rotten portion, returns and asks him why the child was left to rot. She attempts to restore the rotten portion but without success, it is too rotten to revive. Instead, Bugan makes out of the lower body *lubug*, omen-bringing creatures and natural weather and earthly phenomena. When these omen animals and events in nature are observed, then the people need to sacrifice a chicken. The sweet smell of the chicken cooking encourages the skyworld deities to cure the stricken ones from skin eruptions and also bless them with health, abundant crops and protection from their enemies and evil spirits.[159]

In another tradition, lightning is thought to be the "*Aso,*" or dog, of the paramount god, Kadaklan, sometimes called Kaboniyan of the Itneg people. Kadaklan makes his will or displeasure known by sending his dog *kimat* (the lightning) to bite things. The thunder is the growling of the dog or the pounding of Kadaklan's *gansa* (gong drum).[160] In this context, the lightning design represents the will of God being made known.

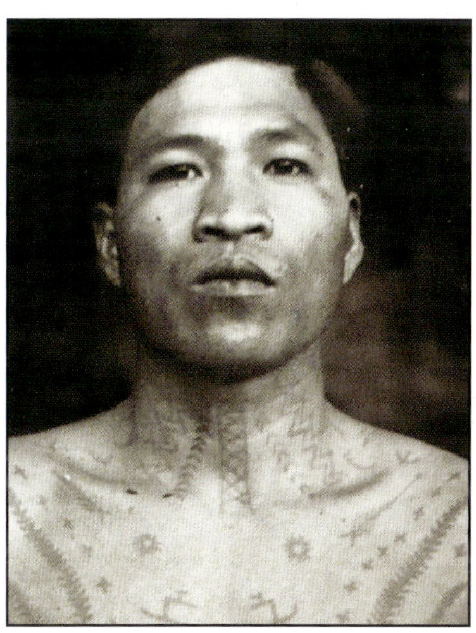

Ifugao man with Kinilat (lightning) tattoos on his neck, ca. 1905

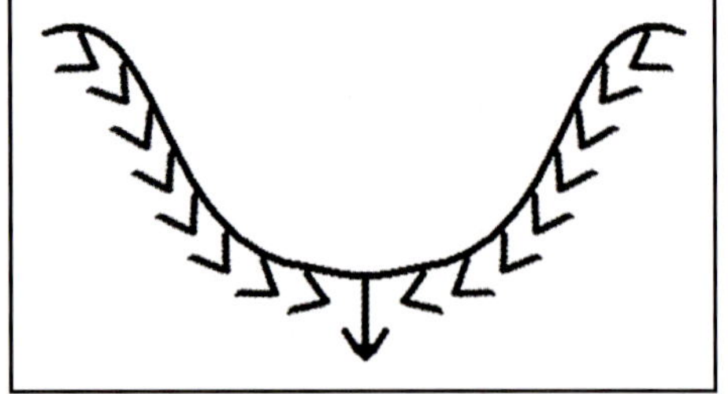

The koling serpent eagle tattoo

Koling

Koling is a Bontoc symbol for the Serpent Eagle, *Spilornis holospilus,* that is found throughout Southeast Asia. In Bontoc folklore, *Koling* was once a human boy who, with his brother, was slowly starving under the abuse of a cruel mother. One day, while collecting firewood in the mountains, the boy climbed a tree and cast down his bones, one by one, saying, "Here is some wood for our mother." At last all his bones had been tossed down and he was transformed into the *koling.* The other brother was afraid to descend the mountain by himself, but the transformed older brother told him from the skies that he would watch over him.[161]

This tattoo conveys the idea of being watched over by a presence from the heavenly or sky world. Like other bird tattoos, it also symbolizes communication from the heavenly realms. It is placed in the upper-center of the chest below the collarbones.

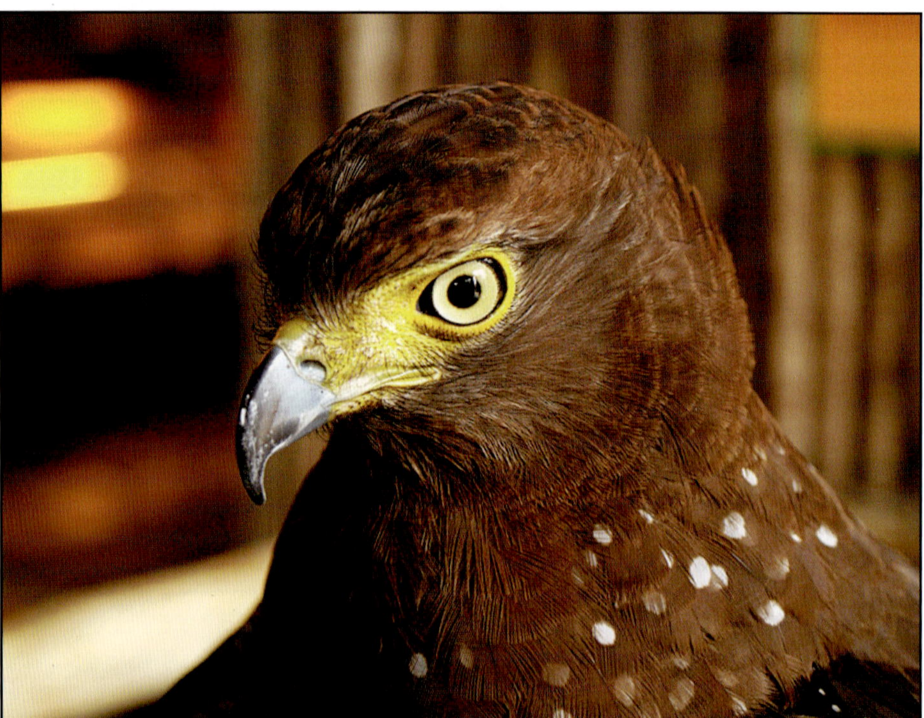

The Philippine Serpent Eagle Spilornis holospilus by RunningToddler. Photo courtesy of Charles P. Laigo. http://commons.wikimedia.org/wiki/File:Ark_Avilon_Phil_Serpent_Eagle.jpg Used under GNU licence. http://commons.wikimedia.org/wiki/Commons:GNU_Free_Documentation_License i

Filipino Tattoos: Ancient to Modern

Padok

This design is from the Ibaloi people of the Benguet region of Luzon. It represents the well established river (*padok*) winding its way through the land. The design is different than the zigzagged lines of other water symbols, although it carries similar meanings and, as with all water, it is a necessity for the continuation of life. This type of water design also has been seen on mummies found in the region, so it evidently has been tattooed for several hundred years. It was formerly tattooed on men, but now is found only on a few elderly women of the region.

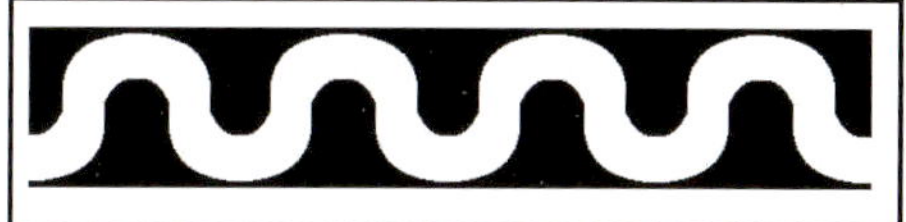

The padok or river design of the Ibaloi; it may be related to the Pinulikawkaw design of the Ifugao.

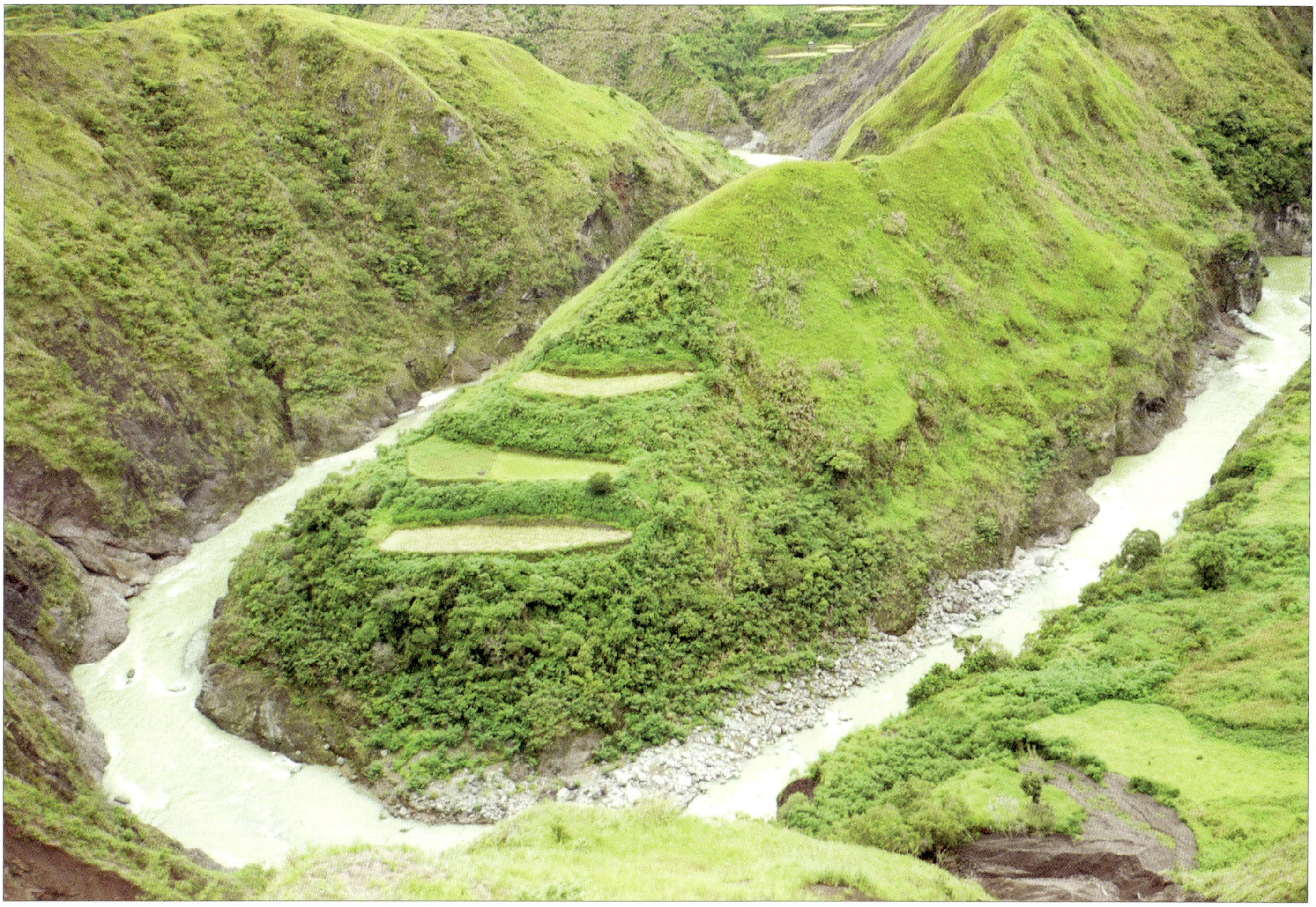

A portion of the Chico River which resembles the padok design. Photo by the Author

The tattooed arm of an Ibaloi girl, showing the padok river design, 1905, by Dean C. Worcester

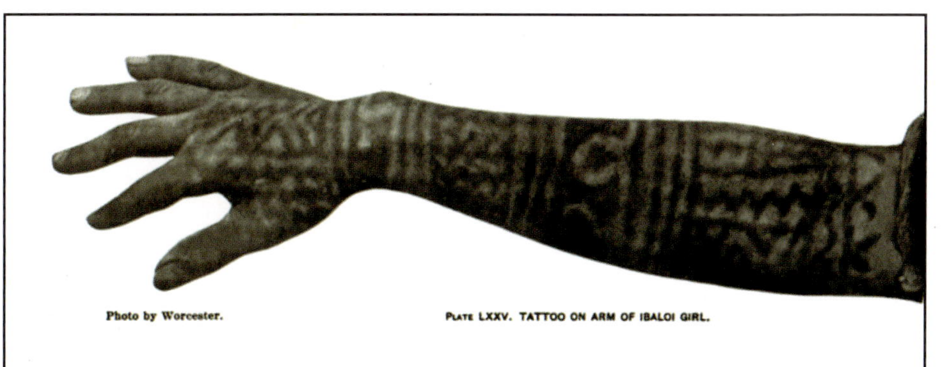

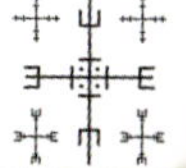

A Selection of Filipino Tattoo Motifs

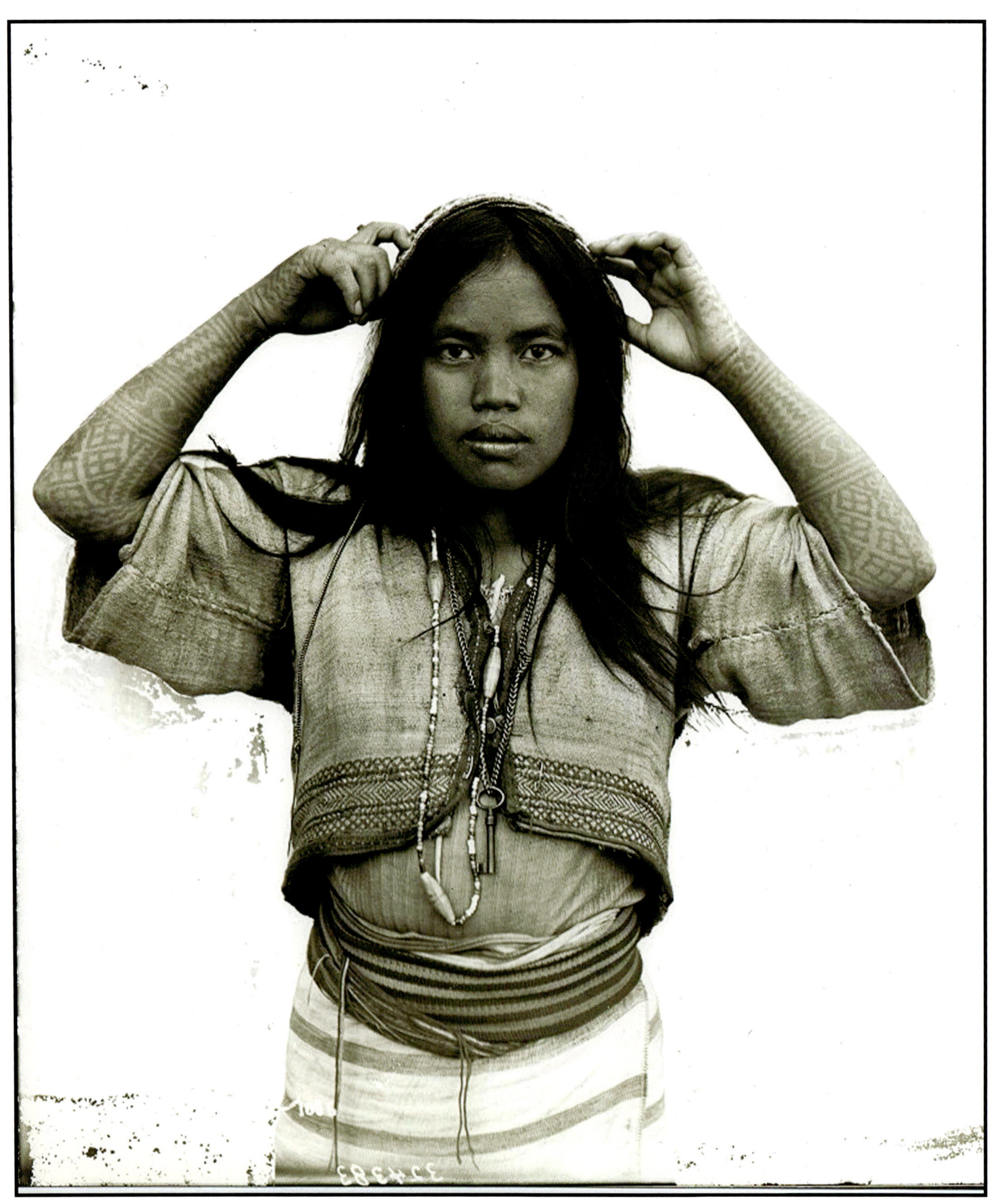

An Ibaloi woman displaying her tattooed arms that bear the Padok designs, 1904

Filipino Tattoos: Ancient to Modern

Pang-ti-i´

This design, in some areas, is used as a form of the *gayaman* tattoo. However, according to Manong Jotoc of the Bontoc province, it represents rice stalks, or *Pang-ti-i´*, heavy with grain and bent over, ready to be harvested. For an old Bontoc warrior, the *Pang-ti-i´* design incorporated into his *chak-lag* chest tattoo symbolized the successfully taking of heads in battle. This design suggests the bountiful harvest, having an abundance and good fortune for the wearer and his family. In a larger sense, the tattoo implies that the wearer will have an abundance of posterity, as the fertility of the fields, domesticated animals, and women are all dependent on the spiritual power that comes from a successful headhunt.

Among other groups, such as the Ifugao, this design is another representation of the *gayaman* (centipede). Sometimes the Ifugao place the legs at right angles to the base line for this design. This design conveys the power of the centipede to figuratively "bite," as in the context of a headhunt. The relationship between the headhunt and an abundance of harvest is illustrated in the tattoo design. Some villages placed symbols in the perspective of the wearer of the tattoo while other villages oriented the designs from the perspective of the viewer. In the application of the *pang-ti'i,* sometimes the tattooist would reorient the direction of the design as its wrapped around a body to maintain the desired upwards or downwards direction of the motif.

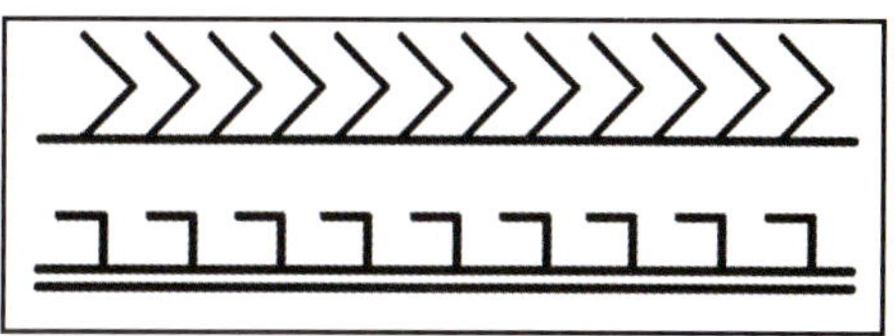

Pang-ti'i designs

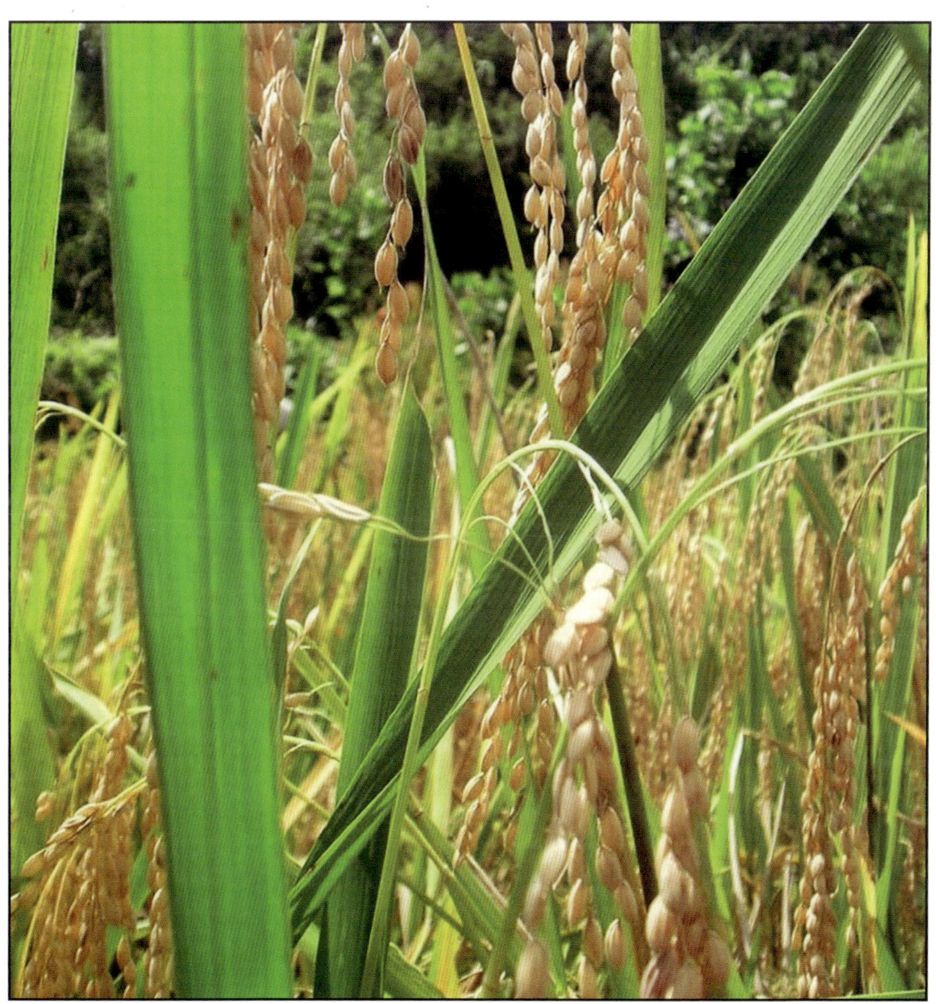

A stalk of ready-to-harvest rice, heavy with grain called pang-ti'i. by Shubert Ciencia. http://www.flickr.com/photos/bigberto/924700551/ Used under licence of creative commons share and share alike 2.0. http://creativecommons.org/licenses/by/2.0/

A Selection of Filipino Tattoo Motifs

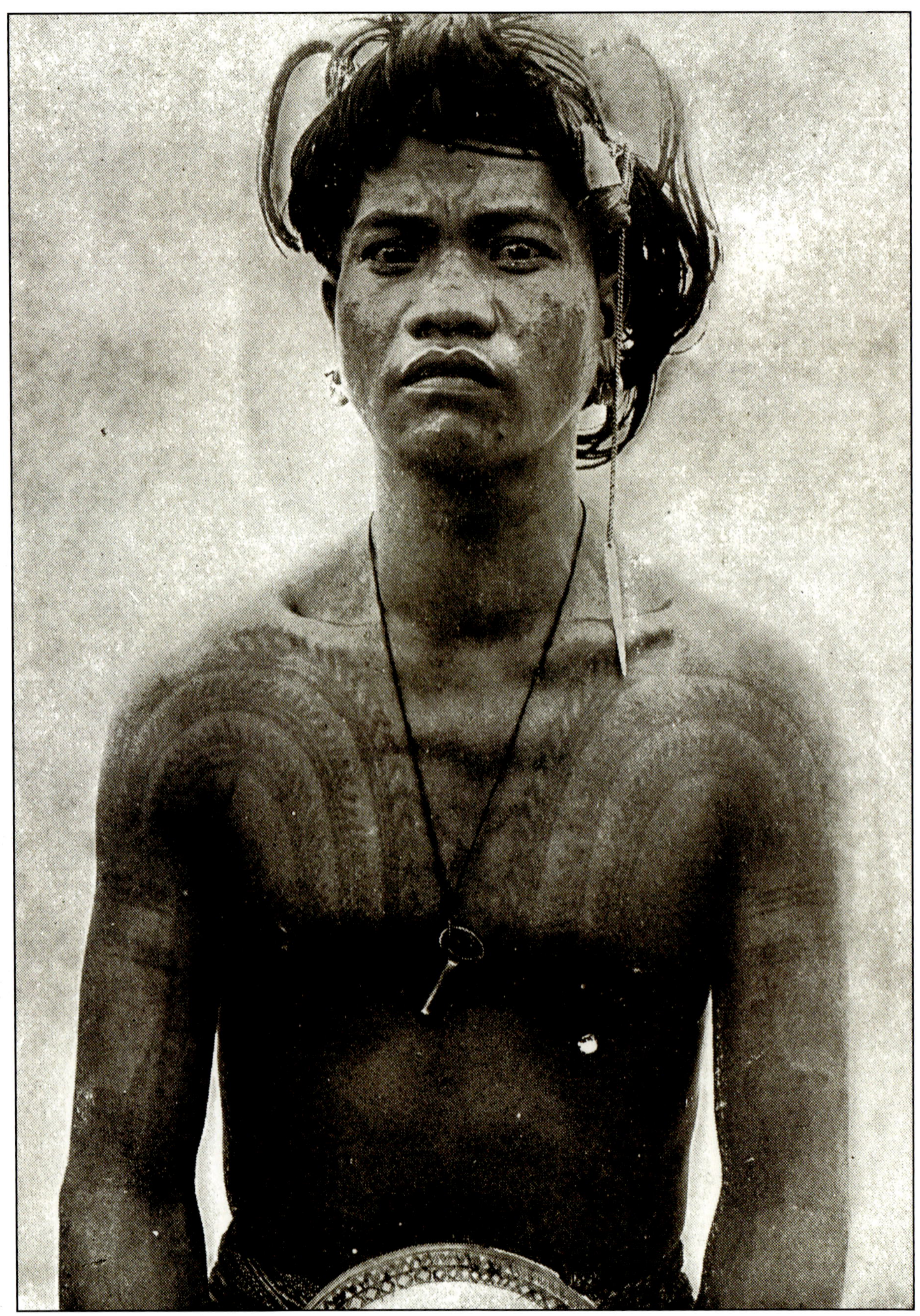

A Bontoc man with the pang-ti'i design as part of his chak-lag chest tattoo, circa 1905

Filipino Tattoos: Ancient to Modern

Pongo

Pongo were tattooed bands of various designs worn by both Bontoc and Ifugao peoples. Generally, they were worn around the arms by women in the Bontoc area.[162] Bontoc men sometimes wear *pongo*-like armbands, but these are usually called *fatek* and made with bolder lines and simpler patterns. *Pongo* tattoos were also worn by the Ifugao women. *Pongo,* or *pung-ngo,* in general refers to the arms, according to Manong Arthur B. Butic, a native Ifugao living in the United States. Manang Gabie M. Buduhan, another Ifugao immigrant in the United States, explains that in her dialect of Ifugao the word "*pongo*" could also be a corrupted form of "*pango,*" which refers to expensive neck beads worn by wealthy Ifugaos. The most expensive beads are called, in her dialect, *Achangyan;* each bead was made of gold rolled in amber.

The pongo tattoo refers to the affluence, wealth or prosperity of the wearer. Beads were often worn around the neck and also on the arms. To have pongo tattoos was like having expensive beads permanently adorning the skin. In fact, those who were abundantly tattooed were usually those who could afford to pay for their tattoos. There were several designs used for pongo tattoos, including triangles, plants, water, and diamonds.

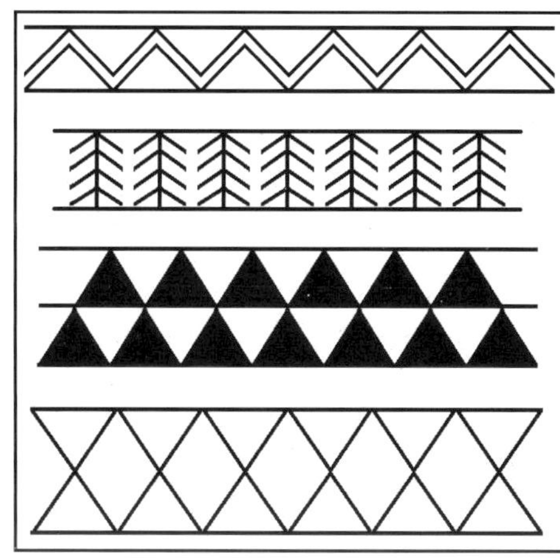

Various types of pongo tattoo patterns

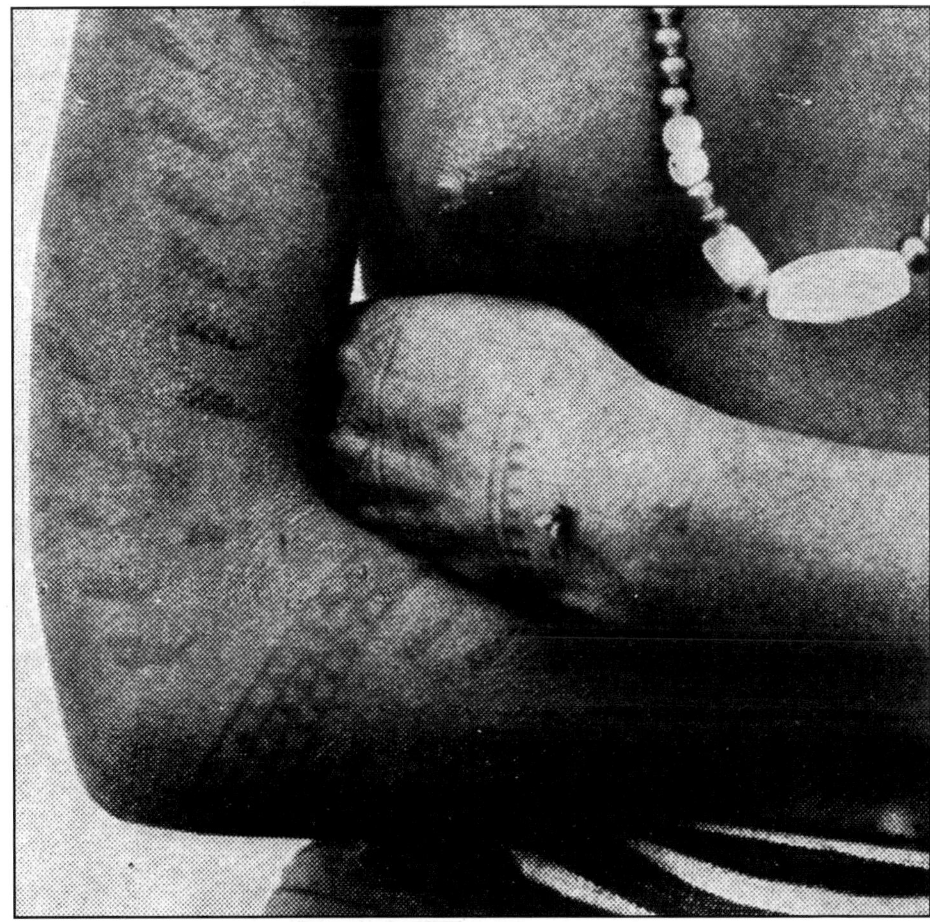

Detail of an Ifugao girl's arms with pongo designs. She also wears the al-alam design on her hand and the inangkid designs on her arms.

Scorpion

The Ifugao have different words for the scorpion depending on their area. Sometimes they are called "*alumpihan*," a term likely borrowed from the Tagalog word "*alupihan*." Another word for scorpion, in Ifugao, is "*ipi'ipit*," conveying the idea of its pinching ability. In some areas of Ifugao, such as in Kalanguya, the scorpion is called "*gayaman*," the same as the centipede, because both animals are aggressive and poisonous. In fact, the scorpion tattoo is designed to look like a shortened version of the *gayaman* (centipede) tattoo. Scorpion tattoos were placed on successful warriors of the Ifugao region in days past. According to Manong Hospicio Dulnuan, poisonous snakes, centipedes and scorpions in tattooing describe the person wearing them as being as deadly when he attacks, as the poisonous animals he has tattooed on his body. Therefore, the scorpion was a symbol of the warrior himself. Dulnuan also relates that people in general were cautious when dealing with a man adorned with this tattoo; its obvious symbol of his strength in battle accorded him their respect.

The scorpion tattoo added to a man's psychological strength and was an intimidation factor when dealing with an enemy. In addition, Manong Hospicio relates that Ifugao men depended on mumbaki prayers before going to war. He states, "Ifugaos also believe that the spirits of their

The scorpion tattoo motif and its animal counterpart

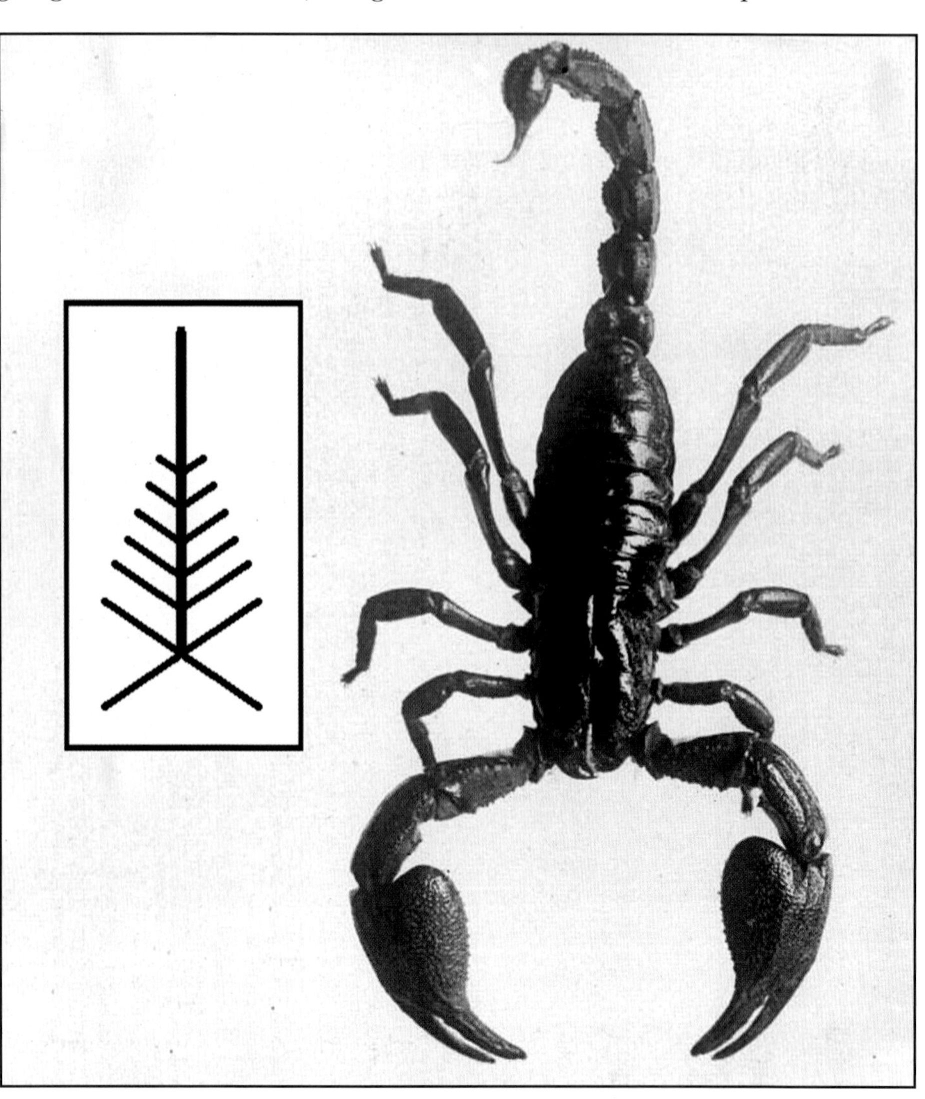

Filipino Tattoos: Ancient to Modern

ancestors play an important role in their lives; that is why the litany of ancestors' spirits is enumerated before a '*baki*' [prayer] is performed. In case of danger, a person shouts to the spirits of his/her parents and grandparents for help. This shout gives the person his fullest strength to fight and protect himself. Although the scorpion tattoo represents the strength of the warrior, it also, indirectly, represents the fullness of strength, protection and blessing from the spirits of a person's ancestors. Thus, the intimidation element of the scorpion tattoo was not just because of the strength of the warrior, but also the strength of the man's ancestor spirits.

Tattao/Tinagu

Tattao, or people tattoos, are distinctly anthropomorphic and easily recognized as human figures. Depending on their context, the human figures depicted represent ancestors, family, the person wearing the tattoo, or the victim of a headhunt. In Ifugao tattooing tradition, the human motif (see **figure A**) is often the victim of the headhunting raid, as numerous scorpion figures (raiding parties or warriors) surround the *tinagu*. **Figures B and D** represent dancing men celebrating the successful headhunt. These figures are tattooed with their bolo knives in their sheaths. **Figure C** was a tattoo found in the middle of mummy Apo Anno's back. Given its placement and Apo Anno's history of being a famous hunter, this tattoo represents either Apo Anno himself or an ancestor spirit. Below the tattoo on Apo Anno's back there are numerous tattoos of dogs. **Figure E** is another Benguet tattoo found on mummies in the Benguet region. Given its similarity to the Kalinga Ufeg design (**Figure F**), it is likely to have the same meaning of ancestors and family woven together. Figure F shows the Ufug design with *heads* to show the similarity.

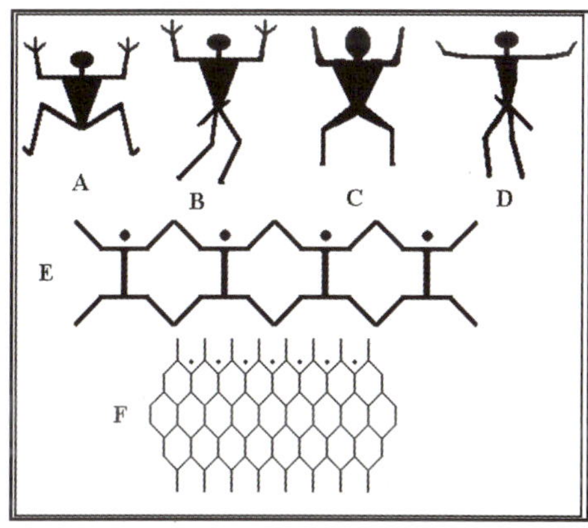

Various types of anthropomorphic tattoo designs, called Tattao or Tinagu

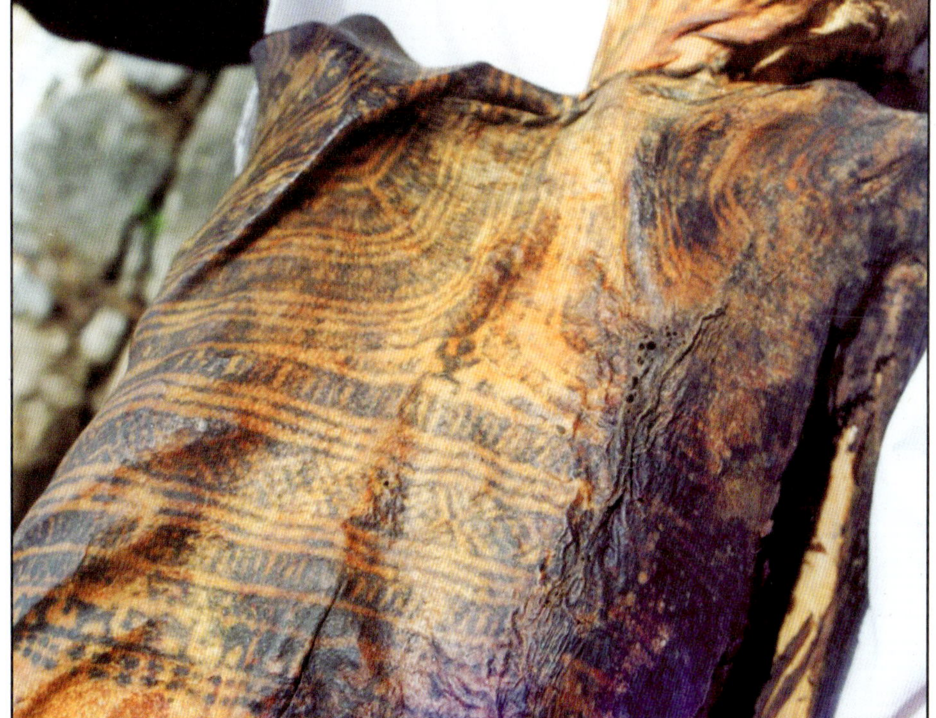

Note the human figure in the middle of Apo Anno's back. Photo by Art Tibaldo

Chapter 8

Modern Filipino Tattooing

The State of Filipino Tattooing Today

When Europeans colonized the Philippines and Pacific Islands, they introduced new social customs and religions that forbade tattooing. Little did these missionaries realize that in abolishing tattooing they were exterminating not only an art form, but also erasing a form of "written" history. Samoa was the only island archipelago in the Pacific Ocean that maintained a continuous tattooing tradition to the present time. To bring their tattooing cultures back from extinction, some Pacific cultures had to go through a cultural revival. Other islands have become so immersed in foreign-introduced ideologies that nearly all remnants of their tattooing culture has been extinguished. The same can be said of the Philippines.

After colonizing the islands, the Spanish went to great efforts to not only Christianize the native peoples but also to convert them to European culture. Many of the lowland peoples of the Philippines were quickly converted to the Catholic faith and were distinguished from their highlander relatives by the term "Indios," and later "Filipinos." Highlander peoples in Luzon who resisted Spanish assimilation became known as "Igorots."

Dok Natividad and family. Tattoo by Nick Arriesgado. Photo courtesy of Roy Arnaldo Cruz

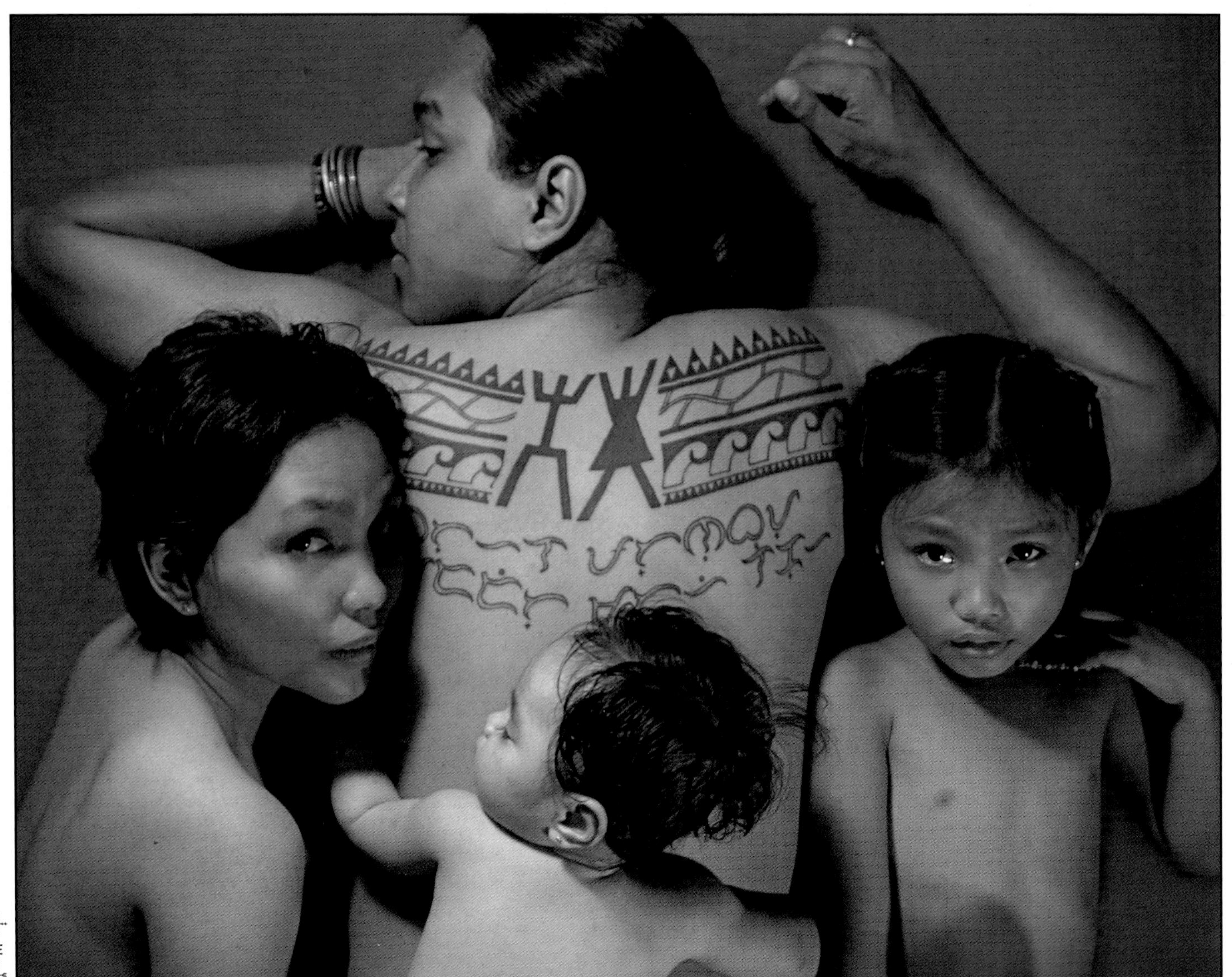

Filipino Tattoos: Ancient to Modern

Spanish invaders were effective in attaching stigmas to the people who maintained their traditions. As they and other nations colonized or invaded these islands, more and more traditional practices and beliefs were forsaken or changed to resemble European practices. Through the many years of foreign occupation, ideology and labeling, the native peoples of the Philippines began to think that there was not only a religious difference between the highland and lowland people but also a racial difference. Tattooing in the Philippine Islands came to be thought of as the practice of an uncivilized and less evolved race, and it has nearly faded from memory.

The last Cordilleran men who are marked with traditional tattoos earned them during World War II (1939-1945) by killing invading Japanese soldiers. At the time of this writing, they are few and in the deep autumn of their lives; the women who still possess tattoos are not far behind them. The last remaining traditional *manfattong* (female tattoo artists) of Luzon can be counted on one finger – Apo Maria Whang-Od. When she dies, the possibility of the extinction of this art form could potentially be realized. Tattooing in the Philippines, especially in the Cordillera, from ancient time until the mid-20th century, had great social, spiritual and aesthetic significance. Today, it should be treasured as not only as an art form but also as the proud marks of a fine heritage. Tattooing provided evidence of the wearer's achievements and visual reminders of the history of the people. Tattooing in the Philippines very literally illustrates the people's relationships to other Austronesians throughout the Oceanic region.

Contemporary Filipino Tattooing

In recent years, tattooing in Western societies has moved toward mainstream acceptance. What once was looked upon as a deviant practice is now gaining popularity as a form of self-expression. Motivations vary from individual to individual. Old and even stereotypical motivations for becoming tattooed still prevail. A desire to be identified with a particular lifestyle, to prove macho mettle, to look individualistic and unrestrained, or to display rebellion against the mainstream of society are strong incentives for some people to become tattooed. In contrast, the ancient perception of tattoos in Austronesian cultures showed a man's or woman's conformity and submission to cultural expectations, not rebellion. Many Filipinos still see tattoos through "Western" eyes that, through the indoctrination of foreign ideologies, particularly among older generations of Filipinos, perceive tattoos as deviant or the marks of criminals. Many groups in the Philippines have been separated so long from their tattooing heritage that the motifs and patterns have been lost. Now, as tattooing in Western society gains popularity as a form of self-expression, the new acceptance of tattoos has bled over to the Philippines through global communication. As a consequence, there are Filipinos who want to be tattooed, and among them are many who are looking for icons or motifs to define them as uniquely Filipino.

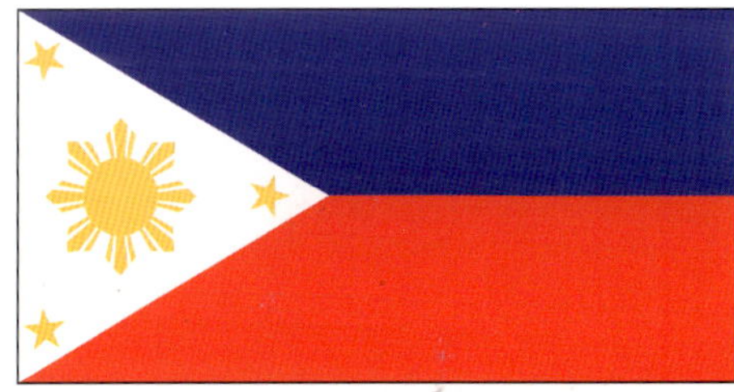

The Flag of the Philippines

An icon popularly chosen as a tattoo today is the depiction of the current flag of the Philippines. Variations of the flag's sun and three stars are tattooed in different artistic settings. The Philippine sun, with eight rays, represents the eight provinces that rebelled against Spain; the three stars represent the three main island groups: Luzon, Visayan Islands and Mindanao.

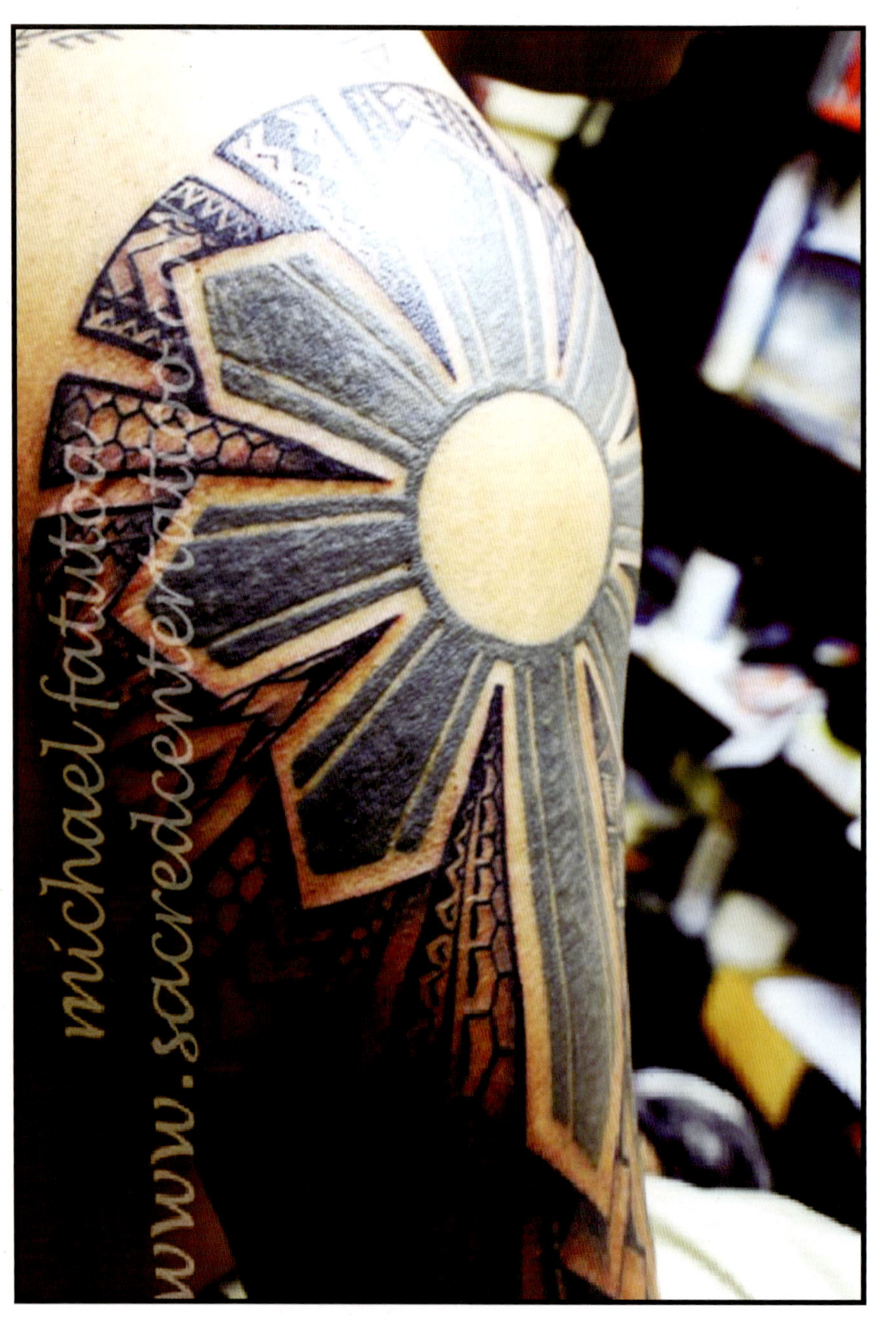

A stylized Filipino sun motif surrounded by Polynesian and Philippine motifs. Tattoo by Michael Fatutoa of Sacred Center Tattoo

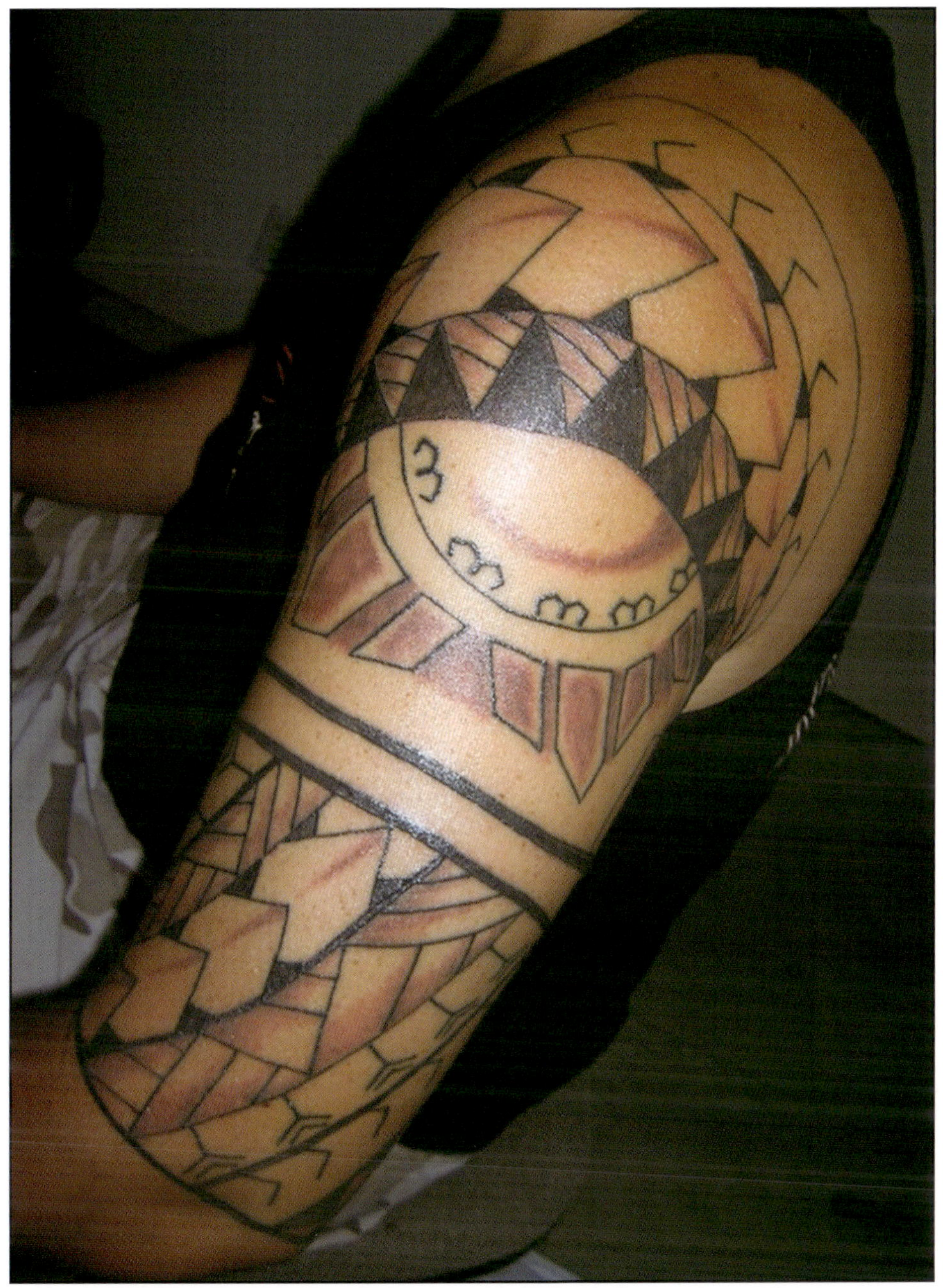

An abstracted Filipino sun motif in a new tribal setting with stylized Philippine motifs. Tattoo by Rodney Alconcel of Bong's Tattoo Shop

Baybayin Tattoos

A popular trend among Filipino Americans is the application of tattoos written in the script indigenously known as "*Baybayin,*" but is more commonly called "*Alibata,*" a Filipino approximation of the word "alphabet" that was coined by Paul Versoza in the early 20th century. The Baybayin script is a phonetic writing style thought to be derived from old Javanese and Indonesian scripts, or having a common origin as these scripts. It was formerly inscribed on bamboo tubes and leaves, as well as ceramics and metal. According to some scholars, it may have been introduced to the Philippines sometime prior to the 9th century, perhaps during the expanse of the Sri Vijayan empire of Indonesia. During this period, the Sri Vijayan empire had ports and small outposts in the Philippines, from Mindanao in the south to Manila in Luzon. Baybayin script was used by many peoples of the Philippines who, over time, developed their own styles of writing. One reason we know that the script was not indigenous, but was introduced to the Philippines, is that until the Spanish modified the script, it did not represent all the sounds of the Philippine languages, especially the final consonant, such as in the word "*langit*" (heaven). In Baybayin script, "*langit*" would have been written as "*la-ngi,*" without the vowel closing consonant "t" at the end. When the Spanish began colonizing the Philippines and converting the natives to Christianity, they introduced the modifier "+" to the script that, when placed under an individual symbol, changed the usual vowel that accompanied symbol to represent a consonant.

The Baybayin phonetic script

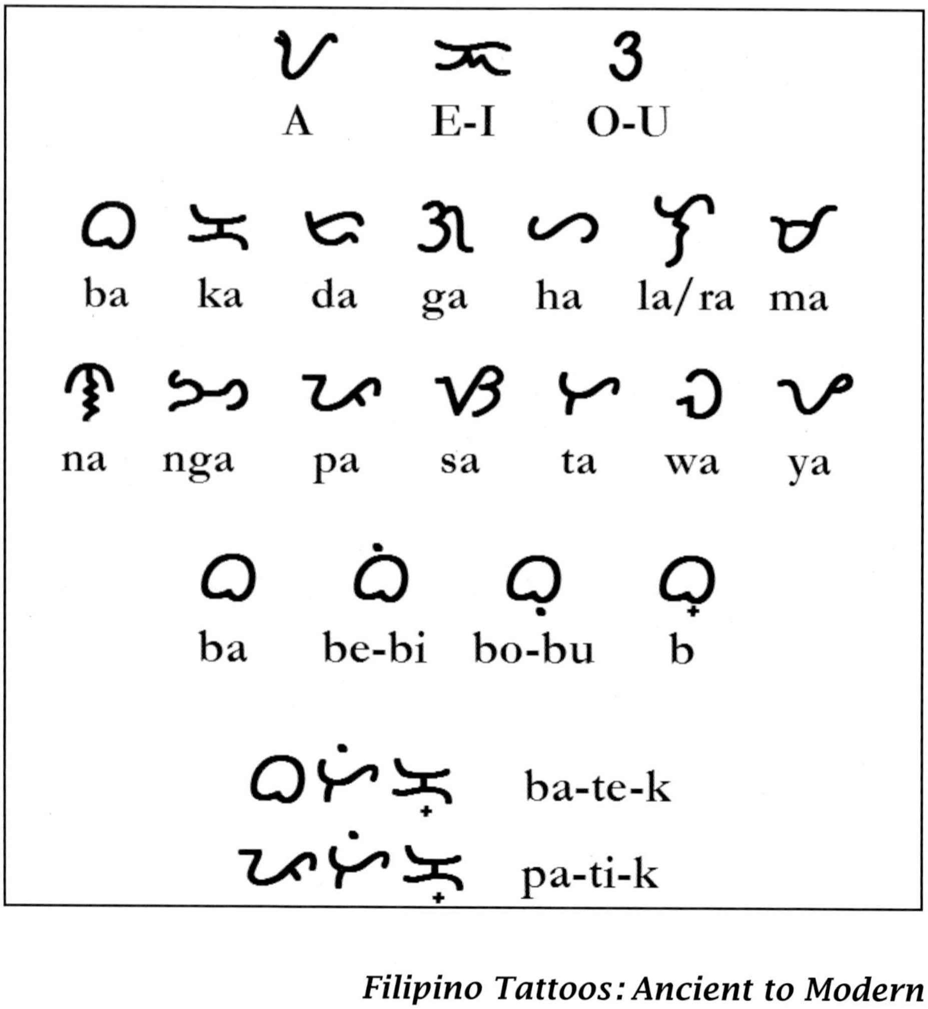

Filipino Tattoos: Ancient to Modern

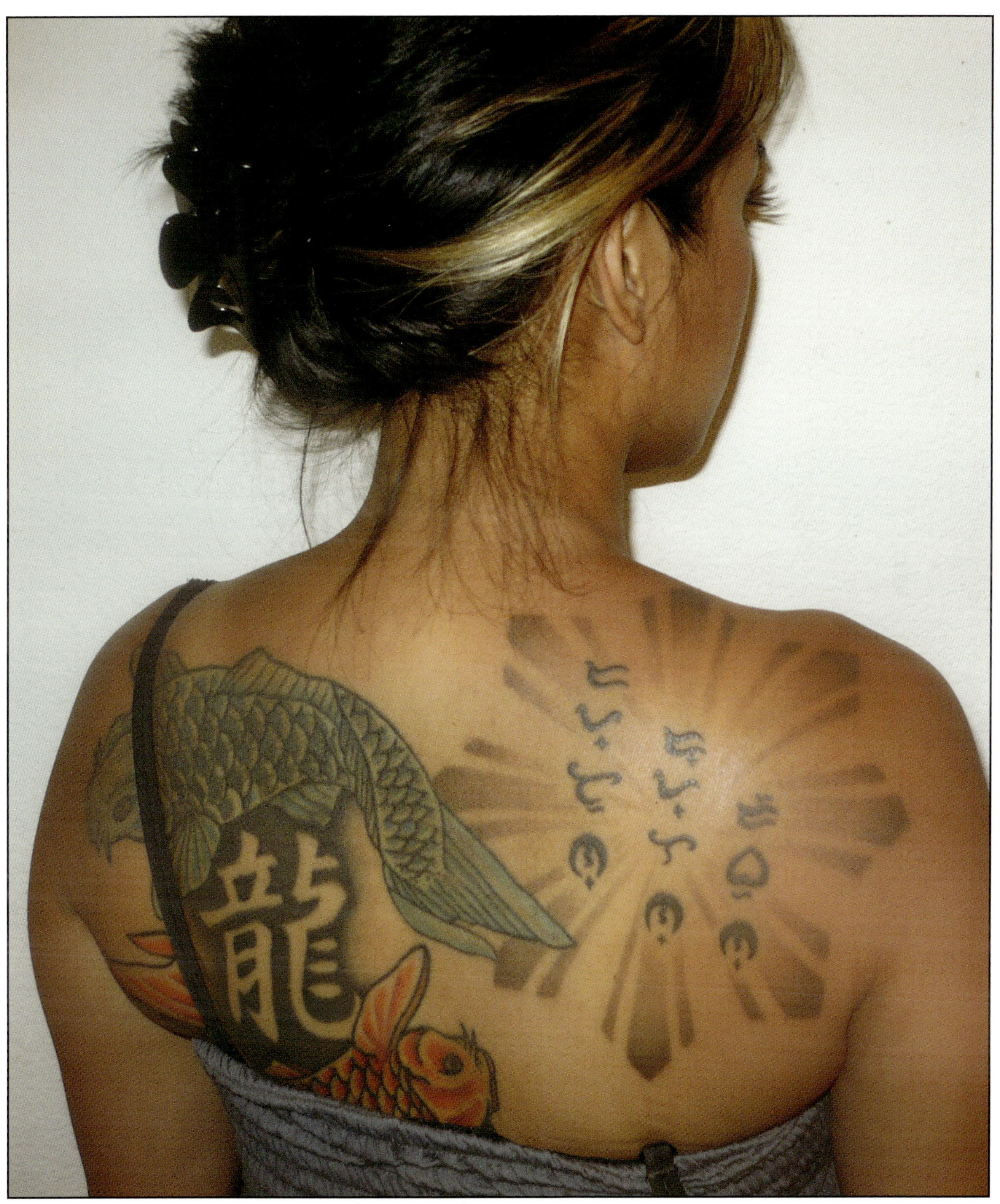

The Author's cousin Lani Damo's tattoo of a Filipino Sun incorporating Baybayin -Tattoo by Chad Cadiente.

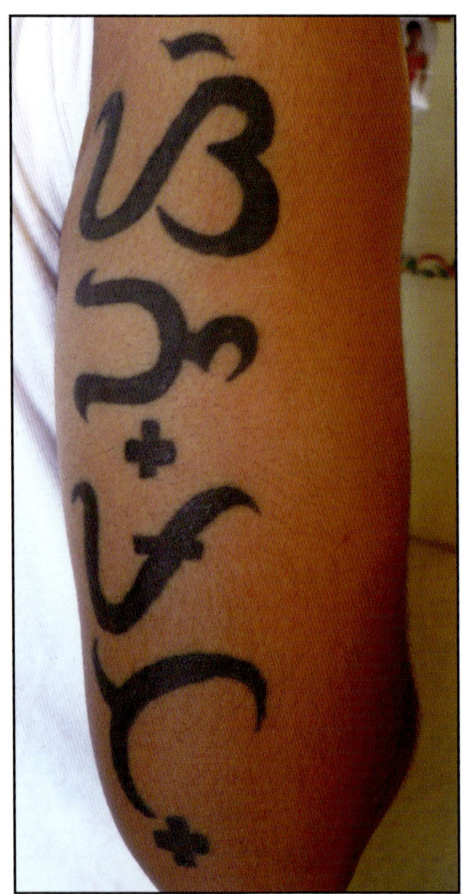

The Baybayin tattoo of Claudell Duldulao

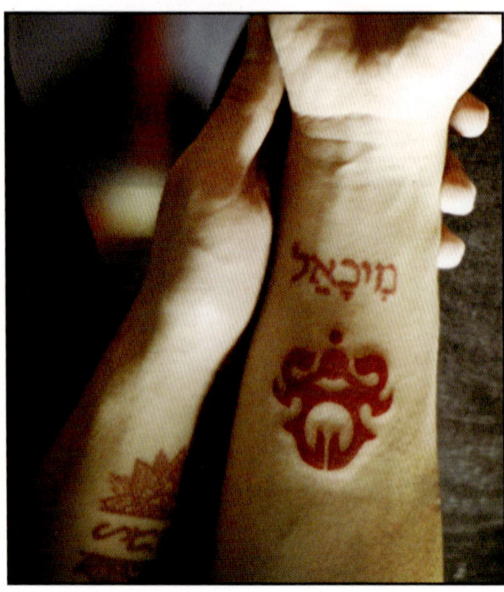

The lingling-o tattoo of Mikhail Quijano. "I designed this [tattoo] based on the basic shape of the Ifugao ornament called the lingling-o, said to bring fertility and supernatural powers to the wearer. It symbolizes many things: courage, the balance of male-and-female energies, and the social standing of the bearer. According to some sources, it also passes through a ritual where the ornament is bathed in blood. Perhaps its most significant meaning is that the bearer's anitos – spirits of their ancestors – may reside in the lingling-o. So here it is, bathed in blood as in the rituals, to mark the end of a tough year. This is for courage, for balance, and for fertility and harvest. This is for all my loved ones who have gone ahead, that they may stay with me forever and guide my hand with what they have taught me." – Mikhail Quijano

The Baybayin script was generally used for commerce, to record transactions such as the Laguna copper plate inscription, discovered in 1989 in Laguna de Bay. The script also may have been used to record important historical events or beliefs.

In the present time, the Hanuno'o of Mindoro still use a version of the Baybayin script. According to one source, the Hanuno'o also inscribed the script onto the skin in the past, but it is unclear whether this was actually tattooed or simply printed on the skin. Since Baybayin was normally inscribed, without using ink, on bamboo and leaves, it is difficult to conclude if it was actually tattooed. Due to the popularity of Chinese and Japanese symbols (*kanji*) as tattoos, many Filipinos have used Baybayin as the Philippine equivalent of *kanji* for tattoos. Certainly, the flowing lines of baybayin make beautiful tattoos and they have become quite popular. Words, such as "*ina*" (mother) or "*ama*" (father), are common as well as the names of children.

Lingling-o Tattoos

Another popular tattooed emblem seen today among Filipinos is the lingling-o, which are commonly described as fertility symbols representing the reproductive organs of a woman. Lingling-o are worn as prestige ornaments in necklaces and earrings made of gold, silver and brass. There are various designs of lingling-o, but most incorporate a C-shaped structure which opens at the base of the ornament. The term "lingling-o" was first recorded by H. Otley Beyer and may be a form of the word for earring in Bontoc, *seng-seng*.[163] Among the peoples of the Cordillera in Luzon, lingling-o are also known as *pinangpanga*, *pinangaan*, *dinumug*, *pinayakan*, etc. and are worn by both men and women as ear ornaments and necklaces. Some groups in the Cordillera string groups of these ornaments together with black thread and wear them in rows around the base of the neck. When strung together as a necklace they are called *balituk* or *uway*. According to Virgil M. Apostol, the origin of the lingling-o most likely comes from India, and derived from the *yoni-linga* sculptures that represent female and male genitals, although often the male's portion of the sculpture is significantly reduced in size in comparison to the female portion.

Similar ornaments have been found in Indo-China, Malaysia, and Indonesia. The *mumuli* of Indonesia is a similar ornament worn as a pendant. It is a great deal larger than the brass, silver or gold lingling-o ornaments of the Philippines. Although the lingling-o is a popular tattoo motif in the present, it was not tattooed in the past. However, it has become an icon in Filipino or Luzon use, and is sometimes incorporated in "new tribal tattoo" compositions. In addition to being used as a tattoo symbol, the ling-lingo has been reproduced in many graphic designs, from business logos to t-shirts and stickers. In recent years, the lingling-o ornament has been mass-produced for commercial consumption by tourists and Filipinos abroad.

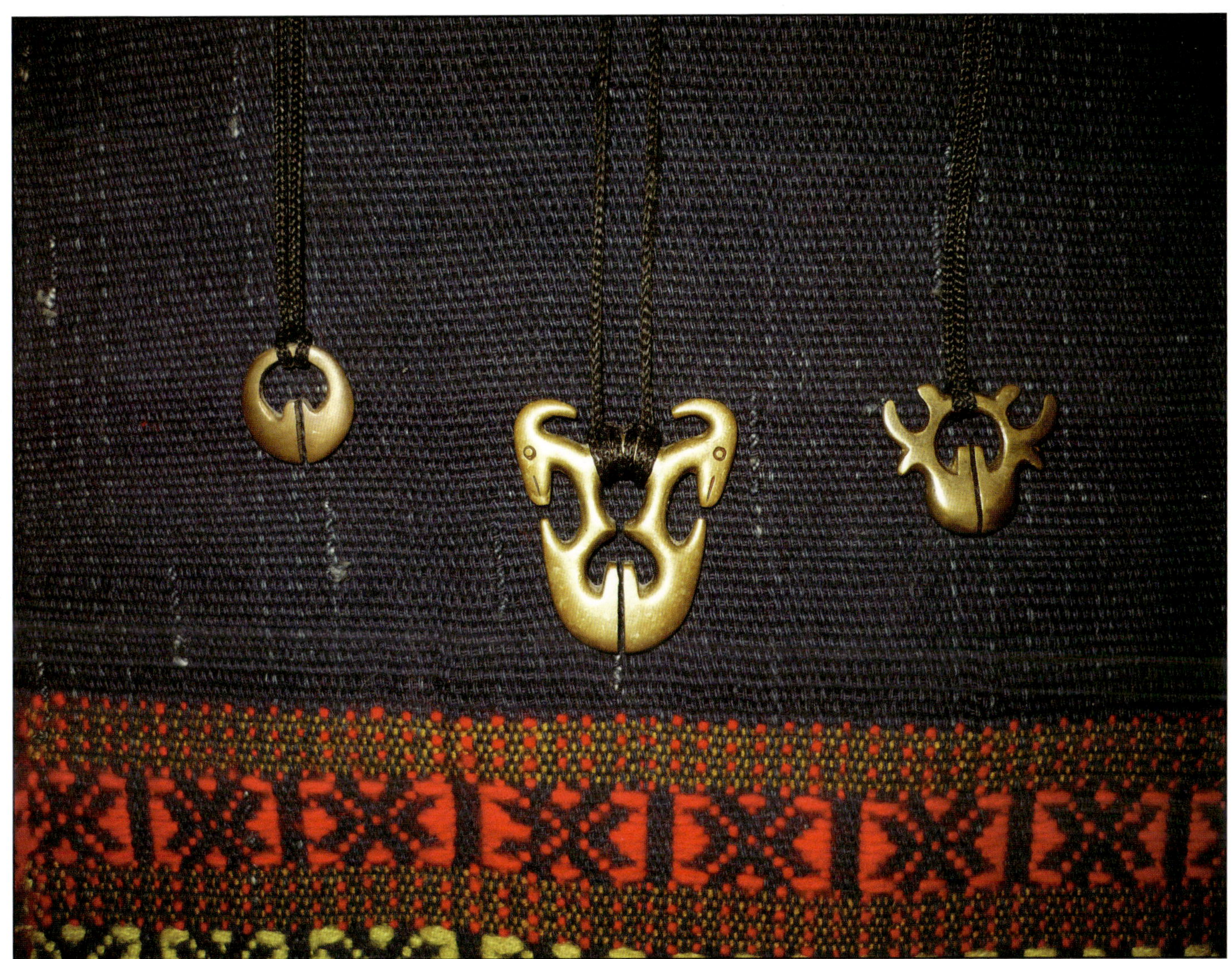

Examples to different types of lingling-o ornaments. Author's collection

New Tribal Tattoos

A popular contemporary form of tattooing is the so-called "tribal look" or "new tribalism." This tattooing style is based largely on old indigenous designs from Polynesia, Micronesia and Southeast Asia. Sometimes the indigenous styles are mixed together to represent a person's mixed ancestry or for aesthetic appeal. Hawaiian-raised, Filipino Leo Zulueta, in the late-1970s, began designing tattoos as stylized versions of traditional tattoos from Southeast Asia and the Pacific Islands. In tattooing these designs (many of which were on the verge of extinction), Leo hoped to preserve the beautiful traditions. His work has raised the awareness of many tattooing traditions from the Austronesian region and inspired others to research their own ancestral tattoos. Because of his pioneering example of cultural preservation, Leo is considered the "Father of Modern Tribal Tattooing."

While this style originated with Leo Zulueta, it has taken on a life of its own. "Tribal tattooing" has rapidly grown in popularity over the last two decades, yet tattooists unfamiliar with the ancient art usually place the designs out of context, since very little of the nature of these symbols is understood. Since traditional tattooing in much of Austronesia

Modern Filipino Tattooing

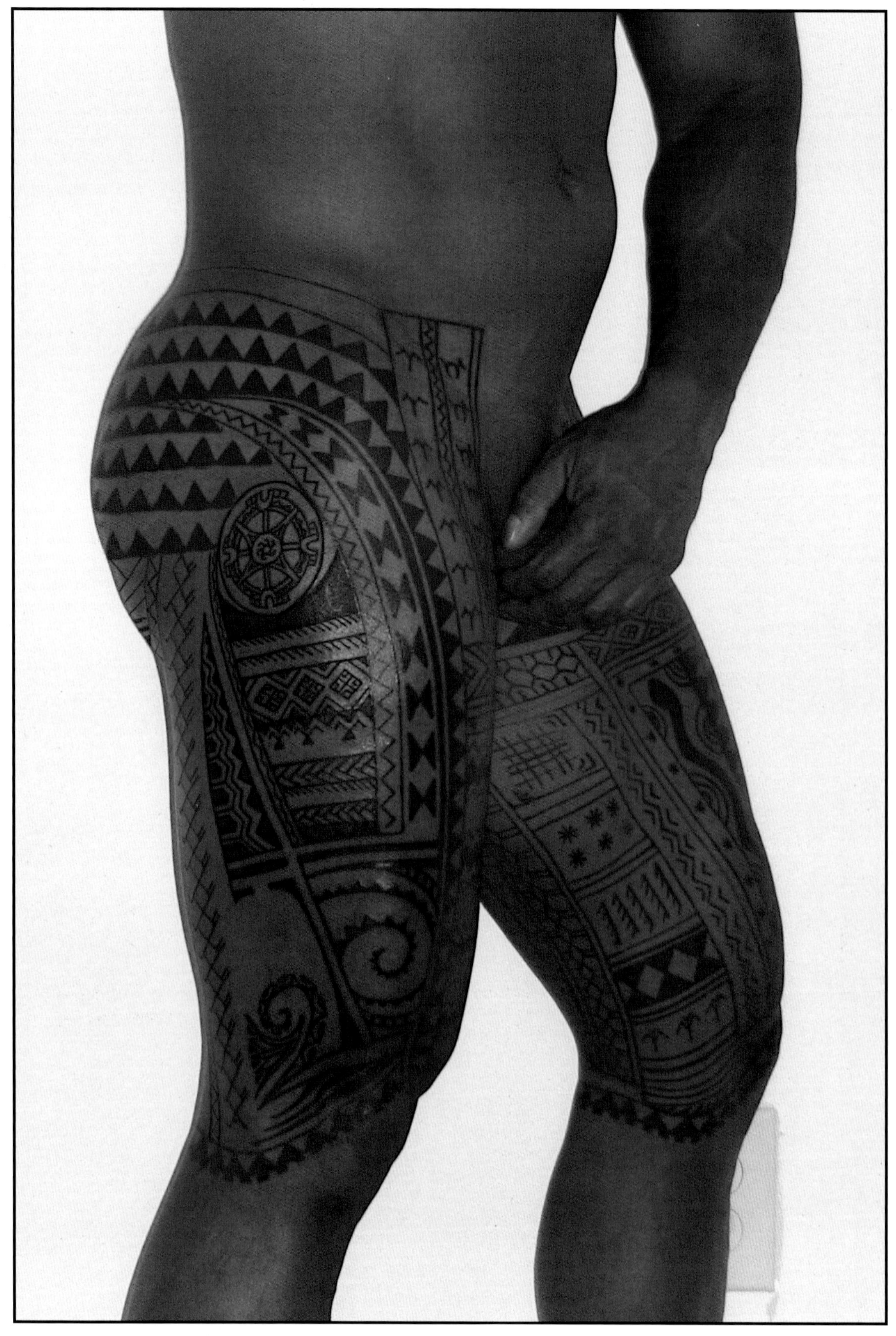

A modern burik worn by Derrick T. based on the drawings by Hans Meyer. Tattoos by Glen Fontilles, Clay Mees and Dennis Mata'asa.

Filipino Tattoos: Ancient to Modern

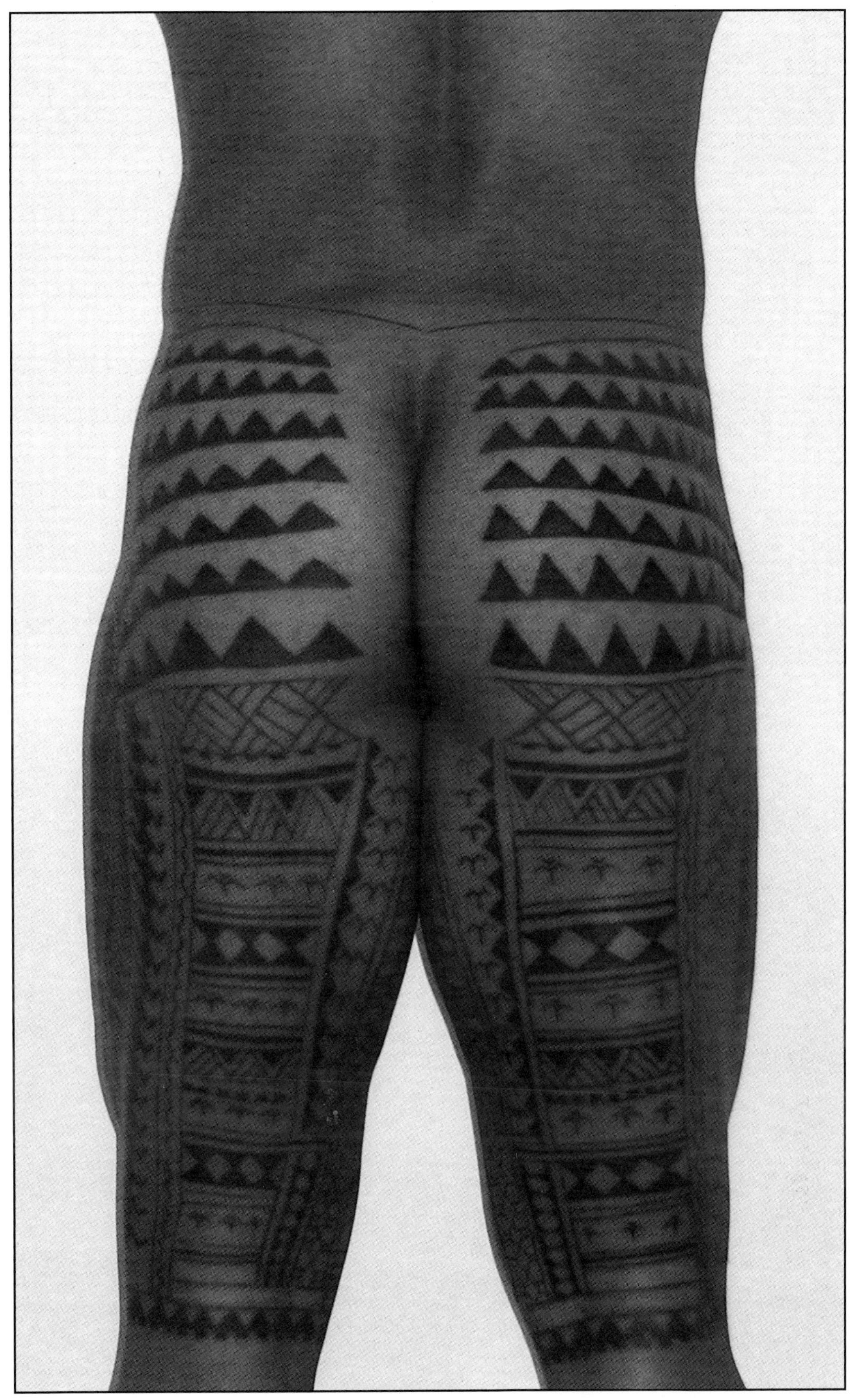

Another view of Derrick's modern burik. Courtesy of Derrick T.

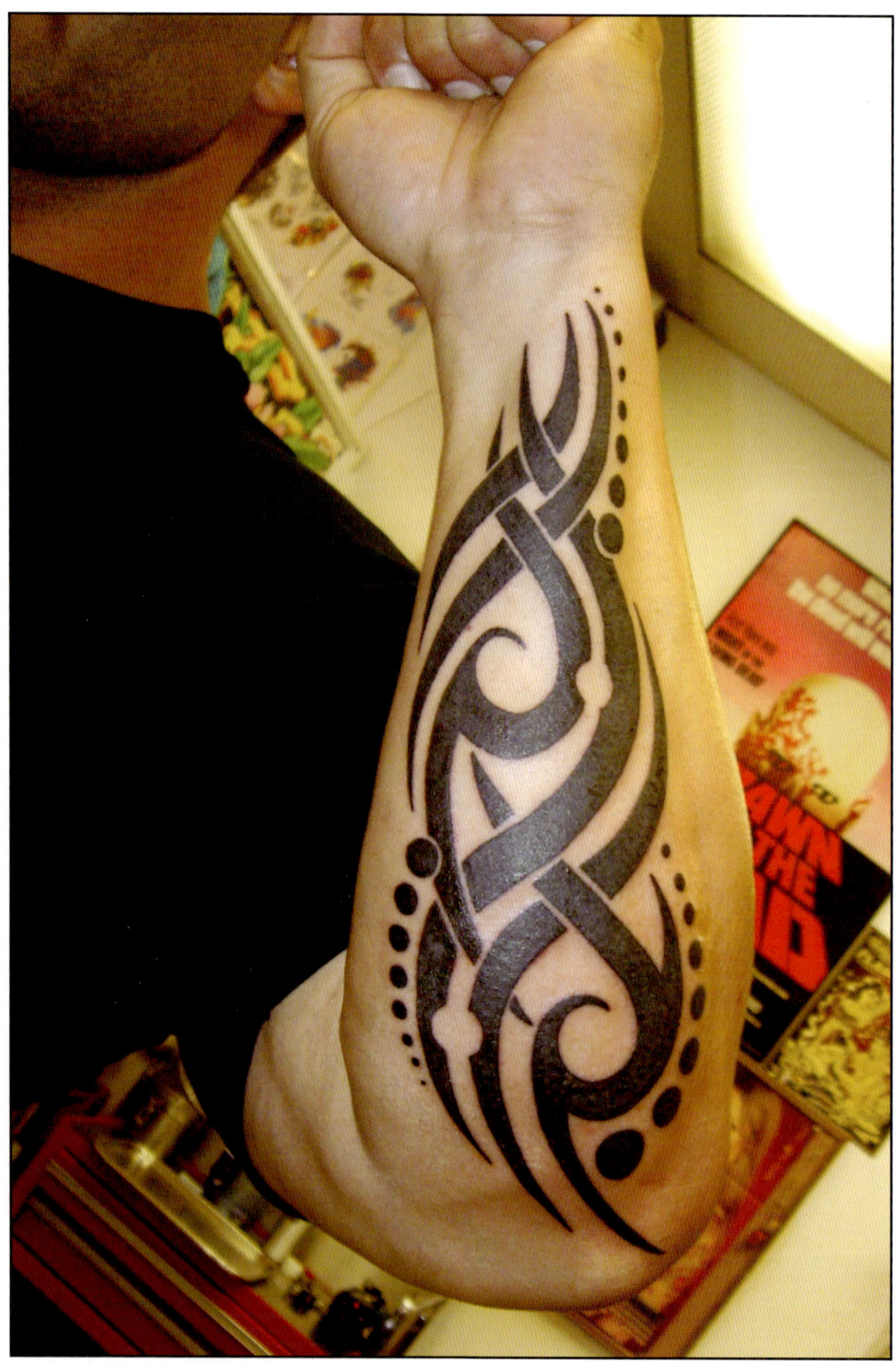

New tribal blackwork popularized by Leo Zulueta. Tattoo by Suluape Angela Bolson

Filipino Tattoos: Ancient to Modern

has largely waned or become extinct due to westernization, the modern "tribal" tattoo now has come full circle and is worn by the descendants of the very peoples who originally inspired the modern art. Due to its popularity, others have sought to emulate the trend by creating "tattoo flash" of these sacred designs. ("Tattoo flash" is a drawn or printed copy of a tattoo design on paper, made strictly to be sold.) Often new tribal tattoos are stylized versions or copies of tattoos used by indigenous peoples. Although one cannot dictate what one person or another puts on their body, it is important to have respect for the history of the designs and their inherent value to the society they came from.

An Old Bontoc Tattooing Tradition

There were two young men who were the very greatest of friends. One day they decided to tattoo each other. One tattooed the other beautifully. He tattooed his arms and his legs, his breast and his belly, and also his back and face. He marked him beautifully all over, and he rubbed soot from the bottom of an olla (clay pot) into the marks, and he was then very beautiful. When the tattooist finished his work he turned to his friend, and said: "Now you tattoo me beautifully, too".

So the young men scraped together a great pile of black, greasy soot from pitch-pine wood; and before the other knew what the tattooed one was doing, he had rubbed soot over him from finger tip to finger tip. Then the black one asked: "Why do you tattoo me so badly?"

Without waiting for an answer they began a terrible combat. When, suddenly, the tattooed one was transformed into a large lizard, the fa-ni'-as, and he ran away and hid in the tall grass; and the sooty black one became the gay-yang, the crow and he flew away and up over Bontoc, because he was ashamed to enter the village after quarreling with his old friend.[164]

[Author's note: In the spirit of the story of Fanias and Gay-yang, and after all I had learned, I felt it was my responsibility to write this book to prevent others from being *tattooed badly*. There is a lot of misinformation about Filipino tattoos. In this work I have tried to show tattooing similarities and differences among various Austronesian cultures. In the desire for traditional body markings, some Filipino individuals who were ignorant of our own tattooing heritage have been tattooed with Hawaiian, Samoan or Maori designs etc. Sometimes because of the close similarity of Austronesian tattoos, some people have assumed it was appropriate for them to wear tattoos of other cultures and claim they are Filipino. I have met individuals with tattoos who are distinctly Marquesan from French Polynesia who were under the impression that the designs were Filipino. Other people have seen unique personal tattoo creations on Filipino individuals and assumed that the motifs or designs were traditional. In an effort to create awareness of the different styles, the following modern examples of some of the popular tattooing styles of the Pacific are offered.]

There is an increasing popularity among Filipino people today to be tattooed with traditional motifs seen in old photographs or copied from patterns seen on some of the remaining tattooed Kalinga or Bontoc peoples of the Cordillera. Caution should be exercised in copying traditional designs. If a tattoo design derives from the Philippines, that does not mean it is acceptable for any person from the Philippines to wear it. A person

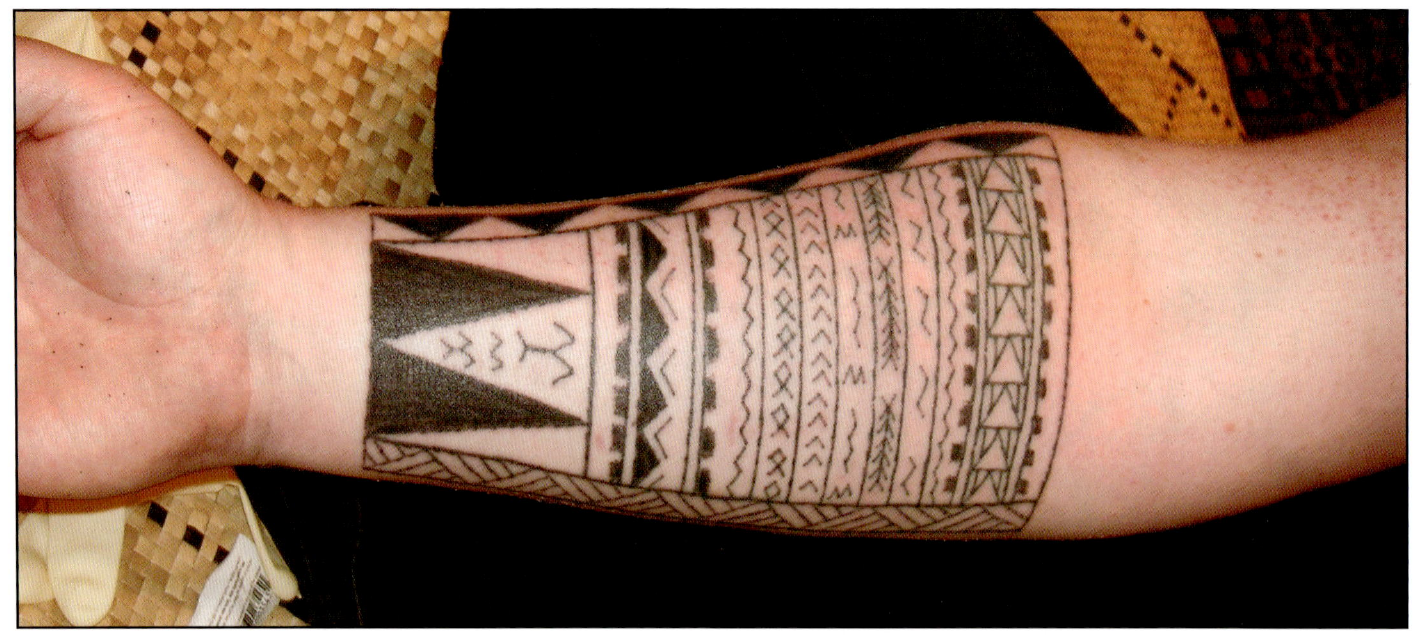

Modern tattooing using Samoan motifs and designs hand-tapped by Suluape Angela Bolson

who recklessly copies designs without knowing their meanings can make embarrassing errors on their skin. For example, on certain occasions men have been seen wearing female tattoo symbols, such as Manobo women's breast tattoos on their arms, just because they saw the design in a magazine or book. Also, some tattoo designs are specific to certain ethnic groups of the Philippines. To some it is inappropriate to wear an ethnic-specific design when that person does not belong to that ethnic group, has no affiliation to that group or does not qualify to wear that design based on their life experience. The ancients believed that tattooing marked not only the body but the spirit as well. So within this context, a person wearing a specific design would be recognized by their specific ancestors after they died. Wearing tattoos that did not belong to you would in effect *alienate* you from your ancestors and possibly sever communication with them. The lesson here is that in reverence to your own ancestors, great care and respect should be exercised in what you decide to do with your body. You are the product of generations of people leading up to you.

Below and opposite: Modern tattooing using Marquesan patterns by Suluape Angela Bolson

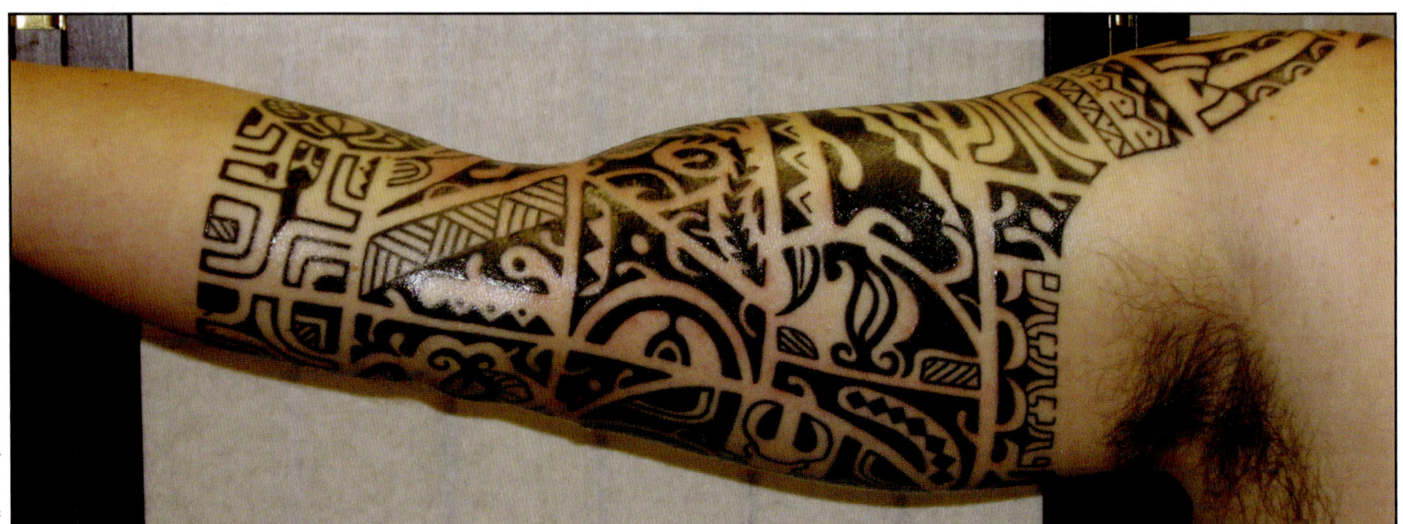

Filipino Tattoos: Ancient to Modern

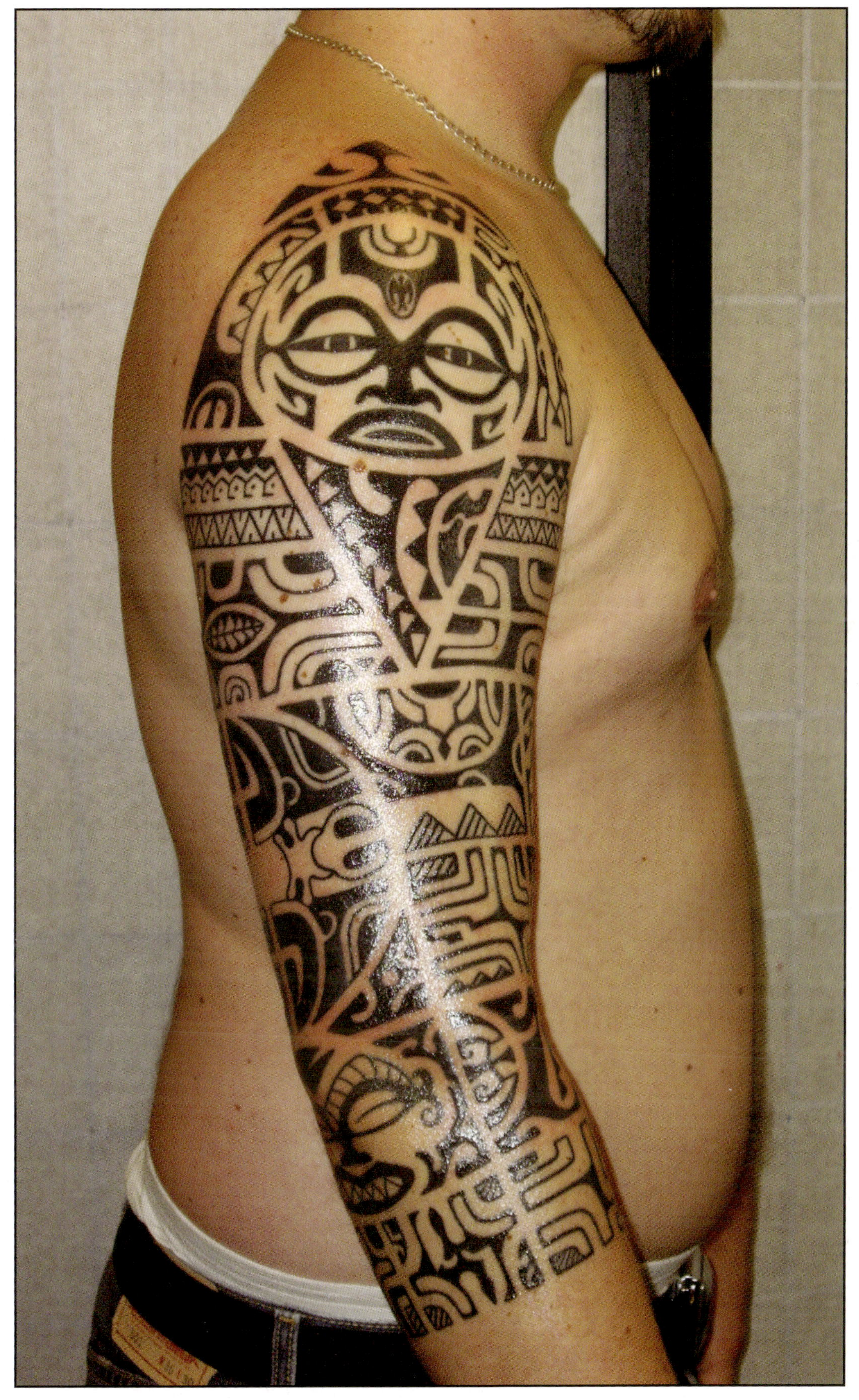

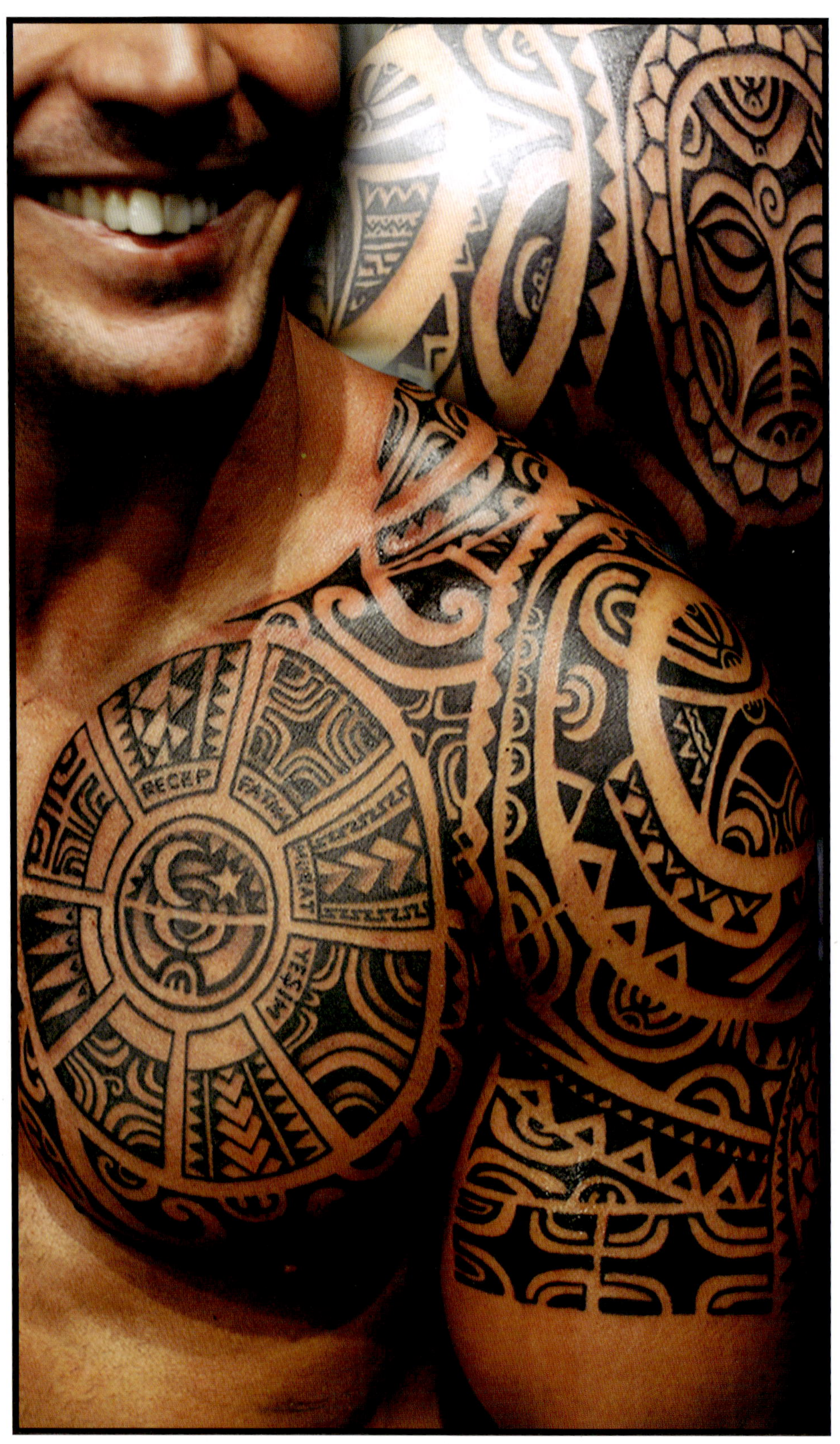

Modern tattooing using Marquesan patterns by Michael Fatutoa of Sacred Center Tattoo

Filipino Tattoos: Ancient to Modern

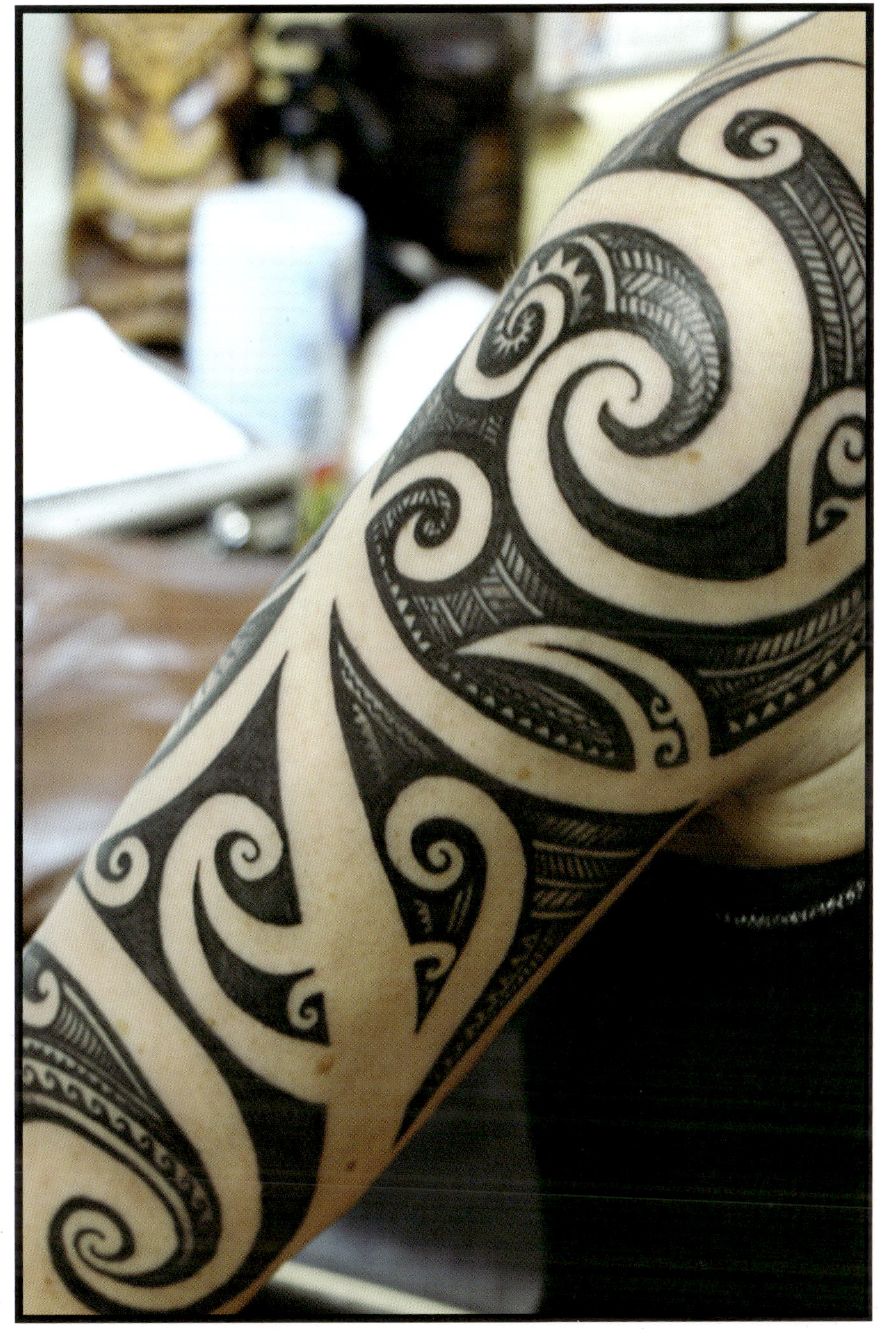

Modern tattooing using Maori designs by Michael Fatutoa of Sacred Center Tattoo

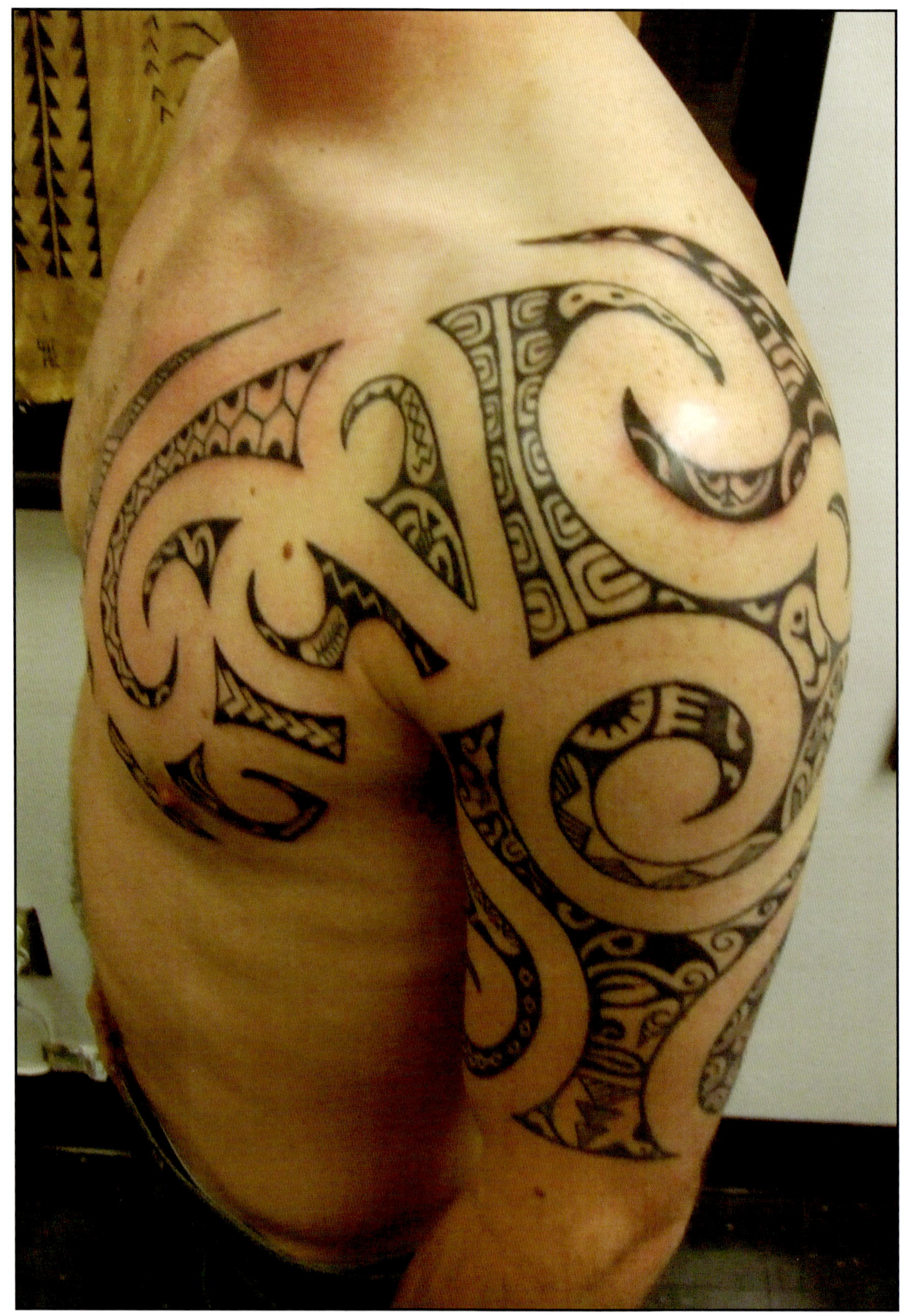

A Pan-Polynesian fusion of different styles by Suluape Angela Bolson

Filipino Tattoos: Ancient to Modern

The following section relates personal stories and images of a few individuals who have chosen to share their experiences and tattoos. Please be respectful and do not dishonor them or yourself by copying their tattoos. Rather, let their stories and designs inspire you on your own journey.

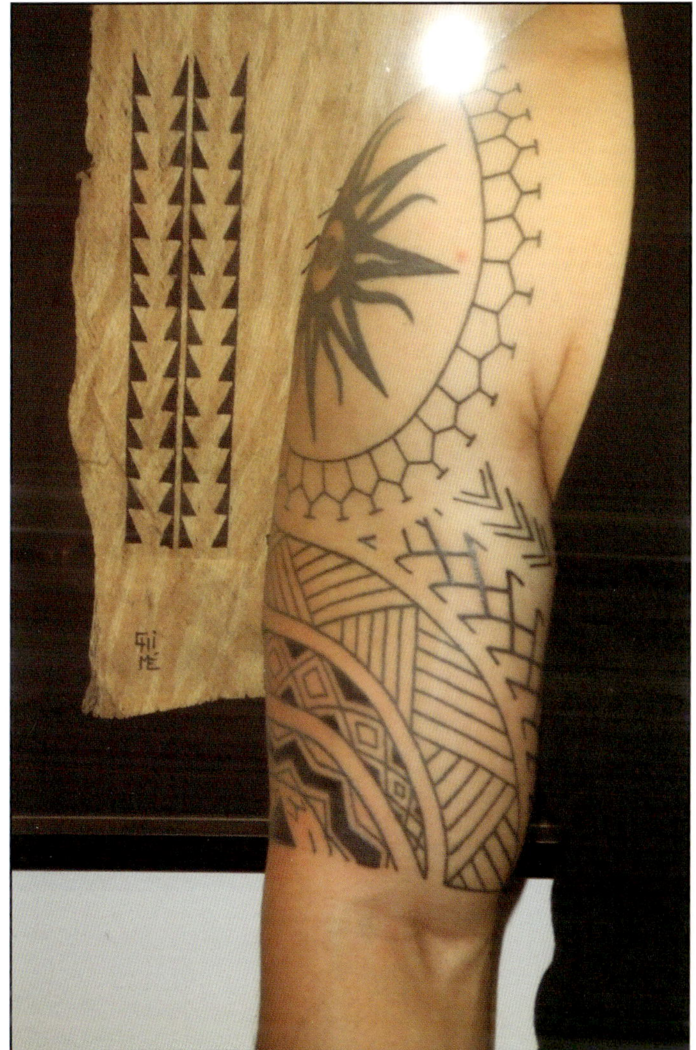
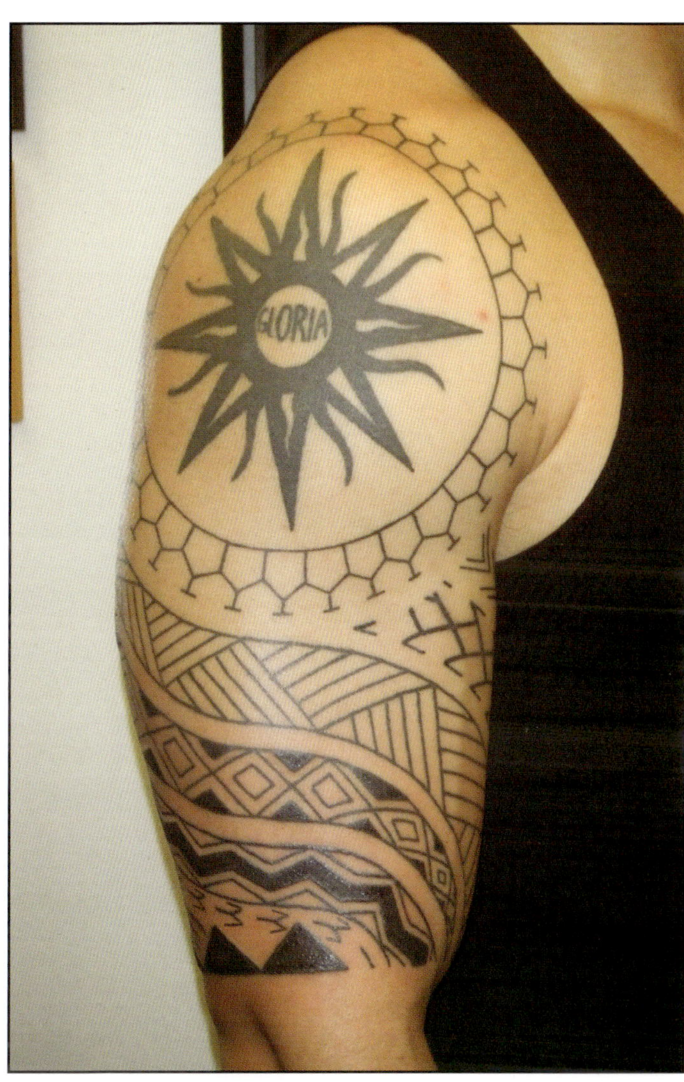

Pages 133-135: A modern composition of traditional motifs and designs from the Philippines for a Filipino-American soldier serving overseas. Tattoo by Suluape Angela Bolson

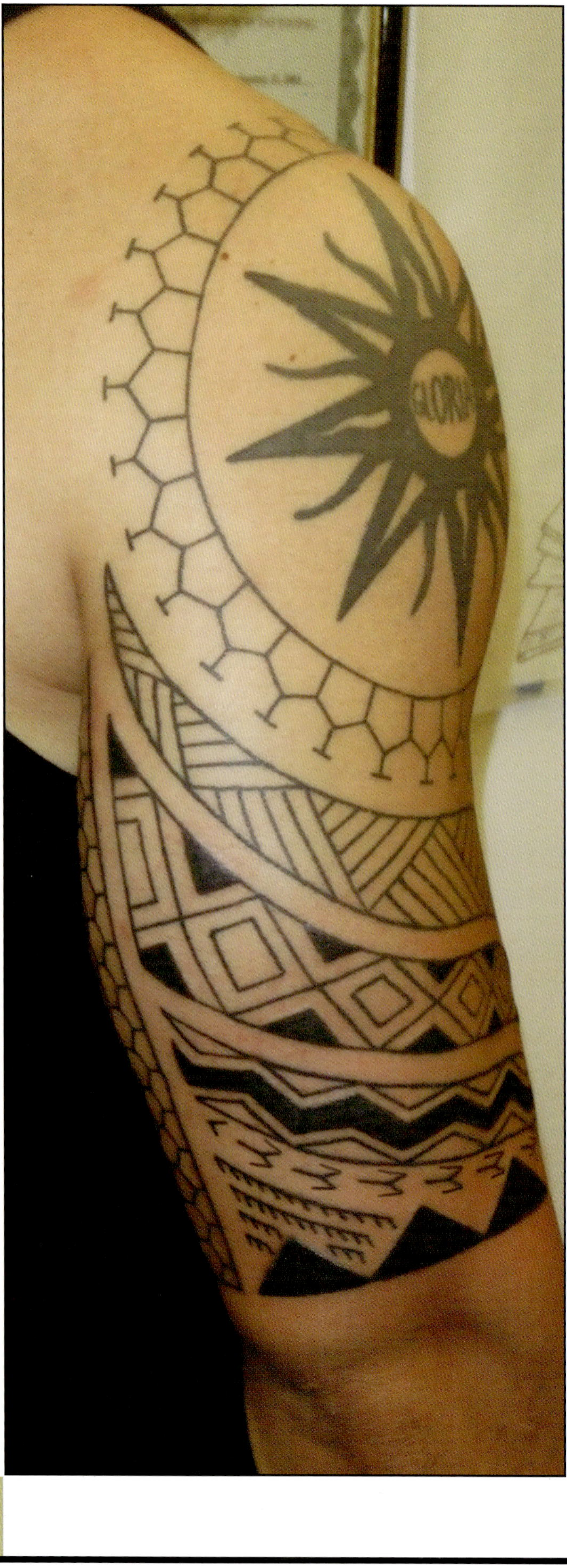

Filipino Tattoos: Ancient to Modern

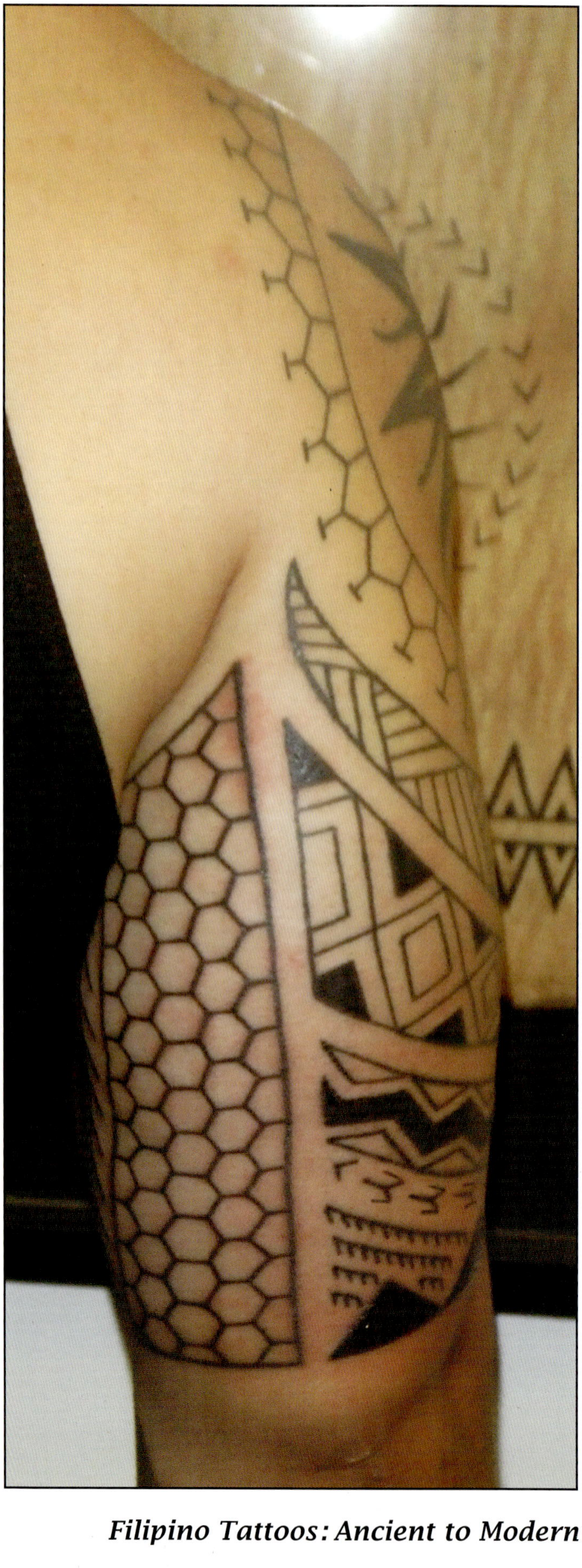

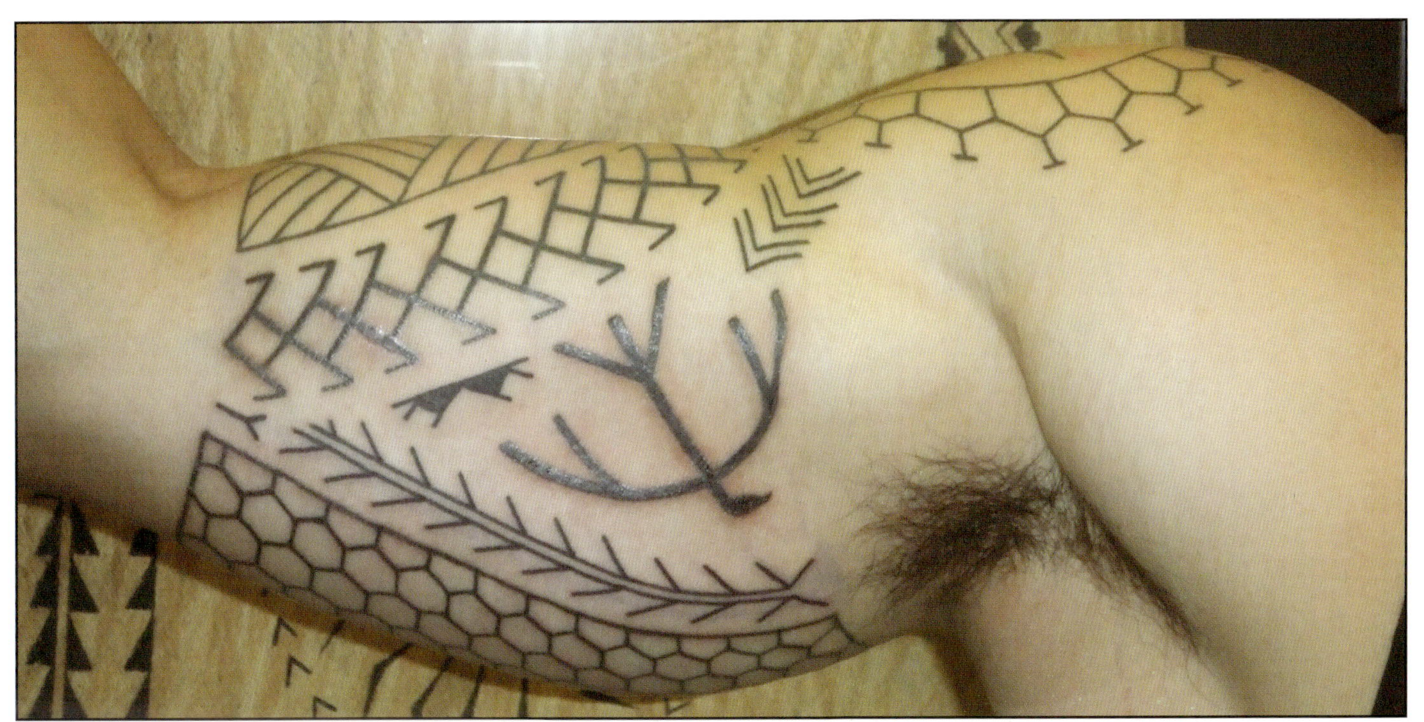
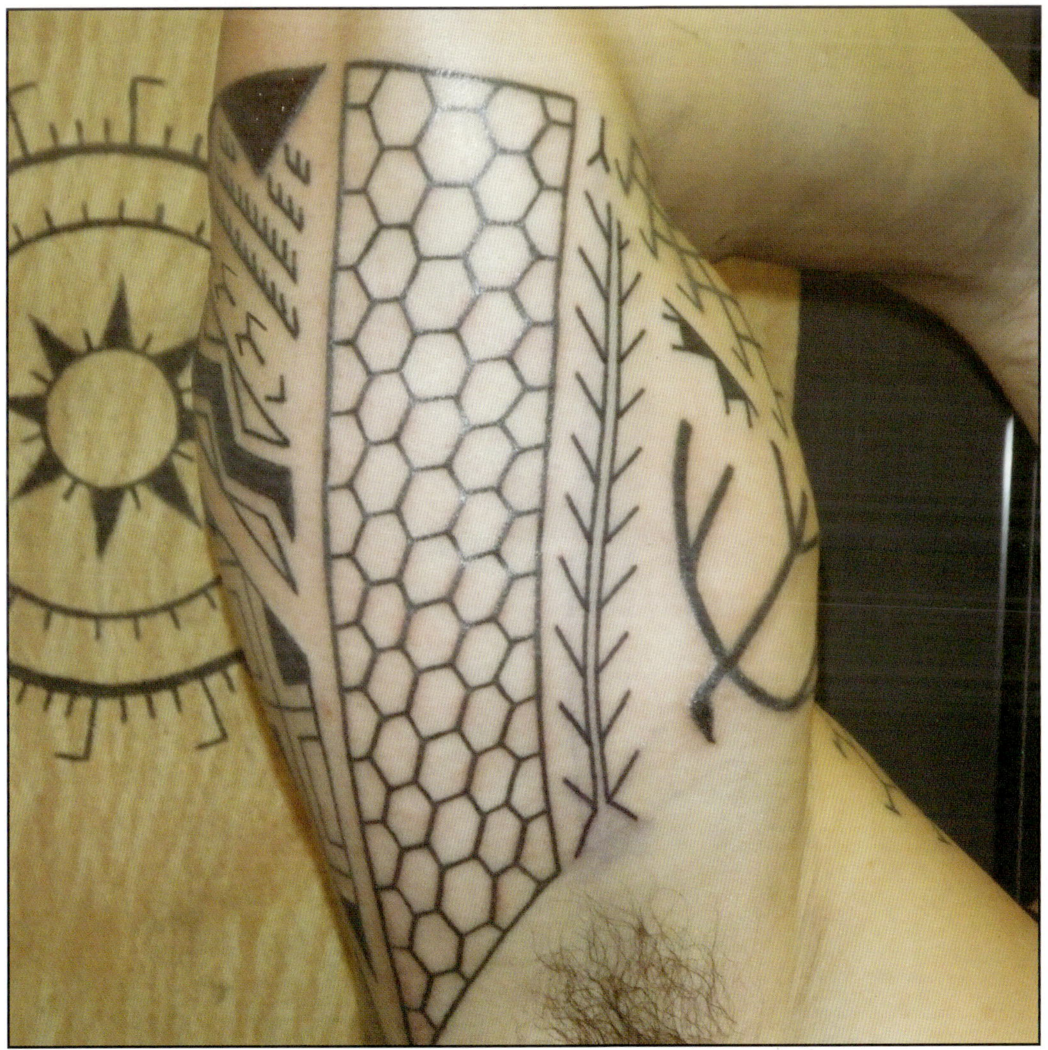

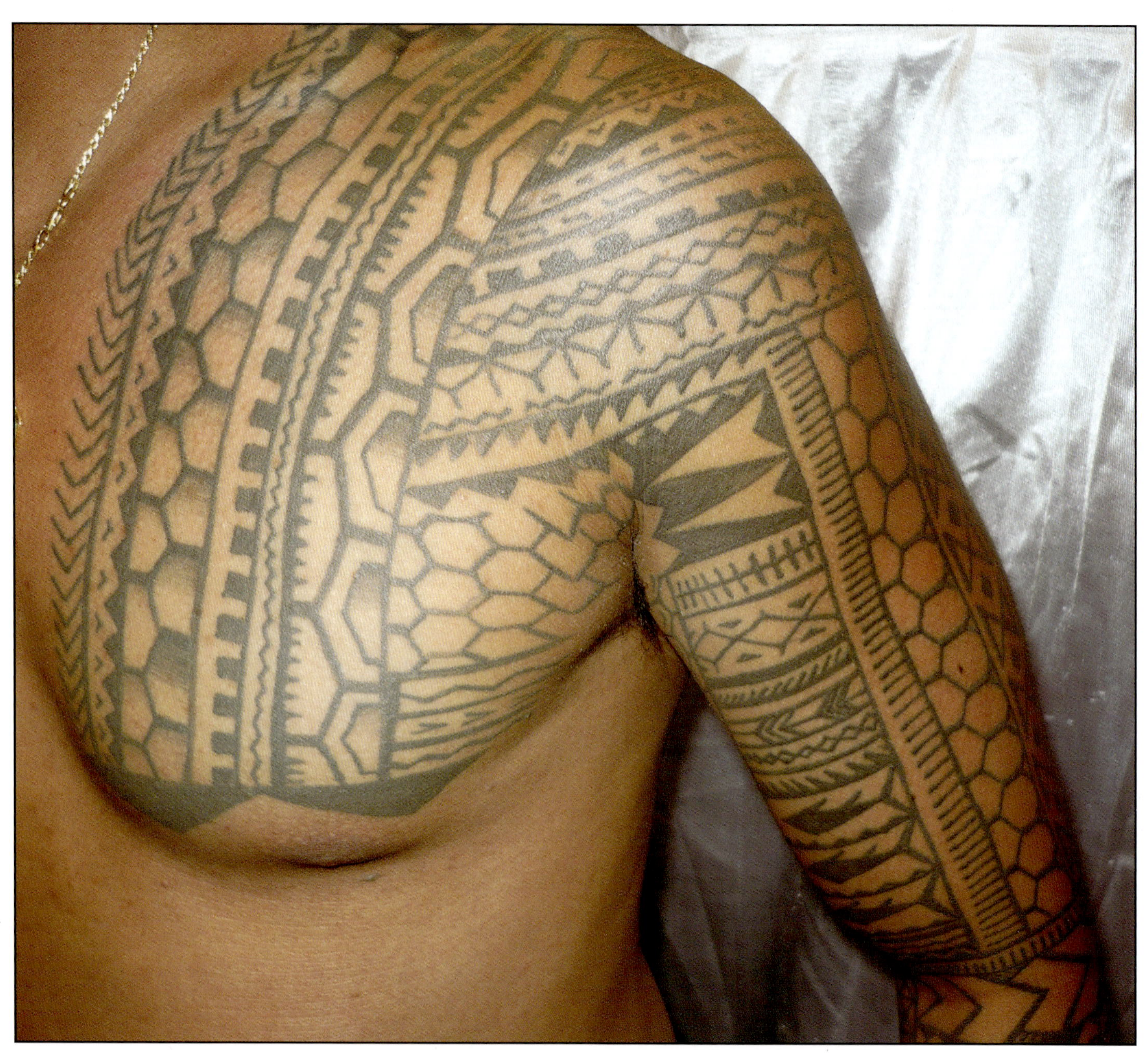

Above and opposite: Tiny's modern Filipino tattoo composition using traditional Filipino designs and a few Polynesian motifs. Tattoo by Michael Fatutoa of Sacred Center Tattoo

Filipino Tattoos: Ancient to Modern

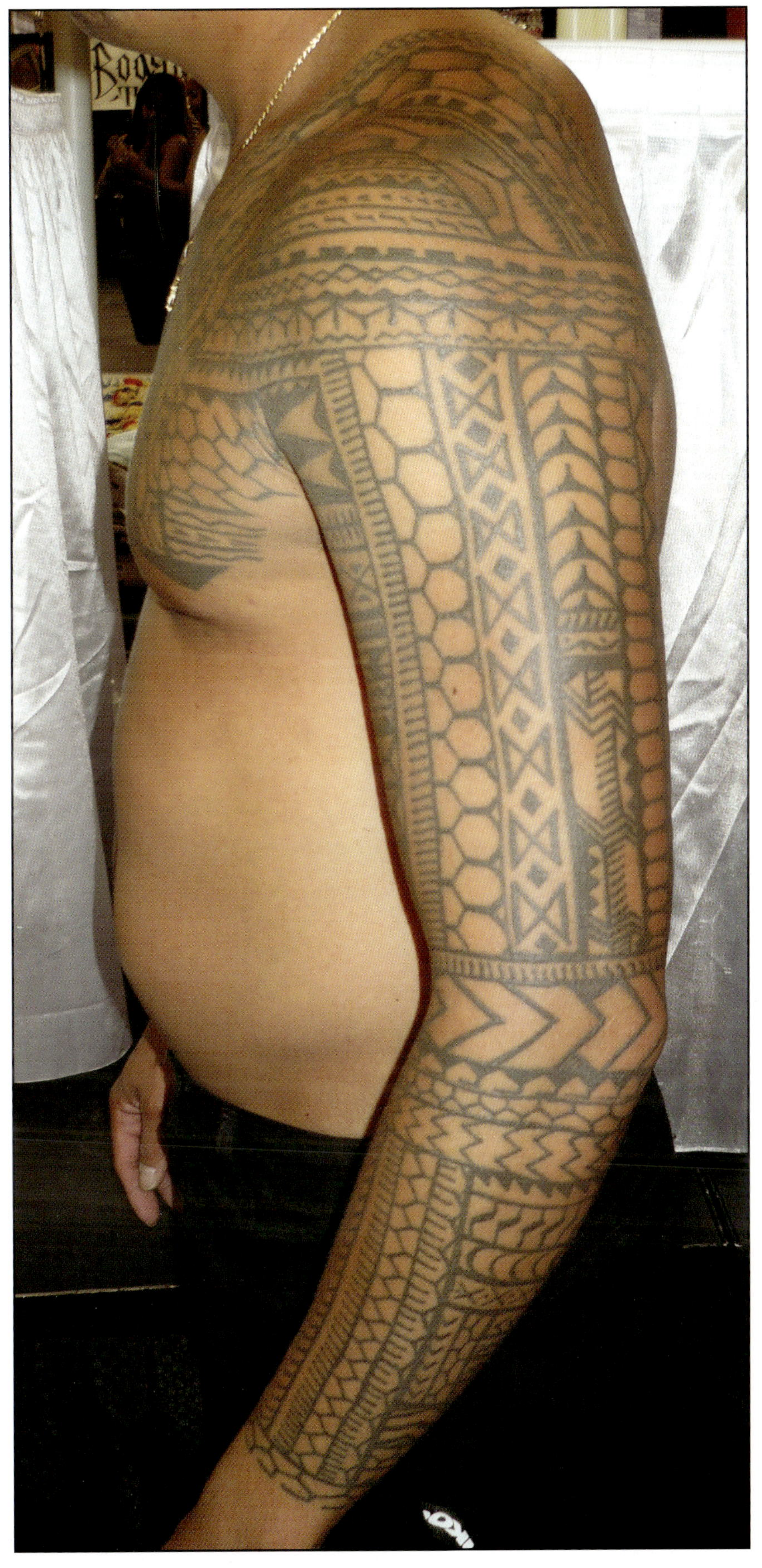

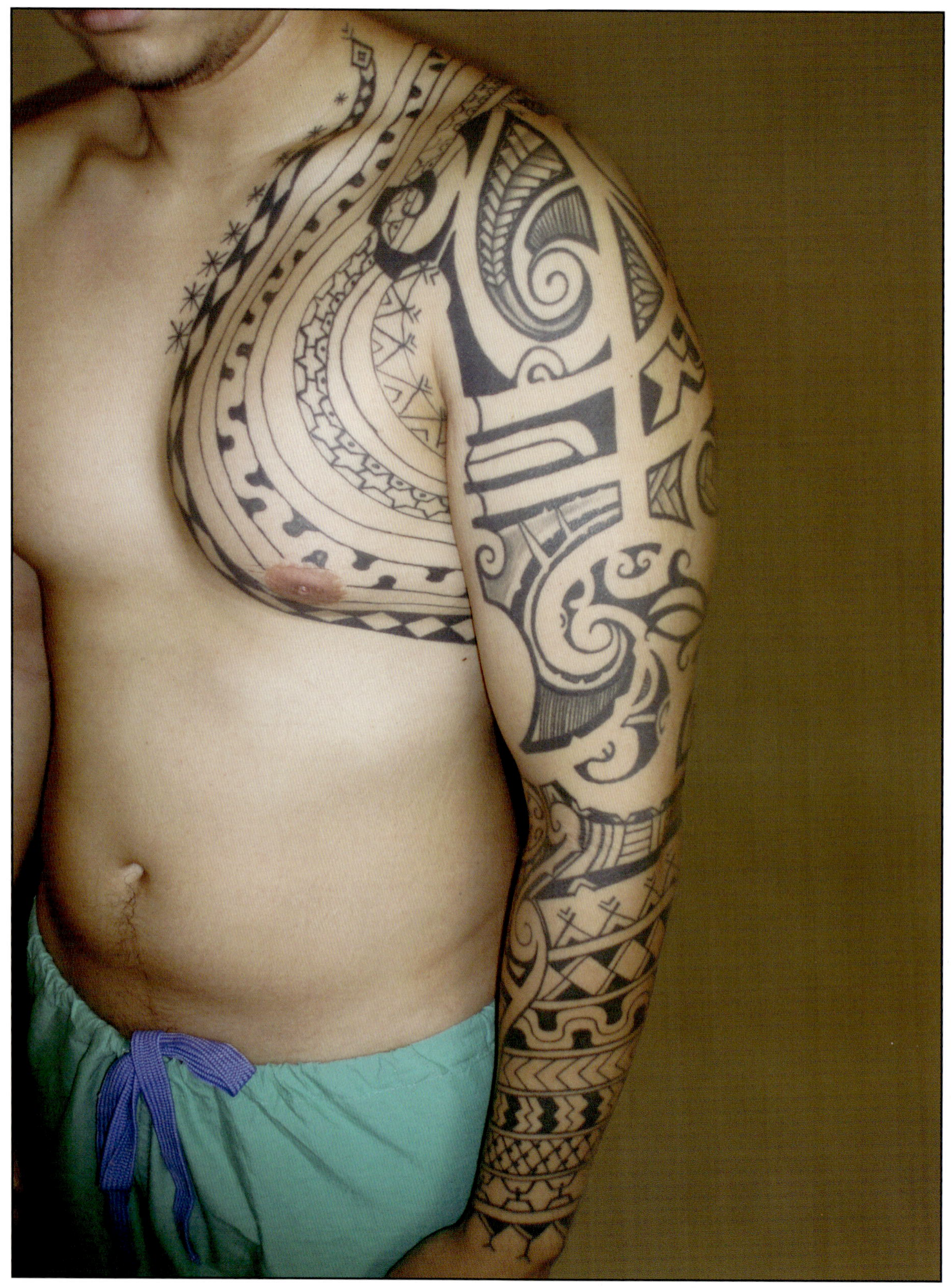

Pages 138-140: Radney Ritarita's tattoos are a combination of Polynesian elements and traditional Filipino elements from the Benguet region. His chest was tattooed by Rodney Alconcel of Bong's tattoo and his arm was tattooed by Orly Lacquiao of Humble Beginnings.

Filipino Tattoos: Ancient to Modern

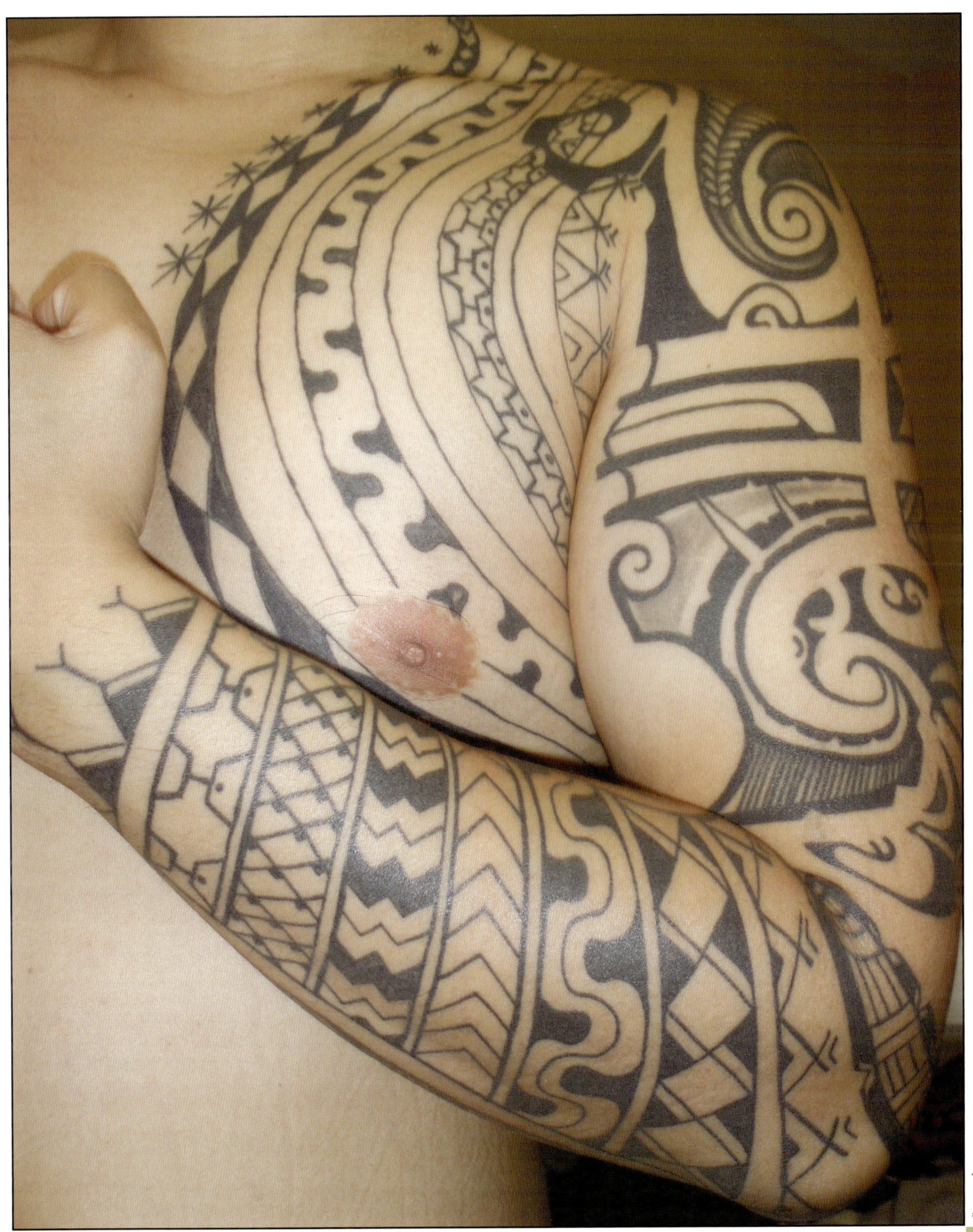

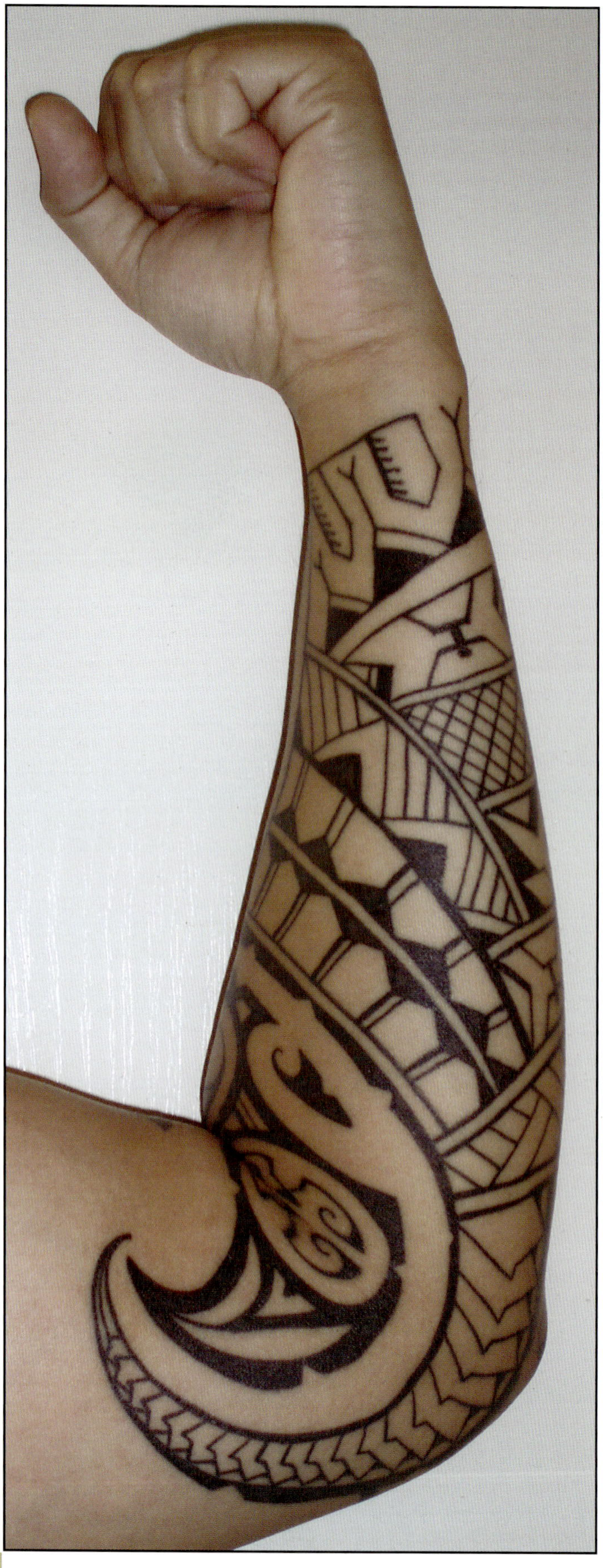

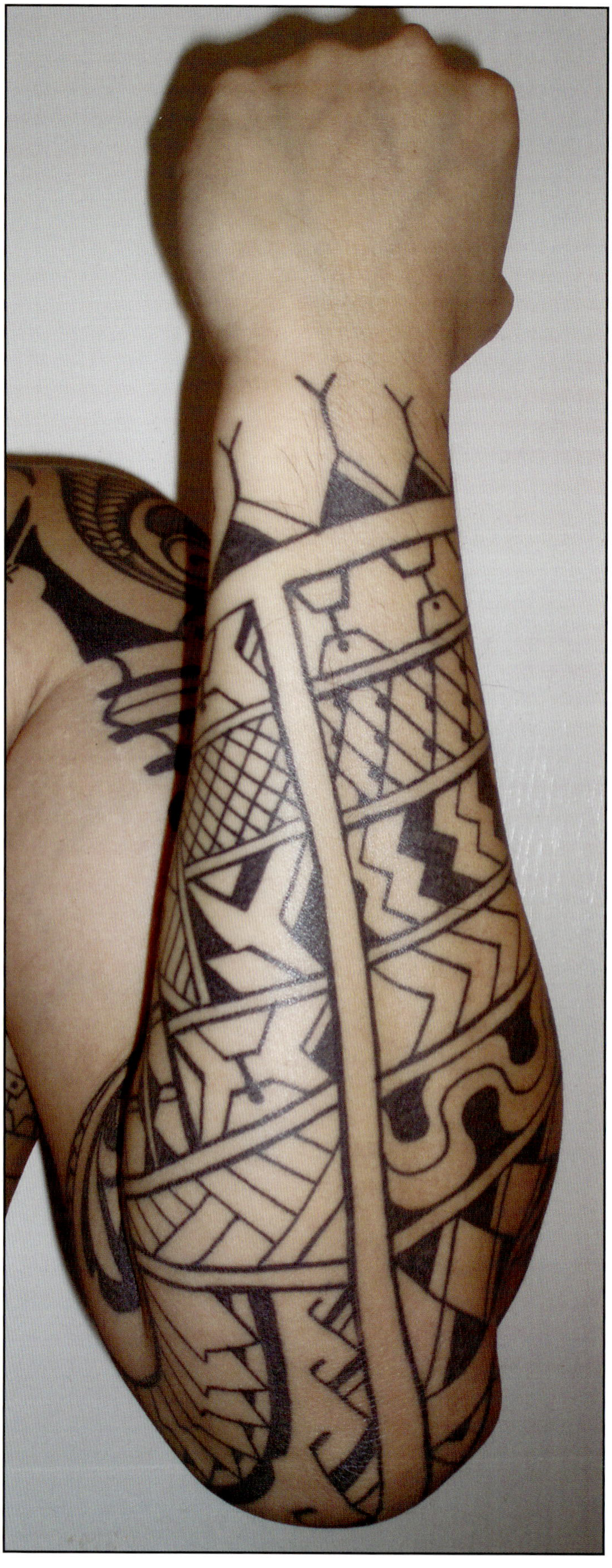

Mary Ann Ubaldo

I am an artist who deeply relates to the Filipino culture. It is a decolonization process (pagbabalik loob) for me of reconnecting with the past to get a better understanding of the present and become able to envision the future. Going through this process strengthens the cultural connection to the Filipino indigenous culture or ideology as a source of grounding. In this way, it promotes cultural and spiritual connection, making it possible for us to identify with one's people and history despite personal, generational, education, economic classes and other forms of differences. Language and the way of writing are foundations of one's culture. By using Baybayin/ Alibata in my art it is a deeper search of our identity and understanding how the loss of language, ancient scripts affects our Filipino identity, that the Filipino culture is the soul of our people, a connection to our folk soul. I could really say, I am on a LAKARAN, that inspired me to do it, a spiritual journey/ pilgrimage, towards understanding a little bit better our spiritual heritage. It is a pilgrimage back to my Filipino cultural roots, a search going back to our KATAALAN.

I see the power of art as a tool to educate and raise consciousness about our indigenous roots. I am reinventing who we are, making sense of what is it to be a Filipino/Filipina, not as defined by colonizers. I believe, there is an inner guiding spirit which I identify as my MUTYA, the spiritual force (diwa/soul) of Inang Bayan (Motherland) that leads me in my art. Through it I am guided by BATHALA and our ancestors.

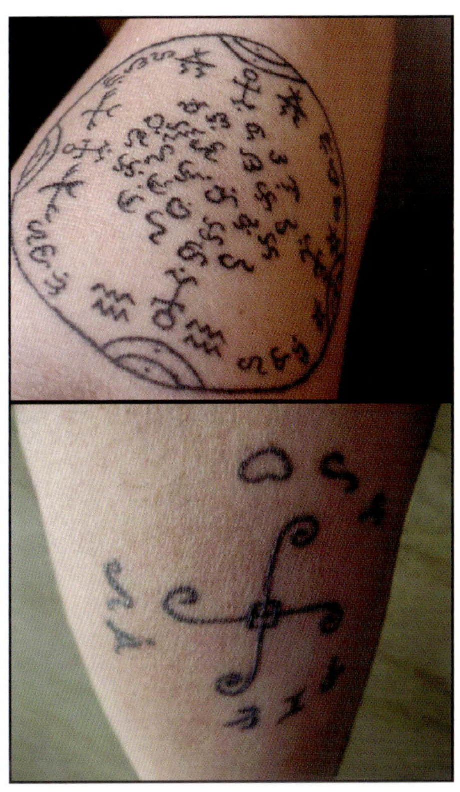

The tattoos of Mary Ann Ubaldo incorporate traditional tattoo motifs and baybayin. Her tattoo is a Kalinga song called Dosayan from the Pasil region of Kalinga written in baybayin. It is traditionally sung with extemporaneous which, in this particular rendition composed by Kalinga artist Arnel Banasan, is a prayer for peace and unity addressed to Kabunian, the creator god of much of northern Luzon. The second tattoo is composed of a variation of a Mangyan cross called pinakuri-kuran and baybayin, which represents Mary Ann's lakaran or spiritual journey.

Margarita Alcantara

I always believe that the ink you choose has some spiritual connection, and resonates with you for a certain reason. I got my first tattoo on my upper back, many years ago when tattooing in New York City was still illegal. I was inspired to get this to mark my own "coming of age" which I could feel in my blood, and I felt I was in fact getting in touch with my "blood" by the time of this first ink. It is a large kapre (Filipino mythological creature) with an anting-anting above it (An anting-anting can refer a protective prayer, or amulet, in my case, it is a prayer.) The anting-anting is in baybayin (the written language in the Philippines before its colonization by Spain.) I got inked in the basement of an East Village shop. I still remember, to this day, that we spent the 3-4 hours listening to Cypress Hill. The piece took a while, because it took up a good part of my upper back, and was completely filled in with black. My arms were sore for the next few days after that from clutching the chair back to my chest so tightly.

The next one was my right arm sleeve, which I got to commemorate my milestone of becoming a woman, in my own eyes. It was a collaborative piece I made with my tattooist, Emma Porcupine, whose shop was in the East Village at the time, and incorporated artwork that I'd found on a classical music CD cover. It has elements of Kalinga tribal art and baybayin. This piece took a couple of hours, as well, and the soundtrack for this one was mostly Elvis and Siouxsie and the Banshees. It was important to me that my tattooist for this piece was female, and Emma is a stellar artist.

My left sleeve was inspired directly by the women of the Kalinga tribe in the Philippines, and was done by tattooist/artist/musician Leslie Mah, of then Diving Swallow Tattoo, in San Francisco. Since the artist also happened to be a friend of mine (I met her through my zine, Bamboo Girl, when she

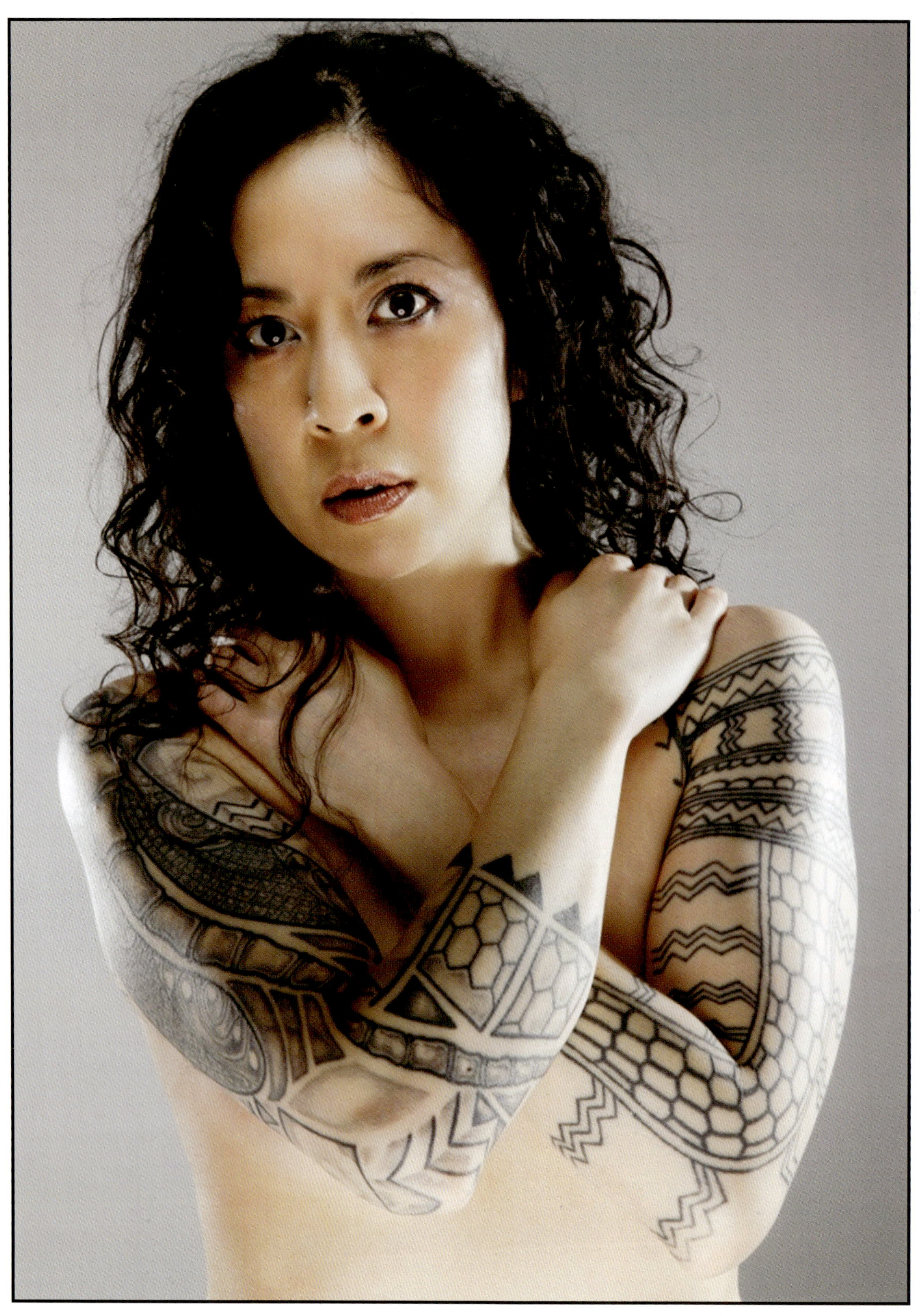

Margarita Alcantara. photo by B. J. Formento

Filipino Tattoos: Ancient to Modern

was in her band, Tribe 8), she was able to ink me after hours. I was really glad to have a female artist of Asian descent tattoo this important artwork honoring my ancestral blood. It is almost complete, and we did as much as we could in the time span of 4-5 hours. I don't think there was any soundtrack to this one. But knowing that the Kalinga women receive this art on both arms and around the neck to symbolize their recognition in their community as life bearers and as women was powerful recognition for me.

My lower back was another large piece, but was more "old school," and was collaboration with artist Emma Porcupine. It is a mermaid, resembling myself, sitting atop three tiers of lotus blossoms. This is my only color piece, and once again marked another important milestone in my life, one of transformation into beauty, after the deportation of my ex-husband.

The full meaning of what each tattoo represents to me is too much to include here; but, suffice to say, they are all symbols to me of my inner strength, my connection to my roots, and my capacity to grow as a woman. I have a lot of stories, and have lived a colorful life already, and my ink is a visible manifestation of this.

I remember when one of our Filipino family friends first saw my ink, she said, "Ay, sayang, you always had such beautiful skin!" (This loosely translates as, "What a shame, you always had beautiful skin!") The funny thing is I feel even more beautiful now than I did when I wasn't inked!

Claudell Duldulao

I was excited to get tattooed the old way, especially when I knew what the designs really meant. I am usually a skeptic and need to have things proven to me. But to tell you the truth, since I got tattooed I've noticed a lot has changed. I used to have nightmares on a regular basis. I would to wake up in the middle of the night feeling like I could not move or speak, like someone was holding me down. Now I am no longer afraid to sleep. I feel

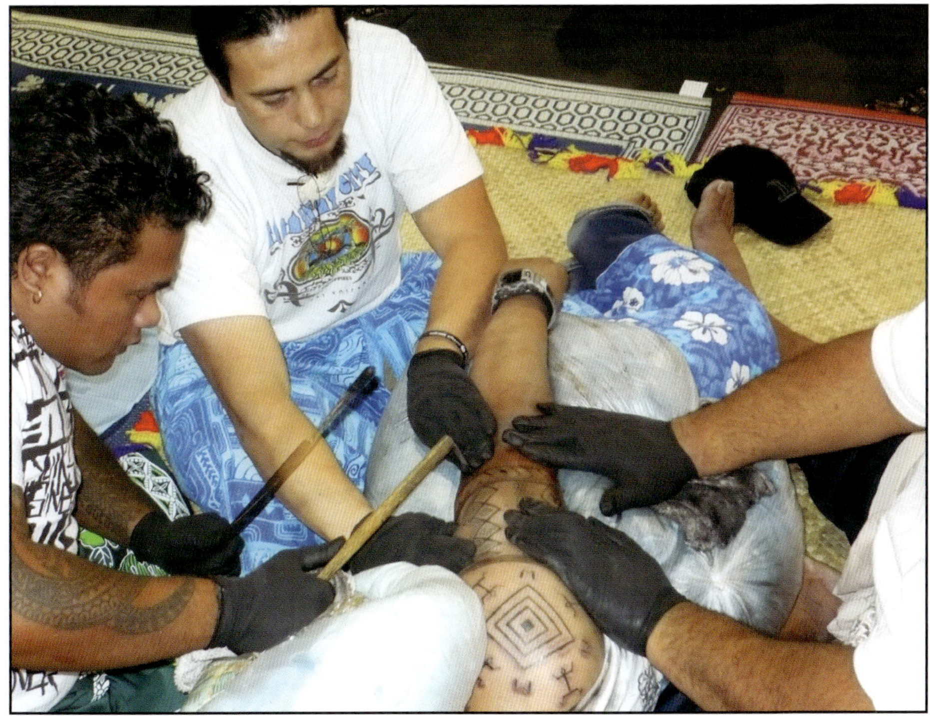

Left and pages 144-145: Claudell Duldulao's experience being hand tapped. Tattoo by Su'a Peter Suluape (Pika)

Modern Filipino Tattooing

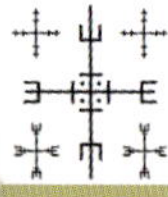

Filipino Tattoos: Ancient to Modern

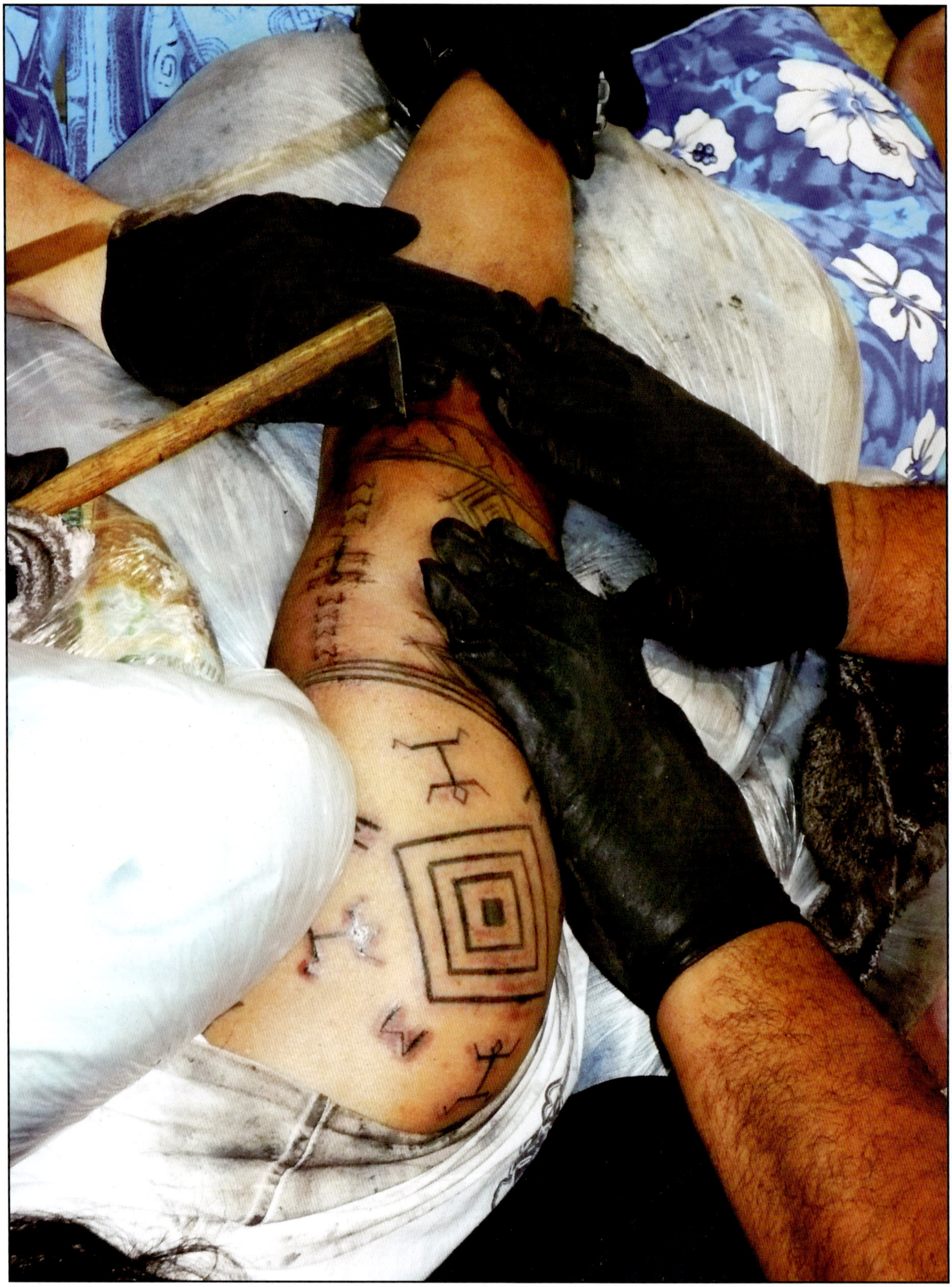

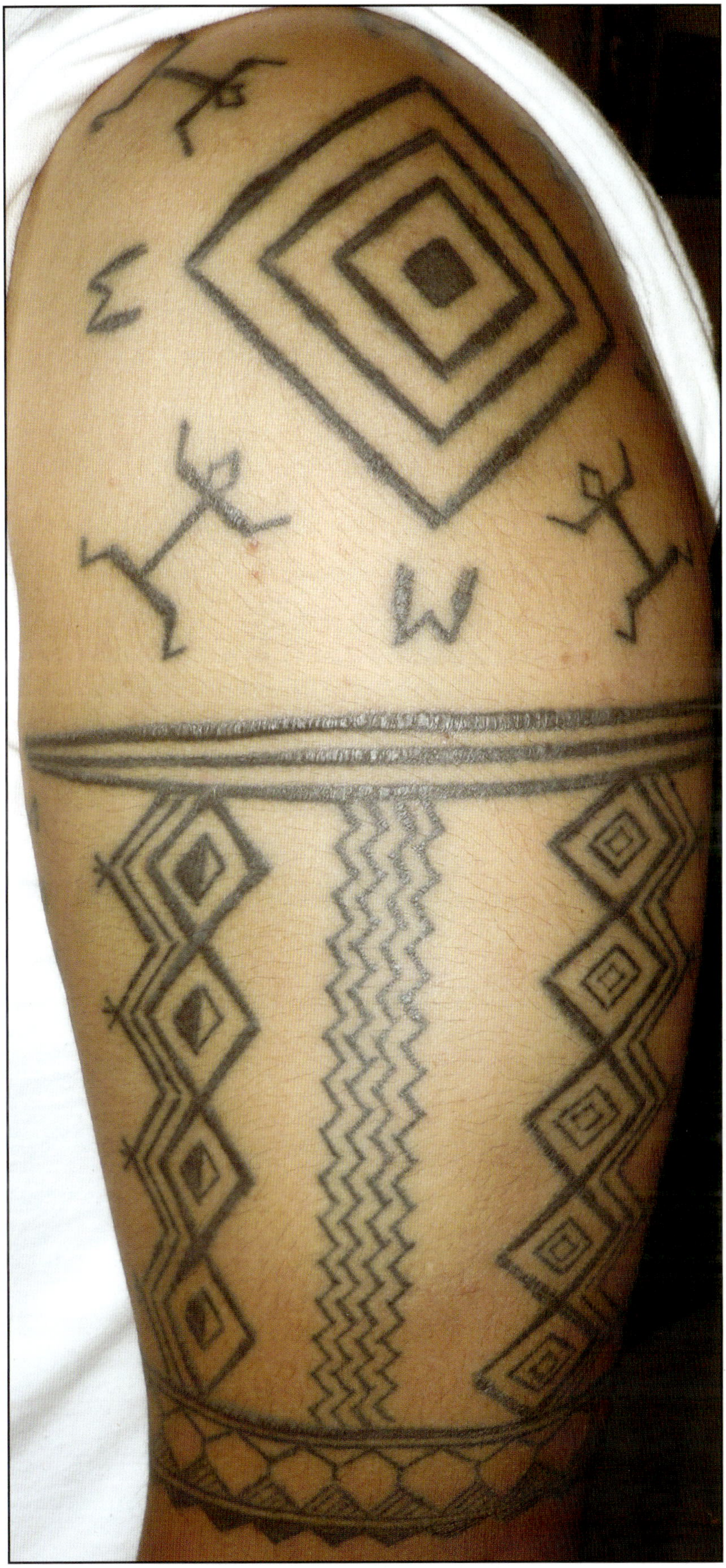

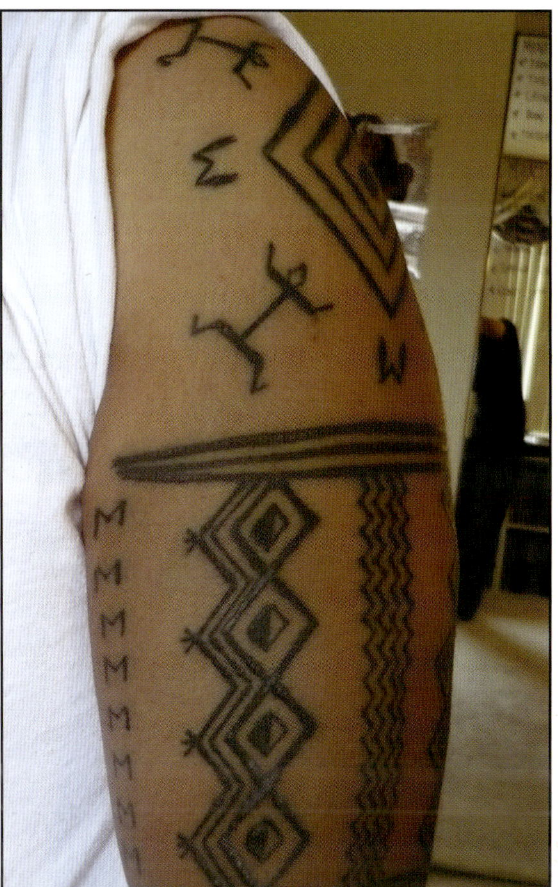

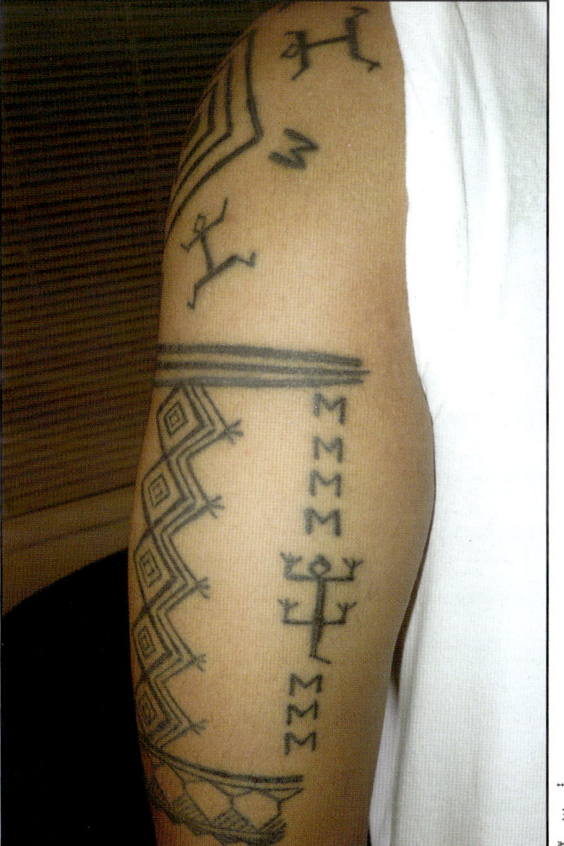

Virgil Mayor Apostol

Long before I considered getting a tattoo, I was unaware of the existence of living tattoo practitioners in the Philippines, and have always told myself that if I were to receive one, it would have to be in a setting similar to being in the deep jungles of Borneo, surrounded by the indigenous peoples like the Iban or Penan performing ceremonies and rituals. Although it took a few years to play with the idea of getting tattooed, I was finally convinced when I relocated to O'ahu, Hawai'i in 2006, after witnessing a large percentage of locals with traditional or contemporary tribal marks. I was eventually guided to local tattoo expert, Keone Nunes, a Hawaiian advocate of Polynesian studies and traditions.

Keone's method of tattooing is of the old school, implementing the use of animal tusk that he shapes himself. What initially impressed me was how he screened and interviewed his clients, getting to know their personality, their spiritual values, and reasons for wanting a tattoo. If they are of Hawaiian ancestry, they are required to research their genealogy. Only then is Keone able to determine the genealogical aumakua (spirit) guide embodied in traditional Hawaiian motif. When I showed him a design incorporating Filipino motifs, and explaining that I am of Filipino origin, he looked over the design and agreed to "tap" this non-Hawaiian design. My initial appointment was set.

By the third session with Keone, I knew that I was in for more pain. When the tapping began, I focused my gaze on a photo of his teacher, Su'a Suluape Paulo, hanging above. I slipped into an altered state, sending my consciousness into my skin being tapped. I then became one with the energy that was passing through the tattoo comb as it was being hammered by the stick. Moving my consciousness through the hammer and into Keone's hands and the rest of his body, I gained the realization of how his body was a vessel for his soul, as well as an awareness of his ancestral line. Through this process, I was also able to reach through to his teacher's ancestors. I felt the spirit of their cultures and traditions passing through onto my skin. Amazingly, the pain that normally accompanied was almost nonexistent! I was ecstatic.

One day, a friend by the name of Iliana, a Hawaiian kahuna, brought me through an initiation process to empower the spiritual warrior in me. As part of the extended initiation, she instructed me to perform a ceremony in order to connect with my ancestors and the spirits of the land, and for the recognition and activation of my "tatau" (tattoos), thus inspiring me to perform the Ilokano kadagaan ceremony intended to carry out the process.

The tattoo designs that I bear are an attempt to reconstruct those that may have been originally worn by the people of the ilukung (valley) regions of the amianan or northern Luzon where my roots are from. Being of Ilokano blood, the main motifs derive from Ilokano and Itneg abel or woven ceremonial textiles. My Ilokano father told me on two occasions that he was also Igorot, while on my maternal side, my great grandfather came from the eastern Ilocos Norte foothills that are occupied by the Itneg and Yapayao. My designs, therefore, are a harmonious blending of motifs from various ethnolinguistic groups from northern Luzon.

The lateral and medial tattoos on my thighs represent the karayan or river of life, its origins, and its eventual merging with the sea. I also have

Filipino Tattoos: Ancient to Modern

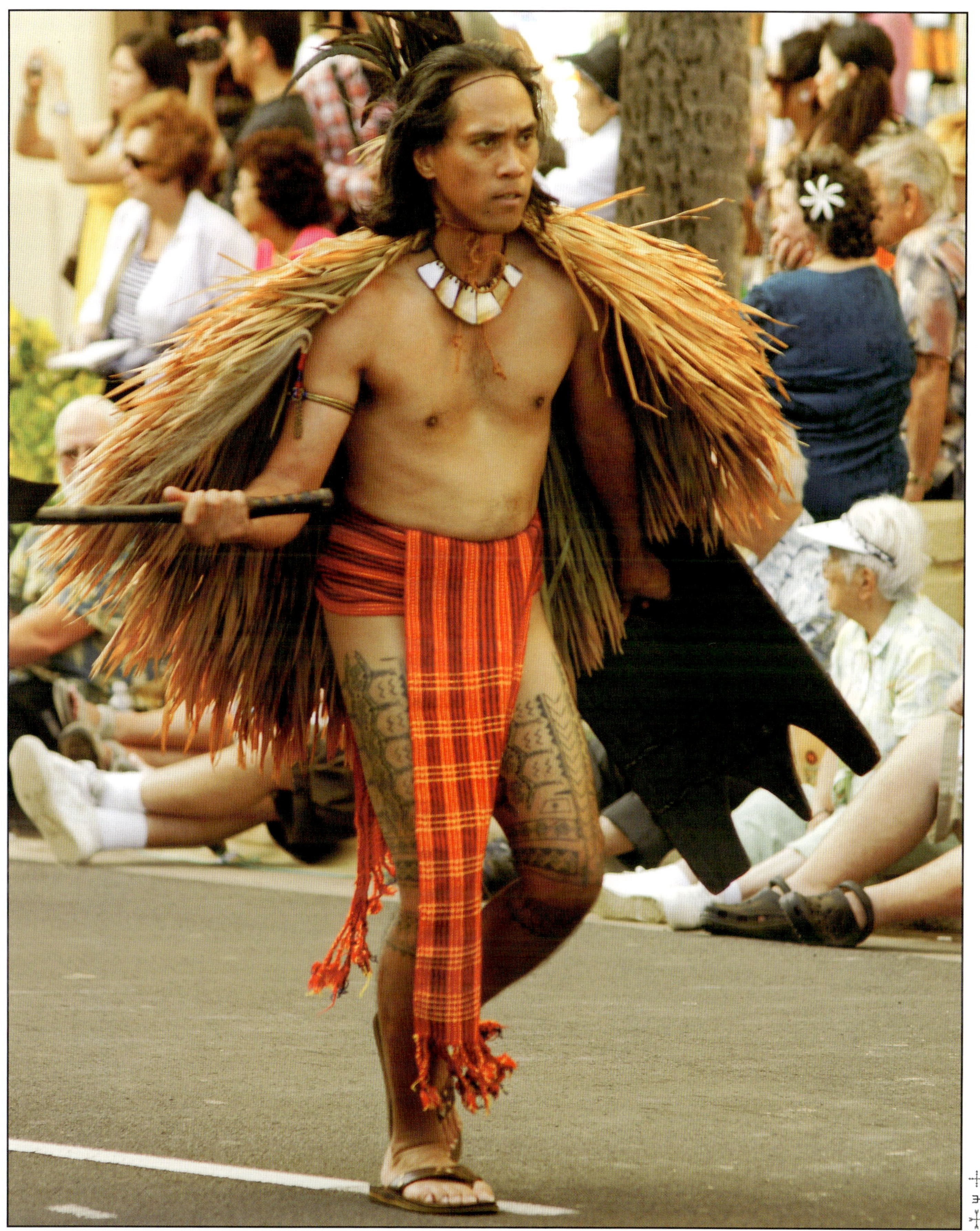

zoomorphic and anthropomorphic motifs based on personal dreams and visions that are prophetic of my life's purpose and destiny. Being permanently marked with these motifs link me to my ancestors and descendants. I do my best to live out the spiritual symbolism behind them, and not to egotistically flash them like others often do. Not too many people would actually see them, unless I wear the ba-ag (loincloth) during ceremonial or cultural performances, or when I wear shorts that expose my thighs when I sit down. They serve as a daily reminder of the commitment I made to uphold and honor who we are, where we came from, and where we are going.

Lane Wilcken

In the early-1990s I began studying the tattoos of the Philippines and Pacific Islands mainly out of curiosity, but as I did so, in the back of my mind there was a part of me that wanted to wear these marks as well. Then in the spring of 2000 I had a series of dreams that made me aware that there was something unseen and substantially deeper to these designs than being just the simple marks of prestige or fertility. After more than a decade of my own research I learned some of the finer points of the canoe pattern of the Isneg people. I soon came to an understanding of its great spiritual and historical significance. One morning driving down the highway back to Las Vegas from Los Angeles I was pondering the importance of the canoe tattoo. While I was lost in thought I suddenly saw in my mind's eye the old ones wearing it back when the fullness of its significance was understood. As I pondered their lives, their work, their dances, and love of their families, my heart yearned within me for my ancient ones. I ached for my ancestors who so carefully preserved their history and beliefs in such an elegant design. Gratitude filled my heart. Chills washed over me and tears welled up in my eyes as I drove. I felt that although their names were lost to me, I was not lost to <u>them</u>. They were aware of the yearnings of their living descendent. I do not want to share all the details of this very personal experience but it was at that moment that I knew I had to have the Andori tattooed on my body for the witness of its significance was already "tattooed" upon my heart. I had known of many Filipino tattoo designs from my research in prior years but I had refrained from being tattooed until I had that moving experience. In making the decision to be tattooed I wanted it to be done in the proper way so as to pay proper respect to those who went before me. I did not want to just go into any old tattoo shop and have someone I did not know tattoo this sacred design on my body.

Some months earlier I had been introduced to Aisea Toetu'u, who is of Tongan, Hawaiian and Filipino descent. Aisea is a traditional tattoo expert, or "*tufuga tatau*," who taught in the Samoan way of tattooing and holds the chiefly "*Su'a Suluape*" tattooist title from Samoa. During one of his visits from Hawaii to California I went to get tattooed by him. But unexpectedly, Aisea's teacher and master, Su'a Suluape Alaiva'a Petelo from Samoa, came into town and was tattooing. Out of respect for his master, Aisea was not tattooing while his teacher was in town.

Petelo is an unassuming man of great humility but commanded great respect of all those around him. His body was covered in tattoos and he wore the *Pe'a*, or Samoan body suit, tattoo. When we approached him, he was tattooing a Polynesian woman around the ankle and she looked very

Filipino Tattoos: Ancient to Modern

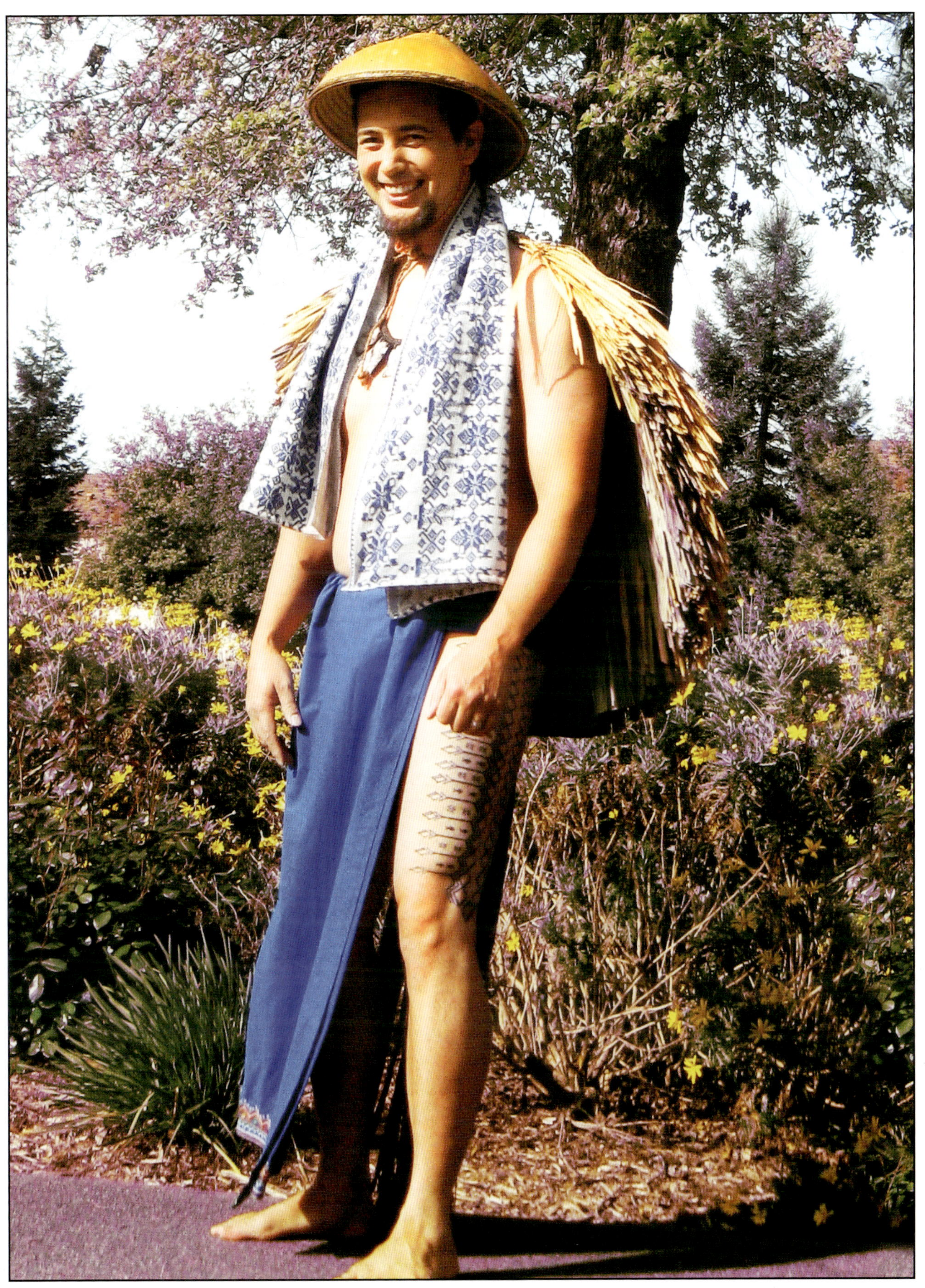

uncomfortable as he worked. I watched the process, and after he finished I was formally introduced to him by Aisea. We sat down together and I tried to be as respectful as possible to the chief who sat before me. As we talked, I shared with him my ongoing research into the links between Filipino culture and Pacific Islander peoples, including tattooing. He humbly listened as he added to my knowledge here and there. He asked if I had any tattoos. I told him, "No, I don't have any." But I showed him the Andori pattern I was hoping to have Aisea tattoo. Then he sat for a moment looking at me. He began speaking in Samoan to his apprentices. They immediately stood up and Aisea told me, "Lane, Su'a has decided that he will tattoo you ... now!"

As they prepared me for tattooing, Aisea explained that Su'a was impressed with my desire to be tattooed traditionally, especially since this was to be my *first* tattoo. He also explained that there were several other people who were scheduled to be tattooed and Su'a had put me in front of them all. I felt extremely honored in spite of the reality that I was soon going to have needles hammered into my skin! I had resolved that I would be strong and refrain from showing pain. Instead of thinking about the pain, I focused on how excited I was to honor my ancestors who were waiting for me to be like them.

Su'a examined my leg where the tattoo was to go and then bowed his head, closed his eyes and appeared to be silently praying before the task ahead of him. He told me to lie down on the woven mat. His apprentices positioned me and held the skin on my leg tight so the marks could be made accurately. Su'a took the tattooing comb, called "*au*" in Samoan, dipped it in the ink and made a few reference marks on my leg. He asked me if I was ready and I said, "Yes." I tried to settle my heart and took a deep breath. With the first strike there was a sharp pain as the multiple needles penetrated my skin. It was a pain similar to being slapped with a wooden ruler or whipped with a thin stick, a sharp burning pain. I held to my resolution to be serene as my friends watched on. But the pain was very real!

During the first fifteen minutes of tapping, I tried to distract myself from the pain by focusing on other objects, listening to others talking, or looking at a particular point on the ceiling. I had read that being tattooed taught a man how to be passive and patient and now I was being educated! As Su'a hammered away at the design (several strikes each second), I found that the more I relaxed the easier it was to manage the pain. Instead of gritting my teeth and tightening my muscles, I relaxed and let the pain flow through me. I reminded myself that this was the same pain my ancestors felt when they received their tattoos, and I should bear it in humility and dignity so as to honor them. I found that the rhythmic tapping of the *au* to be hypnotic. Soon I became relaxed in body and mind, and I honestly felt that I could have lain there all night. A few hours later Su'a finished the Andori on my leg, which stretches from my hip to my knee and covers the outside half of my thigh. Everyone remarked on how well I sat through the operation and the respect they had for me. I felt so proud and grateful to Su'a. Now I was no longer "*mapuraw*" (unadorned), but had the indelible testament of a link to my progenitors forever upon my body.

A Hope for the Future

In the modern world it is quite impossible to return to the old way of living and earning tattoos. Most Filipinos and Pacific Islanders are members of Christian religions and no longer live by headhunting. We have cars and planes to traverse mountains and seas. Many of us living abroad do not even know how to grow our own food anymore, but instead buy it in grocery stores. Once a culture is changed it is nearly impossible to return to "the way things were." Even if left alone, culture is not static; it continues to grow, adapt and change. But there are aspects of an indigenous culture that are valuable and should be perpetuated; this is the case with the tattooing heritage.

In adapting the heritage of tattooing to the modern era, my main concern is that people recklessly use tattooing designs. A danger is that people today may reinterpret the sacred tattoos by devolving them into the brands of petty street gangs. There is also the temptation of taking the catalogue of motifs presented here and making them into tattoo flash. No consideration may be taken about who wears the design or what the true meaning behind it is. In essence, it could be seen as simply a decoration on the skin.

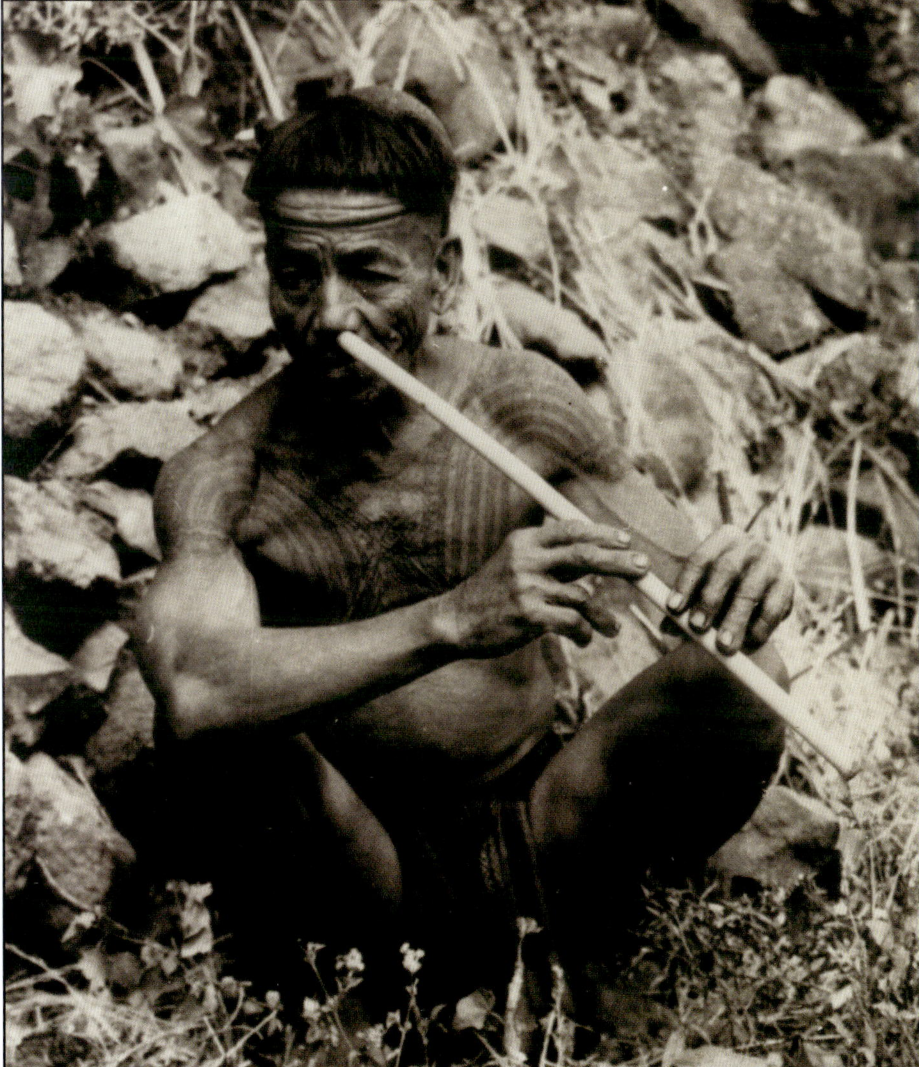

A Bontoc man with a Chak-lag or Head-hunter's chest tattoo playing a nose flute. Author's collection

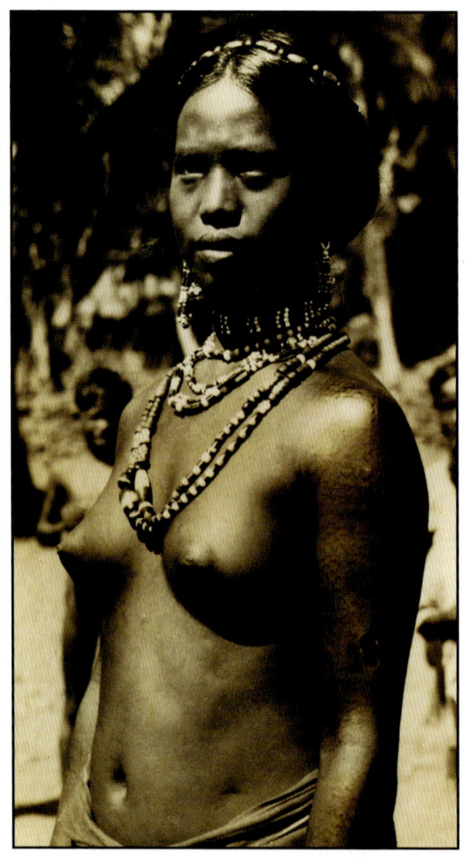

A wealthy young woman adorned with heir-loom beads and tattoos from Lubuagan, Kalinga 1932. Photo courtesy of the Buch-holdt Family Collection

I hope to emphasize that the knowledge, personal character and spiritual values that the tattoo represents are powerful, not the ink in the skin. For example, why would you cover your body in fertility symbols and designs about the continuity of the family or village if you had no desire to have children or serve the community? Or why would you put on a symbol of bravery if you were a coward? The symbol itself will not make you brave.

Symbols may represent and reinforce the valor you already have exhibited, whether it is bravery in the face of an enemy or courage to act on promptings from the spirit world. These ancient tattoos served to reinforce values of bravery and heroism gained through acts of spiritual sensitivity, respect for one's family – both living and dead, personal growth, sacrifice, the obligation to know and perpetuate cultural beliefs, protecting and serving the community, being industrious, and continuing one's lineage. Once you possess these qualities, they enhance your understanding of the tattoos in the proper context. Then, unseen guidance represented by the tattoo is revealed in greater clarity to light the way through this life and the world to come. This is the true "blessing" of the tattoo.

It is my hope that people who choose to be tattooed do not take the emblems of prestige lightly, for they originally were reserved for those who had achieved great acts in their personal lives and within their community. A headhunter, for example, went to battle to right the wrongs made against his village or family. He acted to preserve his people through obtaining a sacrifice and ensuring the survival of the rising generation. His victory was not only his achievement, but a victory shared by the ancestors who guided his path. A warrior did not go on his quests so he could be tattooed. When he returned successful from his mission, it was his privilege to receive a tattoo with the symbols of his guiding *anito* and patterns that displayed the communal prosperity that resulted from his efforts.

In the past, some men humbly resisted being tattooed, even though they were worthy, until they were shamed into having the operation done. The tattoo was the outward mark of the values that were, figuratively, already tattooed upon his heart. The ancestors referred to this as "the tattooing of the soul." The inward marks upon the heart or soul led the man to his victory or achievement. His *tattoos upon the soul,* already gained through his submission or obedience to the counsel of the spiritual realm are the most important to possess. Without them, the marks on the skin are simply vain decoration.

In the past, tattoos were required to be married. Women with tattoos were seen as not only more beautiful but also possessing the emotional and physical fortitude to endure pain and hardship, including the pain of childbirth. For a man, tattooing was a visual marker that he was a person of the highest caliber and character. In a woman's eyes, a man possessing the tattoos of spiritual strength and physical valor showed her that he was an eligible mate worthy of her affection.

Those who wore tattoos without earning them were shamefully compared to the *halo* lizard that was richly patterned but flighty and showed cowardice.[165]

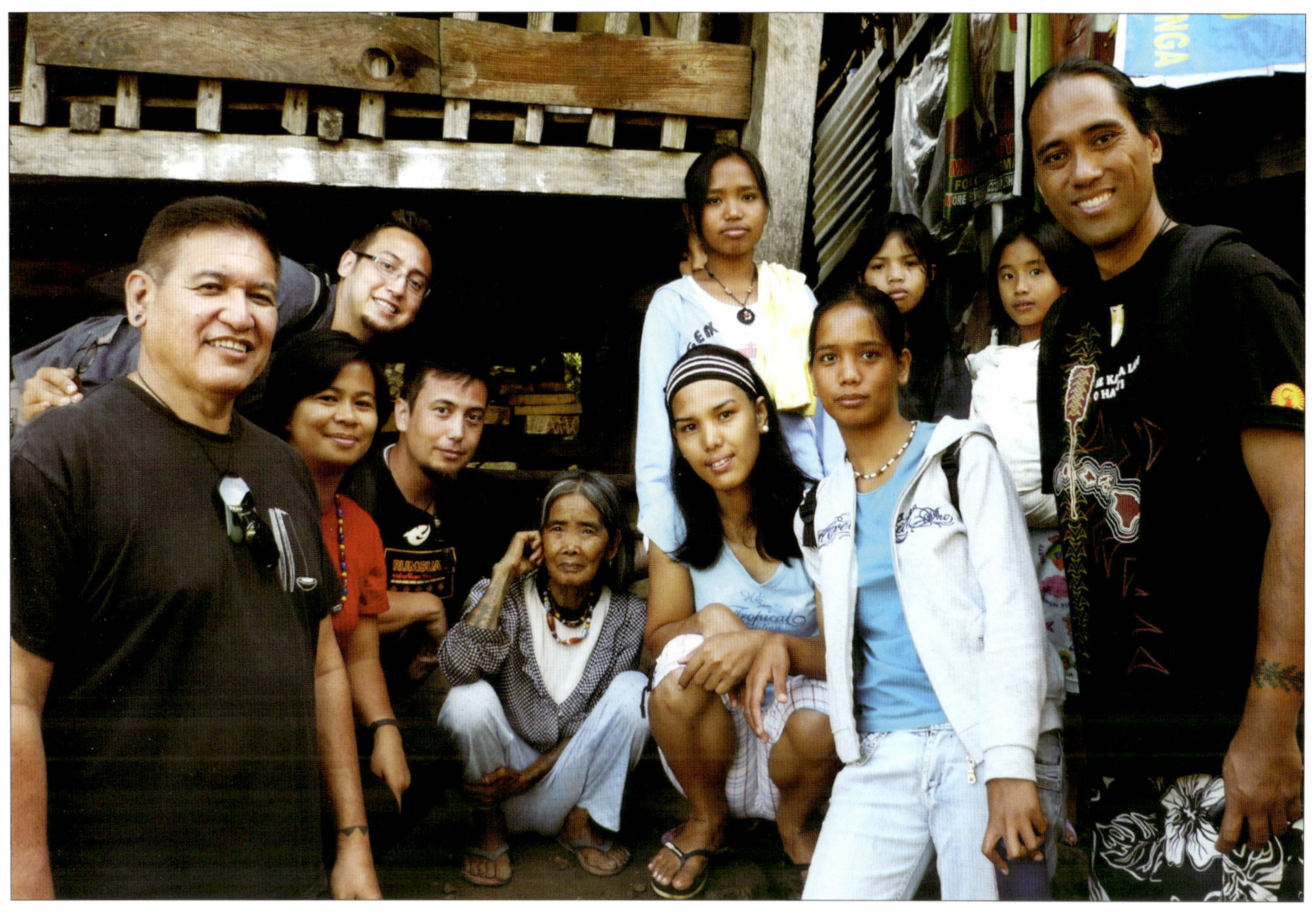

If you decide to become tattooed, *earn the right* by setting and achieving worthwhile goals that benefit your family, community or culture. Seek out your ancestors and they will draw close to you. Research your own history and instill in your soul the values and life experiences that make a person truly worthy of this honor. Then your tattoo will serve as an inspiration to others to strive for qualities you possess. In this way, you will show the proper respect to your ancestors. When gained in the proper context, the symbols of spirituality, character, knowledge and achievement truly become what has been described by some as *magic*.

The Author with Apo Whang-od and friends. (L to R) Keone Nunes, Professor Analyn "Ikin" Salvador-Amores, Jared Wilcken, the Author, Apo Whang-od, our three translators, Vergie, Ella and Rita, Virgil Apostol and three young Buscalan girls.

Appendix

The Creation Myth of the Visayas
Summarized from the Boxer Codex

Before land appeared in the world there was only the sky and the sea that existed from all eternity. There was at this time a bird-of-prey that had to constantly fly between the sky and the sea, with no place to rest. The bird grew tired of its continuous flying so it determined to make the sky and sea quarrel so it could find some place to alight and rest. Flying upwards, it told the sky that the sea wanted to rise up and submerge the sky. The sky told the bird that if the sea did so it would hurl down stones that would restrain it from rising upwards. Instead, the sea would have to flow around the stones.

After this, the bird flew down to the sea and told it that the sky wanted to throw things at it. This angered the sea, which began raising itself up in such great force that the sky began to throw large rocks down upon it. The weight of the rocks restrained the sea, so it returned to its original level.

The bird, seeing the many large stones and islands now in the sea, flew down, having finally found a place to rest. While resting on an island, the bird saw a bamboo with two nodes in the water. [In Panay the bamboo was produced by a marriage between the land and sea breezes.] The surf washed the bamboo up onto the beach where the bird was resting and hit it on its feet. No matter where the bird moved to avoid getting hurt, the surf always made the bamboo go where the bird was and hurt the bird's feet. The bird began vigorously pecking at the bamboo and split open the two nodes on the bamboo.

There emerged from the bamboo a man named Ka-Laki and a woman named Ka-baye. Their names were the origin of the words for man (*lalaki*) and woman (*babae*). After consulting with the fish and birds and receiving approval from the earthquake *Linog*, they were married and had a large number of children. In time there were many children, many of whom were idle and did nothing for their own support. The parents became angry and threw them out of the house.

One day the father came home and, feigning much anger, picked up a stick and yelled at the children, threatening to kill them all. The children fled. Those children who ran and hid inside the house became the various nobles. Those who hid behind the walls of the house became the slaves. Those who hid in the cooking area among the ashes became the negrito peoples. Those children who left the house and never came back became the other peoples of the world.

The Creation Myth of Samoa

Before there were men, the world only consisted of the heavens and the ocean. The great god Tagaloa dwelt in the sky with his son, who was named Tuli. One day Tuli, in the form of a great bird (the Golden Plover), flew between the sky and the ocean. After some time he grew tired, for there was no place for him to land. Tuli returned to the heavens and complained to Tagaloa, who threw down a stone that became the island of Manu'a in the Samoan archipelago. He also threw down other stones that became all the different islands of the sea. [In other versions a single rock rises out of the ocean.]

Now, with a place to land, Tuli flew down and began to live on his island. But this new island rose just barely above the water, and the waves

Filipino Tattoos: Ancient to Modern

of the sea washed over the island. Tuli had to run back and forth to avoid getting wet.

Again, Tuli flew up to the heavens and told Tagaloa his problem. Tagaloa let down his fish hook and raised the rock higher. The name of the rock was *Papa-Taoto* (reclining rock) and after Tagaloa raised it, it became *Papa-Sosolo* (spreading rock), which, upon further exertion from Tagaloa, became *Papa-Tu* (the upright rock). [In other versions Tagaloa commands the single rock, "Be thou split up," and through further actions broke up the single *papa* into its various forms: *Papa-Sosolo, Papa-Taoto,* etc.]

The rock was covered with earth or mold, upon which grass grew. However, after some time, a *fue* (vine) grew up and began to take over the grass. Tuli returned to his father, because there was no man to care for the land. Tagaloa asked, "You have your land Tuli, what grows on it?" Tuli answered, "The *fue*" (vine). Tagaloa told him to pull it up, so he did. As Tuli pulled up the vine, he saw two grubs or worms crawling on the roots. He then flew back to his father and told him of the grubs. Tagaloa then told Tuli, "The fruits of the vine are these grubs. I will fashion them into forms with limbs. I also give a will to each of them. Their bodies must remain opaque and their faces must shine to entertain Tagaloa when he comes to walk the Earth."

Tuli returned to his island and took with him Tagaloa-Tosi (or Gai-Tosi) and Tagaloa-Va'a-va'ai" (or Gai-Va'a-va'ai) who set to work on the two grubs immediately and made them into men. One day, while fishing with nets, one of the men was injured by a fish called *lo*. Soon after, the man died. Tuli was upset that one of his men was dead and returned to Tagaloa to ask what should be done. His Father again sent Gai-Tosi to earth and he reanimated the dead man, but made him into a woman. Presenting the new woman to the other man, the two became husband and wife, and from them sprang the human race.

Endnotes

Chapter 1: Early Accounts

1 Garcia, pg. 334
2 Scott, Discovery of the Igorots pg. 314
3 In the Ilubo area of Kalinga the word for ink is called *merteka*. See Salvador-Amores, Batek: Traditional Tattoos and Identities in Contemporary Kalinga, North Luzon Philippines. Pg. 109
4 Scott, Barangay: Sixteenth Century Philippine Culture and Society, pg. 20
5 Taylor, pg. 6
6 Scott, Discovery of the Igorots pg. 221
7 Alcina, pp. 35-37
8 Gilbert. pg. 29

Chapter 2: Tattoo Process and Tools

9 Salvador-Amores, Batek: Traditional Tattoos and Identities in Contemporary Kalinga, North Luzon Philippines. Pg. 109
10 Salvador, Signs on Skin Beauty and Being. pg. 2
11 Krutak, The Last Kalinga Tattoo Artist of the Philippines. www.larskrutak.com/articles/philippines_/
12 Jenks, pg. 188
13 Salvador, Signs on Skin Beauty and Being. pg. 2
14 Vanoverbergh, Dress and Adornment in the Mountain Province of Luzon, Philippine Islands. pg. 190
15 Kwiatkowski, pg. 12
16 Allen, pg. 122
17 Handy, pg. 10
18 Vanoverbergh, Dress and Adornment in the Mountain Province of Luzon, Philippine Islands. pg. 190
19 Via personal communication with Keone Nunes, Kahuna ka Uhi.
20 Marquardt as cited by Gilbert pg. 50
21 Salvador-Amores, Batek: Traditional Tattoos and Identities in Contemporary Kalinga, North Luzon Philippines. pg. 109
22 Salvador, Signs on Skin Beauty and Being. Pg. 2
23 Scott, Discovery of the Igorots, pg. 311
24 Riria and Simmons, pg. 8
25 Salvador, Ikin. Philippine Daily Inquirer, May 2nd, 2000 Internet Edition.
26 Cole, Faye-Cooper. The Tinguian: Social, Religious, and Economic Life of a Philippine Tribe, pg. 442

Chapter 3: Reasons For Tattooing

27 Vanoverbergh, Dress and Adornment in the Mountain Province of Luzon, Philippine Islands. pg. 188
28 Adapted from Reynolds, et al. pp. 308-310
29 Scott, Discovery of the Igorots pg. 180
30 As cited by Scott, Discovery of the Igorots pg. 308 from Dr. Hans Meyer's "Reisen im Noerdlichen Luzon," (Philippines) Globus, Vol. 43, (1883) pg. 171
31 Dozier, pg. 73
32 Barton, pg. 238
33 Salvador-Amores, Batek: Traditional Tattoos and Identities in Contemporary Kalinga, North Luzon Philippines. pg. 120
34 As cited by Garcia, pg. 267
35 Buck, pg. 209
36 Buck, pp. 78 - 81
37 Newton, pg. 544
38 Salvador-Amores, Batek: Traditional Tattoos and Identities in Contemporary Kalinga, North Luzon Philippines. pg. 118
39 Jenks, pg. 174
40 Jenks, pg. 189
41 As cited by Gilbert, pg. 82
42 Pukui, pg. 139
43 Jenks, pg. 222
44 Cole, Mabel Cook. pp. 37-43
45 Salvador-Amores, Batek: Traditional Tattoos and Identities in Contemporary Kalinga, North Luzon Philippines. pg. 132
46 Scott, Barangay: Sixteenth Century Philippine Culture and Society, pg. 21
47 Scott, Barangay: Sixteenth Century Philippine Culture and Society, pg. 21
48 Scott, Barangay: Sixteenth Century Philippine Culture and Society, pp. 128-130
49 Gell, pp. 135-136
50 Garcia, pg. 347
51 Scott, Barangay: Sixteenth Century Philippine Culture and Society, pg. 62

52 Salvador-Amores, Batek: Traditional Tattoos and Identities in Contemporary Kalinga, North Luzon Philippines. pp. 116, 126
53 Scott, Barangay: Sixteenth Century Philippine Culture and Society, pp. 92-93
54 Salvador-Amores, personal communication
55 Scott, Barangay: Sixteenth Century Philippine Culture and Society, pp. 80-81
56 Scott, Barangay: Sixteenth Century Philippine Culture and Society, pg. 21
57 Jenks, pg. 188
58 Norbeck, pp. 40-41
59 Riria and Simmons, pg. 57
60 Voyage Autour du Monde: Execute Par Ordre du Roi, Sur La Corvette de sa Majeste, La Coquille. 1822 -1825 as cited by Riria and Simmons, pg. 16 B
61 Douglas from, Tattoo: Bodies, Art, and Exchange in the Pacific and the West pg. 37
62 Gell, pg. 145
63 Gell, pg. 228
64 Taylor, pg. 18
65 Vanoverbergh, Dress and Adornment in the Mountain Province of Luzon, Philippine Islands. pg. 241
66 Salvador-Amores, Batek: Traditional Tattoos and Identities in Contemporary Kalinga, North Luzon Philippines. pg. 113
67 Vanoverbergh, Dress and Adornment in the Mountain Province of Luzon, Philippine Islands. pg. 189
68 Scott, Barangay: Sixteenth Century Philippine Culture and Society, pg. 264
69 Scott, Barangay: Sixteenth Century Philippine Culture and Society, pp. 21, 264
70 As cited by Jose Rizal in Garcia pg. 291
71 De Giua, pg. 242
72 Garcia, pg. 345 and Malo, pp. 105 - 106
73 Peralta, pg. 25
74 Newton, pg. 553
75 Gell, pg. 215
76 Scott, Barangay: Sixteenth Century Philippine Culture and Society, pg. 91
77 Dozier, pp. 53 - 54
78 Salvador, Signs on Skin Beauty and Being. pg. 21
79 Via personal communication with Keone Nunes, Kahua ka Uhi.
80 Krutak, Lars. www.larskrutak.com/articles/philippines_/

Chapter 4: Facial Tattooing

81 Dozier, pg. 73
82 Vanoverbergh, Dress and Adornment in the Mountain Province of Luzon, Philippine Islands. pg. 228
83 Riria, Simmons, pp. 25, 70
84 As cited by Jose Rizal in Garcia, pg. 291
85 Scott, Barangay: Sixteenth Century Philippine Culture and Society, pg. 21
86 Scott, Barangay: Sixteenth Century Philippine Culture and Society, pg. 115
87 Handy, pg. 17
88 Kwiatkowski, pp. 21, 24, 25
89 Via personal communication with Keone Nunes, Kahuna ka Uhi as related to him by clients who had facial tattooing traditionally applied.

Chapter 5: Spiritual Aspects of Tattooing

90 Lewis, pg. 771
91 Vanoverbergh, Dress and Adornment in the Mountain Province of Luzon, Philippine Islands. pg. 228
92 Vanoverbergh, pg. 228
93 Garcia, pp. 252-253
94 Orbell, pp. 184-185
95 Sellato, pg. 47
96 Scott, Barangay: Sixteenth Century Philippine Culture and Society, pg. 81
97 Spenneman, pp. 59-61
98 Jenks, pg. 197
99 Barton, Philippine Pagans. pg. 58
100 Jenks, pg. 197
101 Garcia, pg. 311
102 Cole, Mabel Cook, pg. 143
103 Orbell, pg. 63
104 Kamakau, pg. 91
105 Riria, Simmons, pg. 22
106 Constantino, pg. 244
107 Scott, Barangay: Sixteenth Century Philippine Culture and Society, pg. 92
108 Barton, Mythology of the Ifugaos, pg. 81
109 Lasay, pp. 4 -5 and Barton, Mythology of the Ifugaos pp. 143 - 148

110 Velasco, Faye. Tboli, http://litera1no4.tripod.com/tboli_frame.html
111 Emory, pg. 250
112 Via personal communication
113 Tregear, pp. 542-543
114 Gilbert, pg. 40
115 Booth, pg. 61

Chapter 6: Shared Tattooing Motifs with Pacific Isles

116 Jagor et al. pg. 506
117 Handy, pg. 25
118 Kwiatkowski, pg. 7
119 Via personal communication with Keone Nunes, Kahuna ka Uhi.
120 Avea, pg. 29
121 Krutak, The Last Kalinga Tattoo Artist of the Philippines. www.larskrutak.com/articles/philippines_/
122 Avea, pg. 30
123 Allen, pg. 212
124 Kwiatkowski, inside front cover
125 Kaeppler, pp. 167-168
126 Gell, pg. 251
127 Hiroa, pp. 131-132
128 Poignant, pg. 72
129 Salvador-Amores, Batek: Traditional Tattoos and Identities in Contemporary Kalinga, North Luzon Philippines pg. 135
130 Cole, Fay-Cooper. The Tinguian: Social, Religious, and Economic Life of a Philippine Tribe pg. 422, 423
131 Spenneman, pg. 38
132 Kelin, pp. 4-7
133 Avea, pg. 33
134 Vanoverbergh, Dress and Adornment in the Mountain Province of Luzon, Philippine Islands. pg. 204
135 Jenks, pg. 190
136 Spenneman, pp. 36, 42
137 Spenneman, pp. 33, 40
138 Montinola, pg. 95
139 Cole, Fay-Cooper. The Tinguian: Social, Religious, and Economic Life of a Philippine Tribe pg. 433
140 Yabes, pp. 336, 341
141 Pastor-Roces, pg. 66
142 Pendergrast, pg. 39
143 Cole, Mabel Cook. pp. 37-43
144 Cabrera, pg. 145
145 Demetrio, pp. 67 – 68.
146 Salvador-Amores, Batek: Traditional Tattoos and Identities in Contemporary Kalinga, North Luzon Philippines. pg. 131
147 Handy, pg. 25
148 Spenneman, pg. 39
149 Cole, Fay-Cooper. The Tinguian: Social, Religious, and Economic Life of a Philippine Tribe pg. 433
150 Via personal communication with Keone Nunes, Kahuna ka Uhi
151 Pastor-Roces, pp. 57, 61
152 Via personal communication with Keone Nunes, Kahuna ka Uhi
153 Vanoverbergh, Dress and Adornment in the Mountain Province of Luzon, Philippine Islands. pg. 204

Chapter 7: A Selection of Filipino Tattoo Motifs

154 As per electronic correspondence with Ikin Analyn Salvadore-Amores.
155 Vanoverbergh, Dress and Adornment in the Mountain Province of Luzon, Philippine Islands. pg. 204
156 Vanoverbergh, Dress and Adornment in the Mountain Province of Luzon, Philippine Islands. pg. 204
157 Lasay, pp. 4 - 5
158 Moss, pg. 383
159 Barton, The Mythology of the Ifugaos, pp. 143-148
160 Cole, Fay-Cooper. The Tinguian: Social, Religious, and Economic Life of a Philippine Tribe pp. 296-297
161 Jenks, pg. 223
162 Jenks, pg. 188

Chapter 8: Modern Filipino Tattooing

163 Maramba. Pg. 72
164 Jenks, pg. 225
165 Scott, Barangay: Sixteenth Century Philippine Culture and Society, pg. 20

Glossary

Abel: Woven textiles of the Ilokano and Itneg peoples which contain many formerly tattooed motifs.

Aeta: The name for the small Oceanic black peoples of the Philippines. Both Aeta men and women formerly practiced scarification using the sharp edge of a bamboo knife. They are also known as "negritos."

Aitu: Polynesian term used in Samoa, Tahiti, Rotuma, and other islands which represents the spirits of household deified ancestor gods who commonly take the form of certain types of animals such as centipedes, shellfish, sharks, turtles, eels, lizards, owls, and other birds. Care was taken not to eat the representative of the ancestor's animal form. To do so was extremely taboo. Aitu could convey information to their descendants through the movement of behavior of these forms. The term "aitu" is a cognate of the Philippine term "anitu" or "anito," the Tuamotuan, "*vaitu*," the Chamorro "*aniti*," and the Kiribati term, "*anti*."

Anahaw: A type of fan palm *Livistona rotundifolia* of the Philippines. The anahaw is also known as "lapad" in Cebuano and "labid" in Ilokano.

Angalo: Creator god of the Ilokanos and in some parts of the Visayan Islands. He is described as a giant and the ancestor of the Ilokanos. Angalo is also associated with sailing and fishing. Sometimes his name is spelled Angngalo. See Tangaloa.

Anito: Pan-Philippine term which represents the spirits of ancestors or ancestral gods which manifest themselves as certain types of animals and sometimes as specific stones and plants. Common forms of anito are mainly serpents, lizards, and crocodiles but also are manifest as starfish, white roosters, and birds of prey depending on location. Non-animal forms of anito were trees (especially the balete) and also certain stones called "*pinpinaing*." These stones sat at the entrance of the village and were given offerings. The term anito is synonymous to the Polynesian term Aitu and comparable to the Hawaiian concept of `aumakua. Anito is also written "anitu" in some Spanish texts.

Anitu: See Anito.

Apo Anno: An early progenitor of some of the peoples of the Benguet region. His mummified body was stolen and went missing for nearly a century before being discovered and restored to his burial cave. His birth and life was shrouded in the supernatural with his mother supposedly being a fair haired forest spirit. He was said to have been taller and more powerful than the rest of the people. He is credited with introducing tattooing to the region by some.

Apo-ni-Tolao: An Itneg mythological progenitor. One of his wives named Humitao he caught with his magic fishhook after sailing to a stone tower at the end of the world. He is also the husband of Gaygayoma the daughter of Bag-bagak the Morning Star and Sinag the Moon. Their son Takyayen became another progenitor of the Itneg people.

Atang: A food and beverage offering left for ancestor spirits (anito) by Ilokanos.

Atua: A Polynesian term for "god" or "gods" usually reserved for higher deities in Eastern Polynesia. Atua is sometimes used for lesser household or guardian spirits in Western Polynesia.

Au: A Samoan L-shaped tattooing tool of various widths and needles.

**`Aumakua:** A Hawaiian word very similar in meaning to Aitu and Anito and represents household ancestor gods which make themselves manifest by taking the form of specific animals, plants and even certain stones. Common forms of `aumakua are sharks, owls, lizards and mythical dragon-like entities called Mo'o who inhabit fishponds and streams which may have originally evolved from crocodile veneration common in Southeast Asia.

Austronesia: Austronesia is a geographical area which includes the islands of Indonesia, Malaysia, Madagascar, Philippines, Taiwan, Micronesia, Melanesia, and Polynesia. The term comes from the Latin word *auster* meaning "southern wind" and the Greek word *nêsos* meaning "islands."

Austronesian: The term refers to the Austronesian language family which is comprised of main two branches, the Formosan and Malayo-Polynesian branches. The people who inhabit or inhabited Oceania and Southeast Asia who speak or whose ancestors spoke one of the Austronesian languages are known as "Austronesians."

Bag-bagak: An Iteng deity who is the morning star (Venus). His name means, "I advise." His symbol is three concentric diamonds within diamonds. He is the husband of the moon goddess Sinag, the father of Gaygayoma and grandfather of the ancestor Takyayen. Also spelled Baggak, an Ilokano variation.

Batek: Ilokano word for tattoo. It is a cognate of the Kalinga word for tattoo "batok," or the Visayan word for tattoo, *batuk.*

Batok: Kalinga word for tattoo. Batok is a cognate of the Ilokano term for tattoo *batek* and the Visayan term for tattoo *batuk.* Sometimes it is written as the dialectal variation *fatok.*

Batuk: Visayan word for tattoo. It is a cognate of the Kalinga word *batok* and the Ilokano word *batek.*Another Visayan term for tattoo is *patik.*

Bayani: A Visayan term for a warrior or hero. Formerly a bayani was a man who qualified for a tattoo by displaying fitting courage in battle. A similar word in Ilokano which has the same meanings is *Isagani.* Both words are popular names for males.

Bikking: The elaborate chest tattoo of the Kalinga people which signifies headhunter status. It is thought to be an abstract eagle in form. It is also known as "binibiking."

Biro: Visayan word for "soot" and also "tattooing ink" that was made from soot. It is comparable to the Ilokano term for soot, *iro.*

Biyug: Kalinga term for tattooing ink. It is comparable to the Visayan term for soot or tattooing ink *biro.*

Bontoc: A province in the island of Luzon in the Philippines. It is also used as a term for the tattooed people residing within the Bontoc province. The Bontoc people were also referred to as Igorots in the past and were former headhunters.

Burik: A term for tattoos used by Gad'dang and Benguet peoples of Luzon. It means "spotted" or "engraved" in modern Ilokano, but also referred to tattooing in the past.

Chak-lag: The Bontoc and Ifugao term for the headhunter's chest tattoo. It is comparable to the Kalinga bikking tattoo.

Cordillera: A Spanish term referring to the mountain ranges of central and northern Luzon. The inhabitants of this region are sometimes known as *Igorots* and *Cordillerans.*

Dakag: A Kalinga term for tattoos received from participating in headhunting expeditions.

Datu: A man and sometimes woman of chieftain status in the Philippines. A Datu ruled the lower classes, led warriors to battle, commissioned the building of community projects, resolved disputes and executed the law. Similar cognates of this title were anciently had among the Pacific Islands such as the Latu of Samoa, the Fatu of Tahiti and the Haku of Hawai'i.

Datum: The culmination of manhood among the Ilubo people of Kalinga, These men were known as "mu'urmut" and were looked to for leadership and advice. They typically were the peace pact holders between formerly feuding communities.

Fatok: See Batok.

Fattong: A Kalinga word for women's tattoos. It literally means "to put on."

Gayang: The Kalinga word for eagle. It is considered the "Lord of Birds" and messenger of the god Kabunian. The Kalinga's headhunter's chest tattoo (bikking) is supposed to be an abstract representation of the gayang. Ifugao word for "hawk."

Gisi: An L-shaped adze-like tattooing tool with 4 to 6 needles or thorns used by various groups from Luzon in the Philippines. Also known as *kisi.*

Iban: An Austronesian people from Borneo that practice extensive tattooing in association to weaving and headhunting.

Ifugao: A province in the island of Luzon in the Philippines. It is also used as a term for the tattooed people residing within the Ifugao province. The ifugao were formerly headhunters. The tattooing of the Ifugao people was characterized by its free floating elements primarily placed on the arms and chest of the men and on the arms of the women. Tattooing was also placed on the face, legs, and buttocks in former times. The term *i-fugao* means "people of the earth world." The Ifugao are famously noted for their very large and extensive rice terraces.

Igorot: A word used in the Philippines to refer to the inhabitants of the Gran Cordillera or the former Mountain province on Luzon. Typically it is applied to the peoples of the Benguet, Bontoc, Ifugao, Kalinga, and Apayao provinces. It is derived from the archaic Tagalog word *i-golot* meaning "from the mountains."

Ilokano: The formerly tattooed people from the Philippine island of Luzon who live or originated from the provinces of Ilocos Norte or Ilocos Sur. Tattooing was exterminated soon after the Spanish advent due to rapid conversion to Christianity. The appellation *Ilokano* is thought to have been derived from *i-lo'oc* meaning "from the bay." The Ilokano people are one of the most migratory of the Philippine peoples in recent history. They possess ethnic enclaves throughout the Philippines and Hawai'i as well as traveling abroad.

Iro: An Ilokano word for "soot" related to the Visayan word for soot or tattooing ink, *biro.*

Isneg: A tattooed Philippine people of the island of Luzon from the Apayao province. The Isneg were formerly headhunters. Their tattooing covered mainly the arms although tattoos were also placed on the thighs, neck and chest. The word Isneg is derived from *is* meaning "recede" and *uneg* meaning "interior." Thus, *Isneg* means "to recede to the interior" and is a likely description of people who retreated into the mountainous areas of the Apayao province to escape Spanish influence. Some believe that at one time the Isneg people may have been of the same people as the Ilokano people who never converted to Christianity. They are also known as *Apayao*, a reference to their province.

Itneg: A formerly tattooed Philippine people of the island of Luzon from the Abra province. The Itneg formerly practiced headhunting. Their language and weaving traditions are closely related to the Ilokano people. It is thought that the Itneg people people may have been of the same people as the Ilokano people who never converted to Christianity or a combination of pre-Hispanic Ilokano and other mountain tribes. They were also known as *Tingguians* meaning "mountaineers."

Kabunian: Supreme or creator and sky god of the Kalinga and Itneg peoples as well as Ilokano people anciently. In other areas Kubunian figures as a lesser god or is the word for 'god.' In the Benguet area, kabunian is the word for the sky itself. The thunder was thought to be Kabunian pounding on his drum or the barking of his dog. The lightning was Kabunian's dog sent down to "bite things" to show his displeasure. His name is also spelled "Kabunyian."

Kakau: A Hawaiian term to describe the action of tattooing.

Kalag: The word for the soul or spirit in Cebuano (Visayan).

Kalinga: A province in the island of Luzon in the Philippines. It is also used as a term for the tattooed people residing within the Kalinga province. Formerly in the previous century the Kalinga practiced headhunting. At the time of this writing they are one of the few groups in the Philippines where tattooing is still found although those who still wear these designs are old and very few. Both men and women were tattooed with the men wearing the elaborate *biniking* or *bikking* chest tattoos. Women's tattoos covered the arms, hands, shoulders and sometimes upper back and collarbone areas. The term *kalinga* means "enemy, fighter or headhunter."

Keloid: A type of raised scar resulting from a wound that became infected. Keloid scars may sometimes occur in tattooing but are also used by themselves as decorative body marks in scarification.

Kukui: A Hawaiian word for the candlenut, *Aleurites Moluccana.*

Kutao: The name of the ferryman dead souls to the land of the dead, in the old Isneg beliefs. His function is similar to Magwayen of the Visayans and Charon of ancient Greece. His name is sometimes written as *Kitao.*

Labid: The long, inch-wide tattooed stripes that were part of the Visayan male's first tattoo that extended from the ankles to the hips. In Ilokano, *labid* is another name for the *anahaw,* fan-palm tree.

Lufan: The tattooing tool of the Bontoc people of the Philippines. The tool's comb of needles was set in line with the handle of the tool rather than perpendicular to the handle, like the *gisi*. It is also known as *luban.*

Lumauig: Paramount god or demi-god of the people of the Bontoc, Ifugao and Benguet regions of the Philippines. He is usually described as being the youngest son of Kabunian. He is credited with bringing fire to mankind and sometimes forming the world. He is known for his traveling back and forth from the heavens to the earth world, great strength and ability to provide food miraculously. His name is the conjugated form of the word *lawig,* or "fishhook," and figuratively means "one who hooks." His name appears to be a cognate of the Polynesian demi-god Maui who fished up the islands of the sea with his magic fishhook.

Magwayen: The name of the ferryman of dead souls to Sulad, the land of the dead, in ancient Visayan beliefs. See Kutao.

Maingor: An honorific term of address to Kalinga males who were successful headhunters. These men typically wore the bikking chest tattoo. Other cognates include *Mingor, Maingal* and *Maingel,* depending on locality. The word *Maingel* in Ilokano means "brave, courageous, daring and heroic."

Mana: The Polynesian concept of spiritual and authoritative ruling power. Mana came from the ancestor gods and was inherited by one's posterity. Mana could also be earned through great deeds or accomplishments which were sometimes reflected in tattooing. The concept of mana is remembered only in fragments in the Philippines such as in Tagalog where it means, "to inherit." Another remnant is found in Ilokano as *manna,* meaning "power," such as in the phrase *manna kabalin amin,* meaning the "all powerful ability" which is used to describe a deity.

Manbatek: An Ilokano term for a traditional tattoo artist. The term is used in other parts of Luzon wherever Ilokano is used as the *lingua franca* such as in the Cordillera highlands. Cognates used in the Cordillera include *manfatek, manfatok,* and *mambabatok.*

Manfattong: A Kalinga term for a female tattoo artist.

Maori: The Polynesian people of New Zealand formerly characterized by their circular curvilinear spiral tattooing. These designs were primarily placed on the face of a man and the chin of the woman. Tattooing of the buttocks and thighs were also practiced. The Maori are also known for their high development of wood carving which also

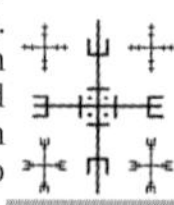

"

incorporates many of the same designs found in their tattooing. In recent years tattooing known as *moko* has enjoyed a resurgence of interest and practice.

Marquesas: These Islands are located northeast of French Polynesia. The people of the Marquesas Islands were the most heavily tattooed of the Polynesian people and were tattooed from head to toe, often with large fully blackened in areas on the face and body. Much of what is considered Tahitian tattooing is actually based on Marquesan motifs and designs. They also were noted for their finely detailed and ornate wood carving which designs were nearly identical to their tattooing motifs.

Moko: The facial tattoos of Maori men and the chin tattoos of Maori women. Moko also sometimes refers to tattooing in general among the Maori. The moko was applied in the past by the traditional pricking method but then included a carving method where the skin was literally chiseled open and soot rubbed into the wounds. This left an incised 3-dimensional grooved tattooed which was unique to the Maori. The word *moko* also means "lizard" and it has been suggested by some that the facial tattoos of the Maori are representative of a lizard.

Moli: The adze-like tattooing tool used by the Hawaiians.

Mo'o: Hawaiian mythical dragon-like beings who inhabit fishponds and streams which may have originally evolved from crocodile veneration common in Southeast Asia. Food offerings were left for them at their favorite haunts. Geckos were thought to be smaller representatives of the mo'o and were also venerated. See `Aumakua and Taniwha.

Moro: A Spanish term for people they encountered in the Philippines that practiced Islam. The term is still applied to Islamic peoples on the island of Mindanao in the Philippines.

Mu'urmut: See Datum.

Pula'ú: A term used in Samoa to describe un-tattooed men but literally means "ordinary." See Puraw.

Puraw: A term used in the ancient Visayas to describe un-tattooed people. It literally meant "natural colored, un-dyed cloth" or "plain." The same word in Ilokano has come to mean the color white, but most likely was used in the same context in the past as in the Visayas before tattooing was exterminated. Puraw is a cognate of the Samoan word *pula'ú*.

Patik: A Visayan term for tattoo. In the Cordillera highlands of Luzon, patik also referred to the tapping stick in a tattooist's tattooing kit. See also Batuk.

Patu-tiki: The Marquesan word for tattoo.

Pe'a: The Samoan bodysuit tattoo which extends from the lower ribs down to below the knees. The term *pe'a* is the Samoan word for the flying fox, a bat which is common in those islands. The small triangle in the small of the back below the canoe motif is called the *tama'i pe'a*. It is thought to be a stylized flying fox and is the most important component of the bodysuit since remainder of the tattooing is based off of it. Men who wear the *pe'a* are respected for their strength of character and are called by the chiefly title *sogoimiti*.

Pintado: A Spanish term meaning "painted people." It was used to describe the tattooed peoples of the Philippines, specifically the Visayan peoples. The Spanish originally called the Philippine archipelago "Las Islas de los Pintados," which means "The Islands of the Painted Ones." See Visayan.

Prince Giolo: An Austronesian man also known as Jeoly who was purchased as a slave with his mother in Mindanao by the English privateer William Dampier in 1692. He was the first example of Austronesian tattooing brought to Europe. His tattoos show that he was likely Yapese or from Western Micronesia.

Samoa: Samoa is nation of islands in Western Polynesia which was formerly called Western Samoa. American Samoa was formerly part of Samoa but is now governed as a territory of the United States of America. Samoa is the only place in Polynesia and one of the few places in Austronesia where the practice of tattooing never languished or fell out of practice. The inhabitants of these islands are referred to in this work as Samoans, who have been instrumental in reintroducing the traditional tattooing techniques to other islands in Polynesia where the practice was abandoned.

Sau-sau: A Samoan word for the hammer stick used to strike the tattooing tool called *au*.

Sina: A Samoan goddess and ancestor who figures in many myths. Sina is known as *Hina* in other parts of the Pacific. She is often associated with the moon or is the moon goddess proper. She is comparable to the Philippine moon goddess of the Itneg people named *Sinag*.

Sinag: The moon goddess of the Itneg people. She is the wife of Bag-bagak, the morningstar. She is the mother of Gaygayoma and grandmother of the ancestor Takyayen, who is the son of Gaygayoma. Her name implies radiance or a ray or light.

Sogoimiti: A Samoan chiefly title for a man who possesses the Samoan body suit tattoo which is commonly known as the *pe'a*.

Tahiti: An island in Eastern Polynesia which is sometimes used to describe the area of the Society Islands in French Polynesia. Tahitian tattooing bore a resemblance to Samoan tattooing but was more restricted covering only the buttocks and hips. Tattooing in Tahiti was exterminated after European occupation but has in recent years enjoyed a revival. Much of what is now tattooed in Tahiti is primarily based on Marquesan tattoo designs and other motifs common throughout Polynesia.

Tangaloa: A Polynesian god. In some places Tangaloa is the paramount creator god or the first god in human form. In other places of Polynesia Tangaloa is a god of the sea. Variations of his name in Polynesia are Ta'aroa in Tahiti, Tangaroa in New Zealand, Tana'oa in the Marquesas Islands, Tagaloa in Samoa, Tangaloa in Tonga, Tagroa sir'ia in Rotuma, and Kanaloa in Hawai'i. Less frequently Tangaloa is known in parts of Melanesia and Micronesia as Takaro in New Hebrides and Loa in the Marshall Islands. He is also found in the Philippines as the giant god Angalo.

Taniwha: Maori supernatural beings that dwell in water. They are guardian spirits or gods who dwelt in deep pools in rivers, lakes, and harbors. They are sometimes described as lizard or reptile-like beings but can take the form of large sharks and whales as well as floating logs. See Mo'o.

Tatak: A Tagalog word which means "to mark, print or stamp." It likely referred to tattooing in the past but fell out of use as a reference to tattooing when the Tagalog people adopted Islam prior to the Spanish advent. It appears to be a cognate of other Philippine words for tattoo such as *batek*, *batok*, and *batuk*. It is currently being used again by some Filipino-Americans as a term for "tattoo."

Tataú: Polynesian term for tattooing. The word "tattoo" is an European corruption of the word *tataú*.

Tek-tek: The hammer stick used to tap the gisi or tattooing tool in Kalinga tattooing. Tek-tek is also thought to be an onomatopoeia which describes the tapping sound of the hammer stick on the *gisi*.

Tonga: The Kingdom of Tonga is located in Western Polynesia and comprises many small volcanic and atoll islands. In former times Tongan royalty traveled to Samoa to be tattooed in a body suit very similar to the Samoan *pe'a*. The inhabitants of these islands are referred to in this work as Tongans.

Tumao: Tumao is a chiefly title from the old social classes of the Philippines. Tumao comes from the word *tao* meaning "person" and suggests someone who is manly, without the taint of slavery, servitude or witchcraft. Tumao were described as *sandig sa Datu,* or "the Datu's support." Correlations are found in Polynesian languages. In the Maori language *tumau* means an attendant or servant, reflecting back to the role of the Philippine Tumao as the support (attendant) of the Datu. *Mau* in Samoan means "to have plenty" while in Tongan *ma'u* means "to acquire or get gain," similar to the Tumaos' wealthy status.

Ugaw: An Ilokano term for the spiritual essence of the food of an atang offering. The ugaw is what is consumed by the spirits called anito.

Uhi: The Hawaiian term for tattoo.

Ukmok: A stylus-like tattooing tool with a single or small group of needles in the tip. The ukmok was used by the Ifugao people of Luzon in the Philippines.

Visayan: An inhabitant of the Visayan islands in the Philippine archipelago. Formerly called *pintados*, or "painted people," by the Spanish due to their extensive tattooing which covered many men from head to toe. Women's tattoos possessed much finer lines and were restricted to either one hand or sometimes both hands. Tattooing among the Visayan peoples was exterminated as the people were converted to Christianity. See Pintado.

Filipino Tattoos: Ancient to Modern

Bibliography

Alcina, Francisco Ignacio. *Historia de las islas e indios de Bisayas*, 1668 3:35-37. Victor Baltazar transcription. University of Chicago Philippine Studies Program 1962.

Allardice, R.W. *A Simplified Dictionary of Modern Samoan.* (1985) Polynesian Press. Auckland, New Zealand.

Anderson, Johannes, C. *Myths and Legends of the Polynesians.* (1969) Charles E. Tuttle Company Inc. Tokyo, Japan.

Aquino, Gaudencio V. *Philippine Myths & Legends.* (1992) National Book Store. Mandaluyong, Philippines.

Argo, Jacques. *Souvenirs d'un Aveugle: Voyage Autour du Monde.* 5 vols. (1868) H. Lebrun. Paris, France.

Avea, Chief Sielu. *Tatau, The Art of the Samoan Tattoo,* (1994) Sielu Enterprises. Hauula, HI 96717.

Barrère, Dorothy B. *The Kumuhonua Legends: A Study of Late 19th Century Hawaiian Stories of Creation and Origins,* (1969) Pacific Anthropological Records number 3, Bishop Museum, Honolulu, HI.

Barton, R.F. *Philippine Pagans.* (1938) AMS Press, New York. NY (1979 reprint of the 1938 edition).

Barton, R.F. *The Mythology of the Ifugaos.* (1955) American Folklore Society, Philadelphia, PA.

Beckwith, Martha. *Hawaiian Mythology.* (1970) University of Hawai'i Press Honolulu, HI.

Biggs, Bruce. *The Complete English-Maori Dictionary.* (2003 reprint) Auckland University Press. Auckland, New Zealand.

Booth, H. T. *Sulu'ape Uili Tasi: Like a Manuel in a Glovebox.* Tattoo Magazine. June 2004.

Buck, Peter H. *Vikings of the Pacific.* (1938) The University of Chicago Press, Chicago, IL.

Cabonce, S. J. Rodolfo. *An English Cebuano Visayan Dictionary.* (1983) National Bookstore. Caloocan City, Philippines.

Casal, Gabriel S. *Kayamanan, Ma'i - Panoramas of Philippine Primeval.* (1986) Central Bank of the Philippines. Ayala Museum. Manila, Philippines.

Casal, Gabriel S. *Tboli Art in it Socio-Cultural Context.* (1978) Filipinas Foundation. Makati, Philippines.

Cole, Fay-Cooper. *A Study in Tinguian Folklore.* (2004) Kessinger Publishing. Whitefish, MT.

Cole, Fay-Cooper. *The Tinguian, Social, Religious and Economic Life of a Philippines Tribe.* (1922) Field Museum Anthropological Series, Vol. XIV, No. 2.

Cole, Mabel Cook. *Philippine Folk Tales.* (1916) University Press of the Pacific. Honolulu, HI.

Constantino, Ernesto. *Ilokano Dictionary.* (1971) University of Hawaii Press. Honolulu, HI.

De Giua, Katrin PhD. *Kapwa: The Self in the Other.* (2008) Anvil Publishing Inc. Pasig City, Philippines.

Demetrio, Francisco. S.J. *Creation Myths among the Early Filipinos.* (1968) Asian Folklore Studies, Vol. 27, No. 1, pp. 41-79. Nagoya, Japan.

Dozier, Edward. *The Kalingas of Northern Luzon Philippines.* (1967) Holt and Rhinehart Publications, New York.

Eugenio, Damiana L. (ed.) (1989) *Philippines Folk Literature, The Folktales.* Quezon City. The University of the Philippines Folklorists Inc.

Figueras, Herminio A. *Some Fragments of the Angalo Legend.* Philippine Magazine March 1934.

Garcia, Mauro. (editor) *Readings in Philippine Prehistory.* (1979) The Filipiniana Book Guild. Manila, Philippines.

Gell, Alfred. *Wrapping in Images: Tattooing in Polynesia.* (1993) Oxford University Press. New York.

Gilbert, Steve. *The Tattoo History Source Book.* (2001) PowerHouse Books. Brooklyn, NY.

Handy, Willowdean, *Chatterson. Tattooing in the Marquesas.* (2008 reprint) Dover Publications Inc. Mineola, NY.

Hiroa, Te Rangi. *Arts and Crafts of the Cook Islands.* (1944) Bernice P. Bishop Museum Bulletin; 179. Honolulu, HI.

Jagor, Fedor et al. *The Former Philippines thru Foreign Eyes.* (1917) Cornell University Library. Ithaca, New York.

Jenks, Albert E. *The Bontoc Igorot. Philippine Islands, Department of the Interior Ethnological Survey Publications, Vol. I.* (1970) New York: Johnson Reprint Corporation, Reprint Corporation. Reprint of 1905 edition.

Kaeppler, Adrienne. *Hawaiian Tattoo: A Conjunction of Genealogy and Aesthetics. Marks of Civilization: Artistic Transformations of the Human Body.* (1988) A. Rubin ed. University of California, Los Angeles, CA.

Kamakau, Samuel Minaiakalani. *Ka Po'e Kahiko: The People of Old.* (1991 reprint) Bishop Museum Press, Honolulu, HI.

Kelin, Daniel A. (editor) *Marshall Islands Legends and Stories.* (2003) Bess Press. Honolulu, HI.

Krutak, Lars. *The Last Kalinga Tattoo Artist of the Philippines.* 2009 www.larskrutak.com/articles/philippines

Lasay, Fatima. *Myth, Mind and Meaning in New Media.* Web published paper. College of Fine Arts, University of the Philippines, Diliman, Quezon City, Philippines.

Lewis, David. *Wind, Wave, Star, and Bird.* National Geographic Magazine.vol. 146, no. 6 December 1974. Washington D.C.

Maramba, Roberto. *Form and Splendor: Personal Adornment of Northern Luzon Ethnic Groups, Philippines.* (1998) Bookmark Inc. Makati City, Philippines.

Marquardt, Carl. *The Tattooing of Both Sexes in Samoa.* (Die Tätowirung beider Geschlechter in Samoa) (1899) [Translated by Sybil Ferner] Papakura, New Zealand, R. McMillan. 1984 reprint.

Montinola, Lourdes R. *Piña.* (1991) Amon Foundation. Metro Manila, Philippines.

Morga, Dr. Antonio de. *Sucesos de las Islas Filipinas.* Mexico, 1609. Translated and edited by J.S. Cummins. The Hakluyt Society, Cambridge University Press, 1971.

Moss, C. R. *Kankanay Ceremonies.* American Archeology and Ethnology vol. 15, no. 4 pp. 343 - 384 October 29th 1920. University of California Publications.

Newton, Douglas. *Maoris: Treasures of the Tradition.* National Geographic Magazine, vol.166, no. 4, October 1984. Washington D.C. pp. 542-553.

Norbeck, Edward. *Folklore of the Atayal of Formosa and the Mountain Tribes of Luzon.* (1950) Anthropological Papers, Museum of Anthropology, University of Michegan No. 5.

Orbell, Margaret. *The Illustrated Encyclopedia of Maori Myth and Legend.* (1995) Canterbury University Press, Christchurch, New Zealand.

Pendergrast, Mick. *Tikopian Tattoo.* (2000) Auckland Museum. Auckland, New Zealand.

Peralta, Jesus T. *Glances, Prehistory of the Philippines.* National Commission for Culture and the Arts. Manila, Philippines.

Poignant, Roslyn. *Oceanic Mythology.* (1967) The Hamlyn Publishing Group Limited, Feltham, Middlesex, England.

Pukui, Mary Kawena. Elbert, Samuel H. *New Pocket Hawaiian Dictionary: with a Concise Grammar and Given Names in Hawaiian.* (1992 reprint) University of Hawaii Press, Honolulu, HI.

Reynolds, Hubert, Fern Babcock Grant. (editors) *The Isneg of the Northern Philippines: A Study of Trends of Change and Development.* (1973) Anthropology Museum, Silliman University. Dumaguete City, Philippines.

Scott, William, Henry. *Barangay: Sixteenth Century Philippine Culture. and Society,* (1995) Ateno De Manila University Press. Quezon City, Philippines.

Scott, William, Henry. T*he Discovery of the Igorots, Spanish Contacts with the Pagan of Northern Luzon.* (1974) New Day Publishers. Quezon City, Philippines.

Scott, William Henry. *Prehispanic Source Materials for the Study of Philippine History.* (1984) New Day Publishers. Quezon City, Philippines.

Salvador, Ikin. *The Cordillera's Vanishing Art of Tattooing.* Philippine Daily Inquirer May 2, 2000 Internet Edition.

Salvador, Ikin. *Signs on Skin Beauty and Being: Traditional Tattoos and Tooth Blackening Among the Philippine Cordillera.* (2004) University of Michigan. Ann Arbor, MI.

Salvador-Amores, Analyn "Ikin," Batek: "Traditional Tattoos and Identities in Contemporary Kalinga," North Luzon, Philippines. *Humanities Diliman* (January-June 2002) 3:1, pp. 105-142.

Sellato, Bernard. *Hornbill and Dragon: Arts and Culture of Borneo.* 1995, Sun Tree Publishers, Singapore,

Spennemann, Dirk R. *Marshallese Tattoos.* (1992) Republic of the Marshall Islands Historic Preservation Office, Marshall Islands.

Swain, Tony. Trompf, Garry. *The Religions of Oceania,* (1995) Routledge, New York, NY.

Taylor, Alan. *Polynesian Tattooing.* (1991) Institute for Polynesian Studies, Brigham Young University - Hawaii Campus. Laie, HI.

Te Rangi Hiroa. *Samoan Material Culture.* (1930) Bernice P. Bishop Museum Bulletin 75, Honolulu, HI.

Thomas, Nicolas. Cole, Anna. Douglas, Bronwen. *Tattoo: Bodies, Art, and Exchange in the Pacific and the West.* (2005) Reaktion Books Ltd. London, England.

Tregear, Edward. *Curious Polynesian Words.* Article LXII, Transactions and Proceedings of the New Zealand Institute Vol. 23, 1890 (1891) George Didsbury Government Printing Office. London, England.

Tu'inukuafe, Edgar. *A Simplified Dictionary of Modern Tongan.* Polynesian Press. Auckland, New Zealand.

Turner, George. Samoa, *A Hundred Years Ago and Long Ago.* (1884) London Missionary Society. Reprinted (1984) Institute of Pacific Studies, University of the South Pacific. Suva, Fiji.

Tryon, D.T. *Conversational Tahitian,* (1970) University of California Press, Los Angeles, CA.

Van Dinter, Maarten Hesselt. *Tribal Tattoo Designs from Indonesia.* (2007) Mundurucu Publishers. Netherlands.

Vanoverbergh, Morice. *Dress and Adornment in the Mountain Province of Luzon, Philippine Islands..* (1929) Publications of the Catholic Anthropological Conference. Washington D.C.

Vanoverbergh, Morice. *The Isneg.* (1932) Publications of the Catholic Anthropological Conference. Washington D.C.

Worchester, Dean C. *Head-Hunters of Northern Luzon.* National Geographic Magazine Vol. 23 no. 9. September 1912. Washington D.C.

Worchester, Dean C. The Non-Christian Tribes of Northern Luzon. (1906) Philippine Journal of Science, vol. I no. 8.

Yabes, Leopoldo Y. *The Adam and Eve of the Ilocanos.* Philippine Magazine (PM) July 1935 pp.336, 341.

Index